Collection of Ancient Chinese Cultural Relics

Compiled by Expert Committee of Chinese Society of Cultural Relics

Vol. VII

The Liao, Jin and Western Xia Dynasties

916-1234

The Yuan Dynasty

1271-1368

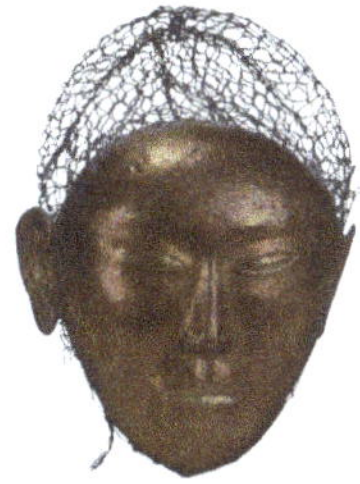

English iteration is with ATF Press

Vol. Ⅶ The Liao, Jin and Western Xia Dynasties /

The Yuan Dynasty

Translated by Guozhen Wang

ISBN: 978-1-925371-50-5 soft
978-1-925371-51-2 hardback
978-1-925371-52-9 epub
978-1-925371-53-6 pdf

Published by:

An imprint of the ATF Ltd.
PO Box 504
Hindmarsh, SA 5007
ABN 90 116 359 963
www.atfpress.com
Making a lasting impact

Contents

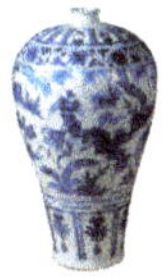

The Liao, Jin and Western Xia Dynasties

Pottery

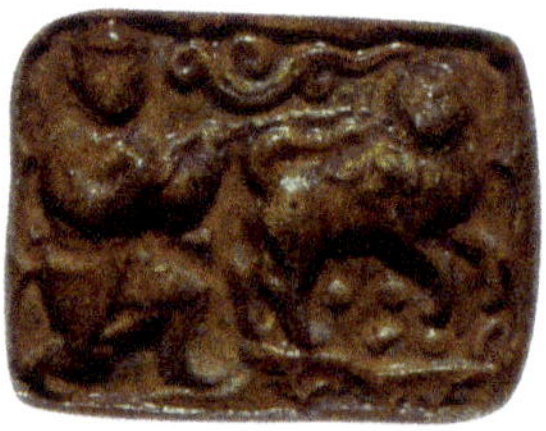

Porcelain

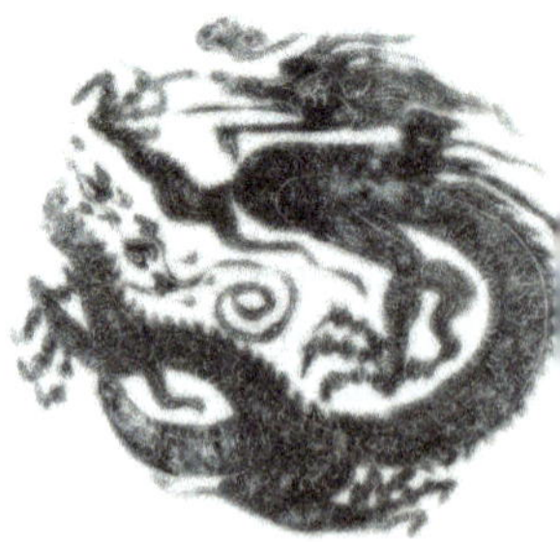

Painting

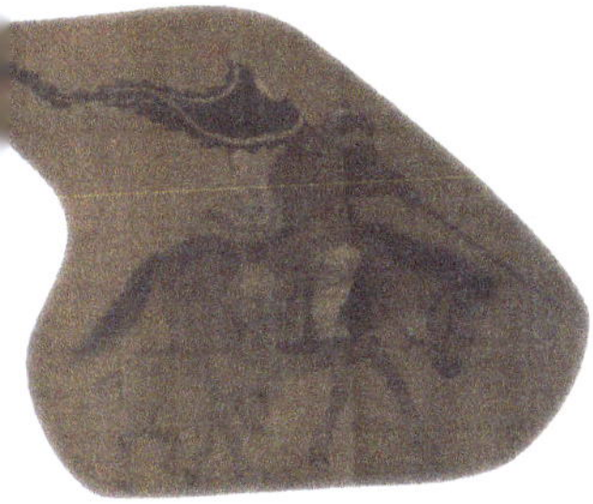

Handicrafts

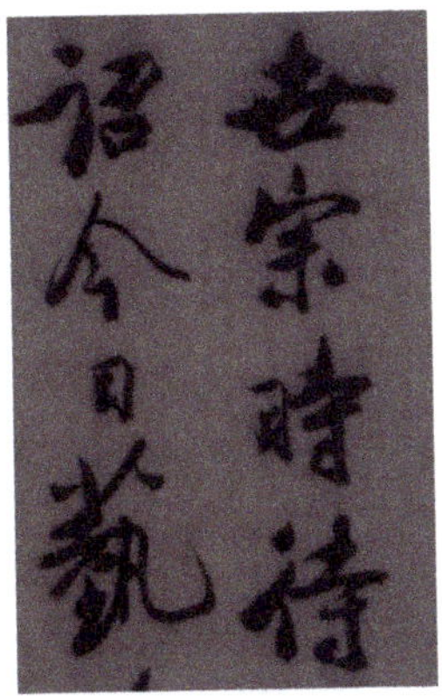

The Yuan Dynasty

Jade Ware

Porcelain

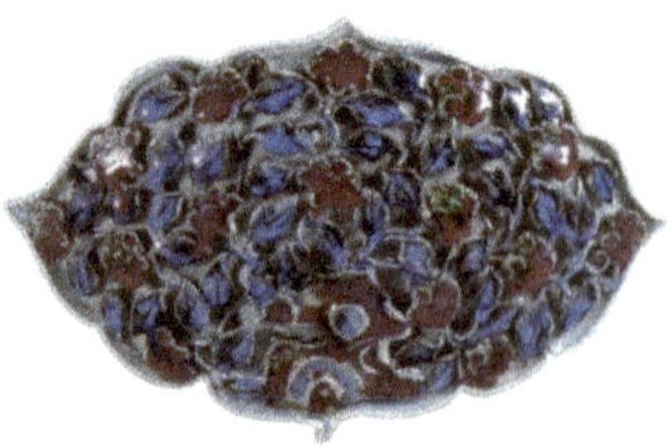

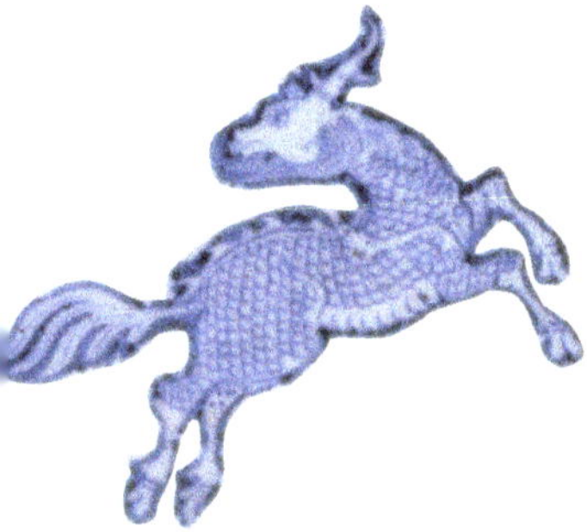

Painting

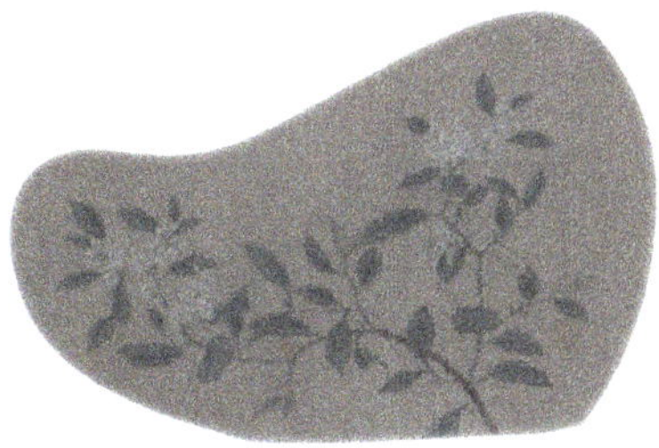

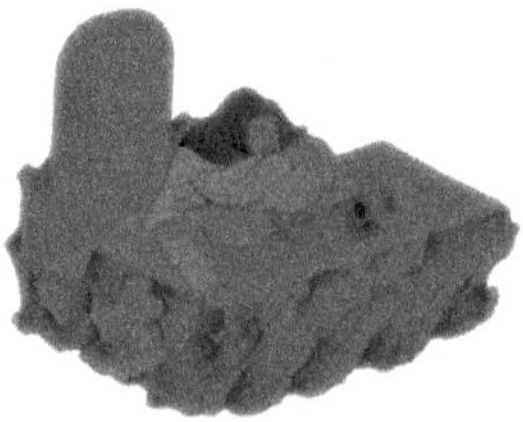

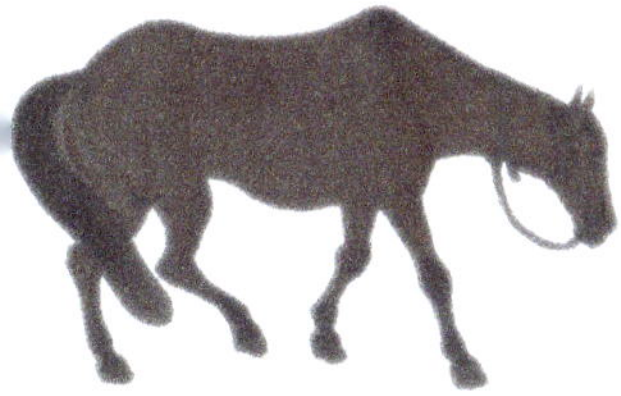

Calligraphy

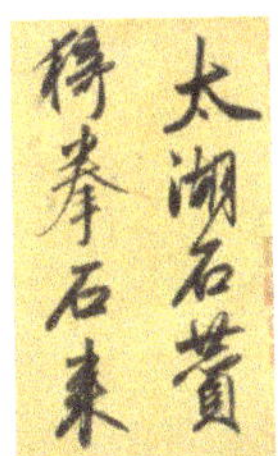

Handicrafts

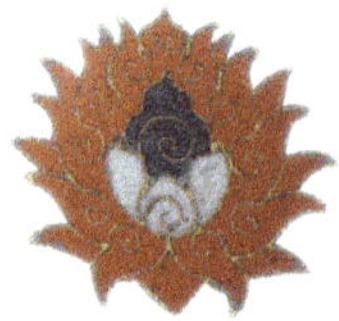

The Liao, Jin and Western Xia Dynasties

916-1234

Preface

During the Northern and Southern Song Dynasties, northern nomads established a number of separate regimes-the Liao, the Western Xia and the Jin. In the northeast, the Khitan people founded the Liao Regime in 916 and it was destroyed by the Jin in 1125.

The nomads of the Khitan tribal people emerged during the fifth century. In the early years they migrated irregularly from north to south along the course of Xianbei Mountain, and subsequently, they led a nomadic existence around the Laoha River (Xilamulun River) Basin present-daythe Zhaowuda area in Inner Mongolia . Early in the tenth century, when the Khitan nationality was beginning to grow in strength, Yelue Abaoji fought a number of battles and expanded his territory after he had unified all the tribes. During the reign of Emperor Shengzong, the Liao concluded the Chanyuan Alliance with the Northern Song Dynasty and was granted 16 prefectures from Yan to

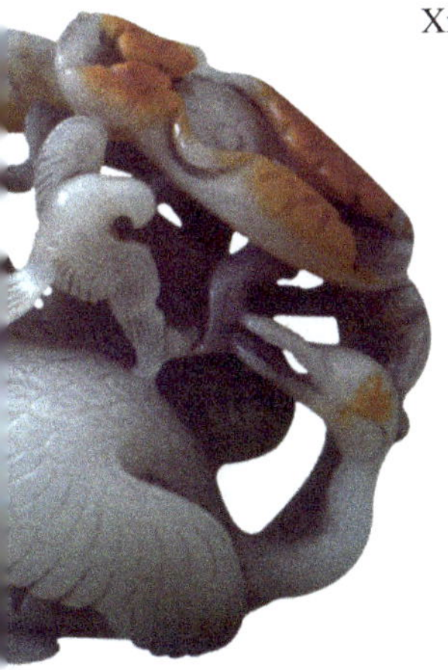

Liao. Hence, the Liao became more and more powerful and was able to resist the Song Dynasty in the south for long periods.

Taking the place of the Liao, the Jin Regime was founded by the Jurchen nationality in 1115. They originated in the north. After many years of fighting, the Jin leader Aguda destroyed the Northern Song and the Liao and occupied all of the Liao territory, as well as a large area in the Central Plain from south of the Yellow River to north of the Huaihe River. As a result, the Jin stood in opposition to the Southern Song government. But they were destroyed by an alliance between the Mongols and the Song in 1234.

The Western Xia, which existed at the same time as the Song and the Liao, was founded by the Tangut people in the northwest in 1038, when the Tangut leader Li Yuanhao proclaimed himself emperor. In all the Western Xia saw 10 emperors spanning a history of more than 200 years. The Western Xia regime mainly occupied the area which is today Ningxia, Gansu, Shaanxi, Inner Mongolia and most of Qinghai, and they provided stiff opposition to the Song and the Liao. During its golden age, the Western Xia held a territory that spanned more than 20,000 li. It covered the northern desert area and the area from the Yellow River in the east to Yumen in the west. Its capital was at Xingqingfu (today just southeast of Yinchuan City in Ningxia). It was destroyed by the Mongols in 1227.

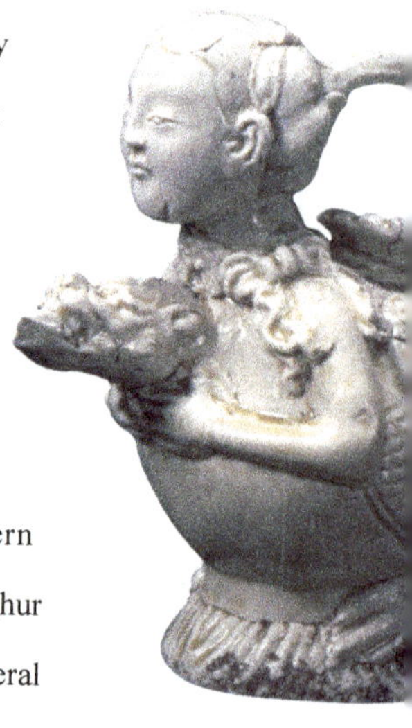

In this period there were other regimes, such as the Dali State established by the Bai nationality in southwestern China, the Ganzhou Uighur, Gaochang Uighur and Khotan Uighur states founded by the Uighur people in the northwest, and several separatist regimes based around the Tubo Regime established by Tibetan people in Gansu and Qinghai. The political situation was very complex.

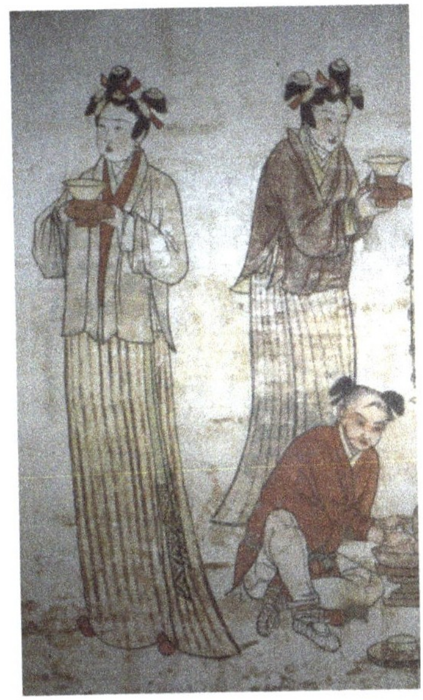

The Liao, Jin and Western Xia were all founded by nomadic peoples, but under the influence of the Han people, who had a long history, the politics and cultures of these nomadic peoples took on a kind of duality. They would preserve the traditions of their respective nationalities, but also they would absorb the culture of the Han people and gradually they even converted to Han customs. Many rulers actively sought to learn Han culture and attained a very high cultural level in that respect. In this context, the arts of the Liao, the Western Xia and the Jin displayed a colorful and unique style.

As an important traditional craft, jade objects were usually manufactured by Han craftsmen. Heavily influenced by Tang and Song Dynasty culture, many objects followed the features of those dynasties in terms of shape and ornamentation, and excellent traditions were also inherited in terms of technology. But they were also made for the use of their own nationalities and thus they also represented many characteristics of nomad peoples and were deeply influenced by their own politics, economy and aesthetics. For example, the Jade Ornament of Spring Water Pattern shows a scene of a falcon attacking a wild goose, which reflects the hunting life and the national character of the Khitan people.

The ceramic industry attached great importance to the absorption of advanced porcelain-firing skills from the Central Plain, and a group of skilled craftsmen migrated to these areas. As a whole, the ceramic industry in these areas were inferior to those of the Central Plain-they had fewer workshops and were smaller in size - but porcelain of some considerable quality was still produced there and different national styles were developed as well as skills and techniques in terms of shaping and adornment. The Liao state followed the lead of the Han people in establishing official kilns inside Shangjing Linhuangfu. In spite of their small size and relatively short duration of usage, these kilns still produced high quality, artistic work.

In the Liao, Jin and Western Xia Dynasties, calligraphy and painting were relatively underdeveloped and there were few great calligraphers or painters. Those few works that survive today were heavily influenced by the styles of the Northern and Southern Song Dynasties which in turn owed their origins to Han culture and art. Nevertheless, these works still enriched the canon of arts of that time. In particular, some mural paintings in Liao and Jin burial chambers represented distinct features of that time and of those nationalities in terms of subject, content and painting skill, and they cannot be ignored. Moreover, the Khitan, Jurchen and Western Xia people created their own written languages which enriched their national cultures and they provide invaluable historical and cultural resources.

Large numbers of gold and silver objects have been unearthed-objects used in everyday life for funerals, for adornment, for worship and for other uses. They each have their distinctive national characterstics, despite the influence of Han traditions in gold and silver ware. This combination of national characteristics and Han styles, makes for a fascinating melding in terms of gold and silver objects. Weaving crafts also developed to some degree, as we can see in the weaving and embroidery works unearthed from Liao and Jin tombs.

Jade Ware

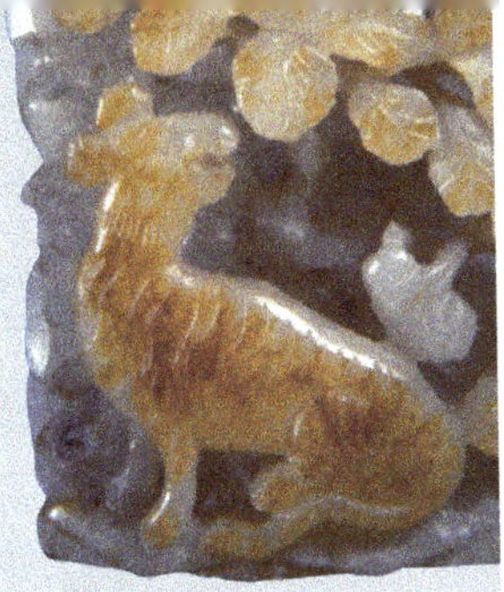

Most jade objects of the Liao Dynasty were unearthed from tombs in Inner Mongolia, Liaoning, Hebei and Shanxi. Of these, the most magnificent jade objects were unearthed from burial tomb of a Chen princess and her Liao husband in Jerim, Inner Mongolia in 1985. Dozens of pieces were discovered in the tomb, and these precious jade objects show all of the basic features of the jadeware of the Liao Dynasty.

Jade was more popular in the Jin than in the Liao Dynasty. The Jin received tribute from the Uighur and also imported materials from the Western Xia in order to get Hetian nephrite and jade for their craftsmen. In order to ensure the quality of the jade ware, the Jin government, in the course of its expansion, captured a large number of jade craftsmen from the Liao and Song regions. The imperial palace of the Jin Court established a special workshop and an "Institute for Producing Jade Books and Treasures" to satisfy the court's demands for jade. The unearthed jade objects of the Jin Dynasty were mostly discovered in tombs present-dayHeilongjiang, Jilin, Inner Mongolia, Shanxi and Beijing. Of these, those tombs with most unearthed jade objects included Zhongxing Ancient Town Ruins and Tomb at Suibin County in Heilongjiang, Aolimi Ancient Town Ruins and Tomb in the lower reaches of the Songhuajiang River, and the Jin Tombs at Fangshan and at Miliangtun Village in Wangzuo Township of Fengtai District in Beijing.

Jade objects from the Liao and Jin Dynasties were usually made by Han craftsmen who were influenced deeply by Tang and Song cultures, so many objects carried forward the shaping and adorning features of the Tang and Song Dynasties. Moreover the most popular motifs included variations on themes like happiness, longevity and luck. These jade objects also represented some characteristics of nomadic people. In both of the northern nomadic nationalities-Khitan and Jurchen - fishing and hunting still dominated, so of course this was reflected in the subjects they chose and landscapes employed naturally included mountains and rivers, and scenes from the land where these nomads live. The Jade Ornament of Spring

Water Pattern and Jade Ornament of Autumn Mountain Pattern both portray the Nabo life of the Khitan and Jurchen peoples, and they reflect a very high artistic attainment and a unity of form and spirit. The common pattern of Spring Water portrays a scene of a falcon attacking a swan, while the pattern of Autumn Mountain shows some Jurchen people hunting deer in autumn.

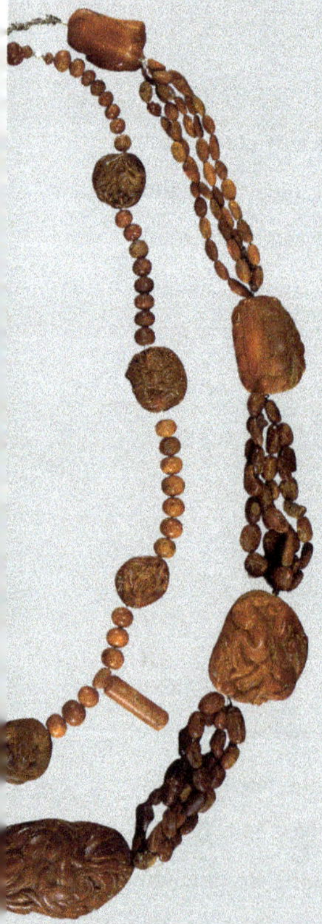

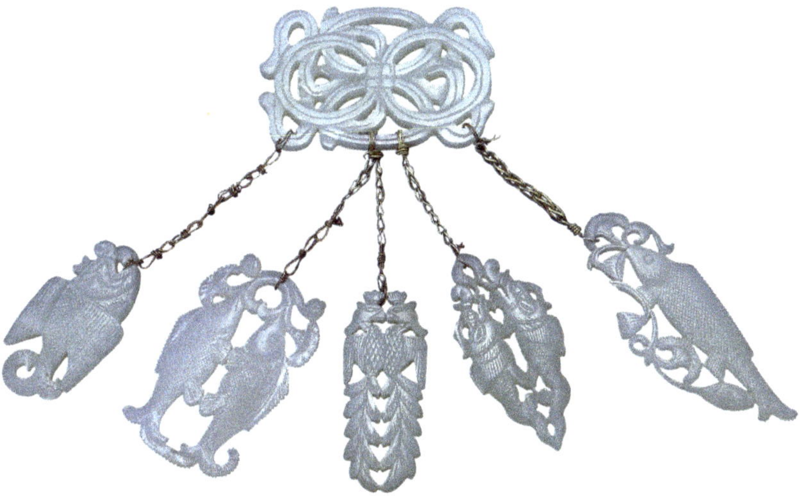

1. Jade Pendant Suite in Animal Shapes

Liao

Length: 4.9-7.5 cm   Thickness: 0.6 cm

Unearthed from burial tomb of a Chen princess and her Liao husband in Naiman Banner, Inner Mongolia in 1986

Preserved in the Inner Mongolia Institute for Archaeological Research and Cultural Relics.

This is an ornament made of Hetian nephrite. The object is flat with carved designs and intagliated roller patterns. The upper part of the biggest piece is decorated with patterns of twisted lotuses and under it hangs five gold chains, each of which is connected to a piece of jade ornament. The middle of the five pieces is decorated with two-phoenix patterns, and other pieces are decorated with patterns of fish holding lotuses and flying fish - both single and double.

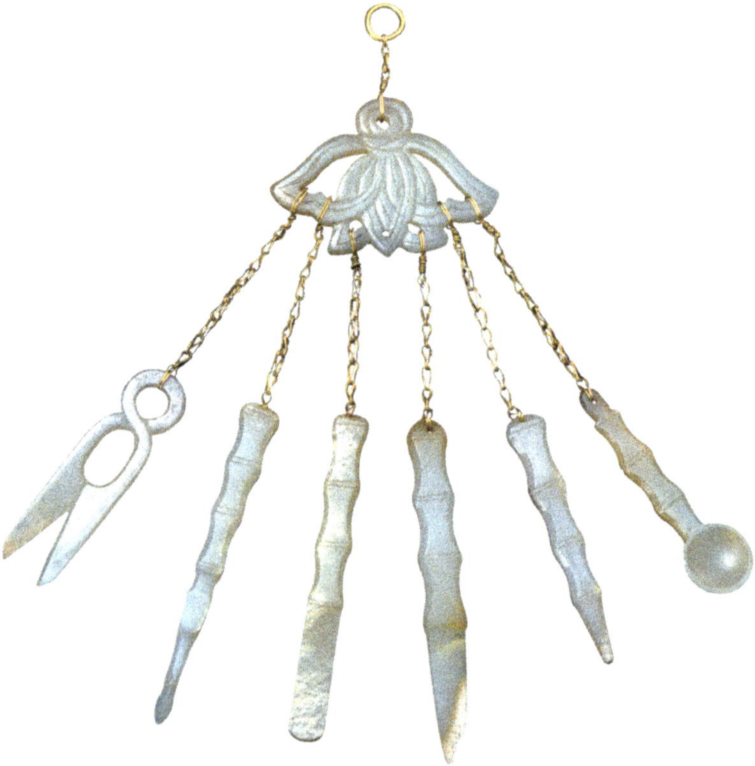

2. Jade Pendant Suite in Tool Shapes
Liao
Length: 6.5 cm   Length of Gold Chain: 5 cm
Unearthed from burial tomb of a Chen princess and her Liao husband in Naiman Banner, Inner Mongolia in 1986
Preserved in the Inner Mongolia Institute for Archaeological Research and Cultural Relics
This is an ornament consisting of seven jade pieces. A jade ring, carved in the shape of a flower, hangs from a gold chain at the top and there were six gold chains at the bottom. Each of the lower chains is connected to a jade tool, and these tools include a pair of scissors, a long awl, an adze, a knife, a short awl and a spoon.

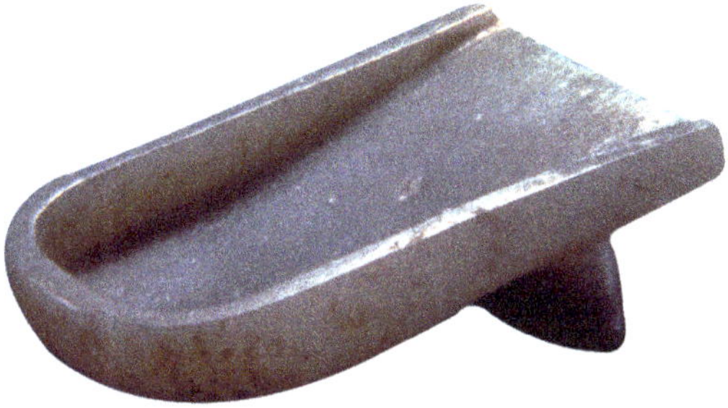

3. Jade Inkslab

Liao

Height: 2.6-4.1 cm Length: 12 cm Width: 7.1 cm

Unearthed from burial tomb of a Chen princess and her Liao husband in Naiman Banner, Inner Mongolia in 1986

Preserved in the Inner Mongolia Institute for Archaeological Research and Cultural Relics

This is a study object made of dark green jade with grey white mottles. It is a circular engravure in the shape of a dustpan. The grinding surface is sloped and the ink-pool is deep. Under its flat bottom are two short square feet.

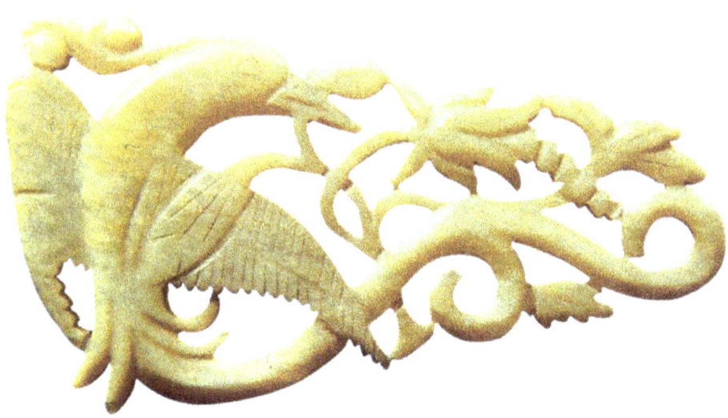

4. Jade Phoenix

Liao (or Jin)

Height: 7 cm Width: 3.8 cm

Unearthed from No.4 Tomb of the Prince's Graveyard at Xinxiangfang, Harbin, Heilongjiang in 1983

Preserved in the Heilongjiang Provincial Museum

This is an ornament made of yellow, glittering and translucent jade. It was carved in shape of a paradise flycatcher holding a flower in its mouth and flying with spread out wings. The pattern is decorated with intagliated lines.

5. Jade Ornament of Autumn Mountain Pattern

Liao (or Jin)
Height: 6.5 cm   Width: 4.5 cm   Thickness: 1.6 cm
Preserved in the Palace Museum in Beijing

This is an ornament made of grey jade which retains its original color - purple red - in some parts. This oblate object is engraved in relief with decorations of intagliated lines. On one side, there is a crouching tiger looking back in the lower part and two running deer in some woods in the upper part, and the whole scene makes use of the jade's original color-yellow. On the other side, there is a hawk standing in a tree in the lower part, and two flying magpies and a sun along with the inscription "阳" (sun) above.

During the Liao and Jin Dynasties, in autumn when the sky was clear and the air was cool, emperors would always go hunting in the woods, a scene often called "autumn mountain".

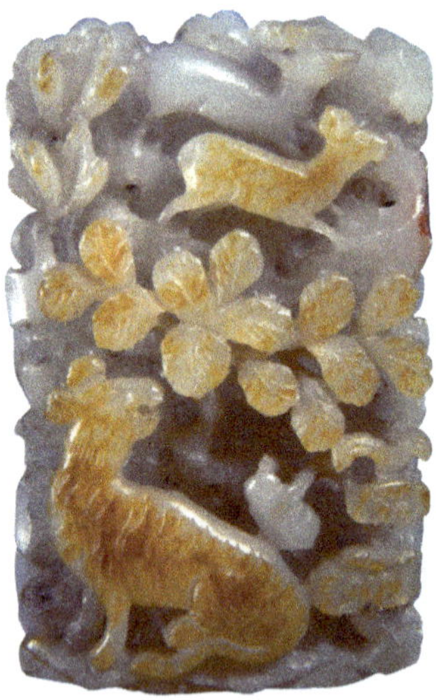

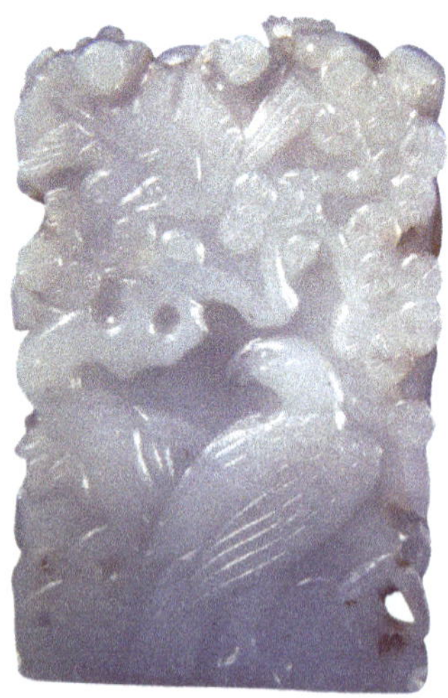

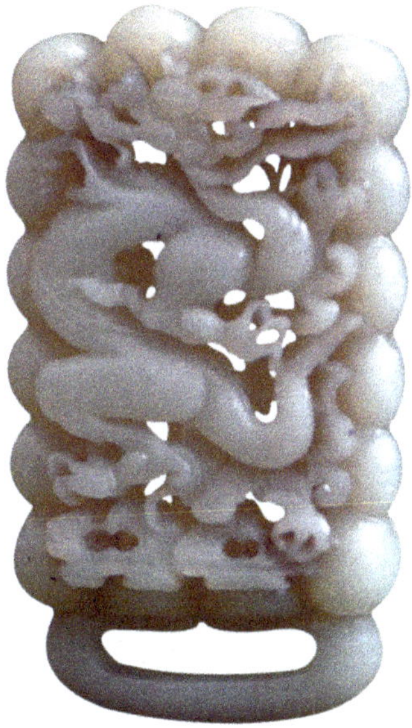

6. Jade Belt with Dragon Pattern

Liao

Length: 9.1 cm Thickness: 2.5 cm

Preserved in the Palace Museum in Beijing

This is an ornament made of white jade. It is compressed and oblong, and was decorated, by means of layered piercing, with the pattern of a dragon playing with a pearl in the clouds. The margin was designed using a bead pattern. A flat hole crosses the object which would have been used for putting on leather belts. On the lower part is a long-circle penetrating hole.

7. Jade Belt with Spring Water Pattern

Liao

Length: 8.5 cm Thickness: 2.2 cm

Preserved in the Palace Museum in Beijing

This is an ornament made of bluish white jade with some brown spots which are due to erosion. It is compressed and oblong, and on the obverse side was carved a wild goose stretching its neck towards some waterweeds. In the sky a falcon is getting ready to attack a wild goose. On the lower part is a long-circle penetrating hole. On the reverse side the center sinks somewhat and the surrounding margin was designed with a thick frame without ornamentation.

Falcons live in the lower reaches of the Heilongjiang River and feed on wild geese and swans. They can be tamed and used for hunting.

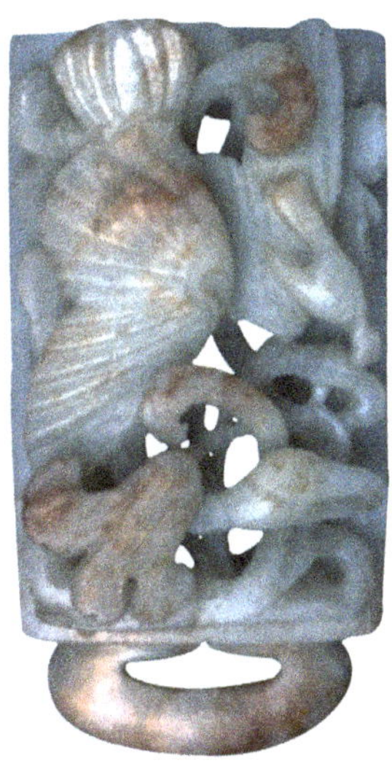

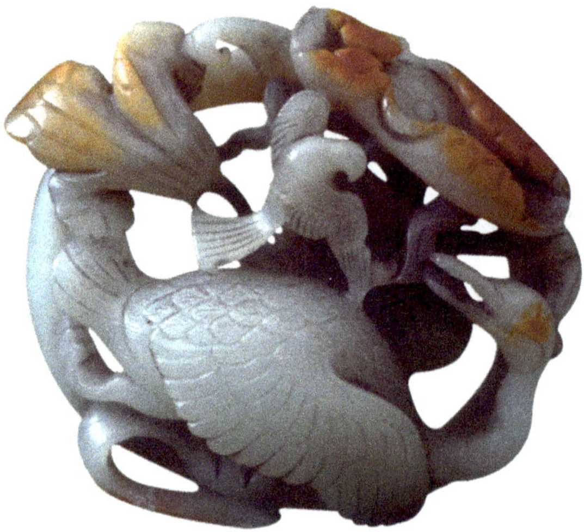

8. Jade Ornament of Spring Water Pattern
Liao (or Jin)
Length: 7 cm Thickness: 2.1 cm
Preserved in the Palace Museum in Beijing

This is an ornament made of grey jade with some yellowish brown spots which are due to erosion. Its obverse side bulges, and on its reverse side the center sinks to a circle and the surrounding is flat. On its obverse side was carved, by means of layered piercing and intaglio, a falcon attacking a wild goose. There are carved lotus leaves as decoration.

During the Liao and Jin Dynasties, kings, princes and aristocrats would go hunting for swans and wild geese every spring, which is called "Spring Water". The pattern of falcons attacking wild geese is called "Spring Water Pattern".

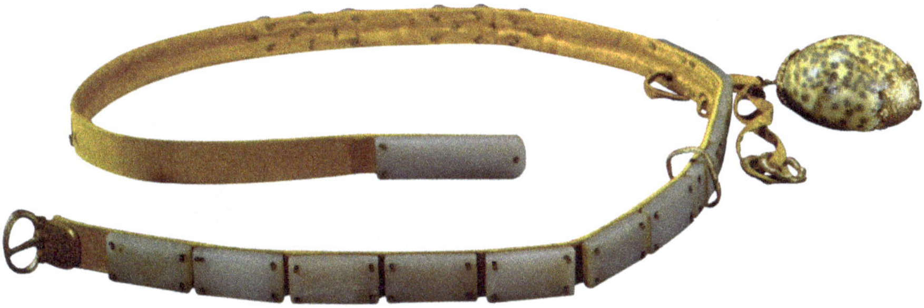

9. Jade Belt with Gold Buckles

Jin
Length: 11 cm for each jade slice
Unearthed from Fuyu, Jilin in 1958
Preserved in the Jilin Provincial Museum
This is an ornament made of white jade and consists of 19 jade plates and 29 gold nails. Of these jade plaques, 12 pieces are oblong, 6 are peach-shaped, and another is an elongated pointed tablet. These plaques are plain with nothing but mortises used for fastening them to leather. This belt was also decorated with gold buckles and rings and some shells.

10. Jade Boy Pendant

Jin
Height: 5.1 cm Thickness: 1.8 cm
Unearthed from Zhongxing, Suibin, Heilongjiang in 1973
Preserved in the Heilongjiang Provincial Museum
This is an ornament made of grey jade with some spots which are due to erosion. There is a circular engravure in the shape of a boy wearing a gauze cap, jacket and trousers, holding banana leaves in his left hand, and walking with his legs somewhat bent.

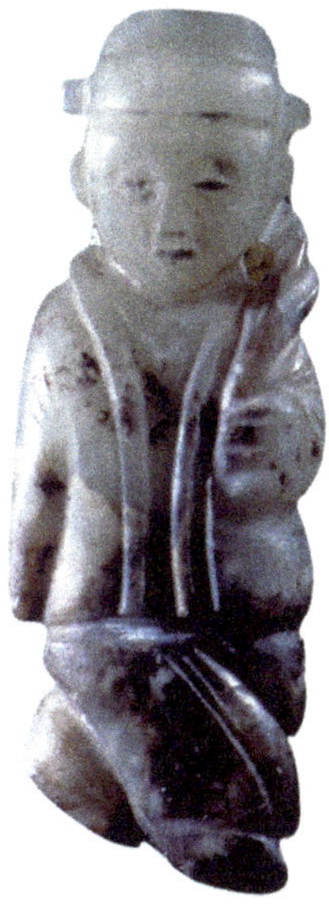

11. Agat Bowl

Liao

Height: 3.1 cm Top Diameter: 7.4 cm
Bottom Diameter: 4.4 cm

Unearthed from burial tomb of a Chen princess and her Liao husband in Naiman Banner, Inner Mongolia in 1986.

Preserved in the Inner Mongolia Institute for Archaeological Research and Cultural Relics.

This is a drinking vessel made of red agat. This vessel has an open mouth, round lips, a protruding belly and round foot. The belly wall has natural grain and a polished surface.

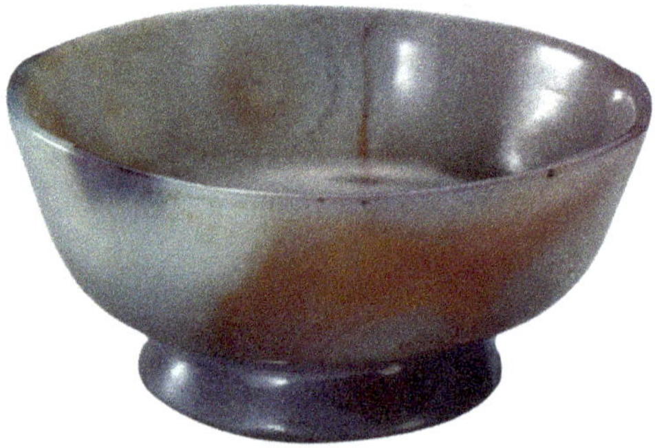

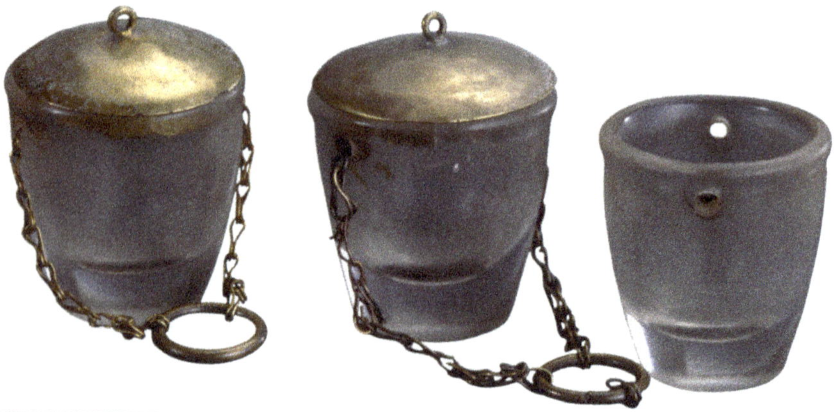

12. Chained Crystal Cup

Liao

Height: 3.5 cm Top Diameter: 2.8 Bottom Diameter:1.8 cm

Unearthed from burial tomb of a Chen princess and her Liao husband in Naiman Banner, Inner Mongolia in 1986

Preserved in the Inner Mongolia Institute for Archaeological Research and Cultural Relics

This is an ornament. The cup has round lips, a barrel-shaped belly and a flat bottom. There are two symmetrical small holes along the mouth. A gold chain crosses each hole and connects with a gilded silver cup which allows it to be worn. Each gilded silver has a hat-shaped gilded silver cover with a small annular button.

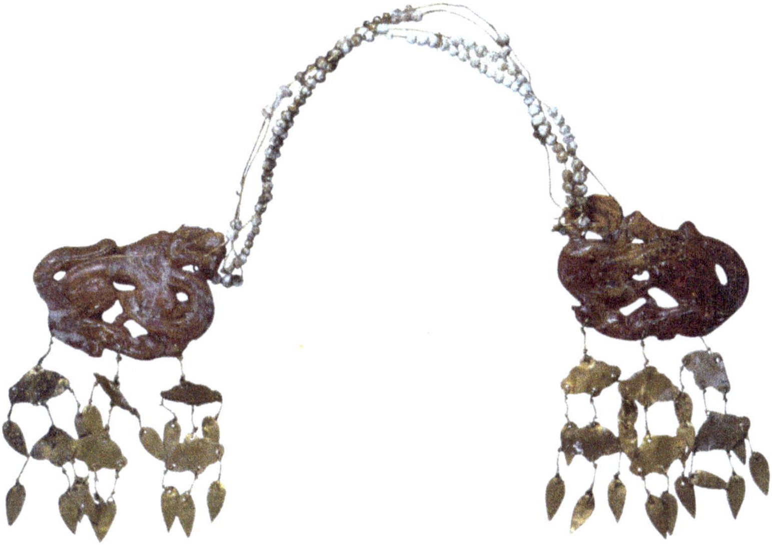

13. Amber and Pearl Headwear

Liao
Length: 5.1 cm
Width: 3.5 cm for the amber ornament with dragon pattern
Diameter: 0.35 cm for each pearl
Diameter: 0.04 cm for gold thread
Length: 1.8 cm Width: 1.1 cm for the gold rhombus sheet
Length: 1.2 cm for the gold sheet in the shape of a pointed leaf
Unearthed from burial tomb of a Chen princess and her Liao husband in Naiman Banner, Inner Mongolia in 1986
Preserved in the Inner Mongolia Institute for Archaeological Research and Cultural Relics

This is an ornament that would have been placed on the head of a princess. This headwear consists of 166 pieces, including 2 amber dragon-shape pieces, 122 small pearls and 42 gold pieces linked by gold wires. These pearls were linked by gold wires and divided into two strings in long loops. Each of the two ends was connected to a dragon-shaped amber piece with three series of gold pieces hanging below.

14. Amber Pendant with Dragon Pattern

Liao

Length: 6.7 cm Width: 4.7 cm Thickness: 2.6 cm

Unearthed from burial tomb of a Chen princess and her Liao husband in Naiman Banner, Inner Mongolia in 1986

Preserved in the Inner Mongolia Institute for Archaeological Research and Cultural Relics

This is an ornament in the shape of a roughly rounded rectangle. On the obverse side was carved a dragon raising its head and swaying its tail. There is a hole crossing the side which allowed for fastening with thread.

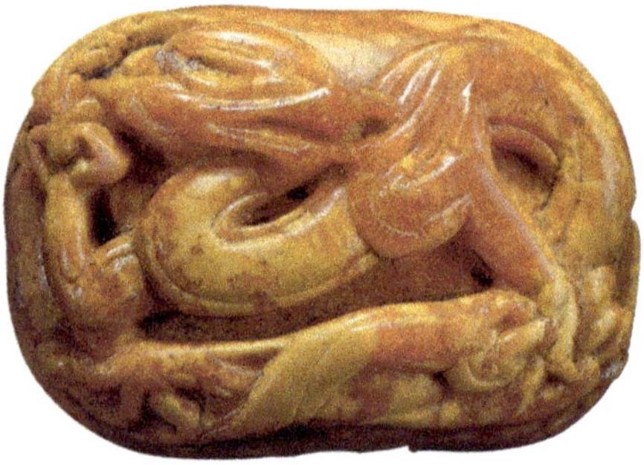

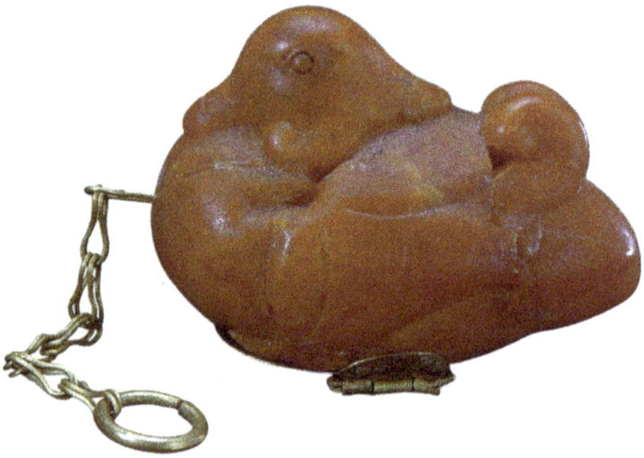

15. Amber Pendant with Mandarin-Duck Pattern

Liao

Length: 2.6 cm Width: 1.5 cm Thickness: 1.6 cm

Unearthed from burial tomb of a Chen princess and her Liao husband in Naiman Banner, Inner Mongolia in 1986

Preserved in the Inner Mongolia Institute for Archaeological Research and Cultural Relics

This is an ornament made of reddish brown amber. It is a circular engravure in shape of crouching mandarin ducks with flat beaks and short tails. They are twisting their necks and closing their wings. There is a hole in the middle of the heads allowing for fastening with thread.

16. Amber Wreath

Liao

Circumference: 113 cm for one suite, 159 cm for the other suite

Unearthed from burial tomb of a Chen princess and her Liao husband in Naiman Banner, Inner Mongolia in 1986

Preserved in the Inner Mongolia Institute for Archaeological Research and Cultural Relics

This wreath is an ornament and consists of two suites. One suite is made of 257 amber beads in 5 strings, 5 pieces of amber relief and 2 plain amber ornaments linked by silver wires; the other suite is made up of 60 amber beads, 7 pieces of amber relief and 2 plain amber ornaments linked by silver wires. The relief designs on these amber pieces are mainly dragon patterns.

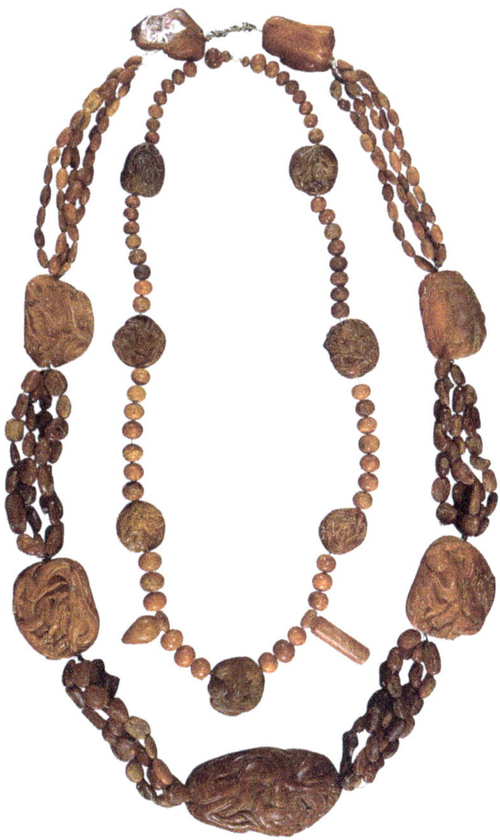

17. Amber and Pearl Earrings

Liao

Length: 13 cm

Unearthed from burial tomb of a Chen princess and her Liao husband in Naiman Banner, Inner Mongolia in 1986

Preserved in the Inner Mongolia Institute for Archaeological Research and Cultural Relics

These ornaments comprise 1 gold hook, 4 amber pieces, 6 big pearls and 10 small pearls linked by gold wires. These 4 amber pieces were all carved into the shape of dragon-fish boats. The boats, with dragons' heads and fish bodies, have cabins, masts, creels, and men rowing and fishing.

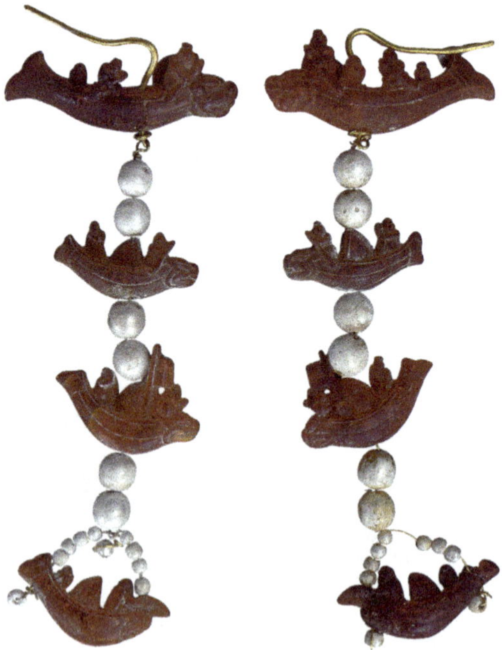

Copper Ware

In the Liao Dynasty, there was not a great amount or a great variety of copper ware. The copper objects mainly included mirrors, cauldrons, bowls, spoons, pots, ewers, counterpoises, bells, gloves and boots made of copper wire, copper masks, and small gilded copper articles for daily use. Of these, the items for everyday use came in many varieties, such as locks, keys and buckles. Copper mirrors were mainly round in shape, like the character "亚" (pronounced Ya), sunflower-shaped or octagonal. And the ornamentation for mirrors mainly included two-fish, Eight-Diagrams, boys, lotus, Glachoma longituba, and peonies and turtlebacks. Mirrors with plain surfaces were also popular. On some mirrors there are lucky words inscribed in both Han and Khitan scripts, a common features of that time.

In recent years many ruins, kilns and tombs of the Jin Dynasty were discovered in some areas in Heilongjiang and Jilins. In terms of variety and shape, many of these unearthed copper items were similar to those produced in the Central Plains. There were copper Buddhas and pagodas besides items for everyday use such as copper mirrors and buckets. Due to the mass production of copper coins, the government of the Jin Dynasty strictly controlled the usage of copper, and many objects at that time were made of iron instead, such as bells and some religious articles. Copper mirrors and seals dominate among copper objects that survive from the Jin Dynasty. Copper mirrors combined many features of Han mirrors, and most of them had wide or rolled-up edges and round buttons, with exquisite or rough patterns. The mirrors were mainly in round in shape some with handles, some without. Other shapes included rhombus, sunflower petals, octagons, or fan.

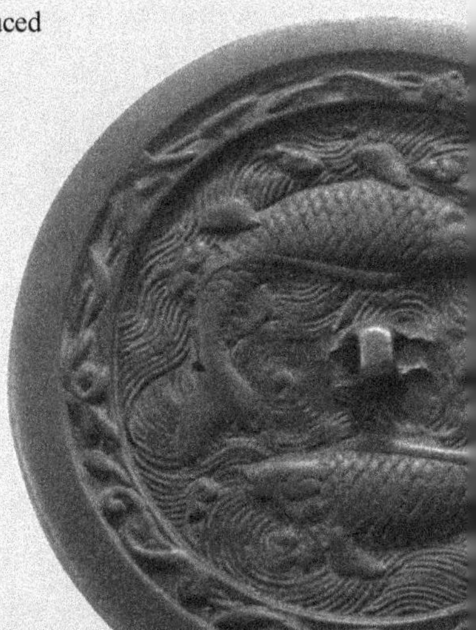

Besides there were also some mirrors with plain surfaces, some with double-fish or double-dragon ornamentation, some with chrysanthemum, lotus, animal, or people motifs. People featured in a wide range of subjects, such as Liu Yi delivering a message, a Wu cow shivering before the moon, stories of the reclusive Nest Father and Fan Shu, or a boy playing with flowers. In the Jin Dynasty, the patterns of the mirrors followed those of the Han and Tang Dynasties. Thus they were typically decorated with connected introverted arcs and stars, clouds, birds and animals. In terms of Tang influence, they were decorated with patterns of unknown animals and grapes. The mirrors were usually inscribed with the names of the places of production, with the names of the officers in charge, and with designated numbers, reflecting the strict controls there were on copper in the Jin Dynasty.

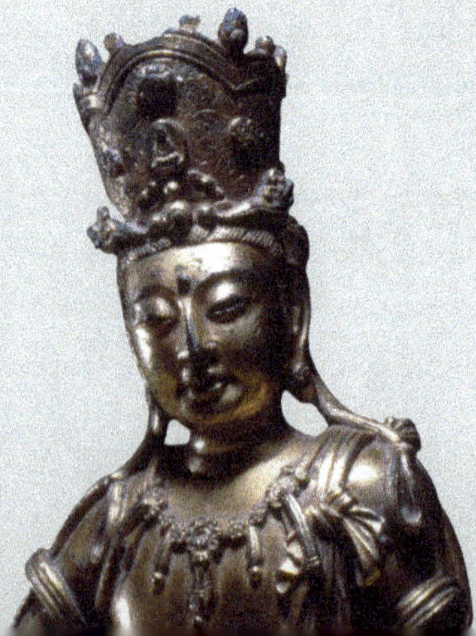

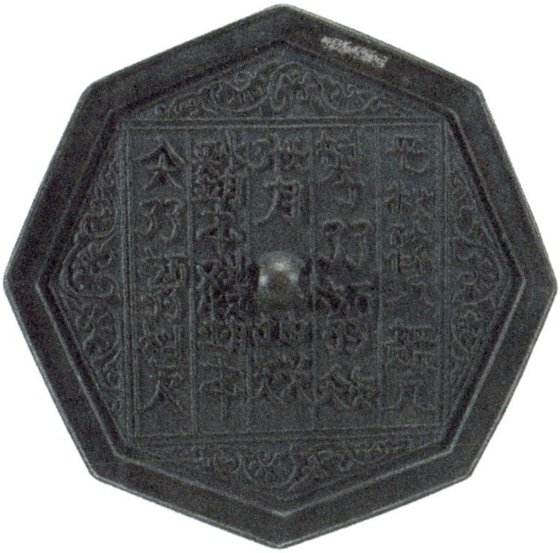

18. Mirror with Khitan Script

Liao
Diameter: 26 cm
Unearthed from Yongfeng, Harqin Banner, Inner Mongolia in 1973
Preserved in the Inner Mongolia Museum

This mirror is octagonal in shape. On its back there is a semi-spherical button in the center and the margin is wide. There is a ridged circle inside and outside the edge. The inside area is in a rounded square. Along each side of the square, there is found intagliated Khitan script, spelling out "longevity", "lasting", "blessing", and "virtue". Between each side of the square and the margin are decorations of leaves and grass in bas relief. On the lower left side on the back are the intagliated characters "Baodi Officer". There is a signature under the script, which reads "Officer".

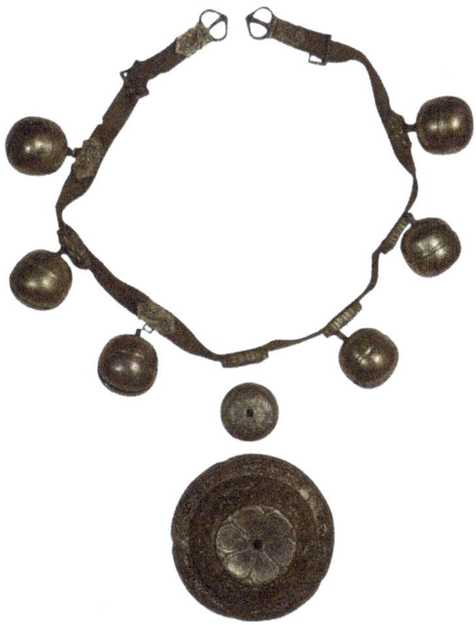

19. Gilded Copper Bells with Buckle

Liao
Unearthed from burial tomb of a Liao princess and her husband, the King of Zengwei at Chifeng, Inner Mongolia in 1953

These are harnesses. Bells were often worn on horses' necks. At the excavation site, some bells were still linked by a leather strap with gilded dragon-pattern ornaments. These bells make different sounds; some sound brilliant and clear and others sound much deeper. The buckles are round with a circle of lotus petals in the center, rolled-up grasses beside, and flowers and grasses in the outer margin.

20. Copper Crouching Dragon

Jin
Height: 19.6 cm Weight: 2.11 kg
Unearthed from Jin Shangjing, Huining Prefecture, Acheng City, Heilongjiang
Preserved in the Heilongjiang Provincial Museum
This was an article for display. The crouching dragon raises its head, opens its mouth, leans forward slightly with its shoulders, lifts its left front leg with its paw clutching a clouds, and stretches forward its right front leg with the other paw on the ground. The tiger is raising up and rolling its tail.

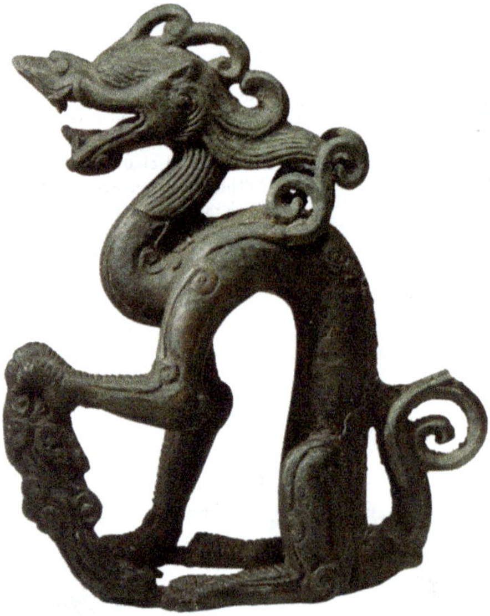

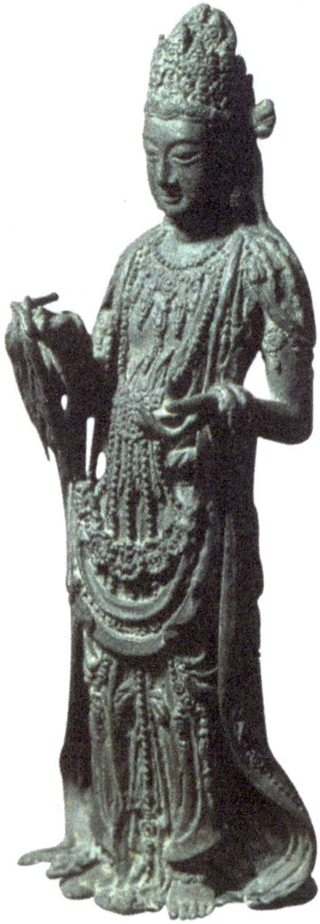

21. Gilded Copper Kwan-yin Bodhisattva Statue

Liao
Height: 21 cm
Preserved in the Shanghai Museum
This is a Buddhist statue. The Bodhisattva wears a crown and has a round face. He lowers his underjaw. His exposed chest is decorated with wreaths and necklaces. He wears a long skirt. He stands up with one hand holding a bottle and the other holding a Buddha.

22. Gilded Copper Kwan-yin Statue

Liao

Height: 18.5 cm

Preserved in the Palace Museum in Beijing

This is a Buddhist statue. The Kwan-yin wears a crown with a rolled-up-grass pattern, and has a round face and a high-bridged nose. His eyes are closed slightly and he smiles with a dignified and amiable manner. His exposed chest is decorated with wreaths and long pieces of silk. He wears a long skirt with one hand supporting his body and the other on his knee. He sits with one leg bent over the other.

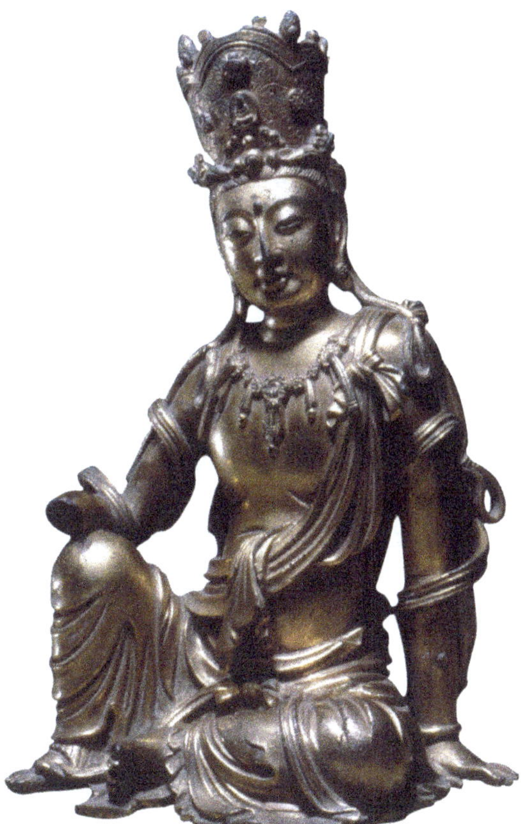

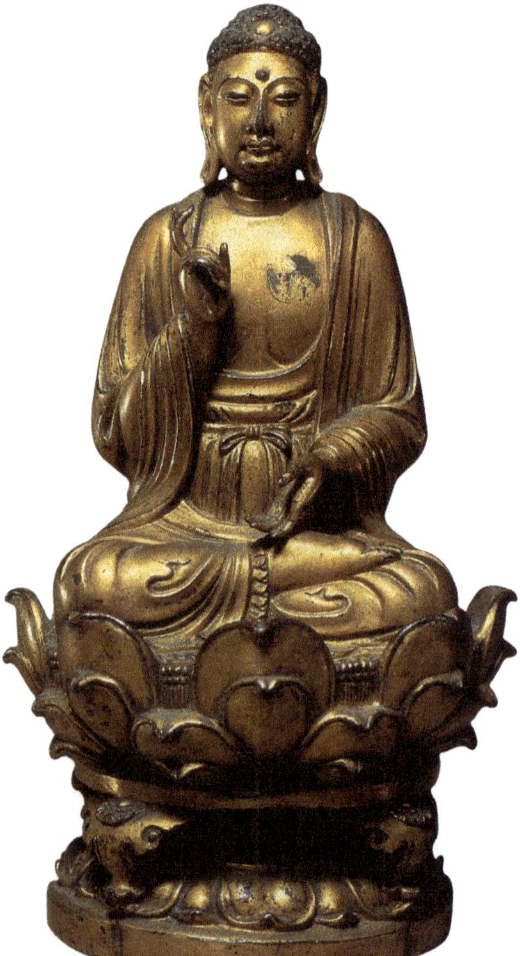

23. Gilded Copper Buddha Statue
Liao
Height: 20.7 cm
Preserved in the Palace Museum in Beijing

This is a gilded copper Buddhist statue. The Buddha has a snail-shaped bun and white hair on his forehead. He looks down with his lips closed and his earlobes are as long as his shoulders. He has a full and round face, and his chest is exposed. He wears a cassock with a hanging collar and a long skirt. He raises his right hand to his breast and holds his left hand on his belly. He sits in a cross-legged posture on a full lotus pedestal.

24. Mirror with Patterns of Mountains, Rivers and People

Jin
Diameter: 36 cm
Unearthed from Suileng, Heilongjiang in 1975
Preserved in the Heilongjiang Provincial Museum
This mirror is round and has a fine, bright, silver grey surface. On the back there is a semi-spherical button in the center. In the inside area there is a scene with some people in relief pattern with mountains, rivers, trees and fields as the background. Mountains, rocks, trees and people can be seen above the button, and rivers and fish below the button. In the inner area there is a narrow circle of twisted branches and rolled-up clouds. The margin is plain and narrow.

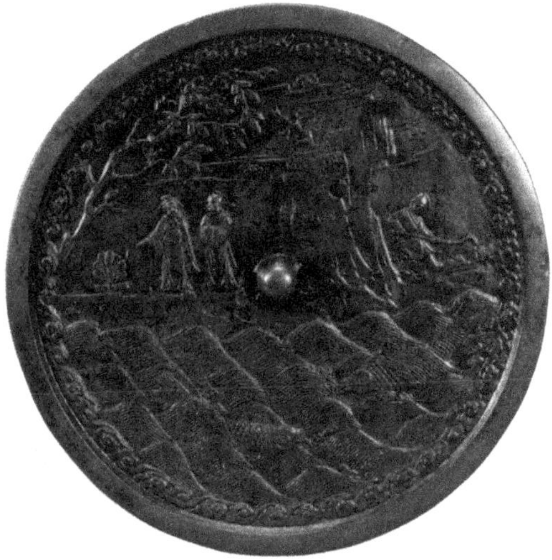

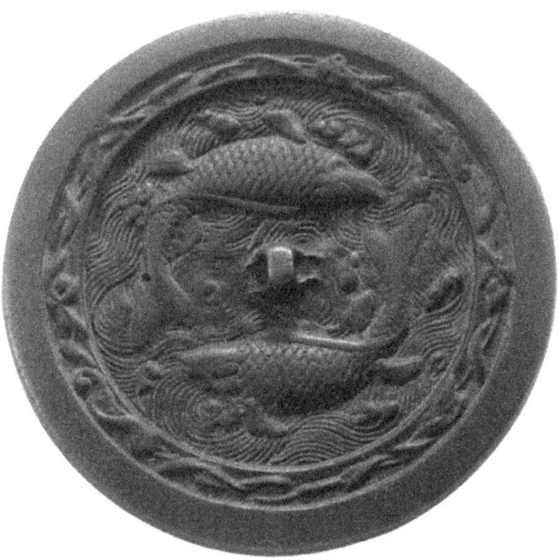

25. Mirror with a Two-carp Pattern

Jin
Diameter: 43 cm Weight: 12.4 kg
Unearthed from Nanyang Village in Acheng, Heilongjiang in 1964
Preserved Acheng County Administration of Cultural Relics
This mirror is round. On the back there is a semi-spherical button in the center and the margin is wide. The major motif is two carps jumping above the water with the head of one touching the tail of the other. Splashing water and waves serve as the background, surrounded by creeping weeds.

26. Gilded Copper Skanda Statue

Western Xia
Height: 58 cm
Unearthed from Xinhua Street in Yinchuan, Ningxia in 1986
Preserved in the Ningxia Hui Autonomous Region Museum
This is a gilded copper Buddhist statue. The Skanda stands up with a square and awe-inspiring face. He wears a helmet with tassels floating in the air. The earflaps of his helmet are rolled up. He wears gold armor with a full-sleeved coat and a shawl around the shoulders. He puts his palms together before his chest and carries a demon-exorcizing pestle. He stands on a half-horseshoe-shaped mountain pedestal. Skanda is a Buddhist guardian deity and is always in the form of a warrior in armor. He is in charge of providing protection from demons.

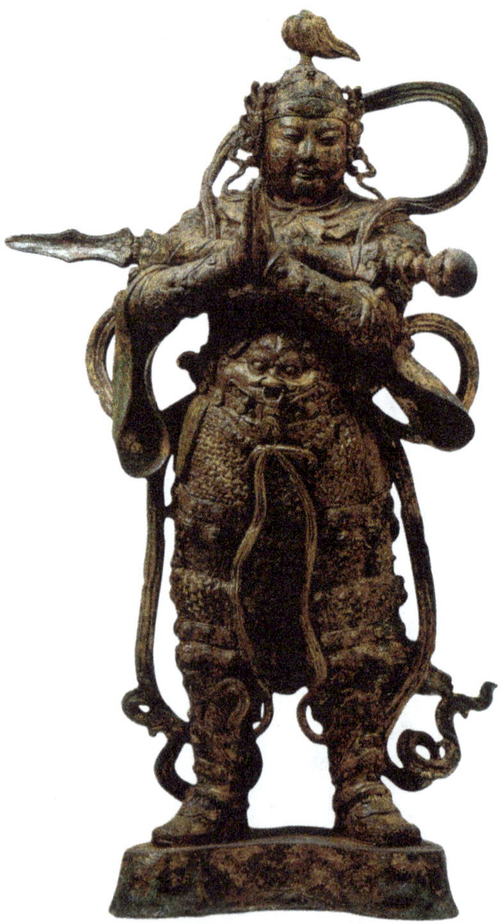

Gold and Silver Ware

Hundreds of pieces of gold and silver ware were unearthed from tombs, pagodas and cellars of the Liao Dynasty in Inner Mongolia, in the west of Liaoning, in the north of Hebei, in Jilin and in Beijing. There is an enormous variety of gold and silver ware from that time and the items were had a wide range of usage covering almost all sectors - articles for daily use, funeral articles, dresses and adornments, sacrificial items and harnesses. Items for daily use mainly included cups, bowls, plates, pots, boxes, refuse vessels, bottles, cases, gourd-shaped ladles, teacup saucers, and alms bowls. Of these, bowls, cups, plates, boxes and refuse vessels were the most common. Funeral items perhaps best represented the distinctive national features, and were perhaps the most important sector for gold and silver usage. Take as an example the two collections of dresses unearthed from burial tomb of the Chen princess and her Liao husband in Naiman Banner, Inner Mongolian Autonomous Region. Before each head was placed a gilded silver crown and the faces were covered with gold masks. Under the princess's head was a silver pillow with gold decorations. Each body had a silver-thread netted around it, a gold and silver belt on the waist and silver boots with gold decorations on the feet. These objects were of the very best quality and were absolutely exquisite. Gold and silver Buddhist ritual objects included bodhi trees, dagobas, ladles and other worship objects are also found in some sites. Most of these were made during the reigns of Emperors Xingzong and Daozong of the Liao Dynasty, with the most common instruments being heavenly palaces and underground palaces used in Liao pagodas. Such objects belong to Esoteric Buddhism, and they show the mix of Khitan and Han cultures. In terms of style, it is clear to see that gold and silver manufacturing in the Liao Dynasty passed through two periods; during the first period, they were influenced mainly by Tang culture and during the second period, they were more deeply

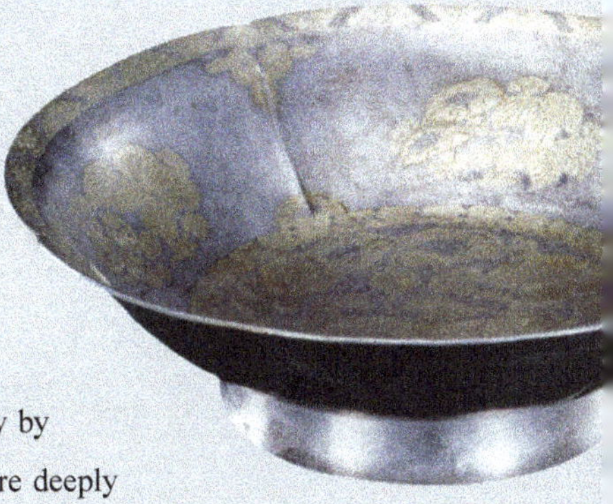

influenced by Song culture.

It is rare to see gold and silver ware from the Jin Dynasty. The best example that remains to us is a silver incense burner with eight ridges and patterns of peonies and sprays. It was made by a Jin folk craftsman and was Unearthed from underground palace of the pagoda in Jinbaoyan Temple in Gu'an, Hebei. This object differs very little from a typical eight-ridged silver piece from the Song Dynasty in terms of craftwork and style. This is probably due to the fact that many Song items would have been available to Jin traders and a large number of gold and silver craftsmen were captured by the Jin Regime after the Northern Song Dynasty collapsed. In addition, a few gold and silver objects were unearthed from ruins of Jin Shangjing Huining Prefecture, Acheng City, Heilongjiang.

A few gold and silver objects from the Western Xia have also been discovered. Representative works include bevel-edged cylinder-shaped gold nail files with two fish, gold earrings engraved with human figures, lotus-shaped gold saucers carved with twisted branches and grasses, and gold bowls carved with phoenixes around lucky patterns, with peonies and passion flowers inside and at the bottom. These objects are simple but elegant, with a style almost the same as gold and silver craftsmanship of the Northern and Southern Song Dynasties.

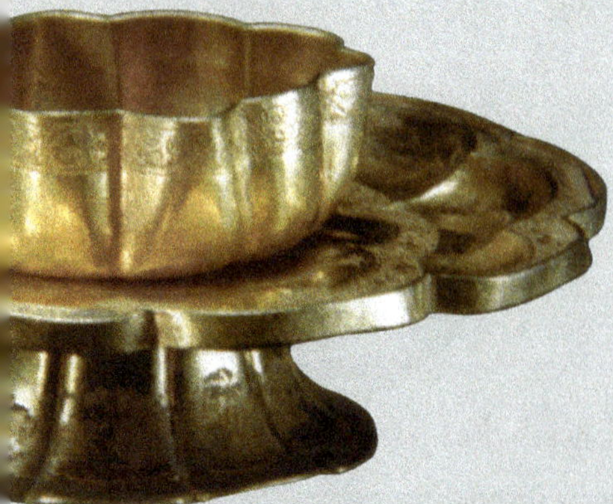

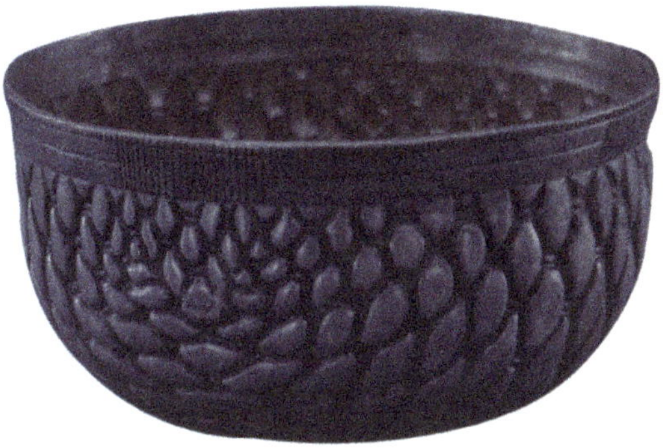

27. Silver Cup with Wicker Bucket Pattern

Liao

Height: 5.6 cm   Top Diameter: 10.4 cm

Unearthed from Bairin Right Banner, Juu Uda Ayima, Inner Mongolia in 1978.

Preserved in the Inner Mongolia Museum

This was a drinking vessel with a wide flaring mouth, straight belly (slightly protruding in the lower part), and a flat bottom. Its neck was chiseled with arced lines and above these arc lines are a series of equidistant vertical lines, giving it the appearance of wicker. The outside of its belly was pressed with patterns like a wicker bucket.

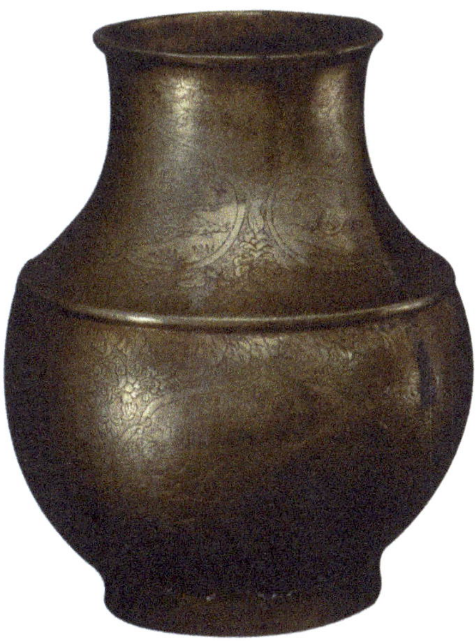

28. Gilded Silver Jar with Dutiful Sons Motif

Liao

Height: 14.8 cm   Top Diameter: 7.6 cm

Unearthed from Tomb of the Liao Dynasty's Yelu Yuzhi at Ar Khorchin Banner, Inner Mongolia in 1992

Preserved in the Inner Mongolia Museum

This was a container with rolled-up round lips, a high neck, ridged shoulders, a round belly and a flat bottom. It was carved with patterns all around. Eight dutiful-son stories constitute the principal decorations, with four on the neck and four on the belly. Around these patterns are flowers and in the lower part of the belly are lotus petal patterns .

Yelu Yuzhi was a cousin of Yelu Abaoji, the Liao Emperor Taizu. He was a ruler of great glory and majesty.

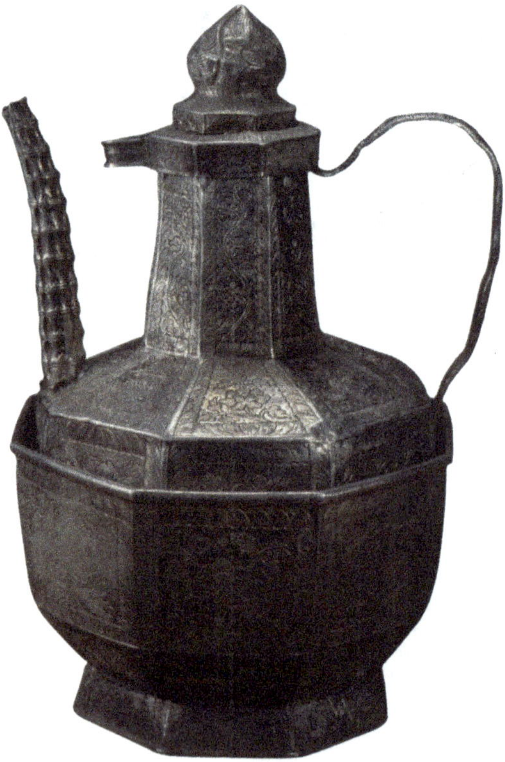

29. Eight-ridged Silver Ewer Carved with Flowers

Liao

Height: 25 cm

Unearthed from Bairin Right Banner , Inner Mongolia in 1978

Preserved in the Bairin Right Banner Art Museum

This is a drinking vessel with a thin neck, broad belly and high shoulders. Its mouth, neck, shoulders, belly and foot are all regular octagons. Its spout is thin and long and is in the form of a series of bamboos. All 32 sides of its body were carved with petals as frames and inside the frames are found intagliated patterns of peonies or twisted lotuses. There is a pointed button on its two-layer cover, which was carved with flower patterns.

30. Loop-handled Silver Pot with Fish-Dragon Patterns

Liao
Height: 43 cm from handle to bottom, 34 cm for pot
Unearthed from Chengzi, Chifeng, Inner Mongolia in 1979.
Preserved in the Chifeng Municipal Station of Cultural Relics.
This is a drinking vessel in the shape of double-fish dragons. It has a straight mouth, long neck, oblate belly, flat bottom and cover. From top to bottom, this sculpture is in the shape of two fish-dragons, head to head and tail to tail, playing with a pearl. Its loop-handle looks like a belt, with each end linked to a small ring. Inside each ring there is a bird-shaped ear with wings spread and a long tail. The handle was decorated with seven three-petal flowers. Its gourd-shaped cover has an expanding margin in the form of a four-petalled flower with a long chain on the neck.

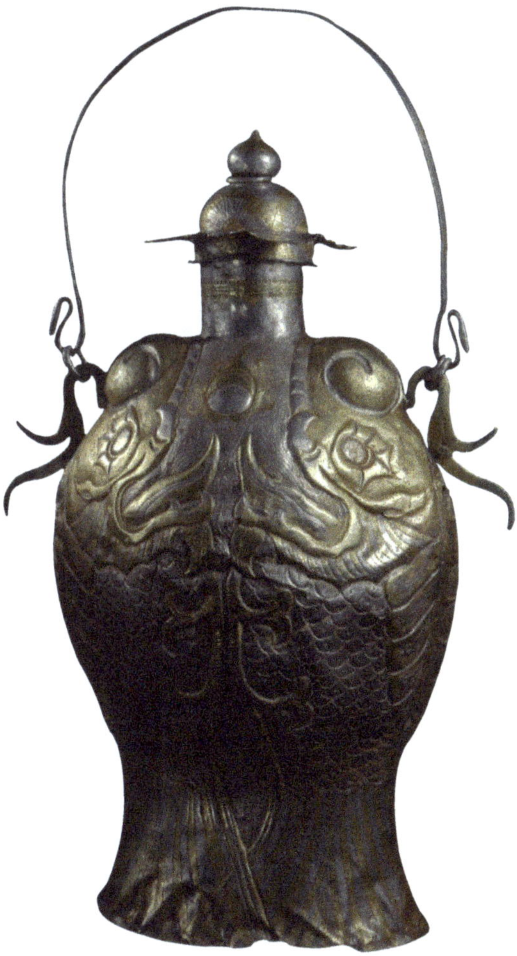

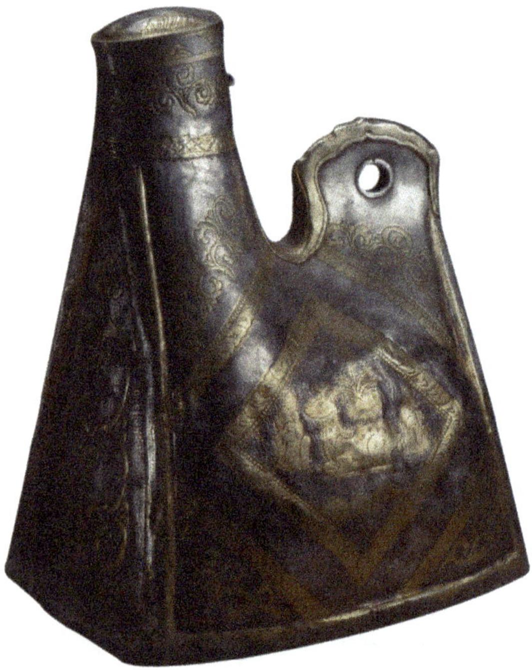

31. Horseshoe-shaped Silver Pot with Deer Pattern

Liao

Height: 26.5 cm

Unearthed from Chengzi, Chifeng, Inner Mongolia in 1979

Preserved in the Chifeng Municipal Museum

This is a horseshoe-shaped container with a straight mouth, small ring and flat bottom. Its cover has a slightly protruding surface with a mortise for a button. Its handle looks like a cockscomb. Its slightly protruding belly has the same designs on both sides: in the center there are two rhombuses in which is a carved crouching deer, and there is a "Buddhist hill" on both the front and back. The left and right sides of its body are triangular in shape, the roe-pattern ground has flower decorations with twisted branches, and the margin has leather strap decorations.

Horseshoe-shaped pots are a kind of leather pot, and were used by the nomadic Khitan people to hold water, milk and wine. They were named for their horseshoe-like shapes.

32. Gilded Silver Case with Dragon-and-Phoenix Pattern

Liao

Height: 21 cm Top Diameter: 25.4 cm Weight: 1800grams

Unearthed from burial tomb of a Chen princess and her Liao husband at the Qinglongshan Mountain in Naiman Banner, Jerim Ayima, Inner Mongolia in 1986

Preserved in the Inner Mongolia Institute for Archaeological Research and Cultural Relics

This was a container with a snap fastener. Its cover is flat and made of silver sheet. Its circular foot was welded to the case. On the surface of its cover is a bas relief of a dragon playing with a pearl. The margin is decorated with a circle of connected beads and transformed lotus petals, and the edge is decorated with patterns of phoenixes and peonies. On its belly are two circles of begonias, one circle of phoenixes, plus a circle of peonies. The bottom edge of the circular foot was chiseled with a circle of connected beads. At the excavation site, there was found in this case a piece of a silver covered pot and three silver boxes.

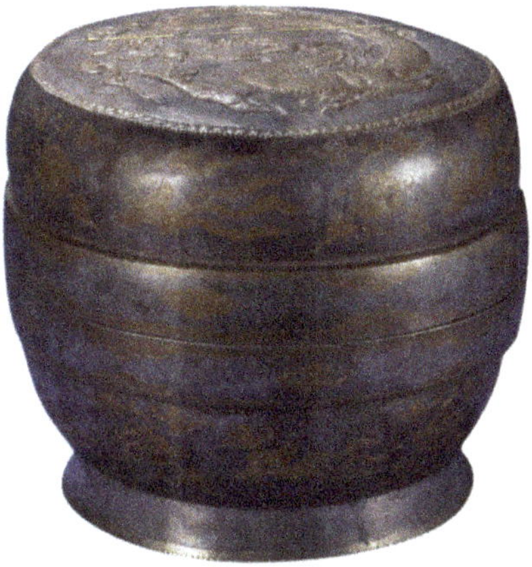

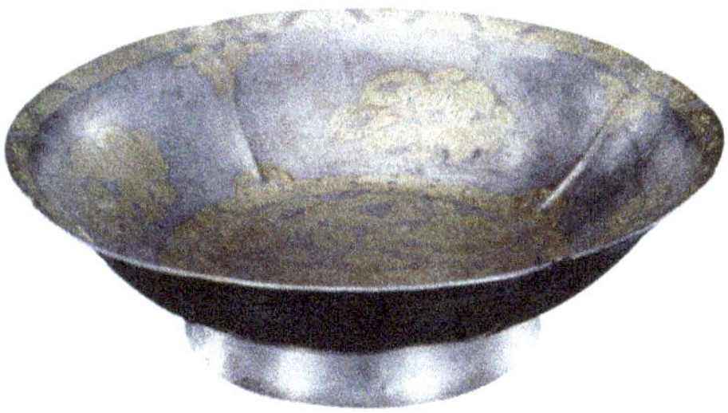

33. Gilded Silver Bowl with Mandarin-Duck Pattern

Liao

Height: 6.9 cm Top Diameter: 22.8 cm Foot Diameter: 11.6 cm

Unearthed from Yongshan Village, Fengzhen City, Inner Mongolia

Preserved in the Inner Mongolia Museum

This was a vessel with a sunflower-shape mouth, oblique-arc belly, and a gently flaring circular foot. The edge of the bowl is decorated with broken begonias, and the inner wall is decorated with four groups of broadleaf rubiaceae flowers. The inside bottom was carved with a pair of mandarin ducks in flowering shrubs; the female duck is in the front, with the male one at the back, and the two mandarin ducks are moving in harmony. Around them are decorations of circular strings and continuous feather-like petals. Some of the decorations are gilded.

34. Silver Teacup and Saucer

Liao
Height: 2.7 cm Diameter: 6.2 cm for teacup
Height: 4.2 cm Diameter: 4.4 cm for saucer
Unearthed from underground palace of the pagoda in Jingjue Temple at Yixian County, Hebei in 1977
Preserved in the Hebei Provincial Cultural Relics Research Institute
This is a set of vessels consisting of a teacup and saucer. The teacup is in shape of flower petals, with a flairing mouth, oblique straight wall and circular foot. The inner wall of the cup was carved with a circle of twisted lotuses. The bowl-shaped saucer has a straight mouth, protruding belly and flat bottom, and is connected with a six-petal sunflower-shaped plate. The edge of the plate rolls down and it has a horn-like circular foot. The margins of the saucer and the plate were both chiseled with twisted lotuses, and the turning-down edge of the plate was chiseled with honeysuckles, with the bottom of the circular foot being carved with a circle of flames.

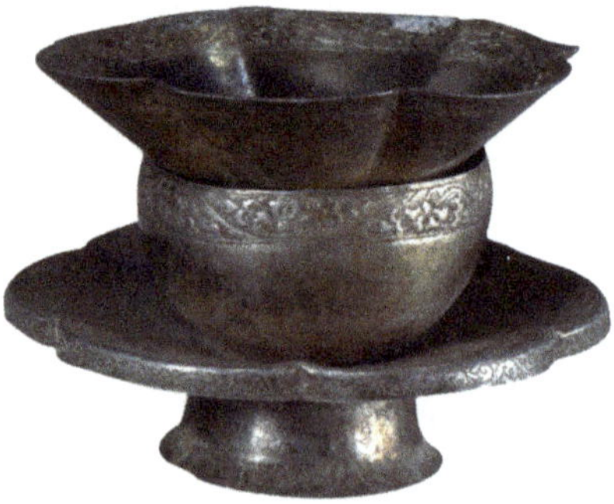

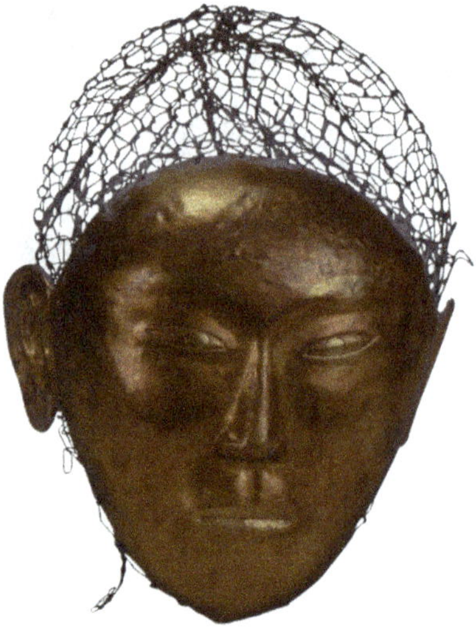

35. Gold Mask for Princess' Husband

Liao
Height: 21.1 cm Width: 18.8 cm
Unearthed from burial tomb of a Chen princess and her Liao husband in Naiman Banner, Inner Mongolia in 1986.
Preserved in the Inner Mongolia Institute for Archaeological Research and Cultural Relics
This is a funeral object. This face-shaped mask was hammered out to show eyes, a nose and mouth. Two open eyes were carved out complete with pupils. The nose has a high bridge. The mouth is closed. There are 26 holes on the frame of the mask with threads of silver wire which connect to the silver-wire net wrapped around the dead body.

36. Gilded Silver Crown Carved with Flowers and Birds

Liao

Height: 30 cm Diameter: 19.5 cm

Unearthed from burial tomb of a Chen princess and her Liao husband in Naiman Banner, Inner Mongolia in 1986

Preserved in the Inner Mongolia Institute for Archaeological Research and Cultural Relics

This is a funeral object and served as a crown for a princess. It was made of gilded silver sheets carved with pierced and chiseled designs. The top of the crown is round with vertical wings on two sides. The opening wings are broad in the upper part and narrow in the lower part. The obverse side the crown and the vertical wings were decorated with pairs of phoenixes facing each other. Around the phoenixes are twisted flowers.

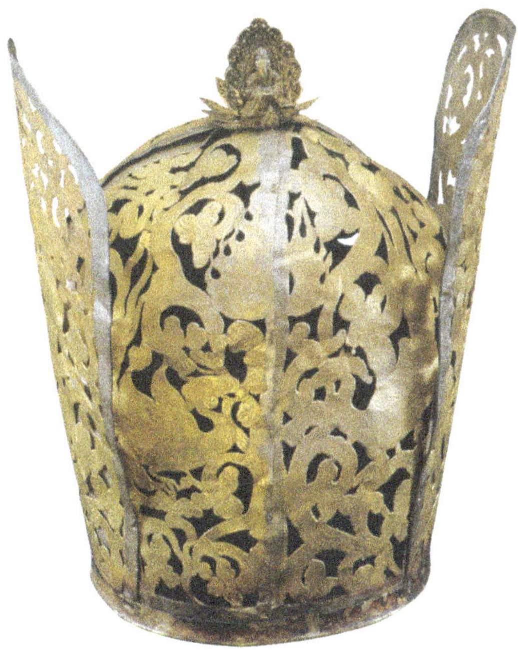

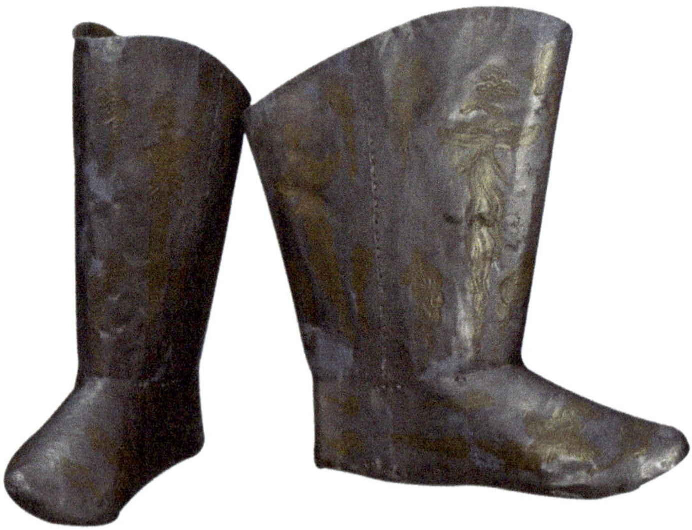

37 Gilded Silver Boots with Phoenix Pattern

Liao

Height: 34 cm Bottom Length: 32 cm Width: 4.5-8.5 cm

Unearthed from burial tomb of a Chen princess and her Liao husband in Naiman Banner, Inner Mongolia in 1986.

Preserved in the Inner Mongolia Institute for Archaeological Research and Cultural Relics

This pair of boots were used as funeral objects. They consist of three parts; legs, uppers and soles. The mouth of the boots is elliptical; the boot legs are broad in the upper and narrow in the lower part and look like fans when viewed from the outside; the toe caps are pointed; the soles are thin and long; and the center of the soles are slightly indented. The surface of the boot legs and uppers was chiseled with gilded phoenixes and clouds. The phoenixes all look like they are getting ready for flying. They were made of silver sheets which were joined using silver wire.

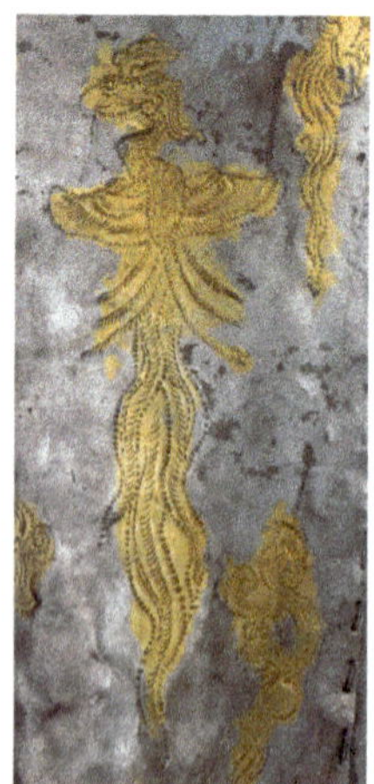

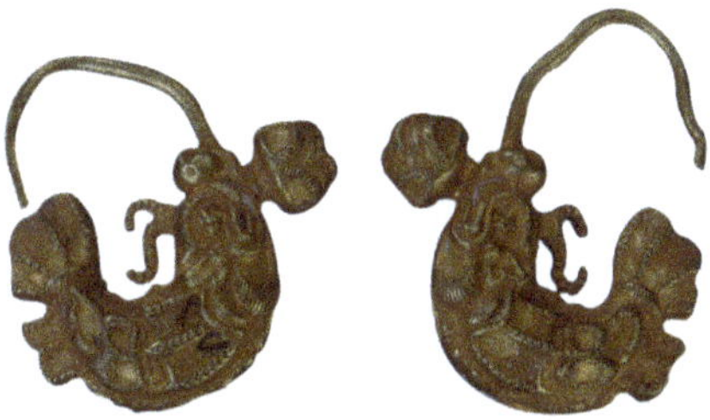

38. Capricorn-shaped Gold Earrings

Liao

Height: 4.4 cm Width: 4.4 cm Thickness: 1.6 cm for one

Height: 4.5 cm Width: 3.5 cm Thickness: 1.3 cm for the other

Unearthed from Liao Tomb of Yelu Yu Zhi at Ar Khorchin Banner, Inner Mongolia in 1992

Preserved in the Inner Mongolia Museum

This is an ornament. Two pieces were made using molds with the resulting parts being jointed together. They are hollow and the surface is carved with detailed decorations. One Capricorn has a two-horn dragon's head and a rolled-up fish body, and the pierced holes are inset with turquoises. The other Capricorn is smaller with a dragon's head with no horn and a rolled-up fish body.

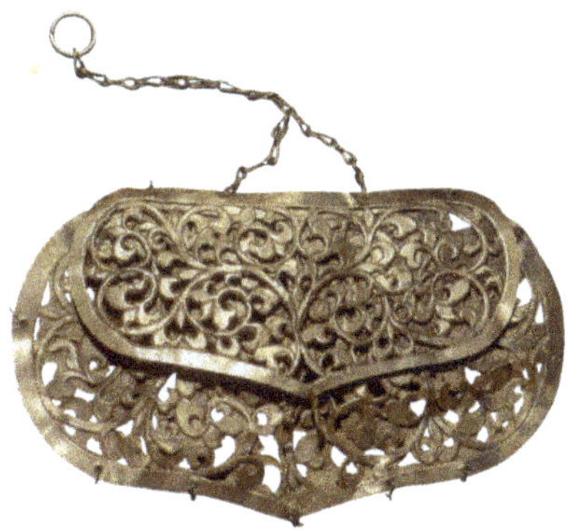

39. Gold Pouch with Carved Designs

Liao

Length: 13.4 cm Width: 7.8 cm

Unearthed from burial tomb of a Chen princess and her Liao husband in Naiman Banner, Inner Mongolia in 1986

Preserved in the Inner Mongolia Institute for Archaeological Research and Cultural Relics

This is an elliptical almond-shaped ornament. It has a cover, chain, and gold ring at the end of the chain for fastening. The major part of this object was made up of two gold sheets of the same size. Each sheet has ten small holes. The cover is smaller than the main part of the object, and it also has holes on the edge which are linked with gold wire. On top of the cover is a small spoon which can be clasped with a small gold ring on the body.

40. Eight-connected-Arc Gold Box

Liao

Height: 1.7 cm Diameter: 5.5 cm for box

Length: 1.7 cm for chain Total Weight: 85grams

Unearthed from burial tomb of a Chen princess and her Liao husband in Naiman Banner, Inner Mongolia in 1986

Preserved in the Inner Mongolia Institute for Archaeological Research and Cultural Relics

This is an ornament. This flat object has a snap fastener for connecting the box and its cover. Two pairs of symmetrical gold buttons were welded to the outside and linked to gold chains. The surface of the box was carved with a pair of mandarin ducks and was decorated with waves and lilies. The outer margin of the box was carved with a circle of protruding connected beads. The bottom was carved with a demirelief of two cranes and some wave decorations and lilies and connected beads. The outsides of the box and its cover were both carved with circles of twisted branches and rolled-up leaves. The designs are fine and smooth, showing extraordinary craftsmanship.

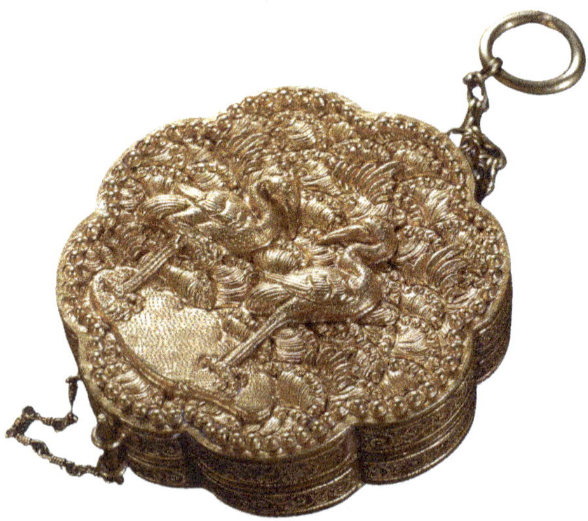

41. Hexagonal Silver Pagoda

Liao
Height: 19.5 cm
Unearthed from underground palace of the pagoda of Jingjue Temple at Yixian County, Hebei in 1977
Preserved in the Hebei Provincial Cultural Relics Research Institute.
This is a Buddhist burial object used for worship. It consists of a base, body and top decoration. Its base is an octagonal girdling Sumeru base decorated with two layers of full lotuses. On each side of the girdle are six sunflower-shaped holes. The hexagonal body was fixed to the base. The top decoration is a hexagonal tented roof and from each corner hangs a bell, with only one missing. On top are lotuses, overlapping bowls and wheels.

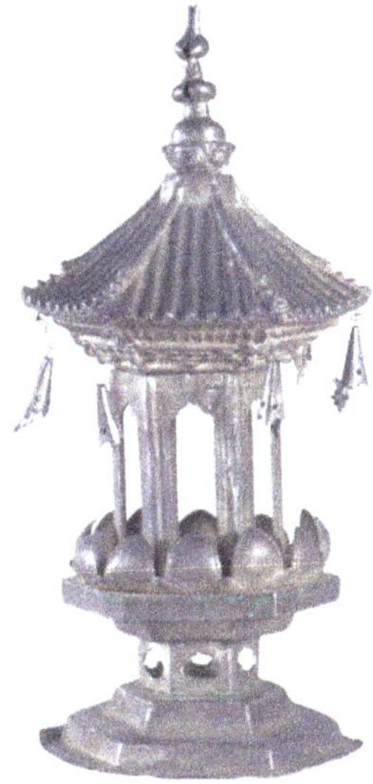

42. Eight-ridged Silver Incense Burner

Jin
Height: 11 cm Diameter: 7.9 cm for top
Unearthed from underground palace of the pagoda of Baoyan Temple at Yuyan Village, Gu'an, Hebei in 1975
Preserved in the Hebei Provincial Cultural Relics Research Institute
This is an incense burner. The body has eight ridges. It has a flaring mouth, round lips, folded shoulders and a small flat bottom. The outside wall was carved with glossy ganodermas, flying butterflies and peonies, and other flowers. On two sides of the burner are rings which would have linked with the handle. Its cover is in the shape of an octagonal monk's hat with a snap fastener. A ring was welded to the cover top decorated with a demirelief of an eight-petal lotus with air holes. The edge of the cover was decorated with lucky clouds. The arch-like handle has a hole with a ring linked to two chains.

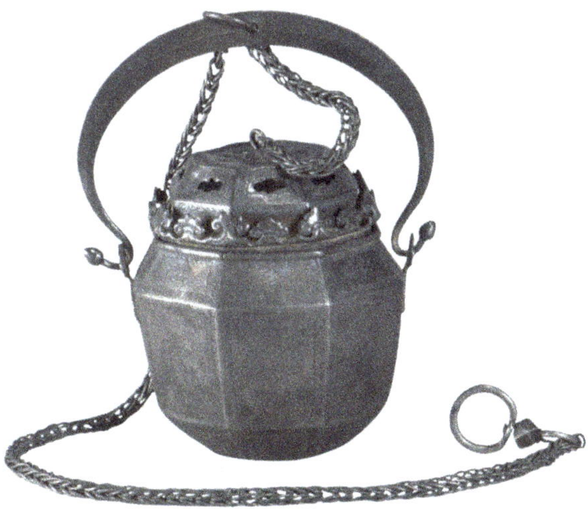

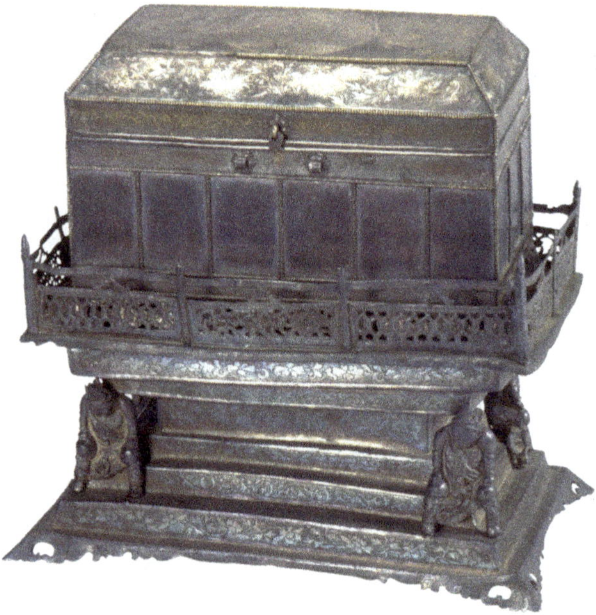

43. Gilded Silver Buddhist Sarira Cabinet

Jin

Height: 28.8 cm   Length: 23.6 cm   Width: 15.5 cm

Unearthed from underground palace of the pagoda at Baoyan Temple at Yuyan Village, Gu'an, Hebei in 1975

Preserved in the Hebei Provincial Cultural Relics Research Institute

This is a Buddhist burial object used for worship. It consists of a cabinet and foundation. The cabinet is rectangular and comes with a cover. The center of the cover was chiseled with two phoenixes holding a clump of flowers in their mouth and on each side of the pattern is a dragon. The oblique top and the vertical edge of the cover and the edge of the cabinet were chiseled with lotus flowers and seeds. The inside of the cover was chiseled with an inscription showing the name of the almsgiver and the time - "the first day of the fifth lunar month of the twelfth year (1134)". The body of the cabinet was chiseled around 18 figures. The foundation is a girdling Sumeru base and the girdle was chiseled with flowers, leaves, clouds and dragons.

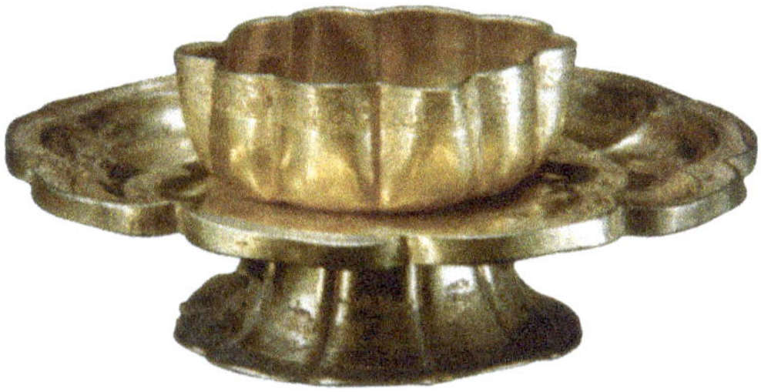

44. Flower-shaped Gold Cup and Saucer

Western Xia

Height: 5 cm Diameter: 12.8 cm for saucer

Unearthed from Western Xia Town Ruins at Gaoyoufang, Linhe, Inner Mongolia in 1958

Preserved in the Inner Mongolia Museum

This is a drinking vessel. The cup, saucer and circular foot are all in the shape of flowers. The cup has a straight mouth and flat bottom. The outside edge was chiseled with a circle of transformed passionflowers. The cup is placed on a saucer with a circular foot. The saucer has a flat belly and broad margin, and both the margin and bottom were decorated with a circle of passionflowers. The circular foot is in the shape of a horn and it also has passionflower decorations on its margin.

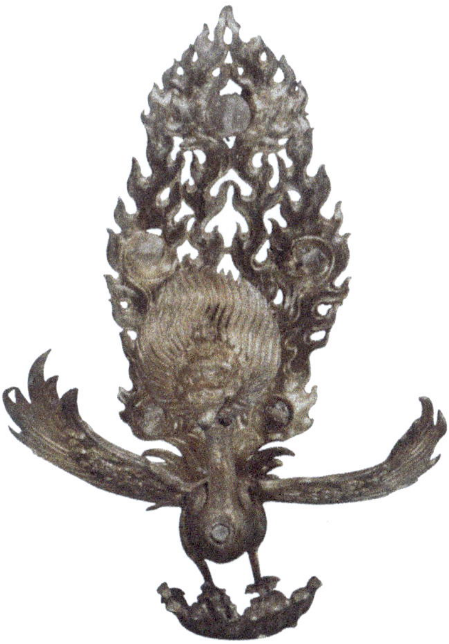

45. Gilded Silver Redpoll Inlaid with Beads

Dali Regime

Height: 18.5 cm Weight: 125 grams

Discovered in the major pagoda of the Three Pagodas in Dali, Yunnan in 1978

Preserved in the Yunnan Provincial Museum

This is a Buddhist instrument. A bird with a crista is ready to fly and its feathers on its neck and tail are all sticking up. Its tail is inlaid with five crystal beads. Its body was carved around with feathers. Under its feet is a lotus seat. All the different parts, i.e. head, wings, body, tail and feet, were all made separately and then welded together after detailed carving. Redpolls were viewed by the Dali people as a guardian deity, guaranteeing the state's prosperity and peace in the land.

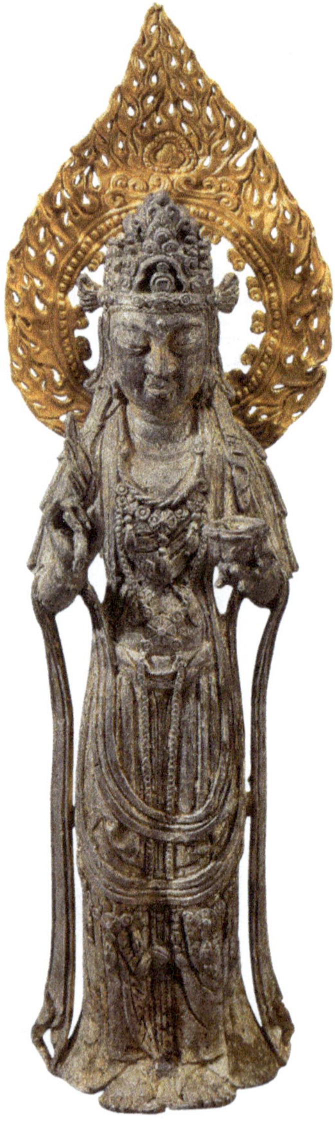

46. Silver Bodhisattva Statue with Gold Nimbus

Dali Regime
Height: 30.6 cm
Discovered in the pagoda in Chongsheng Temple in Dali, Yunnan in 1978
Preserved in the Yunnan Provincial Museum

This is a Buddhist statue. The silver Bodhisattva stands up tall with a serious expression and a low brow. He wears a bun with a coronal. He wears a long coat and skirt, with wreaths as decorations on his chest. He holds a bowl before his chest in his left hand and there are flowers in his right hand. A long strap crosses his two arms and falls down on the ground. Behind him is a gold numbus. There is a halo in the center of the numbus. Clouds are above the halo and patterns of flames are all around the halo.

Pottery

The most representative pottery from the Liao Dynasty is the tri-colored glazed pottery which is a kind of multi-colored low-temperature glazed variety produced on the basis of the well-known tri-colored glazed pottery of the Tang Dynasty. The major kilns in the Liao Dynasty all produced tri-colored glazed pottery. Cases in point include the Gangwa Kiln in Chifeng in the Inner Mongolia, Nanshan Kiln in Lindong, Gangguantun Kiln in Liaoyang in Liaoning and the Longquanwu Kiln in Mentougou District in Beijing. Most of the tri-colored glazed pottery at this time were practical utensils for daily use. Of course, there were still a small number of building components and crestings. As to those items made to be buried with the dead, they are rarely seen. Generally, the style of the porcelain is varied, and includes examples such as the cockscomb-shaped kettle, long-necked vase, mandarin duck-shaped kettle, begonia-shaped plate, square-shaped plate, octagonal plate, jug, eaves tile and crestings. They are mostly decorated with impressed patterns. There are still a certain number of carved, appliquéd and embossed designs. The decorative designs focus on various flowers like the peony, lotus and chrysanthemum. Besides, human and animal motifs can also be seen. The basic glazes are yellow, green and white. Sometimes, red and yellowish-brown are also adopted. But no blue glaze was available. Usually, yellow, green and white glazes are used together. Sometimes, two of them or one of them can be used separately. In this way, according to the number of the glazes used, the tri-colored glazed pottery of the Liao Dynasty can also be subdivided into tri-colored, two-colored and single-colored. The glazing method is usually padding or brushing and glazes in different colors are not mingled together. When fired at low temperature, the glaze neither flows

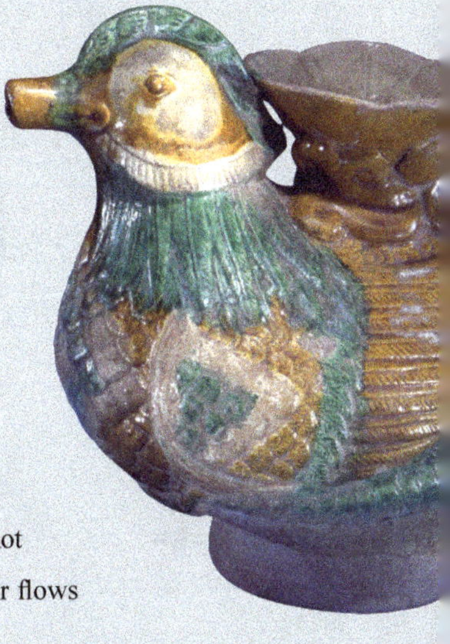

nor infiltrates, thus here is no sagging. Actually, the colorful glazes which consist of what seems like patches look very rigid and unnatural. This also constitutes a unique characteristic of the tri-colored glazed pottery of the Liao Dynasty.

The pottery of the Jin Dynasty mainly refers to pottery figurines. In many tombs, the figurines carved out of high-quality grey bricks were inlaid on the walls to show living scenes of the buried person before his or her death. The firing of the pottery figurines continued the traditions of the Song Dynasty. They are quite similar to those made in the Central Plain areas in terms of decoration, firing technique, appearance and dressing style. There is absolutely no doubt that these pottery figurines represent the highest level of pottery sculpture at that time. Besides, there were a small number of tri-colored glazed pottery produced with the same style as their counterparts in the Song Dynasty, but they are inferior in terms of workmanship.

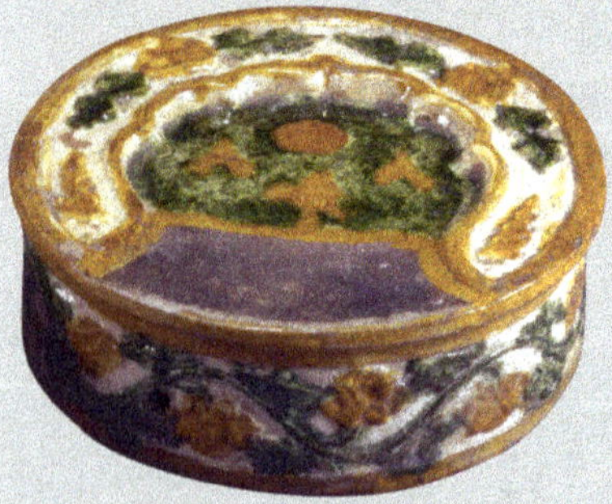

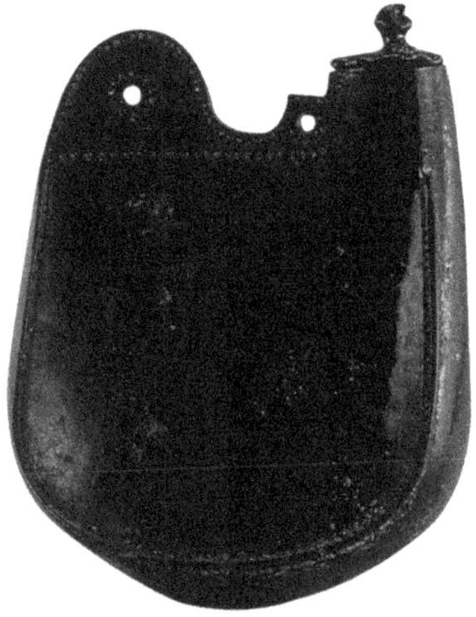

47. Dark Reddish Brown Glazed Cockscomb-shaped Kettle

Liao
Height: 25.5 cm
Unearthed from Faku County in Liaoning in 1974
Preserved in the Liaoning Provincial Museum
With its red roughcast, this container is evenly coated with dark reddish brown glaze which is very shiny. It features an oval tube-like mouth, oblate belly and a lid. The belly is embossed with clay strips much like the seams of leather pieces, on which traces of stitching can be seen.

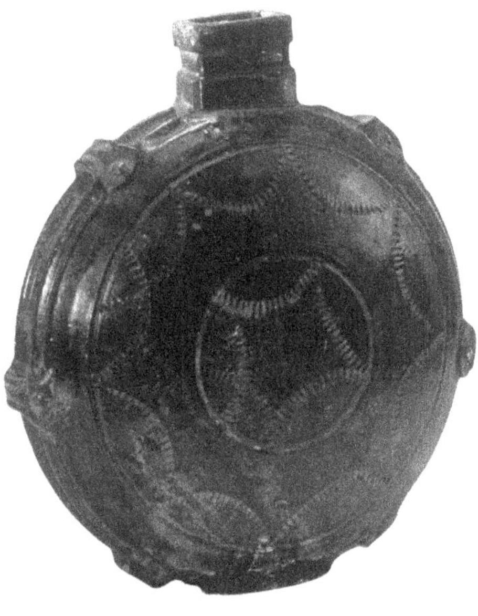

48. Green Glazed Flat Kettle with a Strap

Liao
Height: 26 cm
Unearthed from Ongniud Banner, Inner Mongolia in 1965
Preserved in the Chifeng Museum
With its red roughcast, this container is evenly coated with dark green glaze which is bright and smooth. It has an oblong-shaped mouth and oblate belly. There are grooves on both sides, as well as a pair of tubular ears for the strap to run through, meaning the kettle would have been portable. The belly is decorated with carved running curves in the shape of fine-toothed combs.

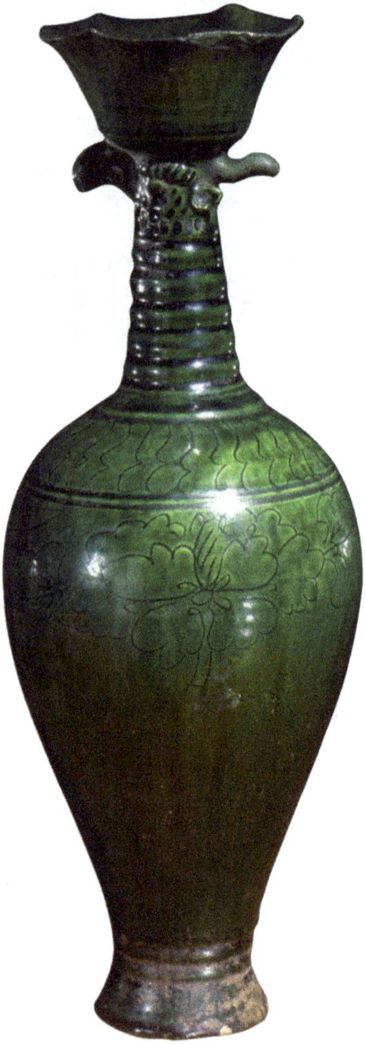

49. Green Glazed Phoenix-headed Vase

Liao
Height: 37 cm
Mouth Diameter: 10.1 cm
Bottom Diameter: 6.9 cm
Unearthed from Tuquan County, Inner Mongolia in 1952
Preserved in the Inner Mongolia Museum

This vase is coated with a green glaze which is even and bright. It is big and high with a lotus leaf-shaped mouth, thin long neck, broad shoulder and a bulging belly. The belly is carved with peonies.

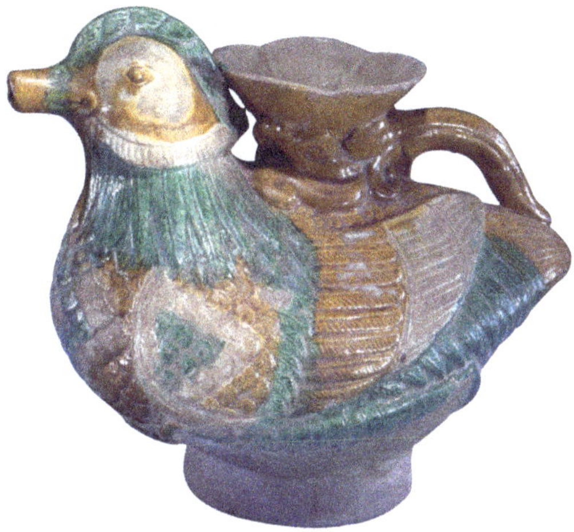

50. Tri-colored Glazed Pottery Kettles in Mandarin Duck's Shape

Liao
Height: 20.1 cm
Mouth Diamter: 8.4 cm
Bottom Diamter: 9.2 cm
Unearthed from Chifeng, Inner Mongolia in 1977 Preserved in the Chifeng Museum
This pair of containers with their red roughcast is covered with three different bright glazes. In the shape of mandarin ducks, they have flower-shaped mouths on the back. Overall, they would have been created on the basis of tri-colored glazed mandarin duck-shaped kettles of the Tang Dynasty.

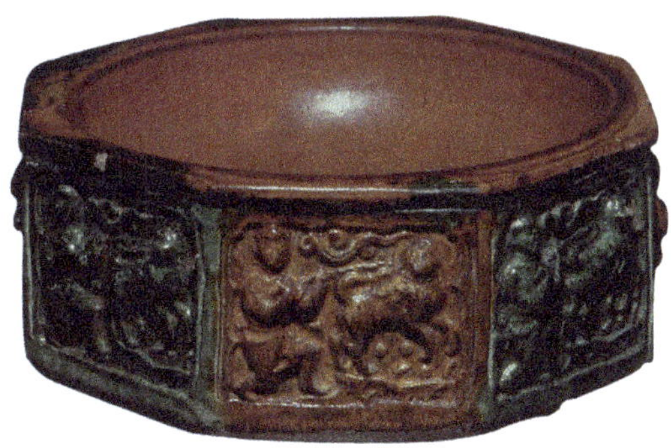

51. Tri-colored Glazed Octagonal Plate with Impressed Design

Liao
Height:9.5 cm Mouth Diameter: 25 cm
Unearthed from Chifeng, Inner Mongolia in 1959
Preserved in the Inner Mongolia Museum
This food container with its red roughcast has an outside which is coated with yellow-brown glaze alternating with green glaze; the inner wall with yellow-brown glaze; and the bottom is unglazed. The plate is in the shape of an octagonal column, flat at the bottom. The inner mouth and bottom are both round. The eight sides of the outer walls are all decorated with impressed patterns of men playing with lions. The men look like natives of West Asia. Some meat remains were found during excavation.

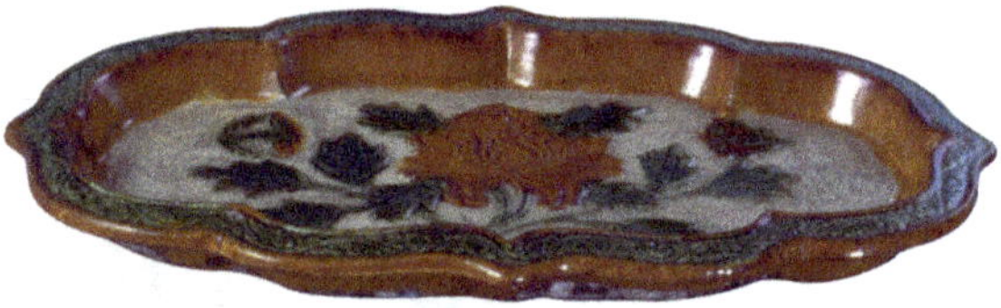

52. Tri-colored Begonia-shaped Plate with Impressed Peonies and Butterflies

Liao

Height: 2.1 cm Length: 30.1 cm Width: 17.9 cm

Unearthed from Xinmin County, Liaoning in 1956

Preserved in the Liaoning Provincial Museum

This was a food container featuring a light yellow roughcast coated with white engobe. The plate, in an eight-petalled begonia shape, has a wide upturned brim, a shallow belly and flat bottom. The white glazed inner bottom is decorated with the impressed peony designs. There are two butterflies flying at both sides of the spray with yellow blossoms and green leaves. The background is white glazed. Along the green glazed brim is an impressed curling tendril design and flower motif. The wall is covered with yellow glaze. The roughcast is exposed at the bottom.

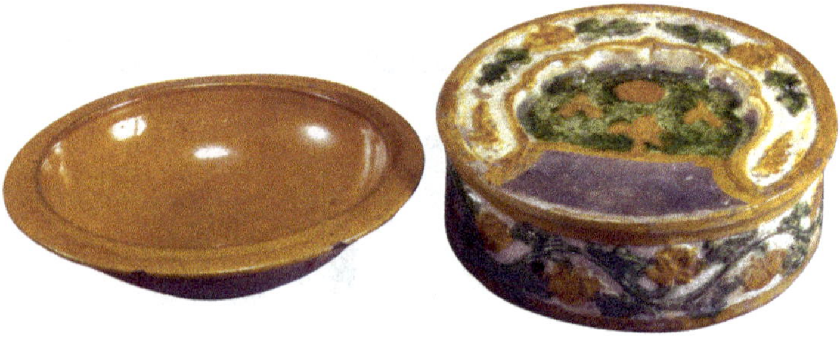

53. Tri-colored Glazed Inkstone with Impressed Scrolling Peony Design

Liao

Height: 8.5 cm Mouth Diameter: 21.6 cm Bottom Diameter: 21 cm

Unearthed from Baarin Left Banner, Inner Mongolia

Preserved in the Inner Mongolian Museum

Decorated in red roughcast, this round inkstone features a wide opening, broad brim, a relatively narrow outer wall and a flat bottom. The unglazed pool for grinding the ink is located in one side, exposing the roughcast. The central part is decorated with animal face and flying bird patterns, as well as a scroll design; the outer ring has a peony and cloud design; and the outer wall has a scrolling peony design and a hollowed-out hole. Besides, the inkstone also comes complete with a nested writing-brush washer. The washer looks like a bowl, and is coated with yellow glaze inside and inscribed with seven small black-inked Khitan characters on the outer wall.

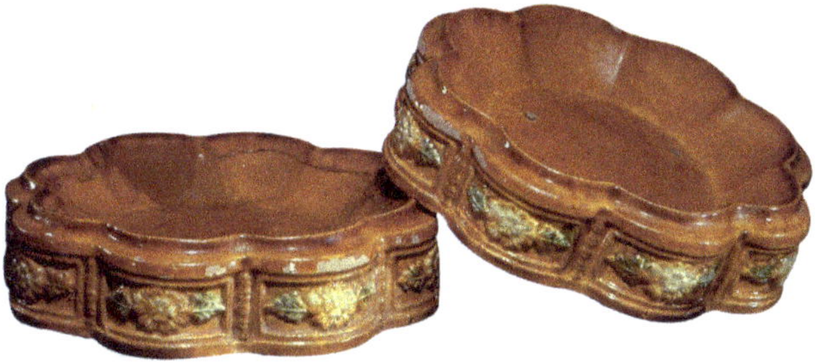

54. Tri-colored Glazed Pottery Box Set with Impressed Decoration

Liao

Extant Height: 4.2 cm Mouth Diameter: 14-15.2 cm

Unearthed from Ongniud Banner, Inner Mongolia in 1977

Preserved in the Chifeng Municipal Administration of Cultural Heritage

This cosmetics set has a red roughcast. The double-layered object once had a lid which has been lost. It has double layers which can be nested into one another. In the shape of a lotus with eight petals, the box is embossed with a peony design on the tri-colored glazed outer wall.

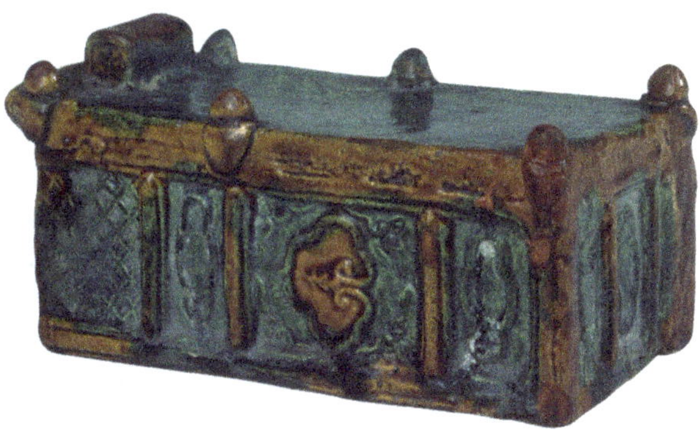

55. Tri-colored Glazed Pottery Bed with Impressed Decoration

Liao

Height: 7.8 cm Length: 15.4 cm Width: 7.8 cm

Preserved in the Liaoning Provincial Museum

This is a clay red pottery burial object with yellow and green glazes. The oblong-shaped bed has six column-headed decorations on four sides and a pillow on one side. The surface is painted with green glaze; the bedside with yellow glaze; and the four sides with green glaze all carved with begonia and cirrus cloud patterns in relief, as well as yellow glazed pillars.

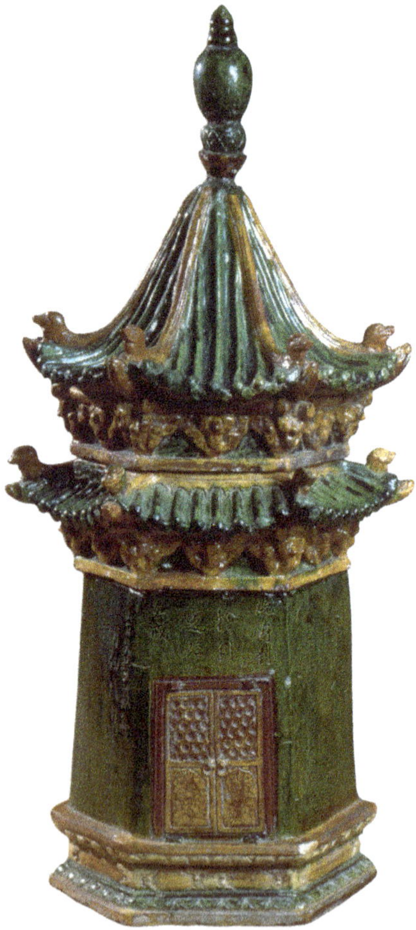

56. Tri-colored Pottery Stupa

Jin

Height: 78 cm Bottom Diameter: 30.5 cm

Unearthed from Youju Temple in the Qilinyuan Village of Lingshou County, Hebei in 1976

Preserved in the Zhengding Administration of Cultural Relics

This burial object a stupa, comprises the body, lower and upper eaves, painted with tri-colored glaze. Imitating the style of its wooden counterpart, this pottery has a hexagonal cross section, waisted base, false door opened in the front and a six-ridged pavilion roof with double layers of eaves, complete with brackets, columns and architraves. All the ridges have animal's heads as decorations at the bottom. The steeple serves as the Baocha. The body carries the inscription "Fired in the second year (1210) of the reign of Daan".

57. Painted Pottery Figurine

Jin

Height: 27 cm

Unearthed from Xinlifeng of Jiaozuo, Henan in 1973

Preserved in the Henan Provincial Museum

This burial object with its off-white roughcast figurine features black eyebrows and hair, red lips and a long neck, which looks sideways. With a black hat decorated with flowers on his head, the figure wears a long gown with narrow sleeves on the upper body, a belt around the waist and an apron covering the abdomen. The feet are wrapped in a pair of black boots and they peek out from under the gown. Standing on a square base inscribed with the Chinese character "Zhang", the manservant holds a basin in his right hand while his left hand swings behind his back.

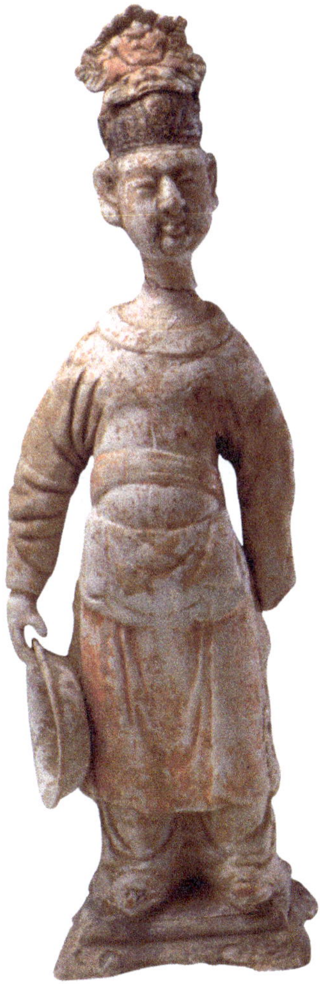

58. Green Glazed Pottery Chiwen (a kind of roof ridge ornament in the shape of a legendary animal)

Western Xia

Height: 152 cm Width: 92 cm Thickness: 32 cm

Unearthed from royal mausoleum of the Western Xia Dynasty in the suburbs of Yinchuan, Ningxia Hui Autonomous Region in 1974

Preserved in the National Museum of China

This building component has a reddish roughcast, and is coated with green glaze. The glaze surface is bright. This object features a dragon's head and fish's body which is covered with scales. The head and tail were fired separately. Actually, chiwen is a kind of ornament used on both ends of the main ridge of the roof. This one, big in size, comes from the royal mausoleum of the Western Xia Dynasty.

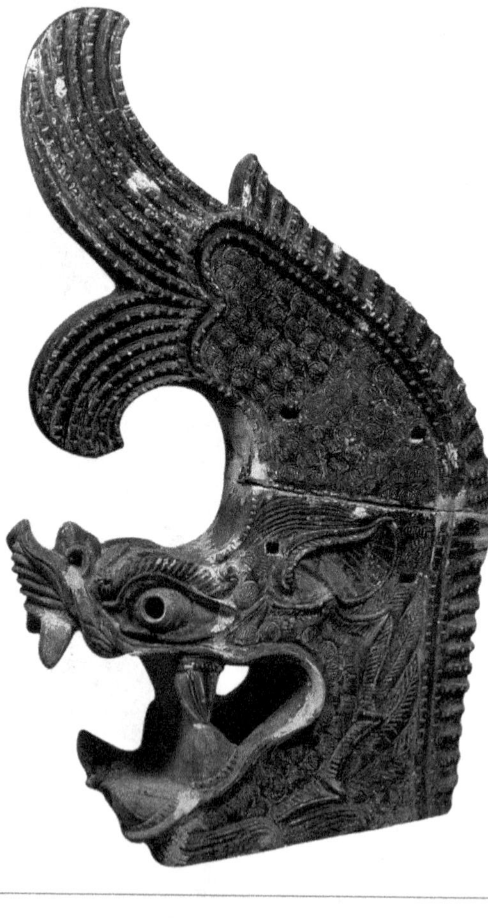

Porcelain

Porcelain in the Liao Dynasty was made from local materials found within the territory of the Khitan. During the Tang Dynasty, porcelain was introduced, and porcelain manufacturing techniques were known to the Khitan in the Five Dynasties. In the early days of the Liao Dynasty, kilns appeared, but in relatively small numbers and on a small scale. When it came to the middle and later period, a large number of Han people moved in, which made it possible for porcelain to advance. Currently, about ten porcelain kiln site built in the Liao Dynasty have been found. Of these, the Shangjing Kiln was run officially in the Liao Dynasty, and the Gangwa Kiln in Chifeng, Gangguantun Kiln in Liaoyang, Longquanwu Kiln and Cijiawu Kiln in Beijing were well known thanks to their size and their productivity.

Influenced by the techniques of the Central Plains area, Liao porcelain did not have a long history of producing porcelain. After absorbing the essence of Central Plains culture traditional Han ways of producing porcelain, Liao porcelain developed its own local characteristics and ethnic styles to create items like cockscomb pot, phoenix head pot, drumstick altar, square plate, crabapple flower plate, and kettle with plate-like mouth and long neck. They are beautiful and practical. Moreover, they are portable enough to meet the daily needs of nomads living on the grasslands. These items of porcelain were mostly decorated with Chinese herbaceous peonies and tree peonies. As the porcelain made in the lands ruled by the Liao Dynasty have a rough roughcast, containing impurities, engobe is always used before painting on the glaze, which is thin but not smooth. Porcelain was glazed only in white, black, and tea dust. But those produced in the Central Plains have a great variety of glazes, including

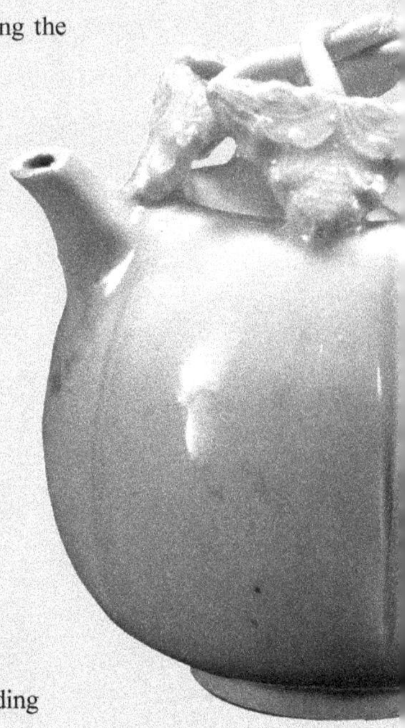

crystalline and transmutation glaze. They don't just employ the normal white, black and celadon. Some are even glazed more than once so that the glaze is thick and good-looking. In particular, the celadon color looks as smooth as jade.

After the Jurchen, who founded the Jin Dynasty, marched southward and invaded, kilns in the Central Plains area were devastated, and many craftsmen moved south, throwing the porcelain industry in the north into a period of sharp decline. The Jurchen forced the Northern Song Dynasty to move its capital to the south, and as a result, occupied a vast area on the Central Plains. They adopted the characteristics and styles of the Ding and Cizhou Kilns of the former Song Dynasty, as the porcelain industry slowly began to recover. A Cizhou Kiln system was formed soon after with Guantai Town in Cixian County, Hebei as the center. Meanwhile, the Ding, Jun and Yaozhou Kilns all began to develop again.

The Western Xia maintained close communication with the Song Dynasty in terms of economy, trade and culture. Its porcelain industry originated in the Cizhou Kiln. Their most representative works were the brown glazed flat kettles with picked designs and brown glazed kettles with picked designs and four loop handles, which were rarely seen outside the regions under the jurisdiction of the Western Xia. These kettles are uniquely shaped, portable and flat, thus meeting the needs of the nomad Tangut people. Besides, the materials used for porcelain in the Lingwu Kiln are of very good quality and are in an abundance rarely seen in other areas.

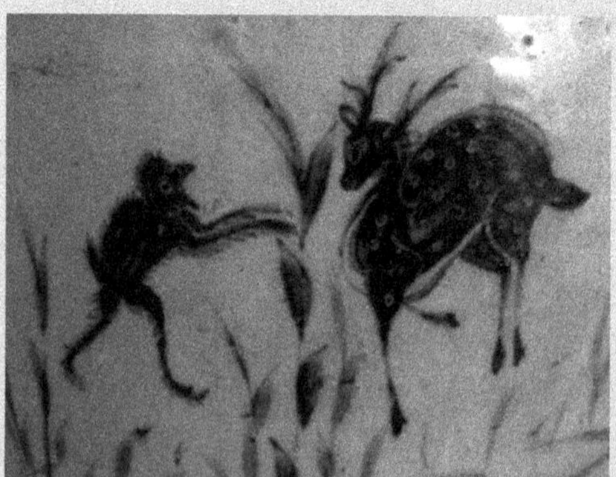

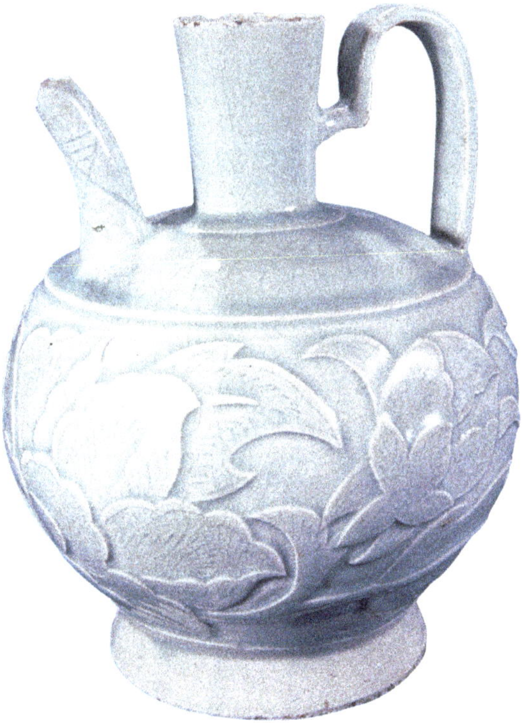

59. Ewer with Peony Designs from the Yaozhou Kiln
Liao
Height: 19 cm Mouth Diameter: 4.1 cm Foot Diameter: 9.3 cm
Unearthed from Pingquan County, Hebei
Preserved in the Pingquan Repository of Cultural Relics

This is a container with a high and straight neck, round shoulder, budging belly and a curved spout handle. The erythrine roughcast is exquisite and hard. Its body is covered with green and yellow glaze, except for the foot. Ice cracks can be seen on the mouth and lower part of the belly. Its handle and belly are decorated with rhombus and lotus patterns, respectively. There are bowstring grains around the shoulder.

60. Flying-fish-shaped Pot from the Yaozhou Kiln
Liao
Height: 9.3 cm Length: 14 cm Width: 7.4 cm
Unearthed from Beipiao County, Liaoning in 1971
Preserved in the Liaoning Provincial Museum
This water vessel in the shape of a Capricorn with its wings stretching out, has its tail rising high and its tail fin extended. The roughcast is refined and hard. Its body is glazed green, and it looks crystal and pure. The vessel is decorated with scales all over.

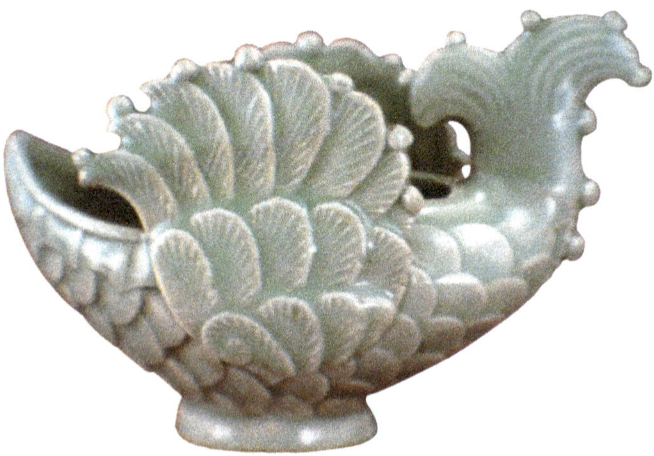

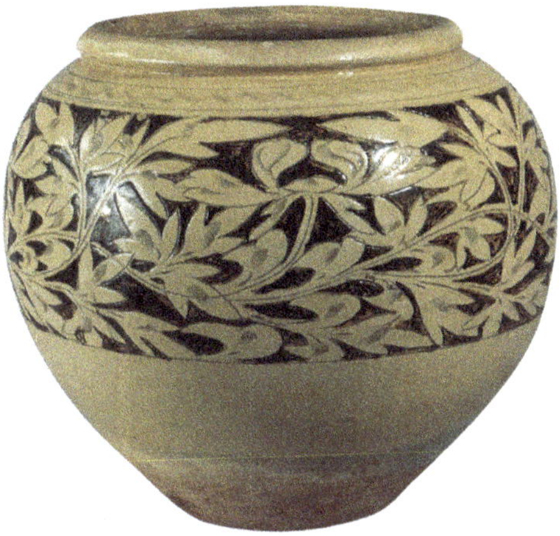

61. White Glazed Jar with Picked Peony Designs

Liao
Height: 29.9 cm
Mouth Diameter: 23.6 cm
Bottom Diameter: 14.3 cm
Preserved in the Shanghai Museum

This container has a big mouth, curled lips, bulging belly and flat bottom. The roughcast is yellowish white, covered with engobe and coated with white glaze, except for the bottom. The shoulder is circled with ripples sandwiched by bowstrings. The belly is carved with peonies, with black color in between.

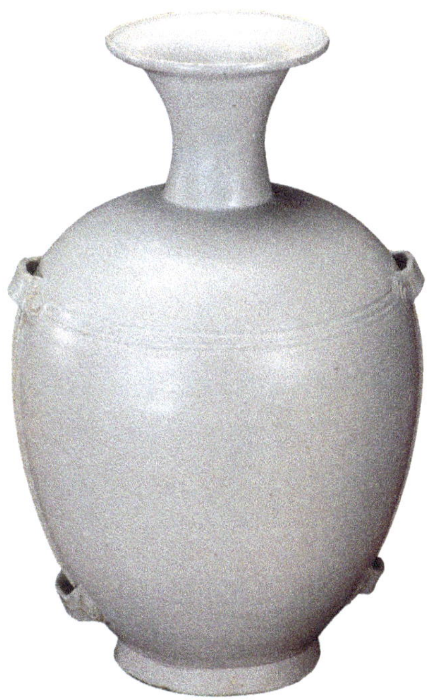

62. White Glazed Portable Kettle with Two Tape Holes

Liao
Height: 36 cm
Unearthed from Tomb of Yelu Yuzhi in the Ar Horqin Banner, Inner Mongolia
Preserved in the Inner Mongolian Museum

This is a container with a plate-like mouth, long neck and big belly. The roughcast is light and refined, and is covered with white glaze. There are fillisters on both sides, and holes to allow for thread to be passed through.

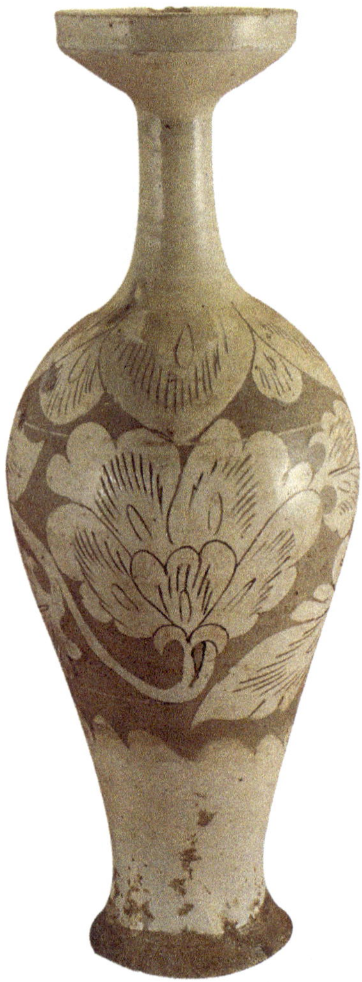

63. White Glazed Vase with a Long Neck and Pink Peony Designs

Liao

Height: 46 cm Belly Diameter: 17.4 cm

Unearthed from a Liao Dynasty Tomb in Faku County, Liaoning in 1974

Preserved in the Liaoning Provincial Museum

This is a container with a plate-like mouth, thin neck and recessed foot. Its bottom slants outward and there is a round foot inside. Its gray roughcast is coated pink, with transparent glaze outside, except for the bottom. Brown dots can be seen indistinctly on the vessel, and fine cracks. The whiting is picked off from the glaze to expose the roughcast, in order to shape the patterns. The shoulder is decorated with nutant petals, and belly peonies. The layout is graceful and simple. This is one of the only findings of this kind from a Liao Dynasty tomb.

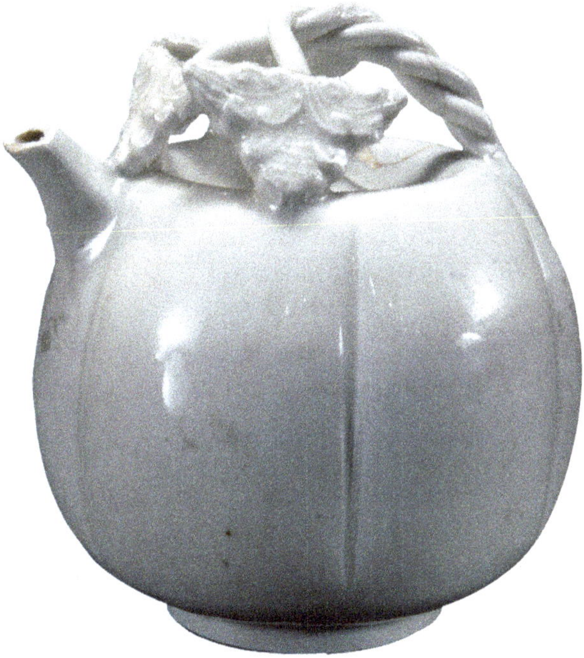

64. White Glazed Kettle in a Melon Shape with a Handle

Liao

Height: 12 cm   Bottom Diameter: 5.4 cm

Unearthed from Chahar Right Front Banner, Inner Mongolia in 1981

Preserved in the Ulanqab Museum

This was a container glazed smooth white. Its mouth is concave, and there is a raised button at the center. Holes are bored on both sides for pouring in water. The kettle has a round belly in the shape of a melon in six parts, and there is a round foot. There is a short spout on the shoulder. A noose–like handle is added on top of the kettle's mouth. The front part of the handle is divided into three sections. Each is decorated with butterflies.

65. White Glazed Cockscomb Pot

Liao

Height: 23.5 cm   Mouth Diameter: 4.1 cm Foot Diameter: 14 cm

Unearthed from Tomb of the Son-in-law of the Emperor Muzong in the ninth year (959) of the reign of Yingli in Chifeng, Inner Mongolia in 1954

Preserved in the Inner Mongolian Museum

This is a container glazed white. Its upper part is flat and the lower round. On the big belly, there is a pipe-like mouth and cockscomb handle with a single hoop. The raised ridge on the belly is meant to imitate a suture line on a bagging pot.

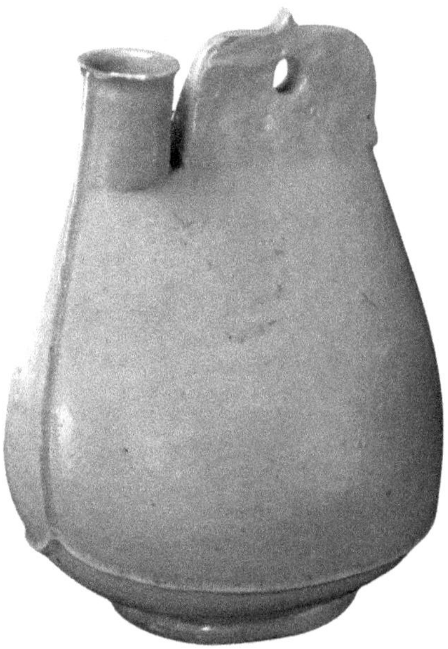

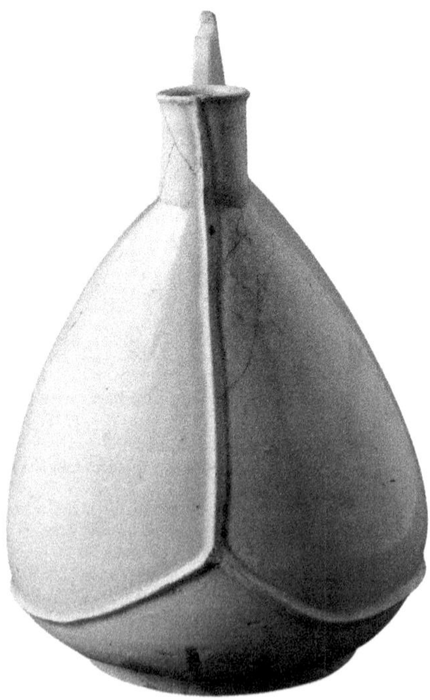

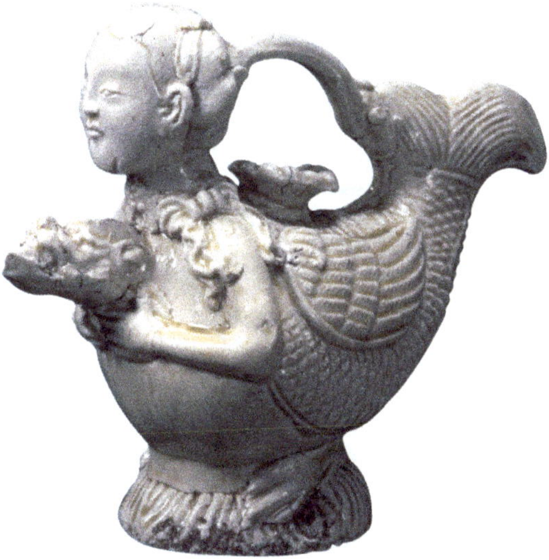

66. White Glazed Pot in the Shape of a Fish with a Girl's Head

Liao
Height: 16 cm
Unearthed from Bairin Left Banner, Inner Mongolia in 1976
Preserved in the Chifeng Work Station of Cultural Relics
This is a container in the shape of a fish with a girl's head. She holds the dragon's head which forms the pot's spout. The roughcast is exquisite, glazed white, and looks pearly and smooth.

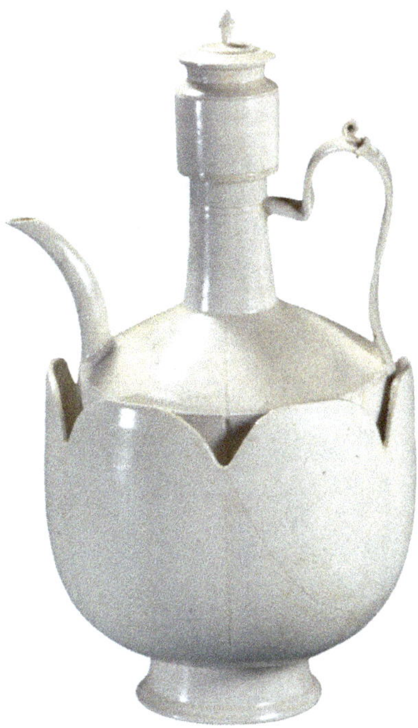

67. White Glazed Ewer with a Lotus Support

Liao
Height: 17.7 cm
Mouth Diameter (for ewer): 3.7 cm
Bottom Diameter: 7.5 cm
Mouth Diameter (for support): 18.1 cm
Bottom Diameter: 9.5 cm
Unearthed from Sanhe, Hebei in 1974
Preserved in the Hebei Provincial Institute of Cultural Relics
This was a set of drinking vessels comprising a ewer and a support. The ewer has a straight mouth, long neck, folded shoulder, budging belly and a lid. There is a spout on one side, and a handle on the other. As for the support, it is in the shape of a lotus with six petals, with a deep belly and a round foot.

68. White Glazed Jug with Lotus Designs and a Lid

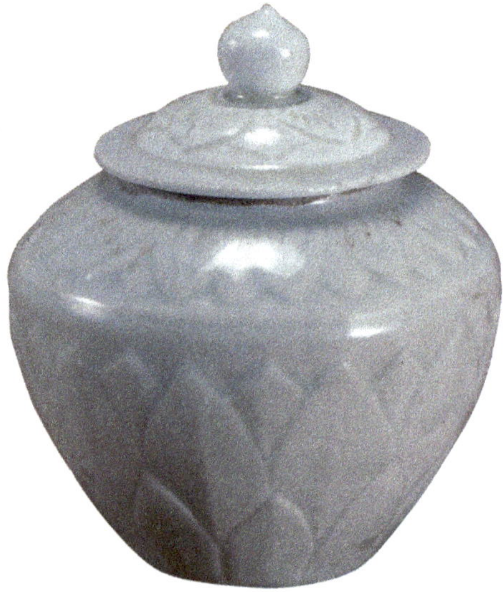

Liao

Height: 11.4 cm   Mouth Diameter: 5.8 cm   Bottom Diameter: 5.1 cm

Unearthed from Tomb of the Princess of the Chen State and her husband in Qinglongshan County, Jerim in the Naiman Banner, Inner Mongolia in 1986

Preserved in the Inner Mongolia Institute of Cultural Relics and Archaeology

This is a container with double lips and slanted shoulder. Its belly converges at the lower part, and the bottom is slightly concave. The roughcast is exquisite and white. Its body is glazed white, shiny and smooth, except for the lid's rim and bottom. The thicker part looks greenish yellow. The lid bulges slightly, with a button on the top. The lid is decorated with dual quatrefoils, the shoulder with dual lotuses, and the belly has a triple upturned lotus. The character "官"(official) is carved on the bottom in running script.

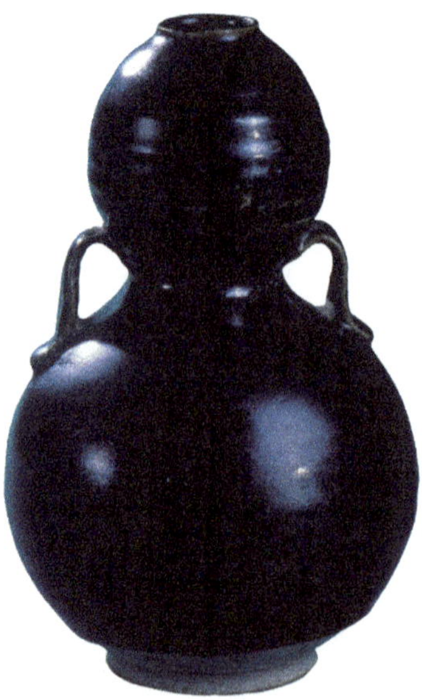

69. Black Glazed Vase in the Shape of a Cucurbit with Dual Loop Handles, Ding Kiln

Jin

Height: 21 cm   Mouth Diameter: 3.4 cm   Bottom Diameter: 7.3 cm

Unearthed from Quyang County, Hebei in 1973

Preserved in the Cultural Relics Preservation Institute in Quyang County

This is a container in the shape of a cucurbit, with a small mouth, bulging belly laced in the waist, and a round foot slanted outward. On the tight waist, there is a pair of band-like handles decorated with tile designs.

70. Plate with Dragon Designs, Ding Kiln

Jin
Height: 7 cm Mouth Diameter: 30.5 cm
Foot Diameter: 12.7 cm
Unearthed from Nong'an County, Jilin in 1985
Preserved in the Jilin Provincial Museum
This is a container with a wide mouth and round foot. The grey roughcast is glazed shiny and smooth, except for the mouth. The inner side is decorated with a circle of concave bowstrings. A dragon is carved on the plate center, which has a thin neck, long tail, four limbs, three paws, two horns, whiskers and scales all over.

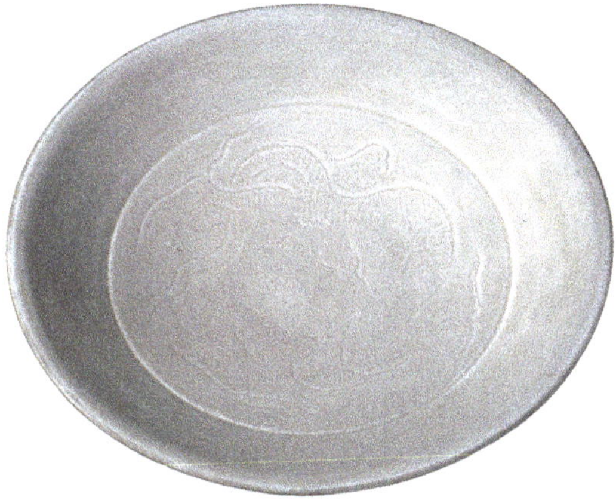

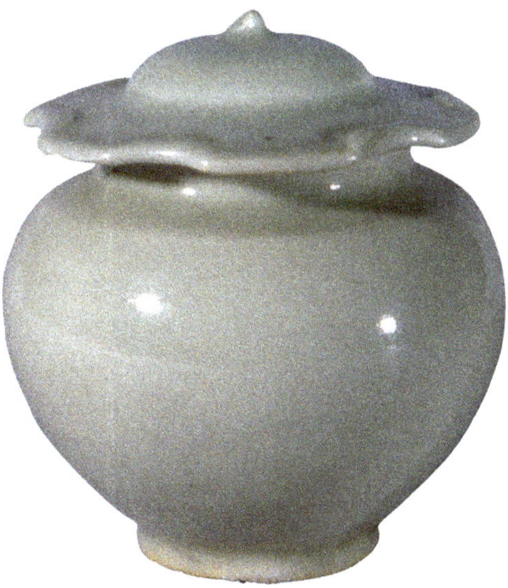

71. Celadon Jug with a Lotus-leaf-shaped Lid, Yaozhou Kiln

Jin
Height: 12.9 cm
Mouth Diameter: 7.5 cm
Bottom Diameter: 6.1 cm
Preserved in the Shanghai Museum
This is a container with a short neck, bulging belly and a round foot. The roughcast is hard and exquisite. It is of glazed celadon and looks mild and smooth. It has a lotus-leaf-like lid, which has a curled rim and bulges in the center.

72. Celadon Bottle on a Beast's Back, Yaozhou Kiln

Jin

Height: 26.8 cm Mouth Diameter: 3.3 cm Bottom Diameter: 9 cm

Preserved in the Datong Museum

This is a container of glazed celadon, and it is smooth and mild. It is composed of an auspicious beast and a bottle on the back. The bottle has a slanting mouth, contracted neck and round belly. A man stands beside the beast, holding the reins.

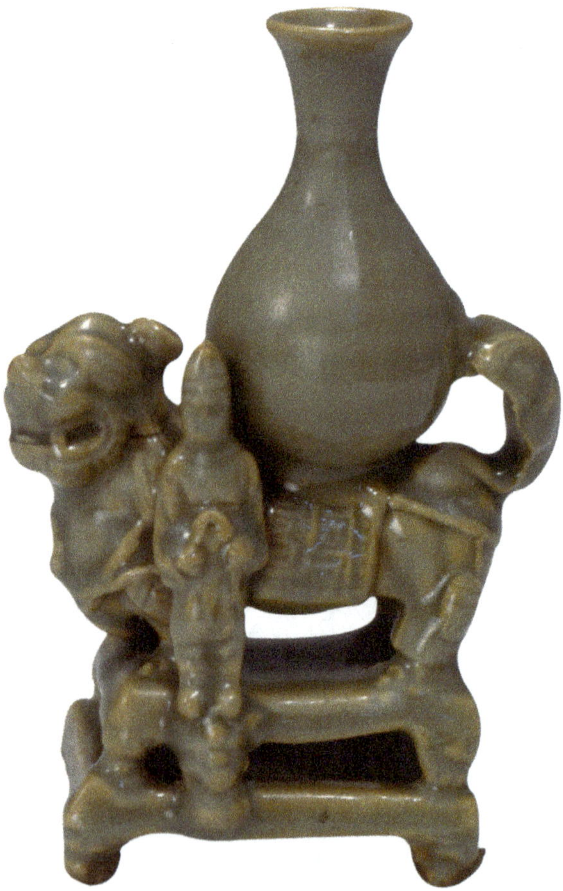

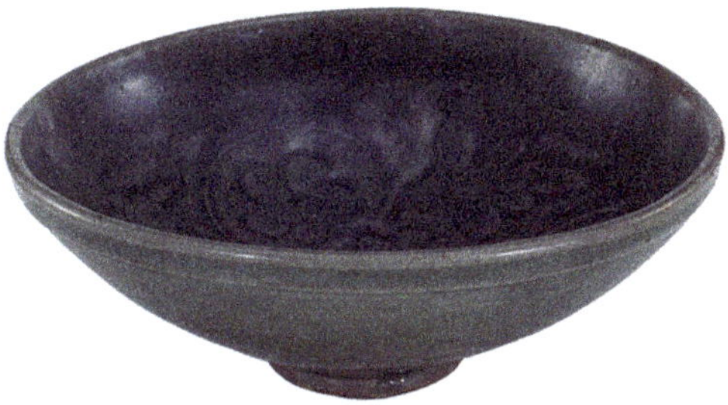

73. Bowl Carved with a Baby Playing among Lotuses, Yaozhou Kiln

Jin
Height: 7.2 cm
Mouth Diameter: 18.7 cm
Foot Diameter: 5.5 cm
Preserved in the Palace Museum in Beijing
This was an eating utensil, with an outwardly slanting mouth, curved body and round foot. The roughcast is thick and refined. The body is glazed yellowish green, and is shiny and smooth. A baby playing among lotuses was carved inside.

74. Three-footed Censer Decorated with the Dragon Pattern, Yaozhou Kiln

Jin
Height: 27.3 cm
Mouth Diameter: 20 cm
Unearthed from a cellar in Lantian County, Shaanxi in 1960
Preserved in the Shaanxi History Museum
This was used for burning incense. The body is glazed celadon, and looks shiny and smooth, elegant and even. It has a square lip, flat rim, contracted neck, broad shoulder, bulging belly and round bottom. The belly is decorated with deformed Kuidragon beasts, and flanges and corrugated patterns which form a partition. The legs are in the shape of a beast's face at the upper part and a tiger's paw at the bottom.

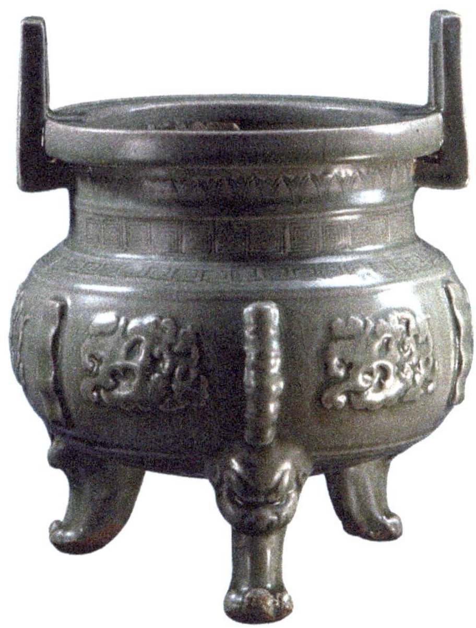

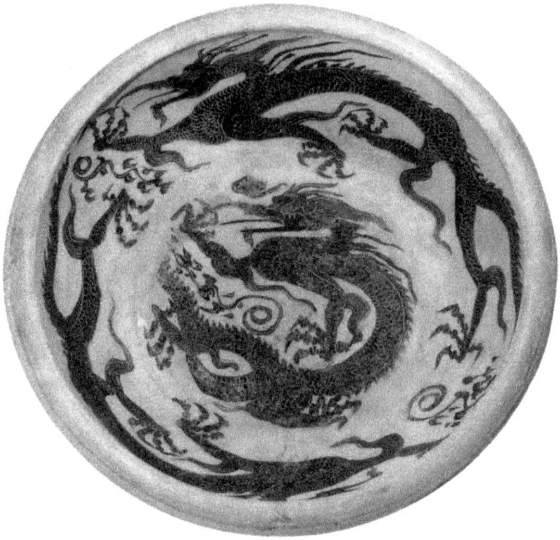

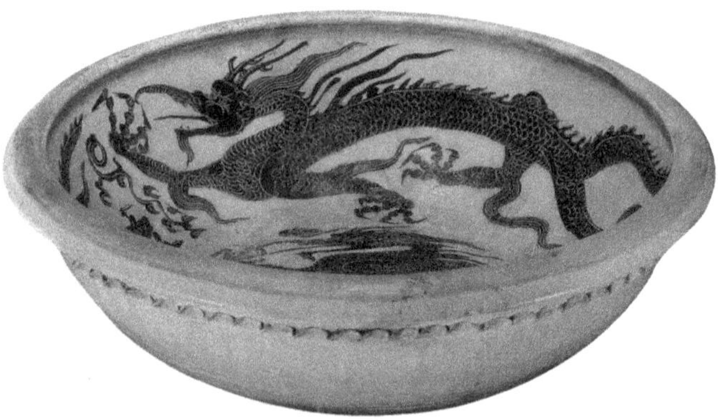

75. Basin with Dragon Designs, Cizhou Kiln

Jin

Height: 20.5 cm Mouth Diameter: 69 cm Bottom Diameter: 40 cm

Unearthed from Site of Guantai Kiln in Cixian County, Handan, Hebei in 1987

Preserved in the Cultural Relics Preservation Institute in Cixian County

This is a container with a slightly converging mouth, a round lip that slants outward, a curved body, shallow belly and concave round bottom. Beneath the lip circles are some piled decorations. Two walking dragons are painted inside, and another curled dragon is depicted on the bottom. This is the largest porcelain basin found so far in the Cizhou Kiln.

76. Tiger-shaped Pillow, Cizhou Kiln

Jin

Height: 12.8 cm Length: 39.6 cm Width: 19.5 cm

Preserved in the Shanghai Museum

This is bedding in the shape of a lying tiger. The grey roughcast is covered with engobe. A bird in a reed field is painted on the oval surface, in black on white glaze. The body is covered with isabelline glaze, and black stripes depicting the tiger. Its ears, eyebrows, eyes and mouth are painted white. A hole can be seen on either ear. The roughcast is exposed on the bottom, on which is written "this was bought by Zhang on the 26th day of the sixth lunar month in the second year (1162) of Dading of the reign of Shizong".

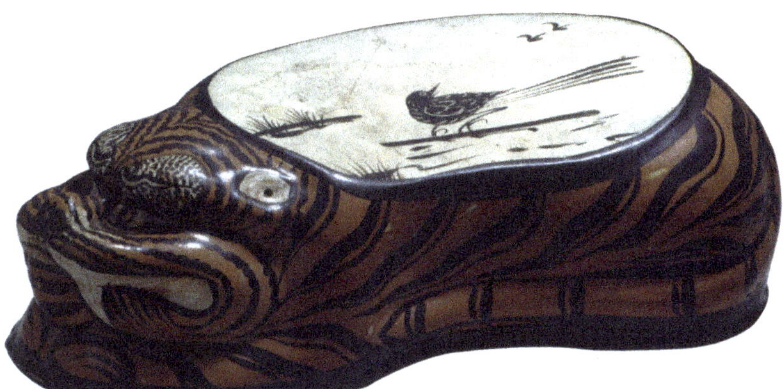

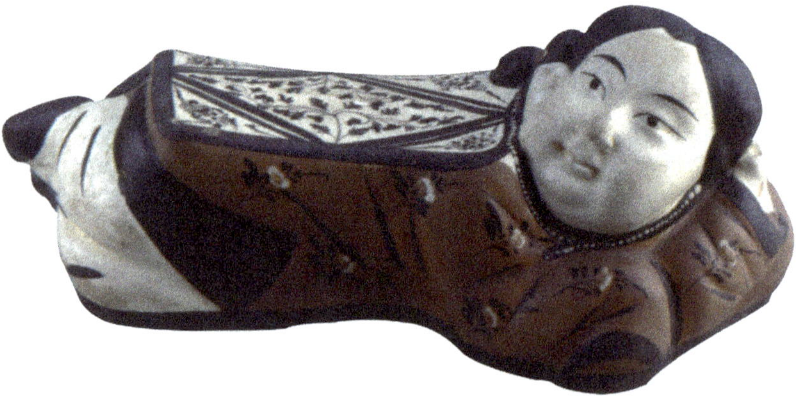

77. Pillow in the Shape of Reclining Woman from Cizhou Kiln

Jin

Height: 12.5 cm Length: 35 cm Width: 15.5 cm

Unearthed from Qixian County, Henan in 1983

Preserved in the Qixian County Administration of Cultural Relics

This example of bedding.has a fine and hard roughcast. The pillow is covered with white glaze and colorful paintings. It is shaped in the image of a woman reclining with one arm supporting her head and her legs naturally bent. Her hair is worn in a bun. Her face is plump, with arched eyebrows and a big smile. Her upper body is wrapped in a brown blouse with narrow sleeves, which is decorated with the pattern of peach blossoms, as well as pearls around the collar. The trousers are white in a narrow-legged style. The pillow surface is painted with white glaze and is outlined in black. In the middle is a diamond-shaped design which contains patterns of lotus flowers and peach blossoms in black.

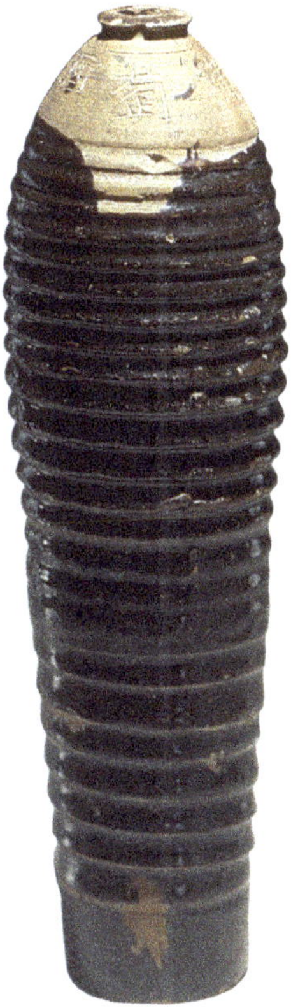

78. Black Glazed Vase with Bowstring Pattern

Jin

Height:43.5 cm Mouth Diameter:9 cm Bottom Diameter: 9.3 cm

Unearthed from Chahar Right Front Banner, Inner Mongolia in 1958

Preserved in the Inner Mongolia Museum

This container is unglazed from mouth to shoulder. The part below the shoulder is covered with black glaze. The enamel is jet-black. This vase has a small mouth with a flat upturned brim, short neck, long belly and a ringed foot. Convex bowstring patterns can be found below the shoulder which carries the inscription "wine bottle". Such vases were usually found in Inner Mongolia, and were commonly known as chicken leg-shaped vases.

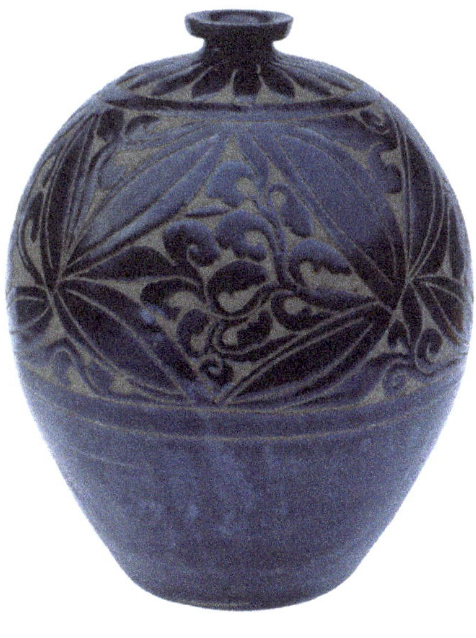

79. Black Glazed Narrow-mouth Vase with Cut Decoration

Jin

Height: 24 cm Mouth Diameter: 4.3 cm Foot Diameter: 11.5 cm

Unearthed from Xiajiagou Village, Tianzhen County, Shanxi in 1955

Preserved in the Palace Museum in Beijing

This vase has a plain roughcast, and is black glazed throughout. The enamel is jet-black. It features a small mouth with flared brim, short neck, broad shoulder, bulging belly and ringed foot. With a cut decoration, it has symbolic chrysanthemum petal designs on the shoulder and curling tendril designs on the belly. The bottom is inscribed with the black-inked characters "Guo She Zhu Dian".

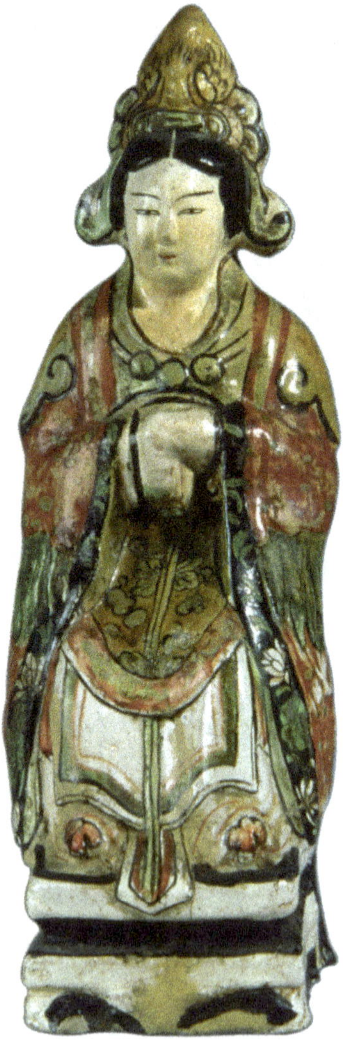

80.Painted Sitting Woman of the Bacun Kiln

Jin

Height:32.9 cm

Preserved in the Shanghai Museum

This porcelain sculpture with a gray roughcast features the figure of a woman sitting still, with a phoenix coronet on her head. Clad in a long gown with wide sleeves, she makes obeisance by cupping one hand in the other before her chest. The clothes, eyebrows, eyes and hair are all outlined in black and are painted with red, yellow, green and brown glazes.

81. Chicken Pot with Rust Coloured Glaze

Jin

Height: 18 cm Bottom Diameter: 7.5 cm

Preserved in the Liaoning Provincial Museum

This container has an off-white roughcast covered with white engobe. It features ivory-white glaze with fine cracks. The bottom is unglazed. The pot is in the shape of a chicken, which is perking its tail up with eyes and beak both opened wide. The beak is used as the spout. On the figure's back is a semi-circular handle which links up with the bottom of the neck and tail head at the two ends. There is a round water injection hole in the ringed foot, which is connected with the water filling pipe inside the pot. The wings and feathers are painted with rust coloured glaze.

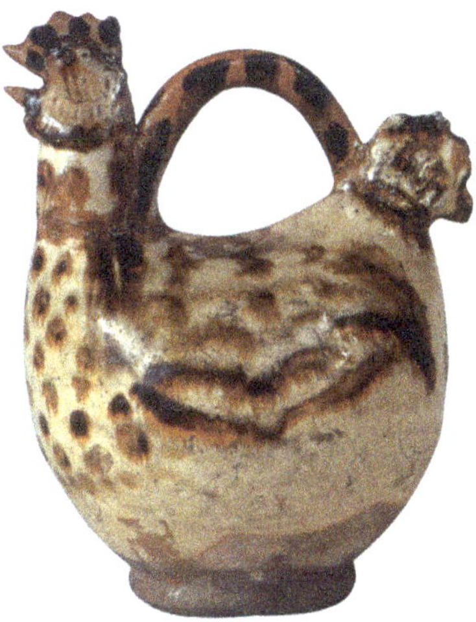

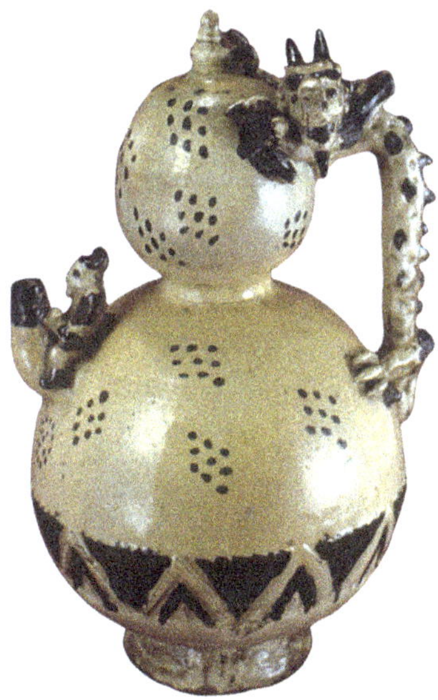

82. White Glazed Gourd-shaped Kettle with Black Flower Design

Jin

Height: 28.4 cm Bottom Diameter: 8.8 cm

Unearthed from Fuxin, Liaoning

Preserved in the Liaoning Provincial Museum

This container is painted with a light yellow roughcast. It is coated with ivory-white glaze which is fairly thick. The roughcast can be seen at the bottom. Shaped into a gourd, the kettle has a dragon-shaped handle, a short spout embossed with the image of a sitting old man. The ringed foot contains a round water injection hole which connects with the water filling pipe in the kettle. So the kettle had to have been put upside down when water was poured in. The kettle body is decorated with underglazed black plum-blossom-shaped spots. The belly features the carved patterns of supine lotus flowers with double layers of petals alternating with tiny fluted designs. Besides, the inverted black triangle pattern can also be seen on the body.

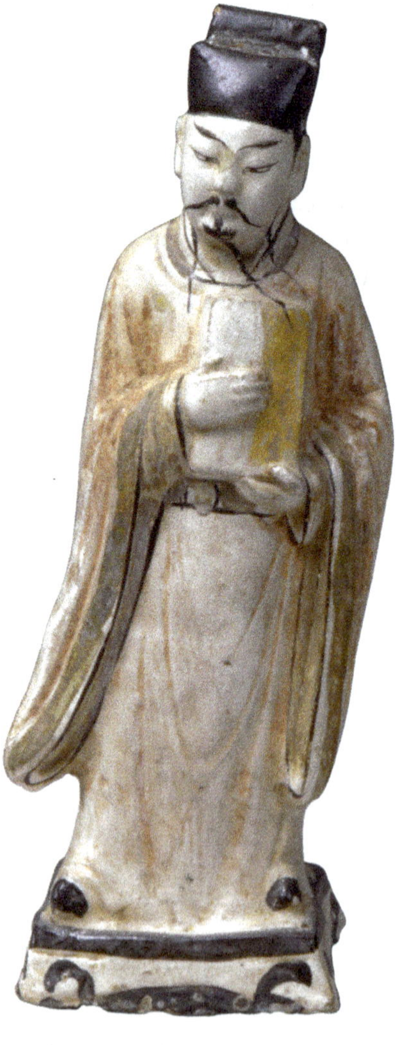

83. Painted Man

Jin

Height: 30 cm

Unearthed from Yangjiayuan Village in Qufu, Shandong in 1954

Preserved in the Shandong Museum

This burial object with its snow-white roughcast appears rough, loose and underfired. The white glazed figurine is painted with red, green, yellow and black colors. Clad in a black hat, this man is well featured, with a long face and moustache. He wears a long gown, a jade belt around the waist and a pair of black shoes with upturned toe caps on his feet. Holding a book in his hands, he stands on a square base.

84. Brown Glazed Jar with Cut Peony Design of the Lingwu Kiln

Western Xia
Height: 21.5 cm Mouth Diameter: 11 cm Foot Diameter: 8.6 cm
Unearthed from Ejin Horo Banner, Inner Mongolia in 1974
Preserved in the Inner Mongolia Museum

This container with a coarse and heavy roughcast has a coat of brown glaze. But the mouth, the lower part of the belly and the ringed foot are naked. The body is something of a globe-shape with a bulging belly. Besides, the jar has a small mouth with a round lip and ringed foot. The belly is engraved with two groups of peony sprays together with the patterns of running curves at both sides, which are circled with cloud and water designs.

The Lingwu Kiln is the most famous kiln during the Western Xia Dynasty. The products of the Lingwu Kiln are heavily influenced by the style of the Cizhou Kiln.

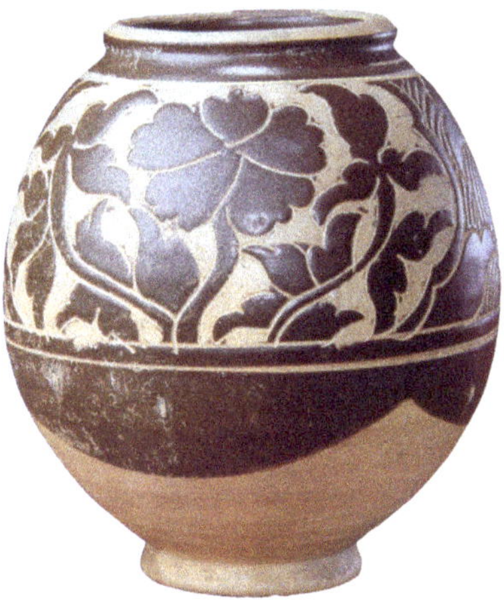

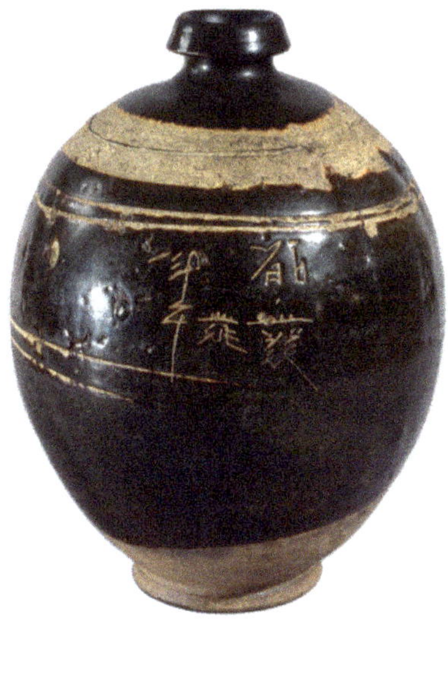

85. Black Glazed Vase

Western Xia
Height: 32.6 cm Mouth Diameter: 5.5 cm Bottom Diameter: 10.9 cm
Preserved in the Shanghai Museum

This container is covered with black glaze. The vase has a ring around the shoulder, which is unglazed, exposing the roughcast inside. The glazed surface is smooth and bright. This object has a small flared mouth, a short neck, a globe-like belly and a ringed foot. The belly has characters cut in intaglio. The first line from left to right looks like the Chinese characters "Dou and Jin" and the second and third lines are obviously Western Xia characters, obviously spelling out a person's name.

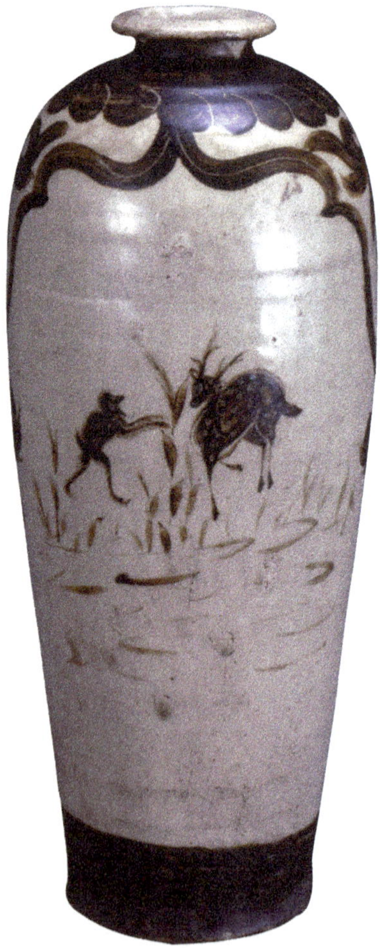

86. White Glazed Vase with Black Design

Western Xia

Height: 42.5 cm Mouth Diameter: 7.8 cm Foot Diameter: 12.7 cm

Preserved in the Palace Museum in Beijing

This vase has a flared open mouth, short neck, broad shoulder, wide ringed foot and unglazed bottom. The part below the shoulder contracts somewhat. The white glazed body is decorated with black designs: there is a ring of symbolic lotus petals around the shoulder. Both sides have two groups of drooping curly leaves; the belly is adorned with traditional auspicious designs of monkey and deer playing on the grassland on one side and two wild geese flying over the reeds on the other side.

Painting

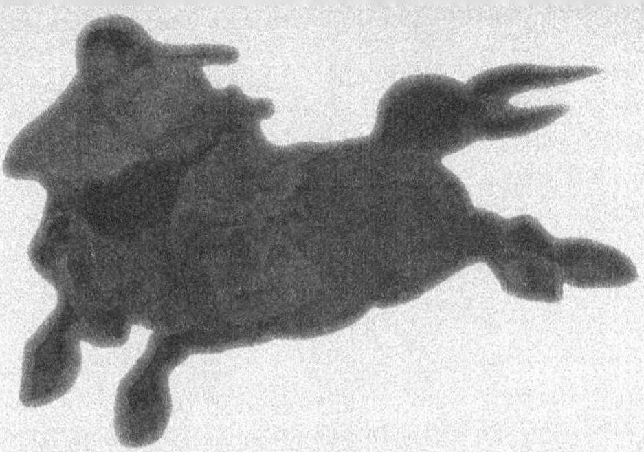

Among the painters in the Liao Dynasty, Li Zanhua, Hu Gui and his son Hu Qian were the most celebrated. Their paintings mainly feature people and horses from the nomadic Khitan people (an ancient nationality in northern China) for whom horses were a vital part of their daily life. Painting of flowers and birds developed slower than in the Central plains. The most indisputable relic in this respect is *Bamboos, Sparrows and Two Hares* unearthed from a Liao Dynasty tomb in Yemaotai, Liaoning in 1974. Because it was discovered in a tomb where the exact date can be confirmed, this is a reliable source for comparative study on works painted during this period.

The surviving paintings from the Liao Dynasty have hardly any simple landscapes. Although a few works do have landscapes as backgrounds to pictures of people and horses, the features of landscape paintings in this period cannot be fully understood. There is one painting from the No. 7 Liao Dynasty tomb in Yemaotai in Faku County, Liaoning, which was named Palying Chess in a Mountain Dwelling. The tomb was built in the early period of the Liao Dynasty. Therefore, this painting is a typical example from the early Liao Dynasty in this respect.

Surviving paintings of the Liao Dynasty are small in number, while paintings on paper or silk are even rarer. In recent years, some mural paintings in tomb chambers were found in Inner Mongolia , Liaoning and Hebeis, areas that once were under the control of the Liao Dynasty regime. Those wall paintings discovered in the Qingling Mausoleum of the Liao Dynasty (Liao Tombs in Baarin Right Banner), Liao Tomb in Baoshan, Chifeng, and Liao Tombs at Xiabali village in Xuanhua, Hebei become more reliable sources for Liao paintings.

Figure painting in the Jin Dynasty blended the style of the Northern Song Dynasty with nomadic elements and achieved an art form with unique national features. Many painters skilled in this respect emerged, including Zhang Yu, Gong Suran, Ma Yunqing and Yang Shichang. They left behind a great deal of artistic treasures. On the other hand, paintings of flowers, birds and beasts of this period reveal the strong influence of the court painting style of the Northern Song Dynasty. This can be clearly seen from existing relics. The drawing achievements of the Jin Dynasty are also reflected in the mural paintings in tomb chambers and temples, like the mural paintings in the Jin Dynasty tombs at Shizhuang village in Jingxing in Hebei, in the wall paintings in the Manjusri Hall of Yanshan Temple in Fanshi County, and in the Amitabha Hall of Chongfu Temple in Shuozhou, both in Shanxi.

The paintings of the Western Xia Dynasty are stood by a batch of Buddha drawings unearthed from Twin Pagodas at Baisikou in Helan County and Hongfota Pagoda, both in Ningxia Hui Autonomous Region. Besides, some wall paintings created in this period and preserved in the Dunhuang Caves are important research sources for Western Xia art.

87. Hu Gui: Go Hunting

Liao

Vertical Length: 32.9 cm   Horizontal Length: 44.3 cm

Preserved in the Palace Museum in Taipei

This was a drawing painted with ink and colors on silk. It depicts a scene where the Khitan people are going to hunt with their eagles. All details are painted exquisitely from the facial expressions to the clothing and baldrics of the hunters, to their eagles, sleuths, horses and saddles. Human and horse hair were dyed in thin colors using a brush made of weasel's hair, while the background has fading plants drawn in tidy strokes. It was affixed with a half-seal (usually used by low-level officials, unlike the full-seal used by high officials), which reads "宣和" (Xuanhe). It has been preserved by the Imperial Household Department of the Song Dynasty during the Xuanhe era of the reign of Emperor Huizong.

Hu Gui, whose dates of birth and death are unknown, was probably active in the ninth to tenth century. His nationality is also not clear with different sources saying he was Khitan, Wusuogu trible, Shatuo or even Fanyang (in what is today's Zhuoxian County in Hebei). He was very skilled at painting Khitan people and horses.

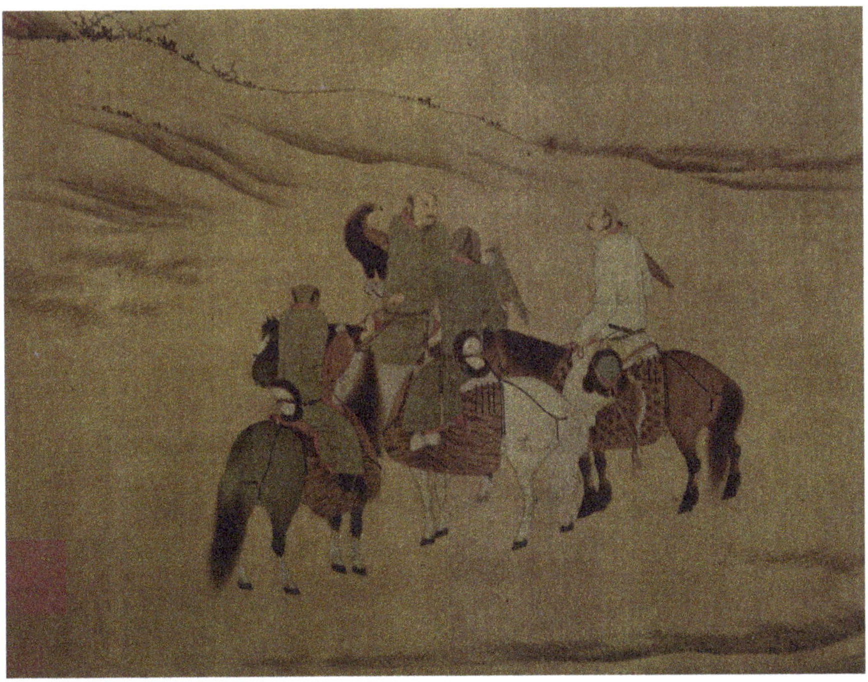

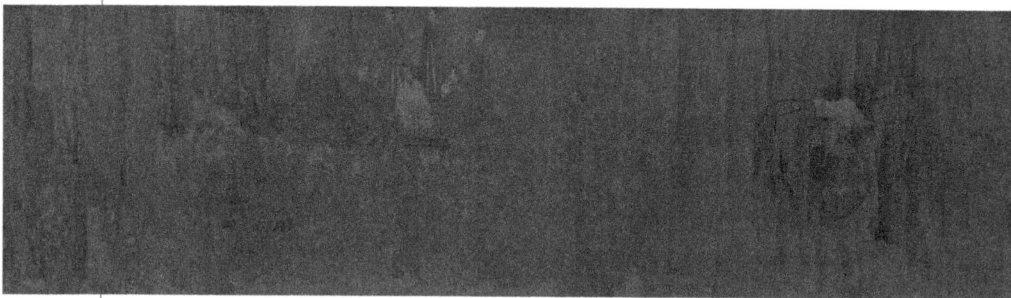

88. Hu Gui: Party Held in a Tent after Hunting

Liao

Vertical Length: 33 cm Horizontal Length: 256 cm

Preserved in the Palace Museum in Beijing

This drawing painted with ink and colors on silk depicts a scene where some Khitan nobles are holding a banquet as they take a break during a hunting spree. In the picture, the Jurchen all have shaved hair, suggesting bold and unconstrained personalities. The horses are plump and sturdy while the background is desolate grassland. The painting style is vigorous with powerful strokes. The scroll has inscriptions by Zhang Zhao and Emperor Qianlong of the Qing Dynasty in the front of the picture, "Sheng Wan Jing Xiao" by Emperor Qianlong is inscribed on the picture part, and annotations by Wang Shi of the Yuan Dynasty, Gao Shiqi and Zhang Zhao of the Qing Dynasty at the bottom. It was recorded in the Precious *Collection of the Stone Moat Squel: Second Edition*, and *Notes on Stone Moat*.

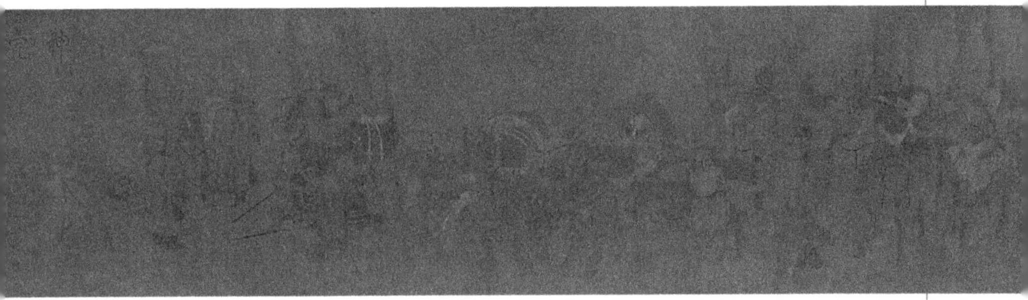

89. Hu Gui: Ethnic Tribal Riders

Liao or Yuan

Vertical Length: 26.2 cm Horizontal Length: 143.5 cm

Preserved in the Palace Museum in Beijing

This drawing was painted with ink and colors on silk. It depicts three men riding on horses and three walking including one man and two women wearing Gugu coronas (usually worn by Mongolian noble women). The figures have vivid and natural postures. The strokes are flexible - they are balanced and vigorous and the colors are simple and unadorned. There is no name of either the painter or recipient recorded on the painting, but there is an inscription by Emperor Qianlong at the beginning and on the painted part. On the panel connecting the beginning and painted part, there is a fake label of Emperor Huizong of Song Dynasty. The painting has 40 seals affixed by connoisseurs from the Qing Dynasty. The *Precious Collection of the Stone Moat Sequel: Second Edition* has a record about it.

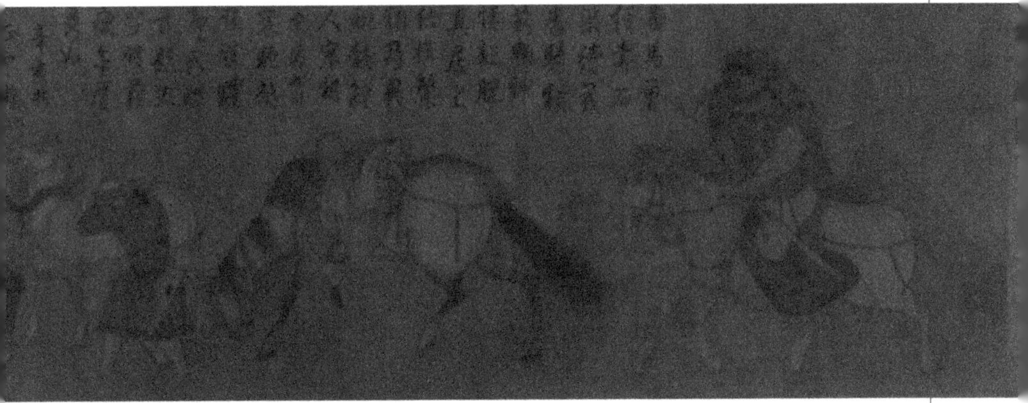

90. Chen Jizhi: Forming Alliances at the Bianqiao

Liao

Vertical Length: 36.2 cm Horizontal Length: 774.9 cm

Preserved in the Palace Museum in Beijing

This drawing painted with ink and paper illustrates the story of Li Shiming, in his capacity as Prince of Qin, who formed alliances with Jiali Khan of the Turks (an ethnic minority in ancient China) at the Bianqiao near the capital Chang'an in 626, the ninth year of Wude of the reign of Emperor Gaozu of the Tang Dynasty. The painting is mainly an adopted line drawing in traditional ink and brush style, with applied colors with light ink. The clothes are drawn with pin-head-rat-tail traces, which is round and smooth with alternating thick and thin lines. The work has the signature "Painted by Chen Jizhi" and a seal "Practice Work by Zhupo Jizhi". At the beginning is the inscription of "Forming Alliances at the Bianqiao Painting by Chen Jizhi" written by Liang Qingbiao of the Qing Dynasty. Besides, it was stamped by Liang Qingbiao and by the Imperial Household Department of Emperor Qianlong, and it was recorded in the *Precious Collection of the Stone Moat Sequel: First Edition*.

Chen Jizhi, who also used the courtesy name Zhupo, was a man of the Liao State. The dates of his birth and death are unknown. This painting is his only surviving work.

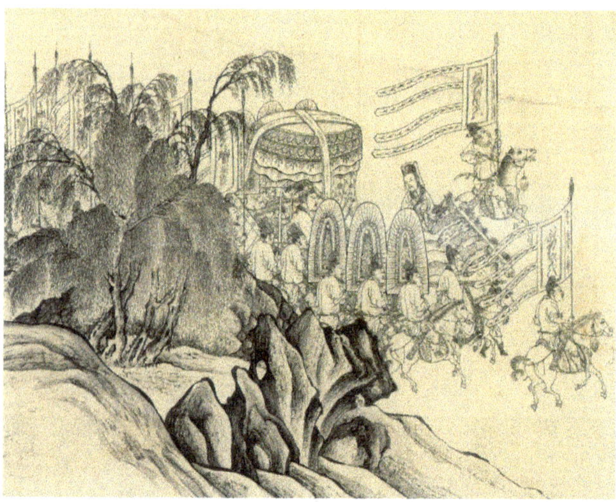

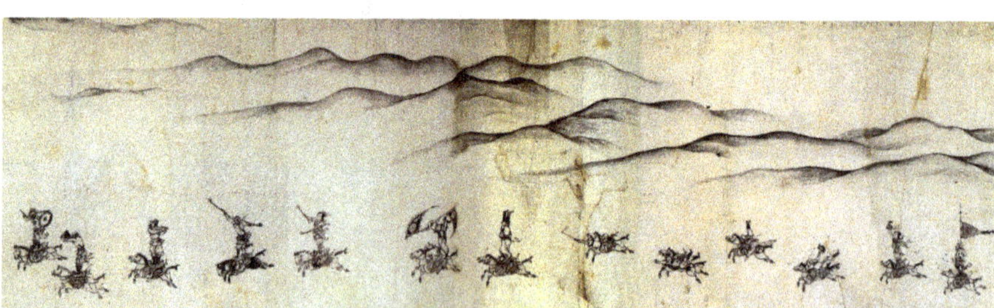

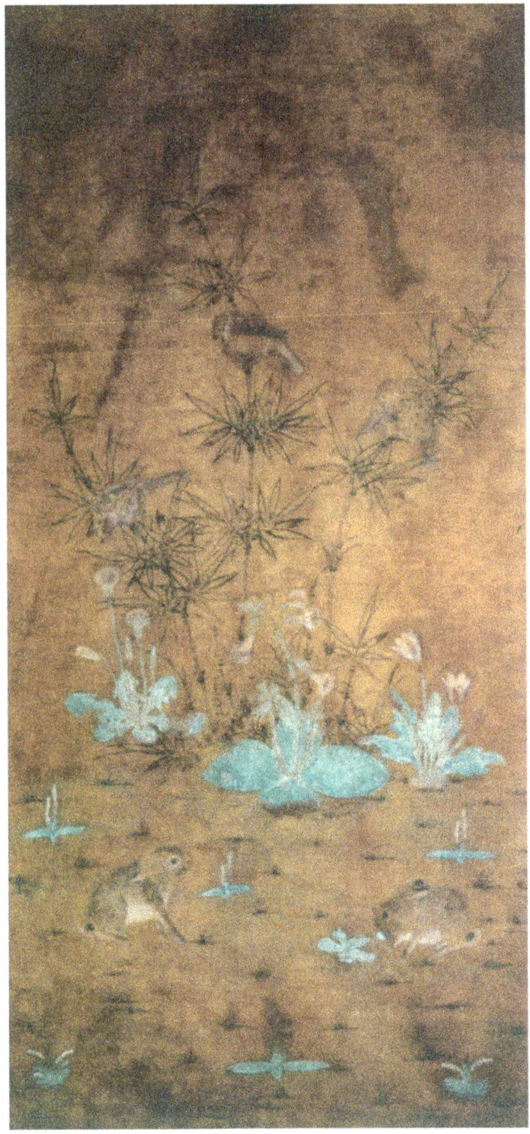

91. Anonymous Artist: Bamboos, Sparrows and Two Hares

Liao

Vertical Length: 114.3 cm Horizontal Length: 56 cm

Unearthed from a Liao Dynasty Tomb in Yemaotai, Faku, Liaoning in 1974

Preserved in the Liaoning Provincial Museum

This drawing painted with ink and colors on silk depicts three bamboos, which were drawn using the method of "double outlines filled with ink", bamboo clumps and some other flowers and plants. Three sparrows are perched on three separate bamboos, standing still, combing their feathers or looking for food. Under the bamboos are two hares, one eating grass and the other looking about. The composition might be conventional but all the contents are vividly depicted. As the only existing flower and bird painting from a Liao Dynasty tomb, it reveals the features of this type of painting in that period.

92. Anonymous Artist: Playing Chess while Waiting for Friends

Liao

Vertical Length: 106.5 cm   Horizontal Length: 54 cm

Unearthed from a Liao Dynasty Tomb in Yemaotai, Faku, Liaoning in 1974

Preserved in the Liaoning Provincial Museum

This drawing painted with ink and colors on silk. depicts a chain of mountains in the main part of the picture with a peak towering in the middle magnificently and many lush peaks in the distance. On the mountain top, there are dense clumps of pines, in which are found courtyards, pavilions and figures either playing chess or on their way to appointments. The wrinkling method is used to draw mountains and rocks in a brief but comprehensive style, filled with peculiar and steep features. The peaks in the distance and pavilions are done in blue and red colors. This work represents the features of landscape painting of the Liao Dynasty.

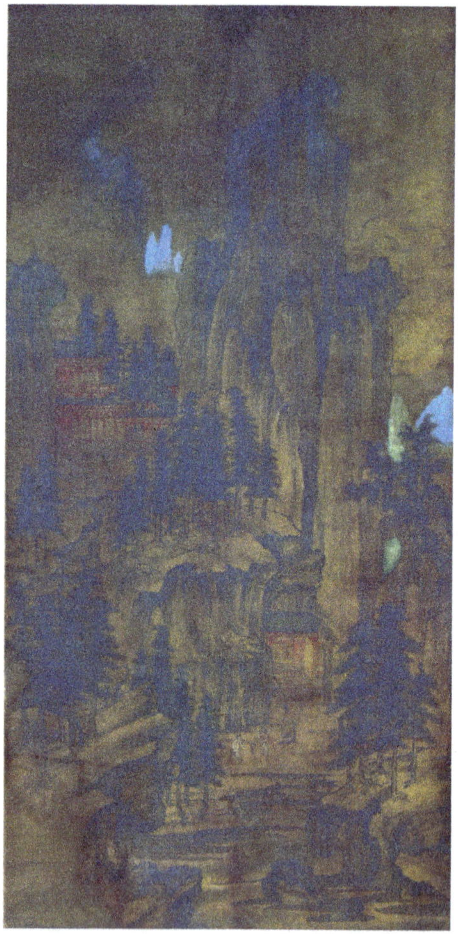

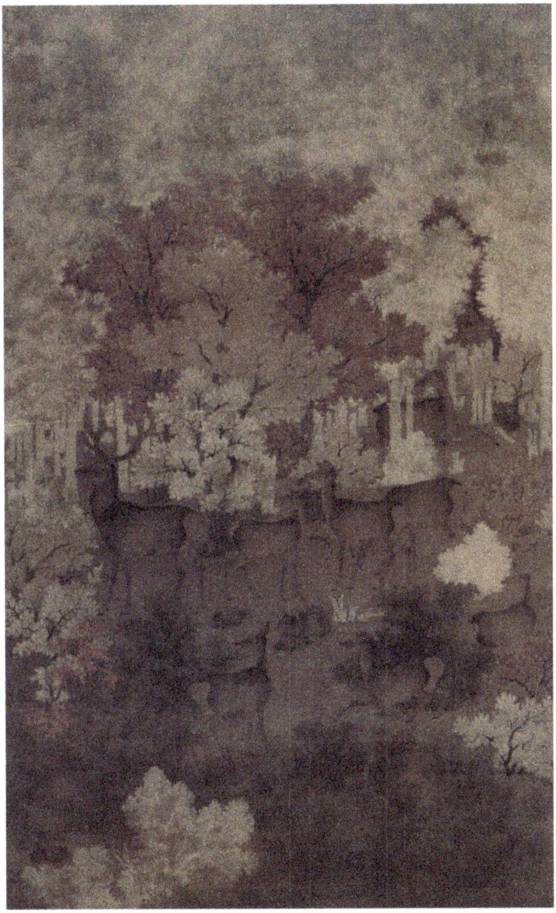

93. Anonymous Painter: Red Maples and Bleating Deer

Liao

Vertical Length: 118.5 cm Horizontal Length: 64.5 cm

Preserved in the Palace Museum in Taipei

This drawing painted with ink and colors on silk depicts dense forest with red and yellow leaves setting off one another. A herd of deer are having a rest in the woods, either standing or crouching, or hiding behind trees, or lingering at the forest border. The deer are painted realistically. The crowns with clear outlines provide a nice contrast. The branches and leaves seem to be drawn with hard fur in a prudent manner, presenting a delicate, pretty and glossy scene. The composition is tight while the color is gorgeous. There is no recorded name of painter or recipient. The painting is stamped by the Imperial Household Department of the Yuan and Qing Dynasties. It was recorded in the *Precious Collection of the Stone Moat Sequel: Second Edition*.

94. A Star-map of Prajvalonisa and Navagraha

Liao

Vertical Length: 94.6 cm Horizontal Length: 50 cm

Found in the Sakyamuni Pagoda of the Fogong Temple in Yingxian County, Shanxi

Preserved in the Shanxi Museum

This drawing painted with ink and colors on hemp paper is slightly damaged in the upper part. The Prajvalonisa holds a cakra sitting on a lotus throne in the lotus position. In front of the Prajvalonisa is the altar on which are some Buddha beads. On both sides stand asterism of Navagraha and on the top of the picture are gods of heaven and constellations. The painting has an inscription, but is partly damaged. It is printed with cut blocks - the lines were printed at first, and then colored. This is the biggest vertical scroll Buddhist painting found in China to date to be printed with wood blocks.

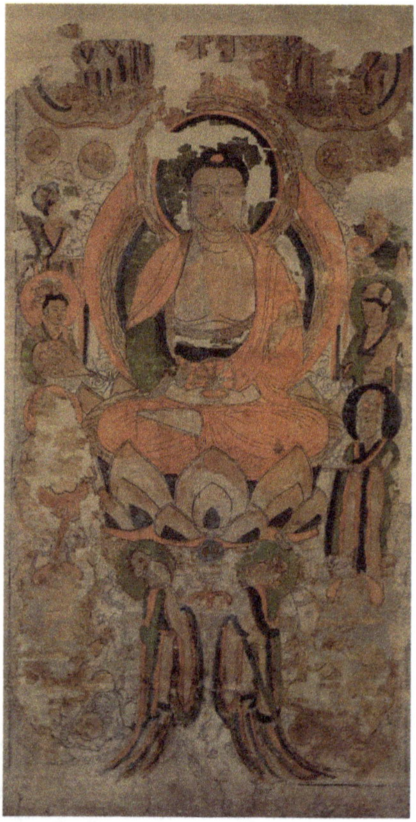

95. San Yue Performance

Liao

Found in the the Tomb of Zhang Kuangzheng in Xiabali village, Xuanhua, Hebei

This mural painted on the west wall of the atria of the tomb depicts eight people standing in two rows. The front row has two men - the one on the left is playing the waist drum and dancing while the right one is dancing. The other six in the back row (starting from left to right) are playing the bass drum, the clapper, the bili (an ancient wind instrument), a flute, a sheng (a reed pipe-like wind instrument) and the pipa (a plucked string instrument with a fretted fingerboard). All are female. The seven musicians wear robes and futous (a kind of soft hat), and are dressed like men. The only dancer wears flowers on her topknot and a long skirt.

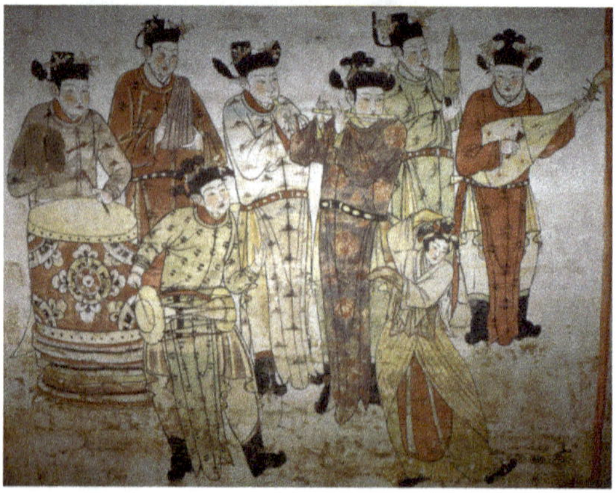

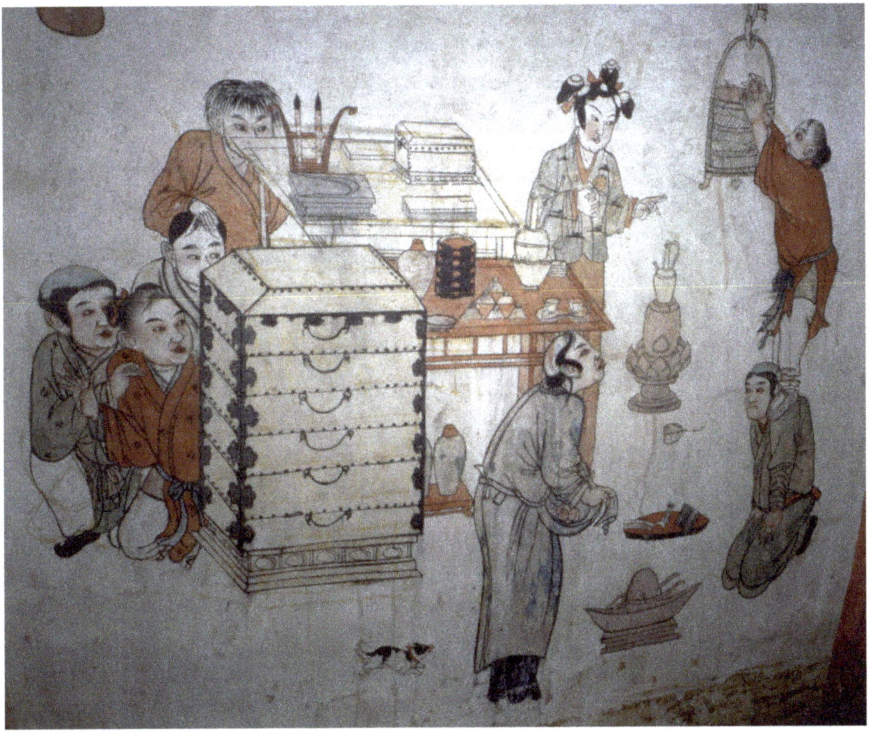

96. Children Playing

Liao

Found in the Tomb of Zhang Wenzao in Xiabali village, Xuanhua, Hebei

This mural is painted on the east wall of the atria of the tomb. It depicts eight persons in two groups. The group on the left has four people. One boy sits on his heels, and on his shoulders another boy stands stretching out his hands towards the peaches in a hanging basket. By their side is a boy lifting up his robe front to catch the thrown peaches. Beside the table is a girl, holding a peach in her right hand and pointing toward the boy fetching the peaches with his left hand. On the ground is a tea roller, a red painted plate and a drinking water boiler. On a red table is a tea set while on the white table are four precious writing table articles-brush, ink, paper and ink pad. The other group on the right have four boys squatting and playing behind a food box and table.

97. Preparing Tea

Liao

Found in the Tomb of Zhang Kuangzheng in Xiabali village, Xuanhua, Hebei

This mural painted on the east wall of the atria of the tomb, depicts five people in two groups. The group in the front row include a maid on the left, who holds a teacup in her hands, and two children on the right, one grinding tea and the other blowing into the boiler. The other group in the back has one maid on the left, holding a teacup in her hands, and a man in Khitan clothes, who looks as if he is fetching in. Behind them is a square table, on which is laid out a tea set.

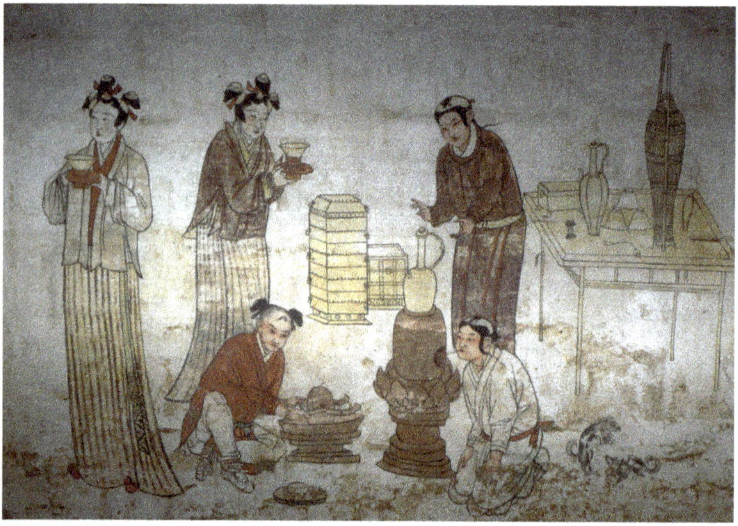

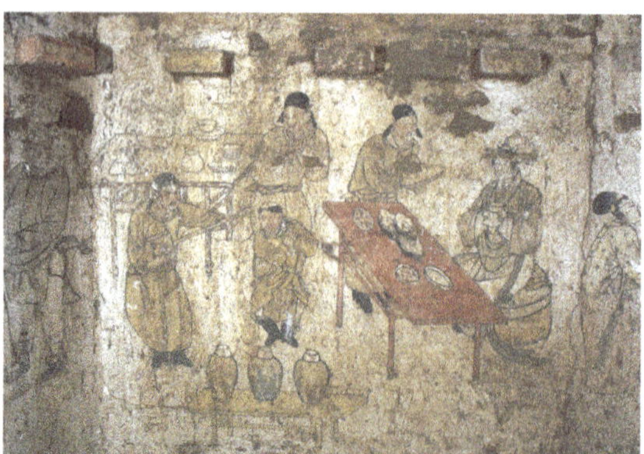

98. Conviviality

Liao

Found in the Tomb of Han Shixun in Xiabali village, Xuanhua, Hebei

This mural painting on the southwest wall of the metacele of the tomb has a woman sitting on a round stool and holding a cup on the right part. In front of her is a table, on which is a plate of food. Beside the table is a servant standing obediently and holding a plate in both hands. In front of the table are two performers putting on a show for the woman. Behind them, on the left side of the painting, is a square yellow table, on which are placed a pot, plates and bowls. On the other yellow bar table are three wine jars.

99. Preparing Tea

Liao

Found in the Tomb of Zhang Shiqing in Xiabali village, Xuanhua, Hebei

This mural painting on the west wall of the metacele of the tomb consists of four parts. From left to right, there is a picture of a woman opening a door; of a woman preparing tea; of servants holding a jar, and of another person opening a chest. The whole painting gives us a lively picture in which busy officials are being served by a group of servants. They were drawn in different postures but there seems a great harmony between them. The painter traced out a scene of the host's home life with careful strokes.

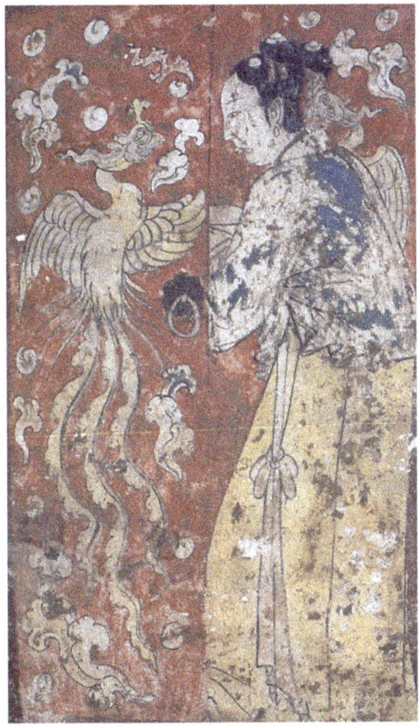

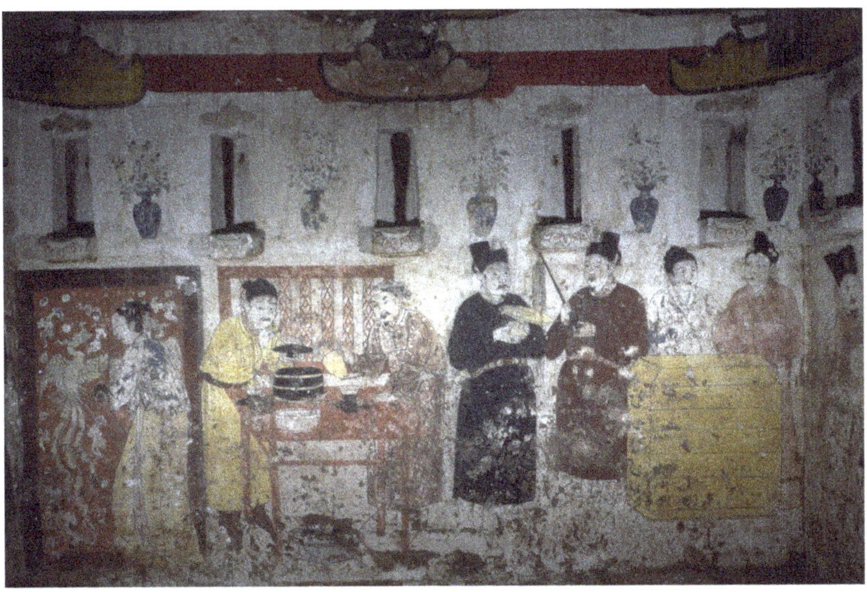

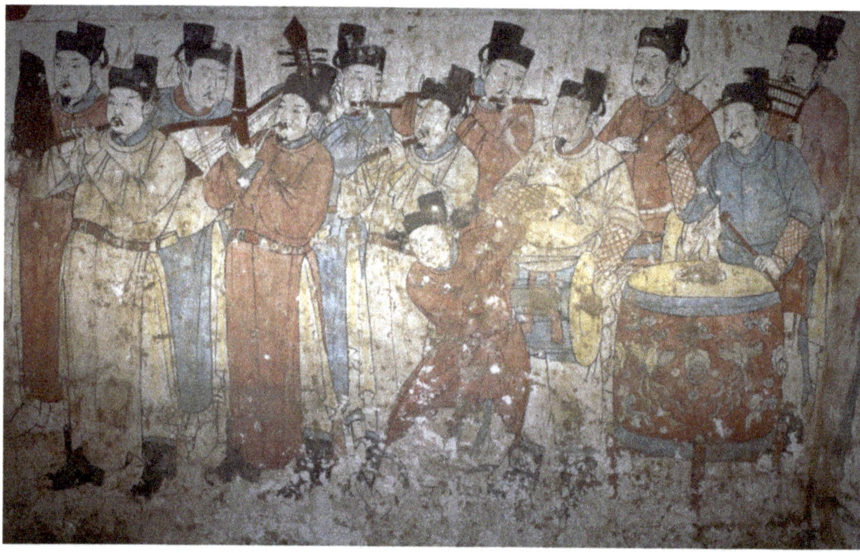

100. San Yue Performance

Liao

Height: 175 cm Width: 225 cm

Found in the Tomb of Zhang Shiqing in Xiabali village, Xuanhua, Hebei

This mural painting on the east wall of the tomb atria has a musical band which consists of 12 persons in two rows. The six in the front row from five are playing the bili (a wind instrument in ancient times), the sheng (a reed pipe-like wind instrument), the xiao (a vertical bamboo flute), the waist drum and the bass drum respectively, and there is one who is dancing. For the other six in the back row,two are playing the clapper, and the 4-stringed Chinese lute, and two are playing flutes, a waist drum and panpipes respectively. All the musicians are wearing black putous (a kind of soft hat), robes with round collars, waistbands and black boots.

101. Ji Jin (Sending a Silken Letter)

Liao

Found in the No.2 Liao Dynasty Tomb in Baoshan village, Ar Horqin Banner, Inner Mongolia in 1994

This mural painting on the south wall of the tomb chamber depicts seven people in two groups. At the front of the left group is the host, and his image is bigger than the others as he orders a maid to give a scroll to a serving boy. In front of the boy is a carrying pole with loads on it. The right group has four maids, holding a book, box and stools respectively. The background is old trees, clumps of bamboo and banana trees. In the top left corner is a poem written with black ink. The painting is elaborate with delicate technique and bright colors, and it reflects the charm of the best ladies paintings of the Tang and Five Dynasties period.

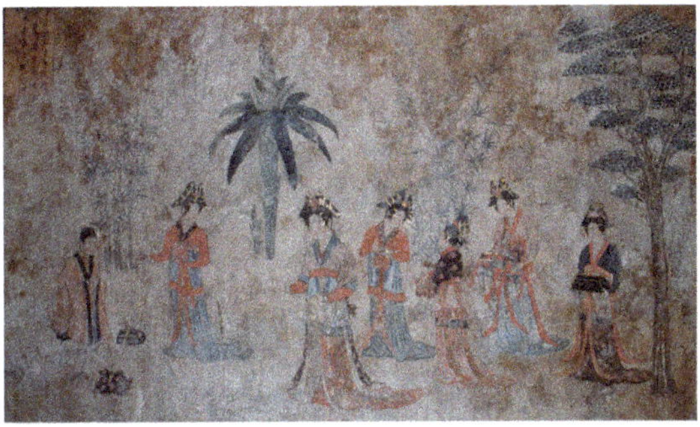

102. Painting of the Figures of Ladies

Liao

Vertical Length: 168 cm

Horizontal Length: 200 cm

Found in the No.2 Liao Dynasty Tomb in Hure Banner, Inner Mongolia in 1974

Preserved in the Inner Mongolia Museum

This mural painting is located on the connection joint between the tomb passage and parvis. It depicts a woman, who is 160 centimeters tall and dressed in Khitan ethnic clothing. She looks serious, as she moves towards the chamber door holding a white covered jar in her hands, seemingly waiting for the host to come out. Behind her is another woman in white. On her right side is a fully-saddled horse.

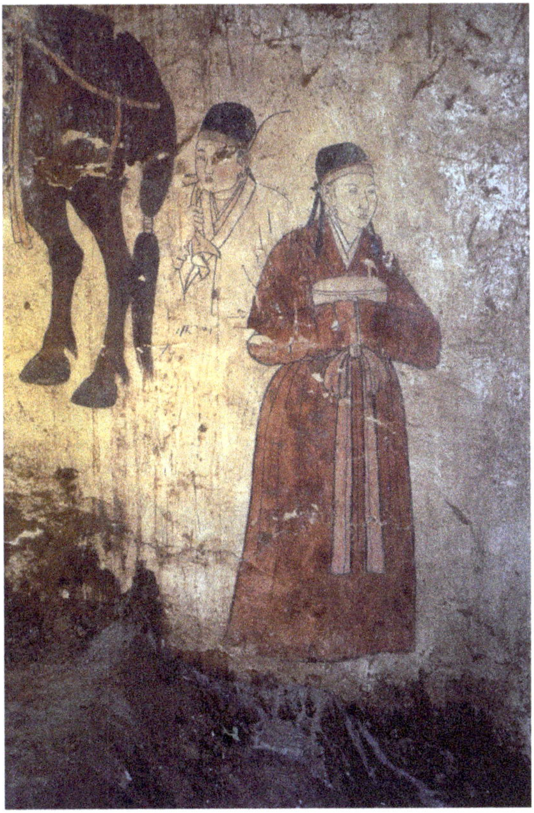

103. Zhang Yu: Wenji Returns to the Han

Jin

Vertical Length: 29 cm   Horizontal Length: 127 cm

Preserved in the Jilin Museum

This drawing painted with ink and colors on silk illustrates the story of Cai Wenji returning to the Han territory at the end of the Eastern Han Dynasty. There is a procession of people marching in the wilderness in the northern part of the country. The first one is a tribal man riding on a horse and carrying a flag. In the middle is a woman wearing a fur hat, tippet and thigh boots. She sits up on the horse and looks ahead. By her horse's side are two grooms leading the horse. Behind her are some Han officials and tribal guards. The painting bears the signature "Painted by Zhang Yu of Zhi Yingsi", a Jin Dynasty palace service department), an inscription and a poem by Emperor Qianlong. It was stamped by the Imperial Household Department of the Ming and Qing Dynasties, and Liang Qingbiao of the Qing Dynasty; and it is recorded in the *Precious Collection of the Stone Moat Squel: Second Edition*.

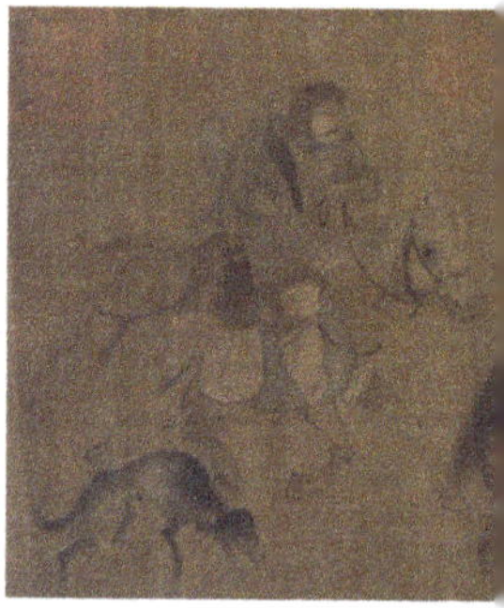

104. Zhao Lin: Six Steeds of Zhaoling Mausoleum

Jin

Vertical Length: 27.4 cm   Horizontal Length: 444.2 cm

Preserved in the Palace Museum in Beijing

This drawing painted with ink and colors on silk consists of six parts depicting six horses from the Zhaoling Mausoleum. Each horse has its name inscribed beside it and some lines of praise written by Zhao Bingwen of the Jin Dynasty. The chief source of the painting is the carved stone horses of Zhaoling Mausoleum. The horses are depicted in galloping postures, and demonstrate their majestic appearances which are full of valor and vigor. It bears the inscription Song of Zhao Lin Stone House (a song of carved horses in the Zhaoling Mausoleum) at the beginning and there are two poems on the front and back of the painting all written by Emperor Qianlong. At the bottom of the scroll is a colophon by Zhao Bingwen. The painting was recorded in the *Precious Collection of the Stone Moat Sequel: Second Edition* and *Notes on Stone Moat*.

Zhao Lin was a native of Luoyang in Henan in Jin Dynasty. He served as Daizhao (an official post in ancient China) in the imperial place under the reign of Wanyan Yong, Emperor Shizong of the Jin Dynasty.

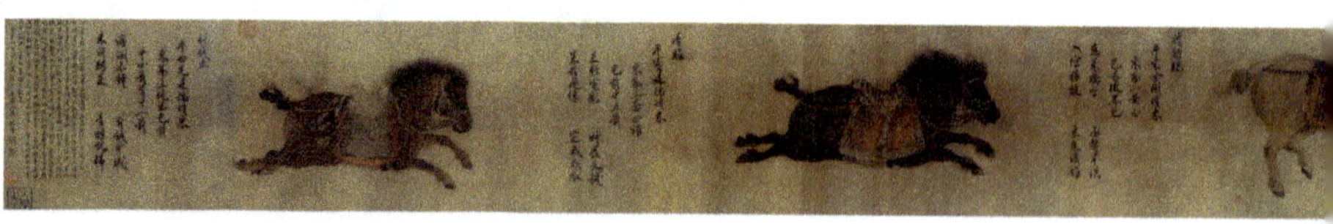

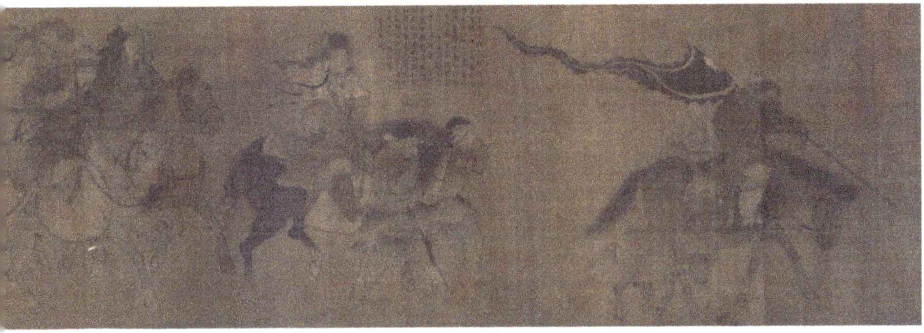

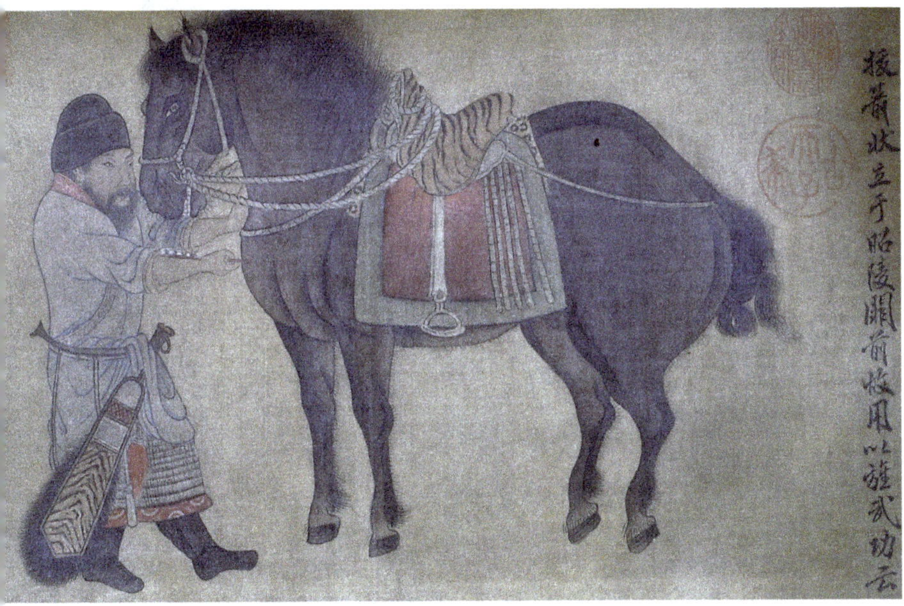

105. Zhang Gui: Magical Turtle

Jin

Vertical Length: 26.5 cm Horizontal Length: 55.3 cm

Preserved in the Palace Museum in Beijing

This drawing painted with ink and colors on silk depicts a magical turtle stretching out its neck, raising its head and exhaling a puff of white smoke. The smoke rises up, forming auspicious clouds, behind which the red sun can be seen indistinctly. The background is a sandy beach and the vast bleak sea. The texture of the turtle is portrayed with dots, lines and different shades of ink. This is the only existing copy of Zhang Gui's work. It has the signature "Emperor's Follower Zhang Gui" and one of Zhang's seals. Besides this, it has 18 seals affixed by the Imperial Household Department of the Yuan and Qing Dynasties and some others. It was recorded in the *Precious Collection of the Stone Moat Sequel: First Edition.*

Zhang Gui, a court painter, was famed in the Zhenglong era of the reign of Emperor Hailing of the Jin Dynasty. He was very skilled at painting figures, something which he learned from Zhou Wenju of the Southern Tang State during the Five Dynasties period.

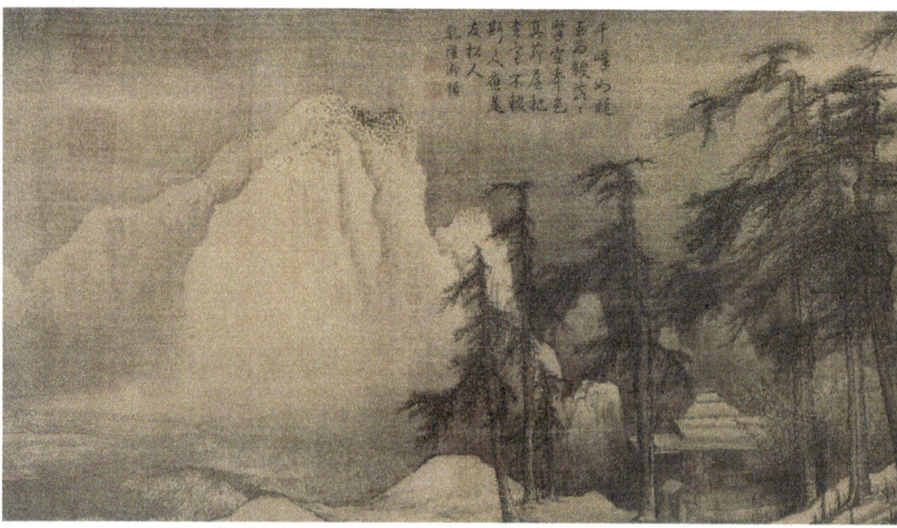

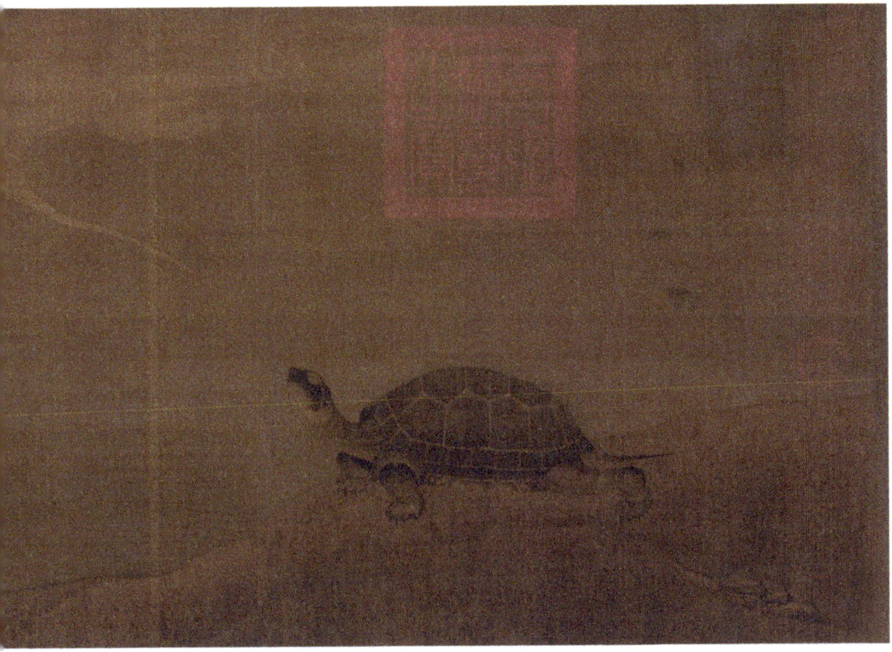

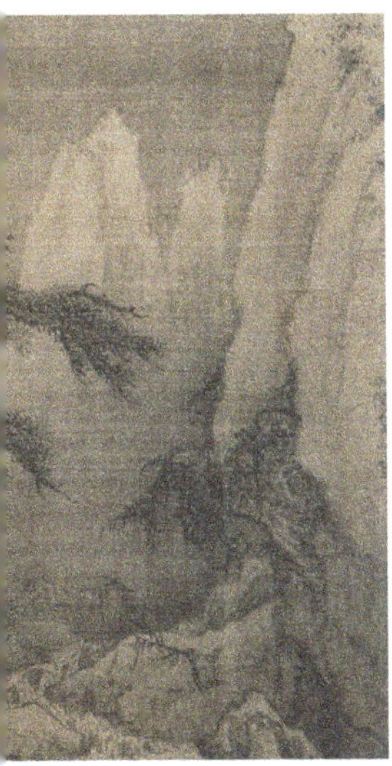

106. Li Shan: Abies Holophylla in Wind and Snow

Jin

Vertical Length: 29.7 cm Horizontal Length: 79.2 cm

Preserved in the Freer Gallery of Art in Washington DC, the United States of America

This drawing painted with ink and colors on silk depicts a line of abies holophylla standing in fog on a snowy mountain. Through the fog there can be seen some bamboos, a courtyard and a stream. This twilight scene in wind and snow spreads out to the trees and the vaguely sketched mountains. The stokes seems to be made carelessly yet all are very well controlled. The signature is "Painted by Li Shan of Pingyang", while the stamp is "Pingyang" in seal script. At the bottom of the scroll are postscripts by contemporaries Wang Tingyun and his son, Wang Manqing.

Li Shan (about 1121-1202) was a native of Pingyang (present-dayLinfen in Shanxi). He was very skilled at painting landscapes, trees and rocks, and in his work he followed the style of Guo Xi and Wang Shen.

107. Gong Suran: Mingfei Going out of the Frontier

Jin

Vertical Length: 30.2 cm Horizontal Length: 160.2 cm

Preserved in the Osaka Municipal Museum of Art in Japan

This drawing painted with ink on paper illustrates the story of Wang Zhaojun (also known as Mingfei) going out the frontier to marry a man of Hun, an ancient tribe in China. The picture shows the scene of the princess and her followers on their journey. The figures all wear Khitan clothing. The lines of the horses and clothes were brushed with light ink, while the wild scenery of the northern-frontier was sketched with thick strokes and light ink. The postures of the figures, dogs and horses capture perfectly the roaring wind, which sets off Wang Zhaojun's calm facial expressions. The signature is "Painted by Gong Suran of Zhenyang", and the stamp reads "Seal of Zhao Fu Shi," a temporary official in charge of political affairs in the army. The scroll has many seals and a postscript at the end.

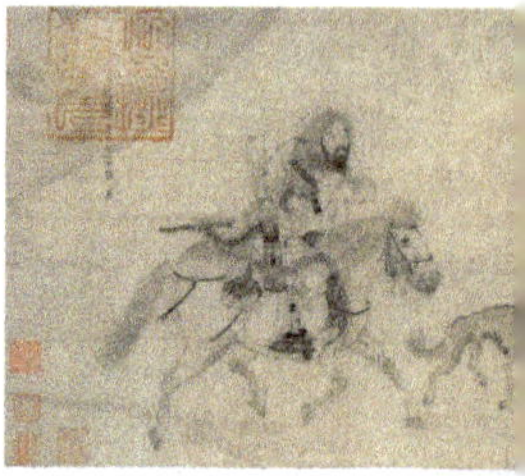

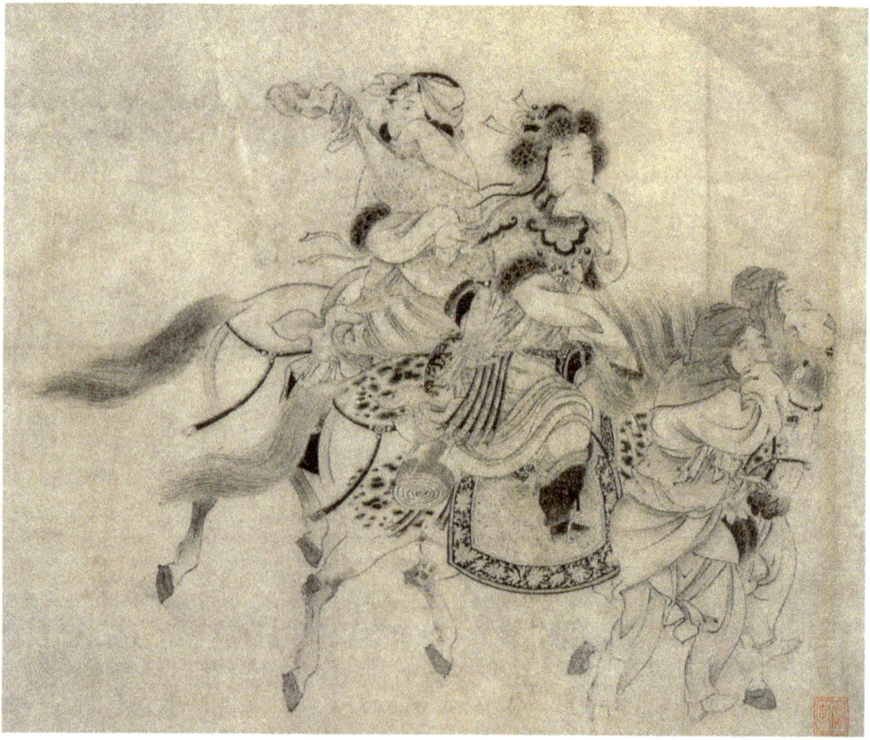

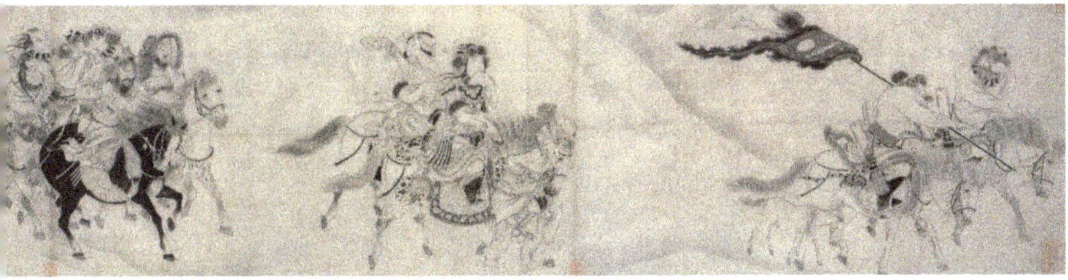

108. Wang Tingjun: Bamboo and Old Tree Branches

Jin

Vertical Length: 38 cm Horizontal Length: 67.9 cm

Preserved in the Fujii Saiseikai Yurinkan Museum of Art in Kyoto, Japan

This drawing painted with ink on paper depicts an old cypress and a bamboo with thick leaves. The painting contains a limited number of strokes yet there are quite a lot of variations, including those written with a dried brush, applied with light ink and hollowed strokes. The bamboo was drawn in a style very like calligraphy. At the bottom of the painting is the painter's own postscript. The bottom of the scroll has an annotation by Xianyu Shu and Zhao Mengfu from the Yuan Dynasty. The work has seals affixed by Zhao Mengfu, Qiao Kuicheng (both of the Yuan Dynasty), Liang Qingbiao and the Imperial Household Department of the Qing Dynasty. It was included in Paintings appreciation and the *Precious Collection of the Stone Moat Sequel: Second Edition*.

Wang Tingjun (1156-1202) styled himself Ziduan and also used the pseudonym Huanghua Shanzhu. He was a native of Hedong (present-dayYongji in Shanxi) but he lived at the foot of Huanghua Hill in Yunzhou (present-dayYuncheng in Shandong). He was skilled at painting landscapes, plum trees and bamboo. He learned landscape painting from Ren Xun, and dead wood, bamboo and rock paintings from Mi Fu. Sometimes he did freehand brushwork paintings too.

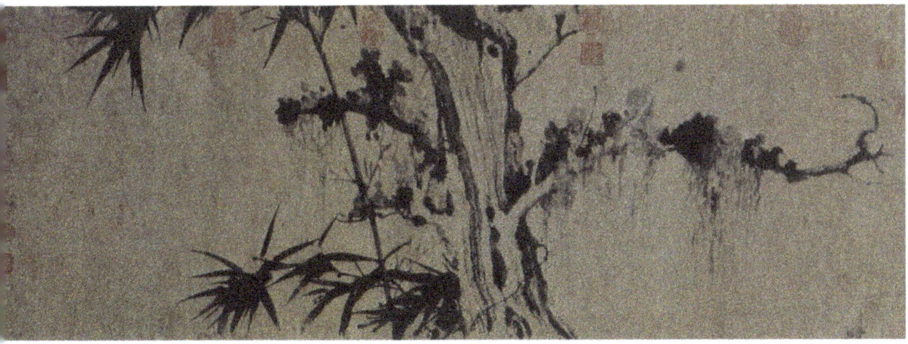

109. Yang Wei: Two Horses

Jin

Vertical Length: 24.8 cm Horizontal Length: 80.8 cm

Preserved in the Liaoning Museum

This drawing painted with ink and colors on silk depicts a scene of a herdsman on horseback ready to tether another horse. The two strong horses are well-shaped while the herdsman is bold with a tense expression. The sketching of the slopes, trees and rocks gives us a great wild and natural background. The signature is "Painted by Yang Wei of Gaotang in 1184".

Yang Wei was a painter in the Jin Dynasty. He was very skilled at painting figures and horses, and at observing objects in detail. Besides this, he excelled at applying colors to paintings.

110. Wu Yuanzhi: Red Cliff

Jin

Vertical Length: 51.9 cm Horizontal Length: 697.7 cm

Preserved in the Palace Museum in Taipei

This drawing painted with ink on paper was painted according to the description of Su Shi's Ode to the Red Cliff. The shades and texture of the rocks and mountains are depicted using light ink strokes and were drawn with a short thin brush. Among the mixture of light and thick lines, some details were added. Compared to the mighty mountain, the trees are tiny but upright. The ink tones are relatively mellow, which makes the mountains appear in majestic layers. There is no signature on the painting but "Last Words on Red Cliff" in seal script are inscribed at the top of the scroll. At the end is a postscript by Zhao Bingwen in large character semi-cursive script, together with a ci (a type of classical Chinese poem) which has the same rhyme as Su Shi's Ode to the Red Cliff. The painting was preserved by Xiang Yuanbian (Ming Dynasty). It was stamped by Xiang Yuanbian and by the Imperial Household Department of the Qing Dynasty, and was recorded in the *Precious Collection of the Stone Moat Sequel: Second Edition*.

Wu Yuanzhi, who also used the courtesy name Shanfu, was a successful candidate in the highest imperial examinations, and was a famous personage with no official post in the Mingchang era of the reign of Emperor Zhangzong of the Jin Dynasty. Most of his artistic work was done in the mid to late years of the Jin Dynasty. He was well versed in landscape painting. His work featured fine strokes and pure but mellow ink tones. The style of his painting is close to that of the imperial-court paintings of the Southern Song Dynasty.

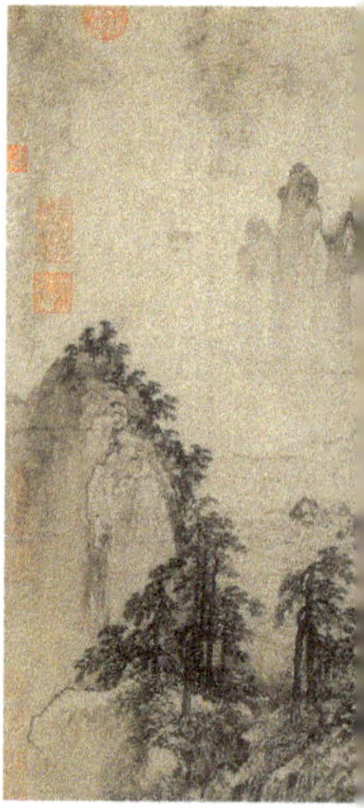

111. Anonymous Artist: Streams, Mist and Clouds

Jin

Vertical Length: 28.8 cm Horizontal Length: 242 cm

Preserved in the Palace Museum in Beijing

This drawing painted with ink on silk depicts a misty and broad open field. With its deep and mighty artistic conception, the work was based on a carefully conceived structure. The mountains and rocks were drawn with thin stiff lines, while the coiling mist and smoke also appears in some features of the landscape paintings by Dong Yuan and Ju Ran. For this reason, a fake signature of Dong Yuan was added over the years. Moreover, other postscripts were forged in the names of the Four Great Painters of the Yuan Dynasty (Huang Gongwang, Ni Zan, Wu Zhen and Wang Meng) and were included at the bottom of the scroll, in an attempt to pass the painting off as one done during the Song Dynasty.

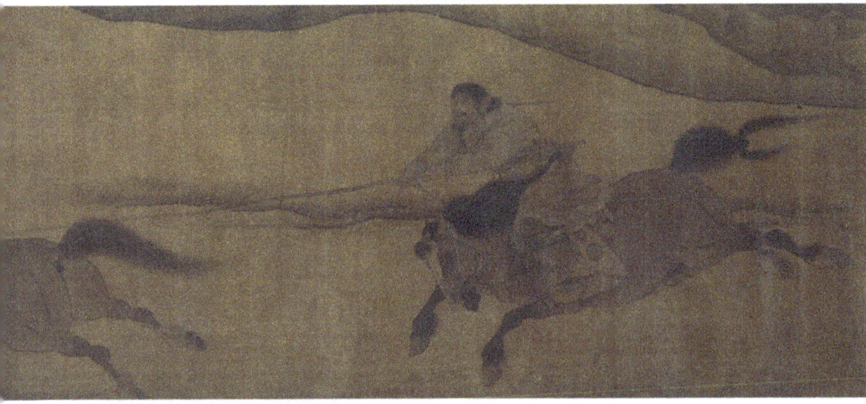

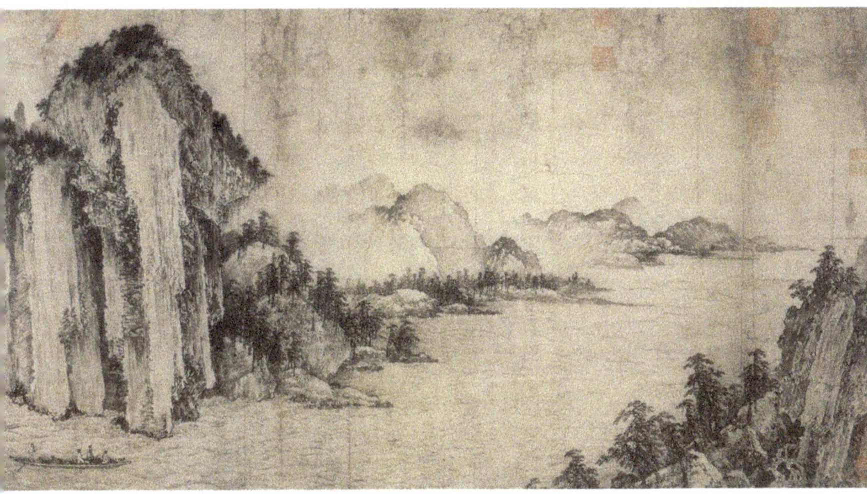

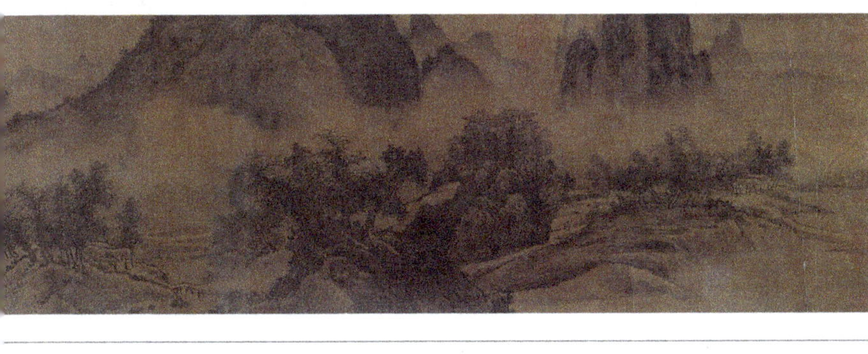

112. Beating the Drum to Announce Good News

Jin

Preserved in the Manjusri Hall of Yanshan Temple in Fanshi County, Shanxi

This temple fresco depicts a scene showing maids in the imperial palace beating their drums to announce the good news of Sakyamuni's birth. It has a title written with ink, which reads "this is the place where we beat the drum to announce the good news of the prince's birth".

Yanshan Temple, originally named Lingyan Temple, was built in 1158, the third year of Zhenglong of the reign of Emperor Hailing. The extant wall painting in the Manjusri Hall is about 90 square meters. It was finished in 1167, the seventh year of Dading of the reign of Emperor Shizong, and it was done by the court painter Wang Kui. It illustrates a story from Buddhist Scriptures.

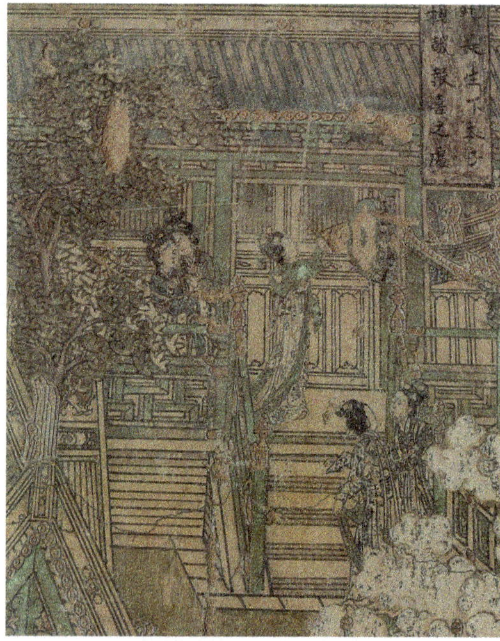

113. Thousand-Armed, Thousand-Eyed Avalokitesvara

Jin

Height: 573 cm Width: 45 cm

Preserved in the Amitabha Hall of Chongfu Temple in Shuozhou, Shanxi

This temple fresco of the gracious Arya Avalokiteshvara has a full and mellow face. On the left and right sides of the face are two faces while on the top of the head are five layers of Buddha heads with a seated Amitabha at the end. The body of the Avalokiteshvara is wound around with all kinds of ribbons which are inlaid with multicolored gems and beads. In front of the chest are six arms with each hand cupping another. In front of the belly are 18 arms, with even more arms on the back. Each hand has an eye in the palm and each also holds a musical instrument-there are over a hundred in total. Those hands and arms form a huge sector. In the lower left and right corner are Vasudeva and Lakasmi.

The one thousand arms of the Avalokiteshvara demonstrate the boundless supernatural power of the Buddha, which can save all living creatures from calamity. The eyes represent the Buddha's inexhaustible wisdom which enables the Buddha to behold the whole world and discover the minutest detail in everything.

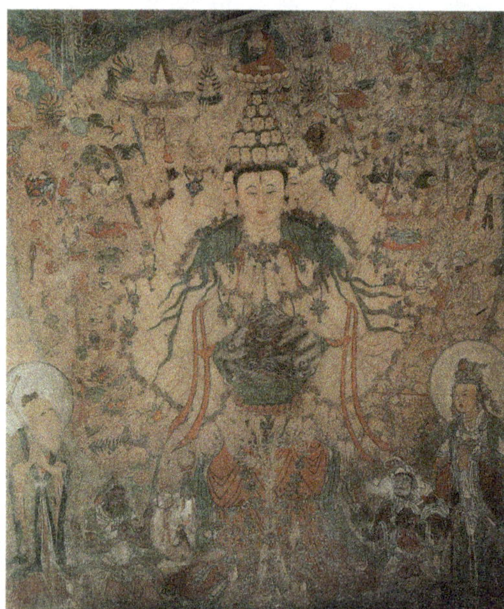

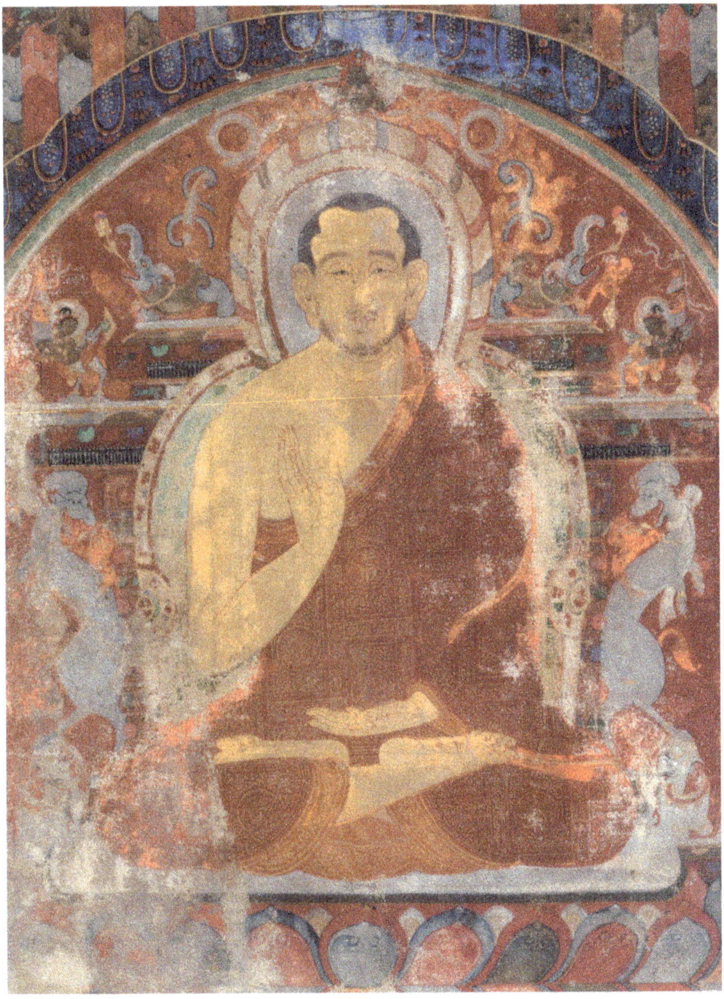

114. Picture of Guru
Western Xia
Vertical Length: 135 cm Horizontal Length: 94.5 cm
Unearthed from twin towers at Baisikou in Helan County, Ningxia Hui Autonomous Region in 1986
Preserved in the Ningxia Hui Autonomous Region Museum
This Tangka painted with color on silk depicts a guru who looks serious and composed. He wears a red cassock with golden design, and his right arm is exposed. In the mudra of the teacher, he sits on the lotus throne in full-lotus position with a halo and a visible aura. The color of the painting is thick and bright.

115. Samantabhadra

Western Xia

Preserved in the No. 3 Cave in Yulin, Anxi County, Gansu

This cave painting of Samantabhadra holding sutras and sitting on the lotus throne in half-lotus position. Under the throne is a white elephant marching on the lotus while the servant beside it is holding the reins tightly. Around the Samantabhadra is a cortege: Brahma, four kings (Dhrtrastra, Virudhaka, Virupaksa and Dhanada), Bodhisattva, and Arhat. The ribbons of those figures are waving while the clouds under their feet are rolling. In the background can be seen pavilions indistinctly in the distance. The figures in the painting are rendered in neat and exquisite lines.

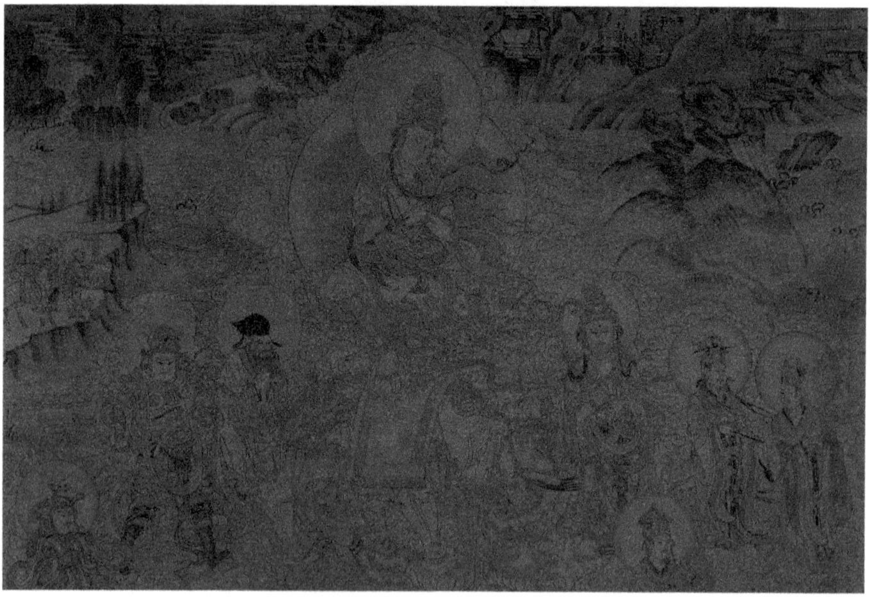

116. Manjushri

Western Xia

Preserved in the No. 3 Cave in Yulin, Anxi County, Gansu

This cave painting is of Manjushri holding a ruyi and sitting on a lotus throne in half-lotus position. Under the throne is a blue lion standing on a red lotus while the servant beside it is holding the reins. Around the Manjushri are Sakka, four kings (Dhrtrastra, Virudhaka, Virupaksa and Dhanada), Bodhisattva, Arhat and some boys, all of whom line up on the clouds ready to sail across a sea. The painting was sketched mainly as a line drawing with some light colors applied.

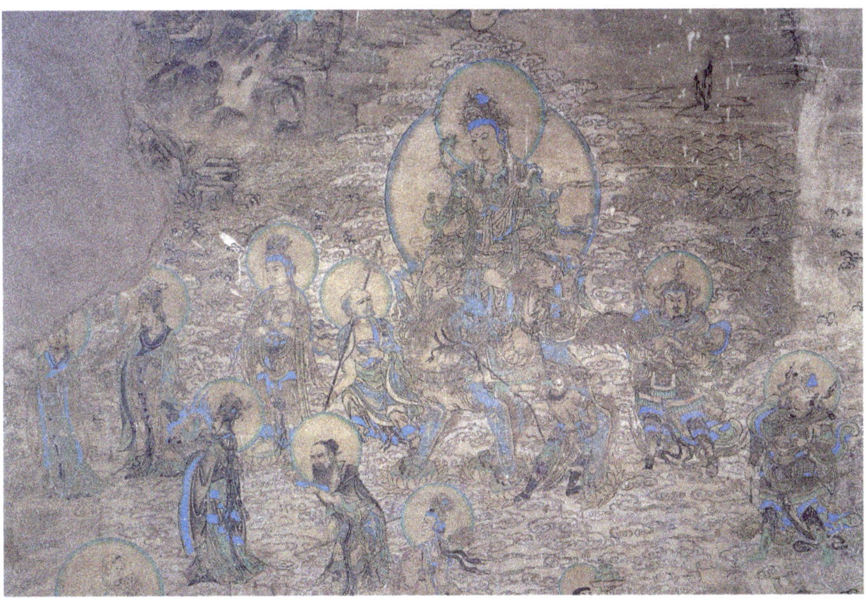

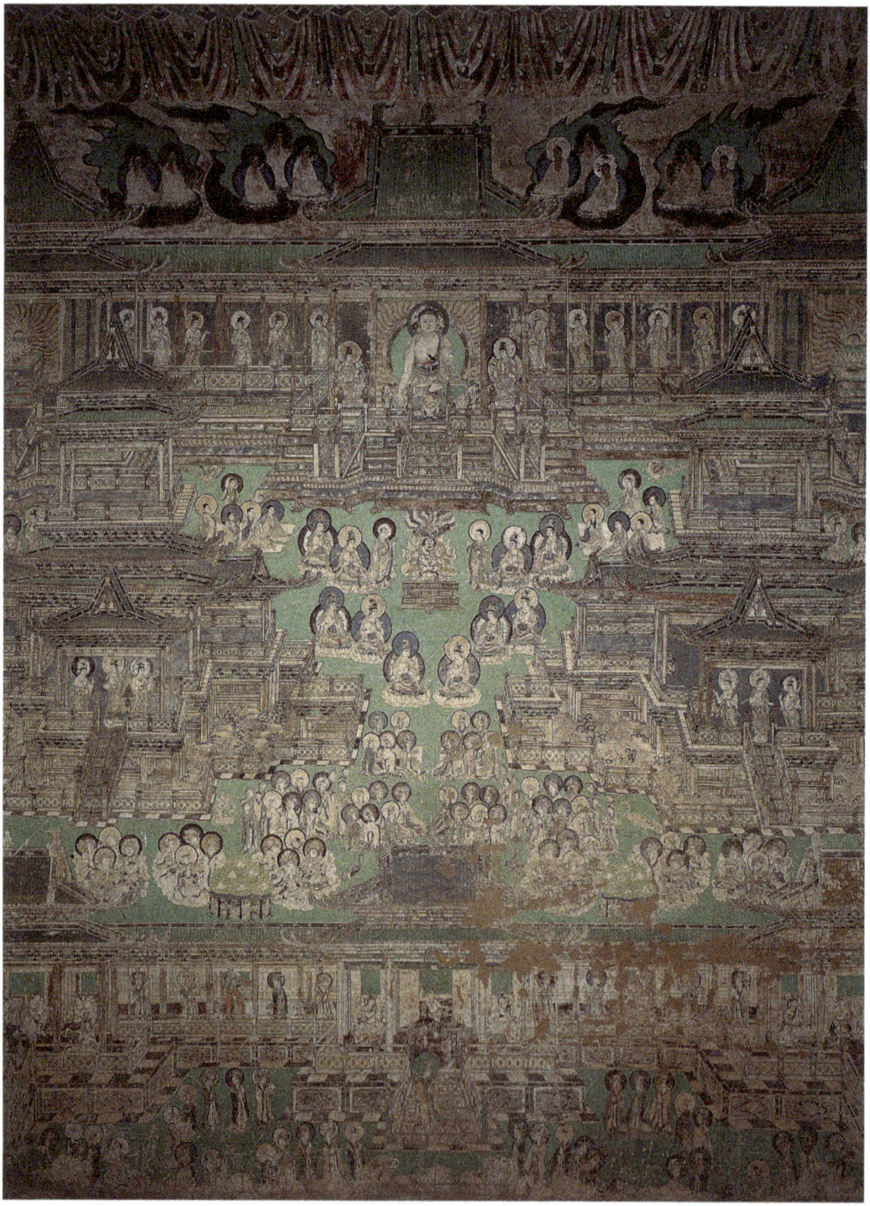

117. Picture of Amitayurbhavana-sutra

Western Xia

Preserved in the No. 3 Cave in Yulin, Anxi County, Gansu

This is a cave painting of the three Buddha of Sukhavati located in the rear court room as the other participants spread out in an X shape, facing the audience. The ruler painting of towers and pavilions can be clearly seen, all facing front. The thick mineral green indicates the presence of a Qibaochi (Lotus pond made of seven treasures), while the water wave design is found in waterside pavilions. Music and dance performances are taking place in the front room at the lower part of the painting. In the Sukhavati (Pure Land) of this picture, there is no Upapaduka (where everything grows out of nothing and appears suddenly, including those gods in charge of the 28 different heavens and hells, and people before they come into being) but rather Upasika, which refers to secular females who believe in Buddhism and practice Buddhism at home.

118. Picture of the Eight Pagodas of Buddha Sakyamuni

Western Xia

Preserved in the No. 3 Cave in Yulin, Anxi County, Gansu

This cave painting of the picture of the Eight Pagodas is about the legend of Sakyamuni. It is 3.7 meters high and 2.2 meters wide. In the middle of the painting is a large pagoda, which occupies most of the wall. The pagoda illustrates the story of "subduing the demons and becoming the Buddha". Different stories about Sakayamuni are depicted on both sides of the pagoda. On the right side are scenes of his six years of ascetic practices, pointing to heaven with one hand and to the earth with the other hand after his birth, his birth under a tree, the thousand Buddhas, and his descent from Trayastrimsa. On the left side are stories where Buddha is being shielded and sustained by dragon kings, taking a bath in Nairanjana. There is a macaque presenting honey, the Buddha speaking the dharma for the first time after he became the Buddha, and subduing the drunk elephant. Over the pagoda is a painting within a horizontal-scroll shape, which depicts Sakyamuni achieving nirvana.

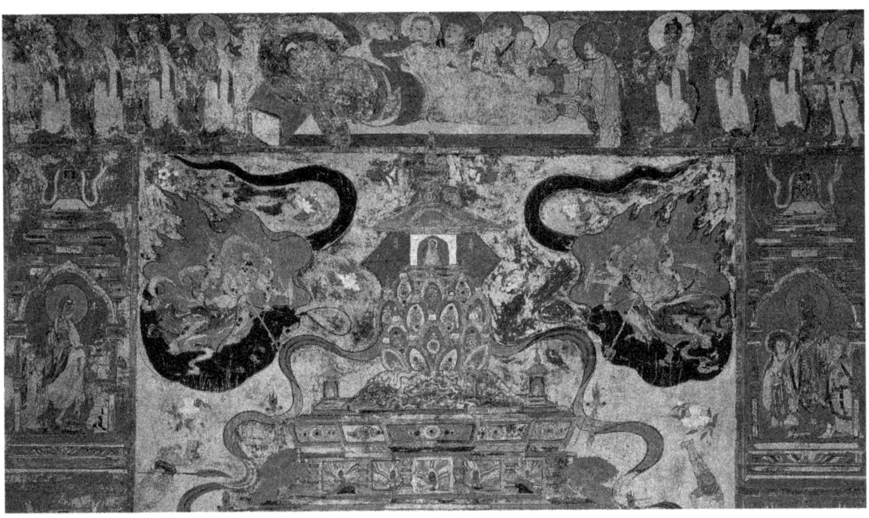

119. Apsaras Beating the Tabor

Western Xia

Preserved in the No. 10 Cave in Yulin, Anxi County, Gansu

This is a cave painting of Apsaras with her hair in a topknot and a halo behind her head. Her face is full with slanted eyes. She wears a coronet and a skirt, and a coat is draped over her shoulders. She holds a tabor in one hand, beating it with the long-handled drumstick in the other. The tabor has coverings on both sides, which are decorated with flower patterns. The figure is strong with short legs - typical of the Western Xia Dynasty. The painting is done with fine strokes and light colors.

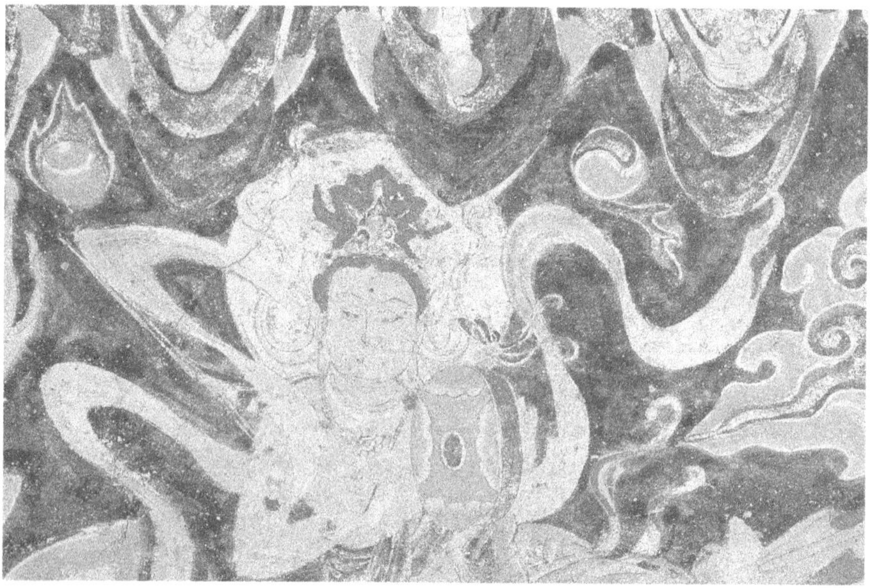

120. Vidyaraja with Two Bodies

Western Xia

Preserved in the Baiyanyao Cave in Aerbasisumu, Etuoke Banner, Yikezhao League, Inner Mongolia

This is a cave painting of Vidyaraja holding his partner in his arms and standing on the lotus throne. It is painted in many colors, but mainly in green, red, black, blue, white and yellow. The pigments are mineral and are still bright and gorgeous even after hundreds of years.

Baiyanyao Cave, also called “Aersai Cave”, is located in the area of Aerbasumu, in the northwest of the Etuoke Banner of the Yikezhao League, Ordos. This is the biggest cave found in Inner Mongolia to date.

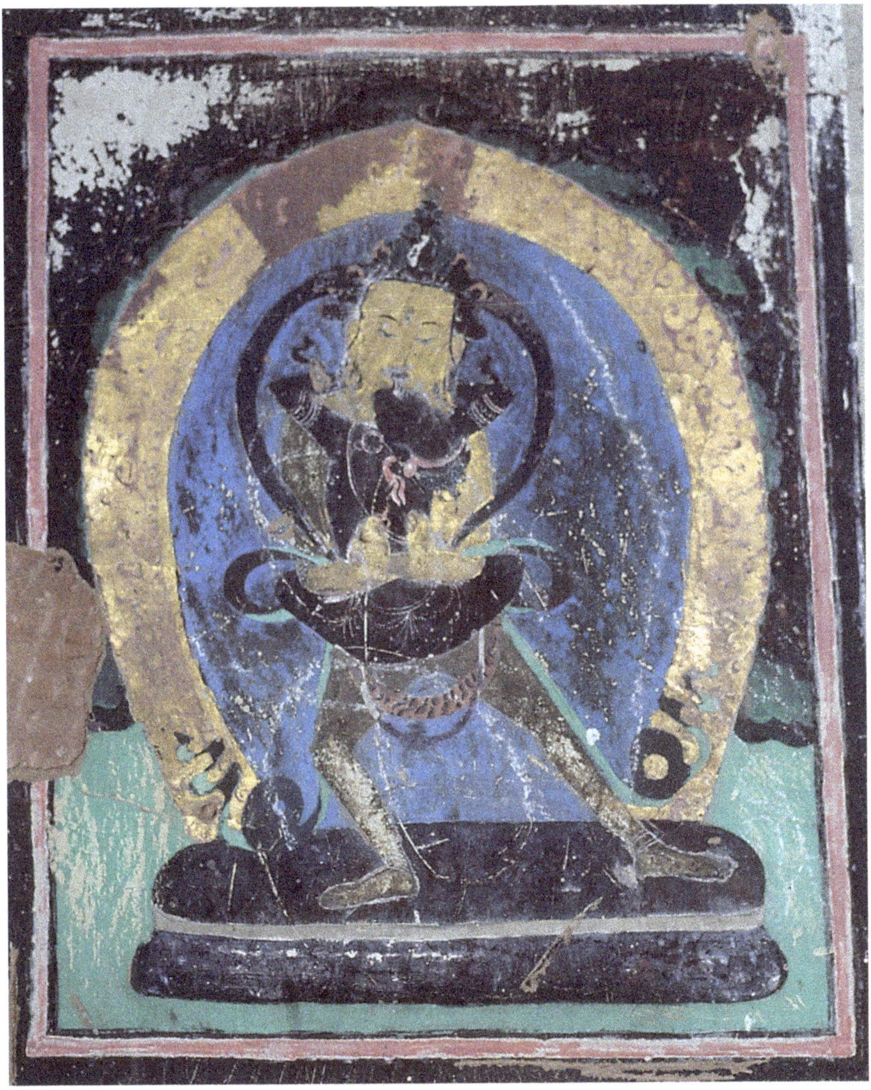

121. Painted Warrior on Board

Western Xia
Length: 15.5 cm Width: 7.5 cm
Unearthed from tree farm of western suburb of Wuwei City, Gansu in 1977
Preserved in the Wuwei Museum
In this xylograph, the warrior wears a military robe with wide sleeves, and he is covered with a suit of armour. He wraps a red scarf on his shoulders and wears a felt cap with red tassels and thigh boots. Standing with his hands folded and raised in front of his chest, the strongly-built soldier looks bold and mighty.

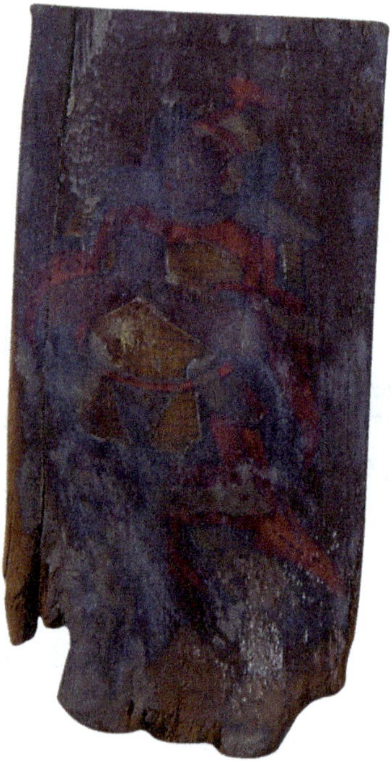

122. Painted Valets on Board

Western Xia
Length: 21.5 cm Width: 12 cm
Unearthed from tree farm of western suburb of Wuwei City, Gansu in 1977
Preserved in the Wuwei Museum
This is a xylograph of five valets. They wear ankle-length robes all in the same style with round collars, narrow sleeves and draggle tails. However they are all dressed in different colors - grey, yellowish-brown, ochre, cyan and blue from left to right. One wears a sword, one carries cloth-wrappers, one holds a tray, one supports a spittoon and one is wrapping around a strip of cloth. They all have hair divided in the middle with hair-tips curling up on both sides. Moreover, two ring-shaped buns hang behind their ears. This is a typical hairstyle of the Tangut people (a well known tribe in ancient China).

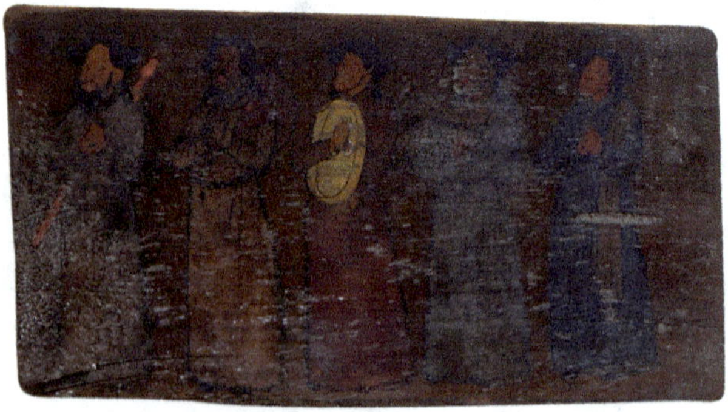

Handicrafts

Khitan characters derive from regular Chinese characters but are quite complicated in structure, and thus are unsuitable to be written in different writing styles. This is why most of the calligraphy during the Liao Dynasty was written using Chinese characters. The elegies unearthed from the mausoleums of Liao Dynasty emperors and their empresses can be regarded as representative calligraphy from that period. There were few calligraphers during the Jin Dynasty. The famous ones include Wanyan Jing and Wanyan Shu, who are both Jurchen people. There were also Han calligraphers such as Ren Xun, Wu Ji, Dang Huaiying, Wang Tingyun, Zhao Bingwen, Cai Songnian and Zhang Zhu. Through their surviving works and relevant historical records, we can find that the writing styles of the Tang and Song Dynasties continued to prevail during the Jin Dynasty, especially the styles of Su Shi and Mi Fu, the two great calligraphers of the Northern Song Dynasty. From this point of view, the writing style of the Jin Dynasty can be seen as a continuation of the Tang and Song period. , The Western Xia people created their own characters based on Chinese characters to record their history. Western Xia characters are square in shape and complicated in structure. Up to now, most of the cultural artifacts relevant to Western Xia characters we have found are broken stone tablets. Generally, they are somewhat similar to the regular script of Chinese characters. Calligraphy in other styles haven't been found so far.

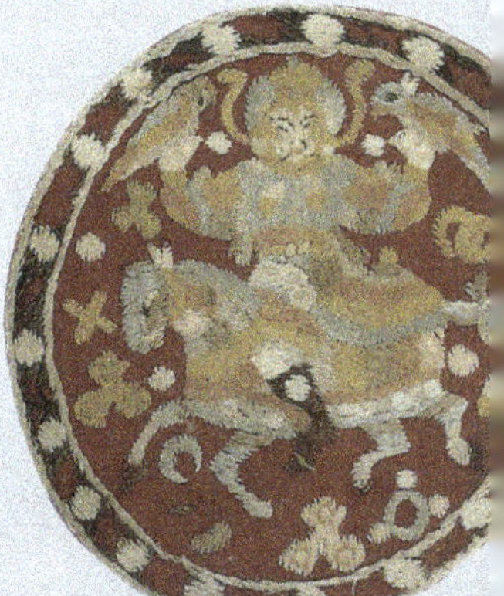

The textile sector is very important among the handicraft industries of the Liao Dynasty. Recent years have witnessed a great variety of silk fabrics unearthed from Liao tombs together with quite a few high-level k'o-ssu, embroideries and textiles which used printing and dyeing designs. They are really rich in variety and decorative design and boast exquisite workmanship, demonstrating the high level of textile production in that period. For instance, six types of silk products in more than 90 specifications were unearthed from Liao tombs in Yemaotai in Faku County in Liaoning. The dyeing and weaving techniques of the Jin Dynasty made advances on the textiles of the Song and Liao Dynasties. A case in point is the clothes found in the tomb of the king of the Qi State during the Jin Dynasty which is located in Acheng in Harbin, Heilongjiang. They are not only rich in style and in terms of material, but they are also blessed with high-level textile technology, exquisite workmanship and beautiful design, and thus are extremely precious.

The wooden furniture found its way into households at an early date. However, few have survived to now. A whole set of furniture made of apricot wood was found in the tomb of Yan Deyuan of the Jin Dynasty in Datong, Shanxi, including a folding screen, towel rack, basin stand, bed, tea table, tables and chairs. Despite the fact they are burial objects, they are well proportioned and perfectly shaped, demonstrating the simple and unsophisticated style of real wooden furniture and they provide invaluable materials for studying ancient furniture.

Few of the seals of the Liao Dynasty can be found now. But the chops left behind by the Jin Dynasty are large in number. Most of them are carved with Chinese characters in seal script. Of course, those carved with Jurchen characters in a seal style can be found, but they are small in number. In addition, there are some inscribed with Jurchen characters on the sides.

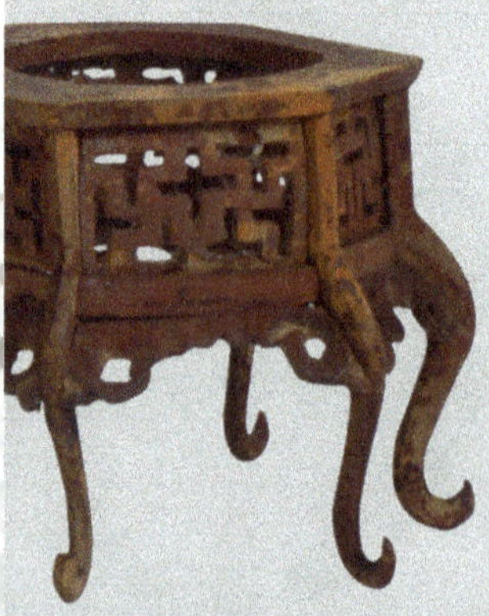

123. Zhao Bingwen: Preface and Postscript of Six Steeds of the Zhao Mausoleum

Jin

Vertical Length: 31.2 cm Horizontal Length: 205 cm

Preserved in the Palace Museum in Beijing

This is a paper scroll in running script. These passages were written on Zhao Lin's famous picture - Six Steeds of the Zhao Mausoleum as the preface and postscript. They show the influence of the styles of both Su Shi and Mi Fu, two well-known calligraphers of the Northern Song Dynasty. The end of the inscription is dated the 15th day of the seventh lunar month of 1220 (the year of Gengchen, according to the Chinese Heavenly Stems and Earthly Branches time-reckoning system).

Zhao Bingwen (1159-1232), also known as Zhouchen and Xianxian Jushi, was a native of Cizhou (Cixian County in Hebei at present). He once worked as a member of the Imperial Academy, and was a grand master and director of the Board of Rites. When he was young, he once studied literature and calligraphy under the guidance of Wang Tingyun and later turned to Su Shi and Yan Zhenqing. His calligraphic works in cursive script are particularly good.

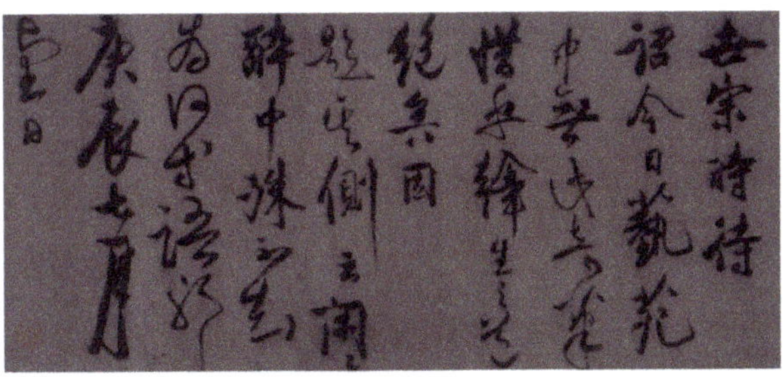

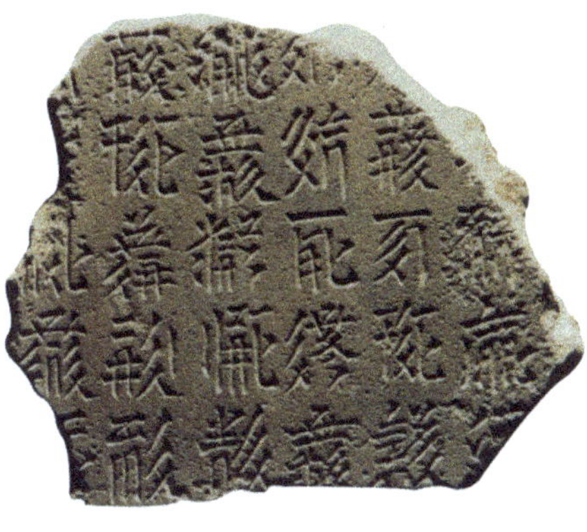

124. Broken Stone Tablet Inscribed with Western Xia Characters Unearthed from Imperial Mausoleum

Western Xia

Remant Height: 23 cm Width: 27 cm

Thickness: 4.3 cm

Preserved in the Ningxia Hui Autonomous Region Museum

The stone tablet is engraved with Western Xia characters in regular style. It contains some records of territory, military affairs and tribes. Of the remaining 27 words in six lines, 21 are intact in terms of strokes. These words with firm strokes are square in shape and are over 3.3 cm large. They provide important materials for studying the calligraphy and history of Western Xia characters.

125. Embroidered Cloth-wrappers for Buddhist Sutras

Liao

Height: 27.7 cm Width: 27.5 cm

Unearthed from Baita Dagoba of the Liao Dynasty in Qingzhou, Baarin Right Banner, Inner Mongolia in 1992

Preserved in the Baarin Right Banner Museum

This is a piece of embroidery. On the red silk outside, there is a ring-like design in the middle, which is sandwiched between patterns of two strings of beads. In the ring is a man on horseback who is clad in a cotton-padded fur cap, cotton-padded fur robe and leather boots, and he has an eagle standing on each of his hands. Furthermore, the interspace inside the ring is dotted with the patterns of Buddhist treasures. Lined with a piece of white thin silk, the cloth-wrappers have a thin silk belt at the corner, which was used for packing.

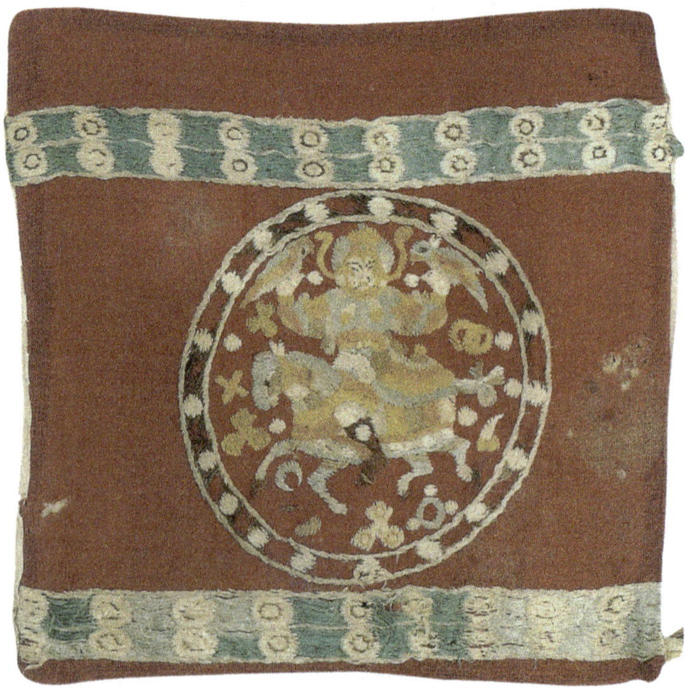

126. Dark Camel Silk Trousers with Embroidered Design

Jin

Length: 142 cm   Height of the Waist: 46 cm

Width of the Part below the Waist: 60.5 cm

Width of the Part above the Waist: 111 cm

Unearthed from tomb of the King of the Qi state during the Jin Dynasty in Acheng, Harbin, Heilongjiang in 1988

Preserved in the Heilongjiang Provincial Museum

The trousers which are wadded with silk waddings have dark camel silk on the outside and light camel silk as the lining. The silk outside with its faint diamond-shaped patterns is embroidered with flowers in staggered arrangement, each group consisting of two sprays.

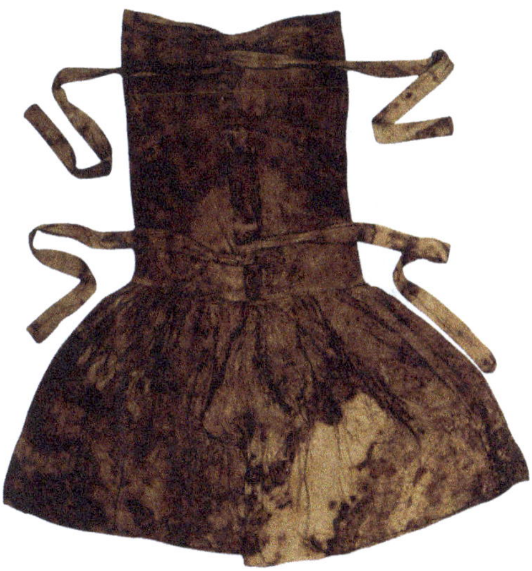

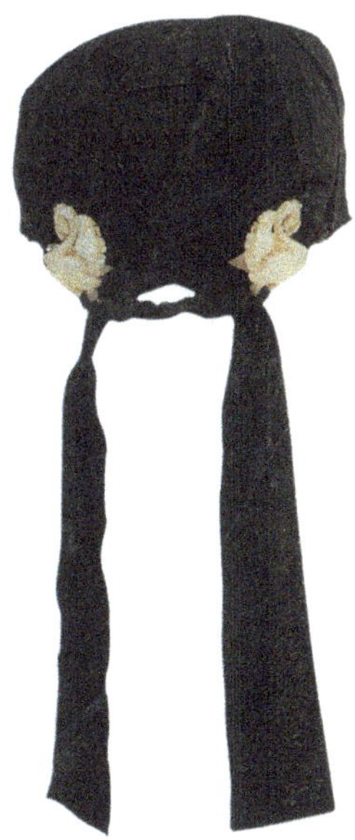

127. Plain Silk Cap with Silk Pendant

Jin

Height: 13.4 cm   Width: 17 cm

Unearthed from tomb of the King of Qi state during the Jin Dynasty in Acheng in Harbin, Heilongjiang in 1988

Preserved in the Heilongjiang Provincial Museum

This is a man's hat. The half-moon hat has a piece of broad belt nailed in the middle from left to right. The front is designed into a semi-circular triangle. Both right and left sides are decorated with a piece of sapphire carved into a goose holding a lotus in its mouth. After twining with the sapphires, a green silk belt hangs down from behind like a pendant.

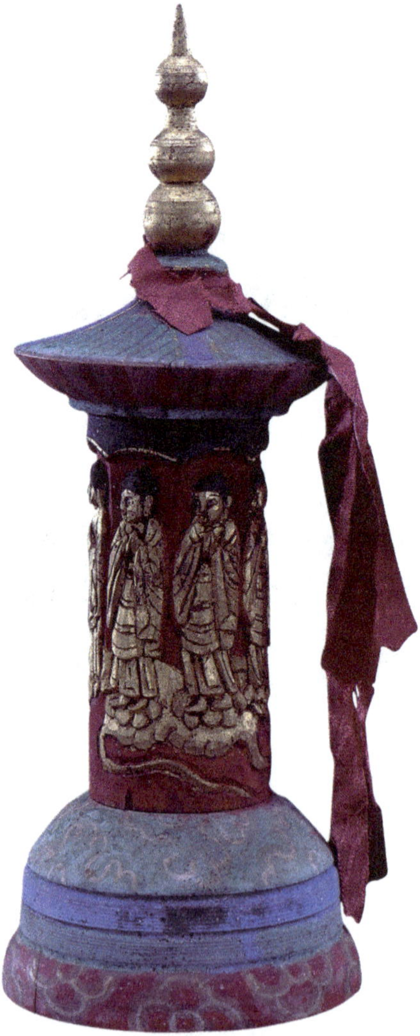

128. Wooden Stupa with Seven Gilded Figures of Buddha

Liao
Height: 23 cm
Bottom Diameter: 9.1 cm
Found in the steeple of the Baita Dagoda in Qingzhou, Baarin Right Banner, Inner Mongolia in 1989
Preserved in the Baarin Right Banner Museum
Made of cypress, this Buddhist stupa is a tenon-and-mortise work composed of a round pedestal, cylindrical body, eaves and steeple. The outer walls are carved with seven standing figures of Buddha depicted with blue hair, which are covered with gold leaf from head to foot. Except for the figures of Buddha, the outside of the stupa is colored with yellow, red and blue. A brocade streamer with an interlayer and hanging fish is tied to the steeple.

129. Wooden Washbasin Stand

Jin
Height: 13.8 cm
Unearthed from tomb of Yan Deyuan in Datong, Shanxi in 1973
Preserved in the Datong Museum
This burial object, made of apricot plank, is coated with red paint. In six prismatic shapes, it has a wide opening in the upper part to hold the basin, and is empty inside. Below the waist is a side stretcher together with four crossed stretchers to shape the design. The oval opening has six edges which combine with the legs. The inlaid side panels are carved with faint 卍-shaped patterns. With a high waist, the washbasin stand has six cabriole legs which means that the legs are in an S shape and end in an outward-curving horse hooves.
There are dozens of various wooden models of farm tools and household furniture which were dug out of the tomb of Yan Deyuan, a Taoist priest in the first year (1190) of the reign of Mingchang during the Jin Dynasty, in the western suburb of Datong city.

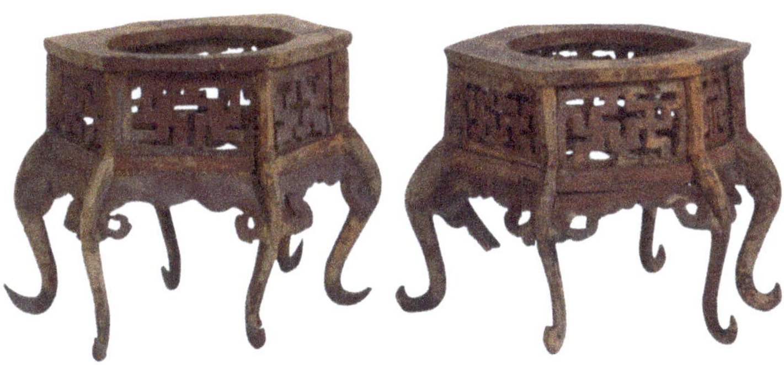

130. Wooden Stupa

Western Xia
Height:76 cm
Unearthed from a forest farm in the western suburb of Wuwei, Gansu in 1977
Preserved in the Wuwei Museum
This burial object, this cypress stupa is comprised of a pedestal, body, top and steeple (or cha). Sitting on a four-tier octagonal pedestal, the body is made up of eight pieces of board and it sports a blue coat. The blue surface is inscribed with yellow incantations in Sanskrit. The top features eight ridges with the eaves turning upwards slightly. There is an inscription found on the inner side of the top, revealing that the stupa is named as "Yuanta". Such a kind of wooden stupa is a burial object unique to the people of the Western Xia Dynasty. This one is the first of its kind dug out from any tomb.

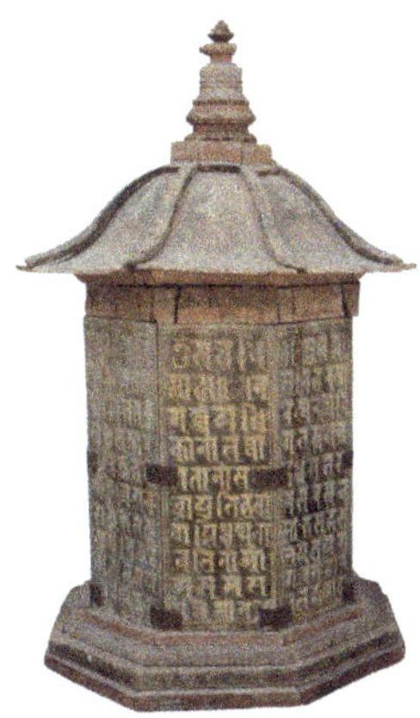

131. Copper Seal for Military Governor

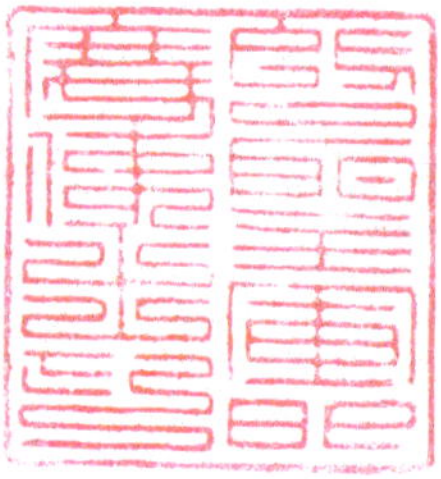

Liao

Height:2.4 cm Width: 5.7 cm Length: 6 cm

Unearthed from Niangniang Yingzi of Zhizushan Township, Fuxin Mongolian Autonomous County in Liaoning in 1972

Preserved in the Liaoning Provincial Museum

This basically square seal has an inverted funnel-shaped knob, inscribed with the red characters "Copper Seal for Military Governor of the Qisheng Army" in seal script. "Qisheng Army" is the military designation of the troops stationed in Yikun Zhou (Zhou, an administratioin division of the Liao Dynasty) under the jurisdiction of Shangjing Dao (Dao, an administration division of the Liao Dynasty). Yikun Zhou is the birth place of the Empress dowager Yingtian, the wife of Yelyu Abaoji who was the founder of the Liao Dynasty.

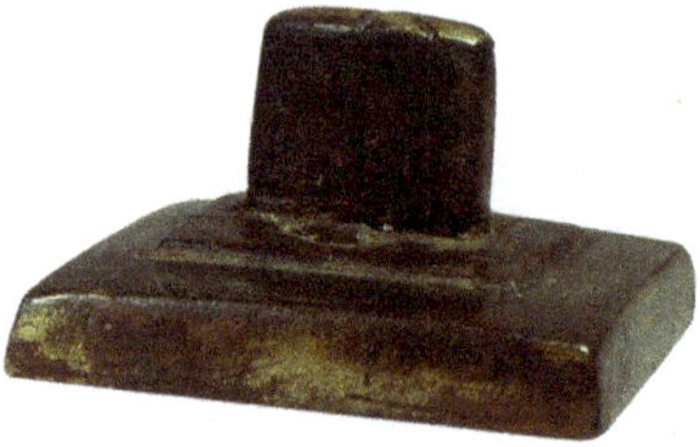

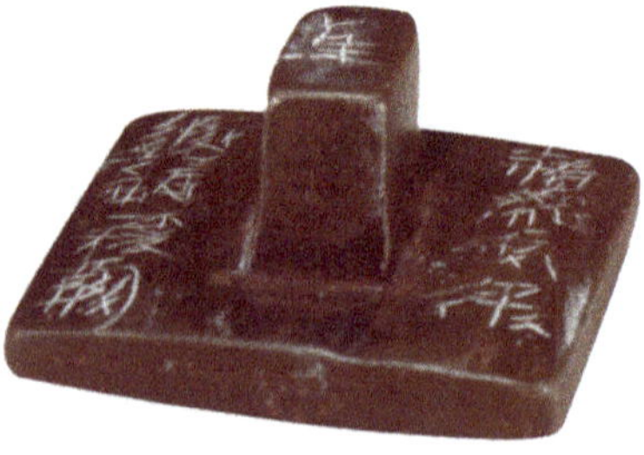

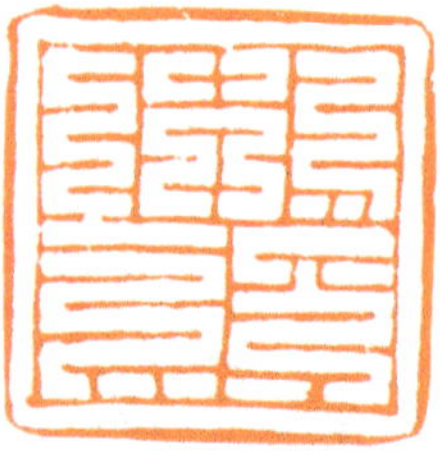

132. Copper Seal Inscribed with Western Xia Characters

Western Xia

Height: 3 cm Length of Margin: 5.5 cm

Unearthed from Ejin Horo Banner, Inner Mongolia in 1956

Preserved in the Inner Mongolia Museum

This square seal has a short rectangular knob. The surface is carved with two lines of white Western Xia characters in seal script, which mean "chieftain" in Chinese. The back is carved with two lines of white Western Xia characters in regular script, which read "the year of xxx" and "Built in Weihan Q162" in Chinese. The knob is inscribed with a line of white Western Xia characters in seal script, which means "Up" in Chinese. This is an official seal of the military officer during the Western Xia Dynasty.

The Yuan Dynasty

1271-1368

Preface

In the early period of Yuan, while the regimes of Liao, Song, Jin and Western Xia were fighting each other, the emergence of the nomadic Mongol people on the northern prairies was hardly noticed. In 1206, Genghis Khan, known as "A Proud Son of Heaven", began building the Mongol empire in the north, adopting as the title of his reign the name Great Mongolia. Through a long-lasting expedition, the group conquered the Western Xia, Jin and Dali regimes, and even extended their reach to the Europe, to the consternation of the Europeans. Despite possessing an unprecedentedly large and international empire, the emperor remained unsatisfied and turned his attention to the Southern Song regime. In 1260, Kublai Khan became the supreme leader and transferred the political center from the northern prairies to the central plain where the Han ethnic group dominated. In 1271, he changed the reign title into "Da Yuan", literally

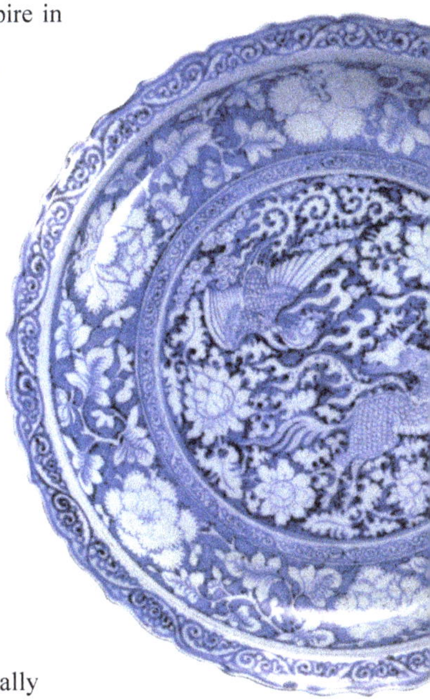

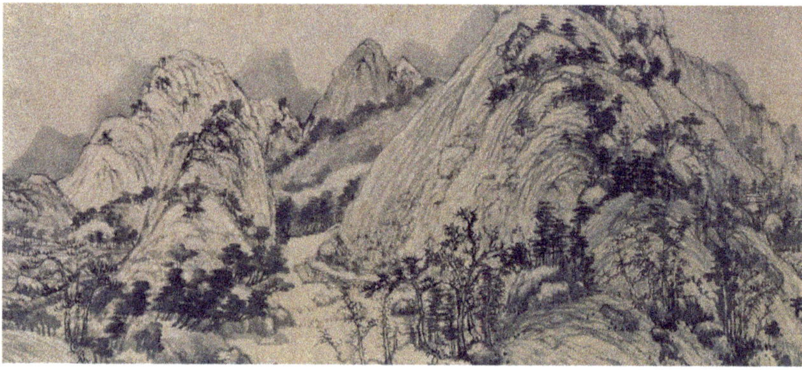

Great Yuan. Five years later, in 1276, the Yuan regime moved south and conquered the Southern Song Regime to reunite the whole country-the first time this had been achieved by a northern nomadic ethnic group in China's history.

Mongol people are the nomadic group, leading a life of migration in search of water and pasture. After Kublai Khan built the Yuan Dynasty, he paid close attention to agriculture, encouraged industrial development, trade and the economy, promoted the handicraft industry and absorbed Han culture as much as possible - all of which facilitated Yuan's development in society, economy and culture. Handicrafts particular gained great accomplishments, due to the absorption and application of foreign advantages through exchange or even in war, which laid a body foundation for development in handcraft and fine arts in the Ming and Qing Dynasties.

The Yuan Dynasty witnessed a culmination of techniques of jade making. For instance, huge jade ware up to about 500 kg could be made, which imitated the ancient style, as Song handicraftsmen had done. The jade wares were classic, laying the basis for the styles of the Qing Dynasty.

Yuan is an important period in China's development of pottery and porcelain, in which porcelain making was greatly developed; it was in this period that Jingdezhen took the central position. The porcelain with colored glaze was added with more popular styles in order to cater to international as well as national markets; this period also saw the diversity of multi-colored porcelain, the colors ranging from blue and white porcelain to three-color glazed porcelain, especially the blue and white porcelain, whose development symbolized the transfer from color-glaze to multi-color, thus being of considerable significance.

Yuan calligraphy was not unique, but inherited the style of the Jin and Tang Dynasties. Its overall style showed a tendency of restoring the ancient modes. The joint efforts of intellectual men and calligraphers somewhat reversed the worsening situation of calligraphy in the Southern Song Dynasty. In the Yuan Dynasty, imperial court paintings fell far behind those of the Song, which had something to do with the painters, amateur or professional, who were intellectuals or officials before and now faced an awkward situation, so they withdrew from the imperial court and lived in mountains and forests to paint for entertainment or for a living. Some painters, who had held high positions, mainly followed the painting tradition portraying men of letters, depicting scenic views and orchids and bamboos. Their painting emphasized the ancient concepts and morals rather than of form, and pursued the essence of feelings. They perfectly combined poetry, calligraphy and painting, strengthening the literary and ethnic flavors of China's paintings. Therefore, the Yuan Dynasty became

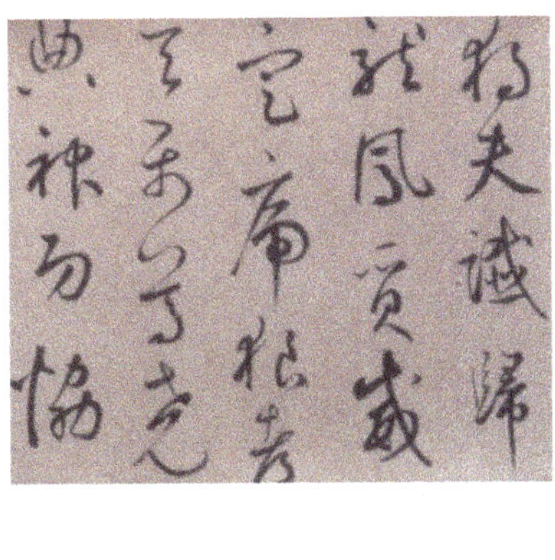

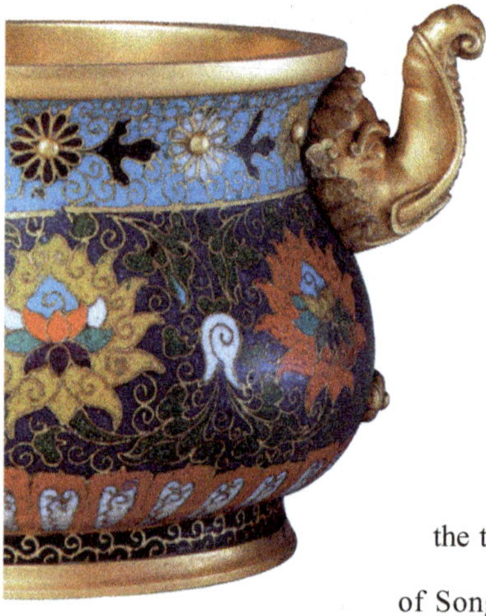

a critical period witnessing significant changes of China's painting.

Progress could be seen also in knitted embroidery goods. There was unprecedented development in knitted gold brocade and the growing maturity of silk fabric weaving. The variety of silk weavings expanded, forming a basis of development of techniques in multi-colored silk fabric weaving. Gesi (weaving done in fine silks and gold thread by the tapestry method) and embroidery developed through absorption of Song traditions. Lacquer ware manufacturing skills were much improved. This period saw some famous lacquer ware artisans including Zhang Cheng, Yang Mao and Zhang Minde. It was also during this time that metal-made champlevé enamel wares were brought to China and combined with traditional Chinese handicrafts and fine arts, thus forming a kind of precious and well-known metal art ware, which was inclusively made and used by the imperial court and rarely seen in ordinary families. In hundreds of years of development, the imperial features dominated whether in shape, pattern or the techniques, showing imperial aesthetic sentiment.

Jade Ware

There was almost no jade carving industry before Yuan conquered Jin. However, after that, especially after the Yuan Dynasty moved the capital to Dadu (present-day Beijing), the formation of ritual system drew lessons from the Jin, Song, and earlier Han and Tang Dynasties. For instance, the part involving headscarf, clothes and vehicles followed the tradition of the Han nationality and jade ware was widely used. As a result, the government recruited a lot of artisans from the Han ethnic group, and an institute in charge of jade carving was especially set up, encouraging great advances in the jade carving industry. Its development culminated in 1266, the third year during Zhiyuan's reign, when the Bureau of Jade Ware Artisanship was set up and the jade ware industry rapidly advanced. The government-controlling pattern in Jin and Southern Song was followed in the Yuan Dynasty, and its capital city Dadu and Hangzhou became two of the biggest jade ware carving centers.

In the Yuan Dynasty, the jade ware including Chunshui and Qiushan Jade that were prevalent in the Liao and Jin period enjoyed popularity as well; traditional Han-group jade ware prevalent in Southern Song were still popular, but some new-type jade wares with Mongol features such as yuya, jade ladle and jade belt buttons were created. Chunshui and Qiushan Jade became more civil in nature. The former gradually became dominated by goose and lotus pictures while the latter favored blessed deer pictures. This trend was kept until Ming and Qing Dynasties. Yuya was a jade ware used to deal with documents. Dated back from Five-Dynasty period, the real objects were discovered in the Yuan Dynasty. Then, yuya were used exclusively by senior officers with imperial approval. Other officials could use only ivory or wooden seals. The jade wares

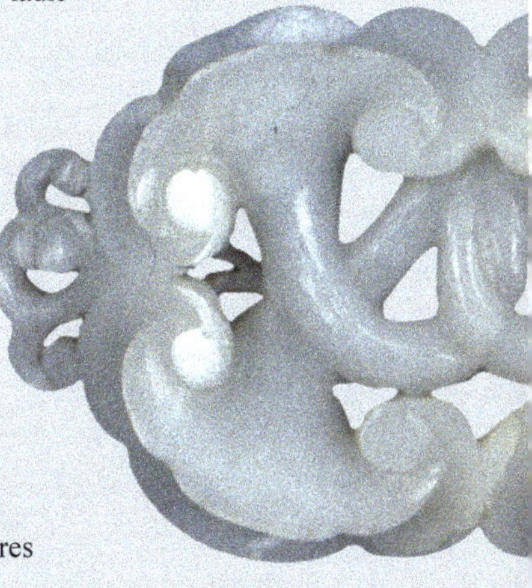

imitating ancient styles were fairly elegant and refined, the most successful ones of which were yuping yuzun and jade ladle imitating the bronze ware of the Zhou Dynasty, making a firm basis for development and prevalence of jade wares following ancient traditions in the Qing Dynasty.

In the Yuan Dynasty, jade wares were carved roughly, with flaws of carving traces. However, from the perspective of pattern and shapes of animals and plants, the styles were diversified and creative with a rustic charm. The traditional themes of carving in the Song and Jin Dynasties were applied, especially dragon and tiger patterns. In the Yuan Dynasty, they were not only widely chosen, but also skillfully handled to make the pattern both graceful and powerful, forming a unique style.

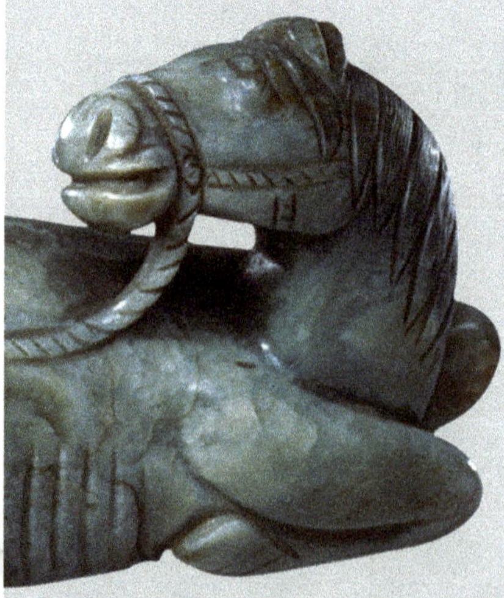

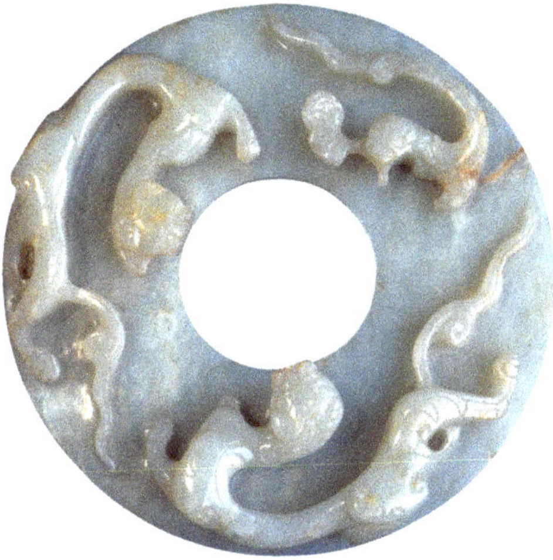

1. Hornless Dragon-patterned Jade Bi

Yuan

Diameter: 11.1 cm

Hole Diameter: 3.7 cm

Thickness: 0.6 cm

Preserved in the Hebei Museum

As a sacrificial vessel, a Jade Bi is a round flat piece of jade with a hole in it. This piece is made of grey jade with grain pattern and specks. On its front side are convex engravings of three dragons, two large and one small, chasing each other and forming a circle. The inner and outer edges on the reverse side are raised, and there are patterns inside and outside the ware. Inside are eight sets of curled cloud patterns, and outside are eight sets of linked cloud patterns. The blank is filled with small nipple patterns.

2. Jade Pendant with Hollowly-engraved Dragon in Flowers

Yuan

Length: 9.7 cm Width: 9.6 cm

Thickness: 0.8 cm

Preserved in the Palace Museum in Beijing

This blue-white jade pendant is flat in the shape of a petal. On the front side is an exquisitely hollowly engraved small dragon playing in the flower, with pores in four directions for tying. The other side is flat with minor engraving traces. This jade pendant shows excellent craftsmanship.

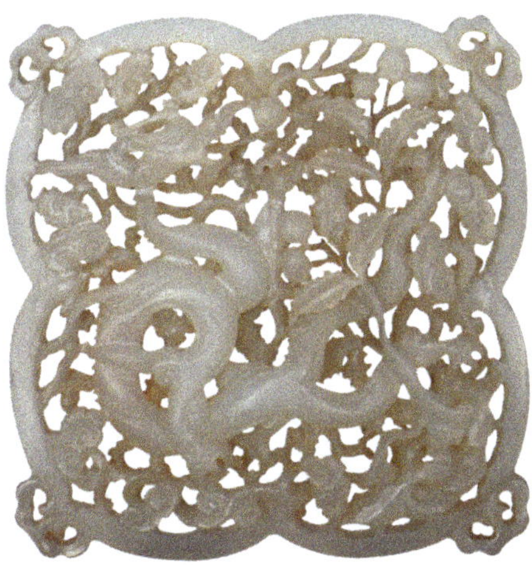

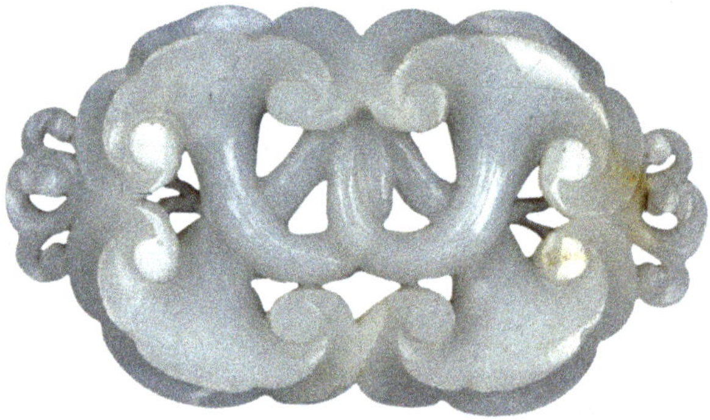

3. Trumpet Creeper-shaped Jade Jewelry

Yuan

Length: 12.8 cm   Width: 7.4 cm

Unearthed from Xiaoxitian construction site of Beijing Normal University in 1962

Preserved in the Capital Museum

This jade jewelry is flat and made of fine white jade, and uses hollow and convex engraving techniques. On its front side are hollowly engraved four intertwined blooming trumpet creepers. The petals are thick and slightly winding, and the floral axis is slender, with two vines on both sides. The other side is flat and smooth, with the center convex and six pairs of pores for looping.

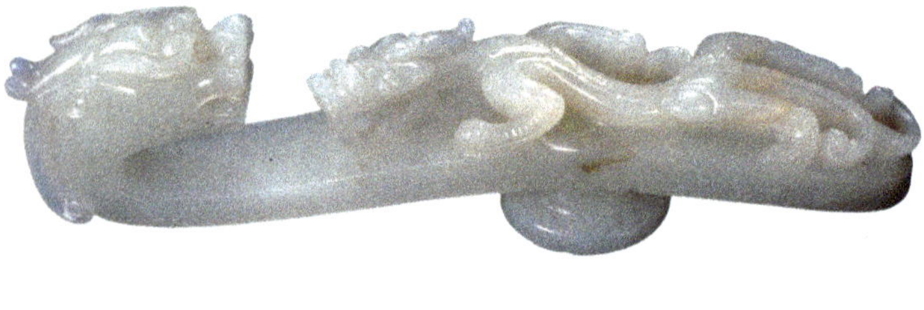

4. Dragon's Head-patterned Jade Belt Hook

Yuan

Height: 3 cm   Length: 13.8 cm   Width: 2.3 cm

Preserved in the Hebei Museum

This jade jewelry is made of white jade, with slightly brown spots yet with luster of suet. The top is in the shape of a dragon's head. The body is an arched rectangle with dragon patterns. A round button sticks out from the other side; it is carved in a slightly convex way with whirlpool lines. The horns of the dragon bend backwards, forming a "V"; the body is an "S" shape. The round button surface is slightly convex, and line-carved with the whorl pattern.

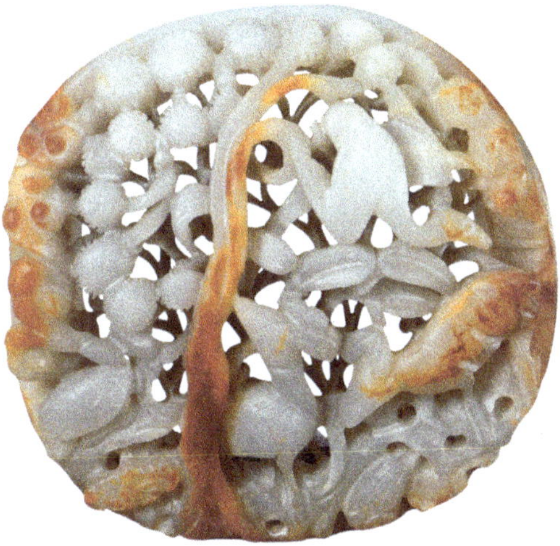

5. Crane and Deer-patterned Jade Jewelry

Yuan

Length: 8.5 cm Width: 7.2 cm

Preserved in the Palace Museum in Beijing

This is made of gray jade, with dark brown spots. On the front side are convex engravings of deer, crane, pine branches and glossy Ganoderma, suggesting longevity, successful career and wealth. The center of the other side is concave, with a ring in the surrounding. There are two pores on both sides for tying.

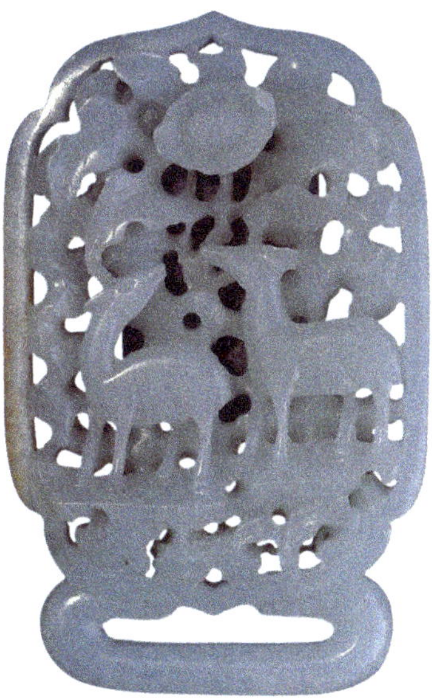

6. Jade Belt with Openwork

Yuan

Length: 6.1 cm Width: 4 cm

Preserved in the Hebei Museum

This is made of white jade, and is long and flat involving openwork engraving techniques. The pattern shows two deer standing on a mountain looking up while surrounded by flowers. The other side is polished. It was used to hang decorations.

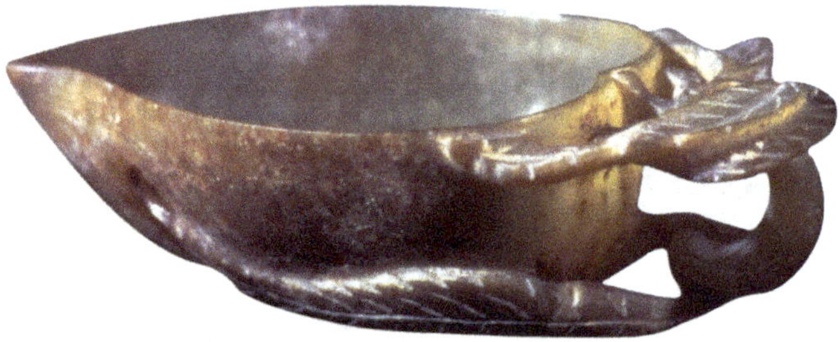

7. Peach-shaped Jade Cup
Yuan
Height: 3 cm Width: 11 cm
Unearthed from Tomb of Qian Yu in Southern Wuxi, Jiangsu in 1960
Preserved in the Wuxi Museum
This drinking vessel is made of gray jade, with sight white spots and black dots, and heavy yellow spots. Where the leakage is most obvious, there is even a tiny hole. The cup is like a half peach, which is cut open evenly. On the outer layer, hollowly-engraved peach leaves extend and form a handle. This is the earliest peach-shaped jade cup ever seen.

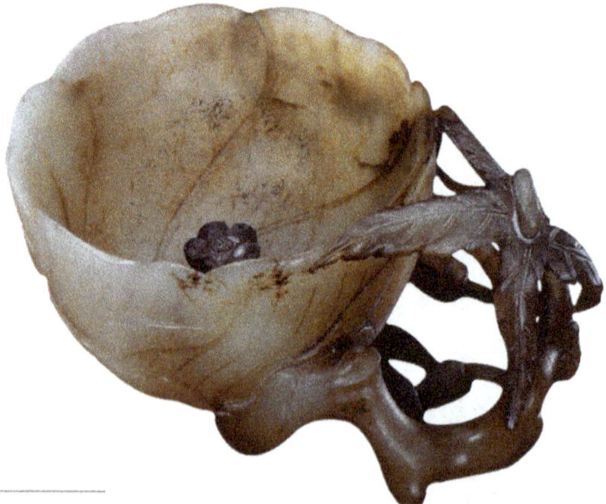

8. Sunflower-shaped Jade Cup
Yuan
Height: 5.1 cm Mouth Diameter: 8.5 cm
Preserved in the Palace Museum in Beijing
This drinking vessel is made of gray and white jade, blackened by fire in some parts. The cup is in the shape of a sunflower. The cup has a round mouth, and the interior bottom is convex and engraved with a stamen. The outer layer is engraved with leaves and twigs that naturally form the handle and stand. This cup is in typical Yuan style, from its shape, pattern, and color to the engraving techniques.

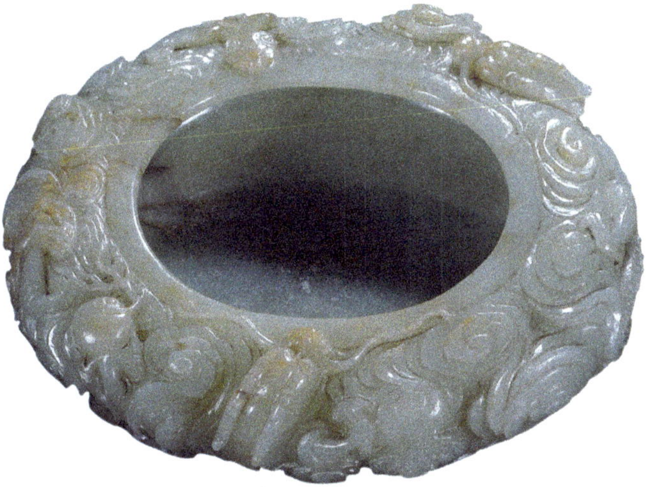

9. Jade Washer with Engraved Dragon

Yuan

Height: 4 cm Outer Diameter: 16.5 cm Mouth Diameter: 9.3 cm

Preserved in the Hebei Museum

As a stationery material, this jade wash is made of white jade glowing with gray luster. The wash is oblate with an oval mouth. Its outer layer is convexly engraved with two big dragons and a small one, playing in a cloud sea. One big dragon is holding a jewel and the other two are chasing each other for the jewel. There are hackle marks on the eyebrow, cheeks, legs and tails of the two bigger dragons.

10. Herdsman-shaped Jade Paper-Weight

Yuan

Height: 5 cm Length: 12 cm

Preserved in the Palace Museum in Beijing

This paperweight is made of blue-grey jade, seemingly to burnt by fire. The engravings include a herdsman and his horse. The horse, kneeling on the ground, is turned towards the rider who has one hand holding the reins and other lying in his lap.The neck is carved with hair and the clothing folds and the horse's hair are all carved in lines, distinct and exquisite.

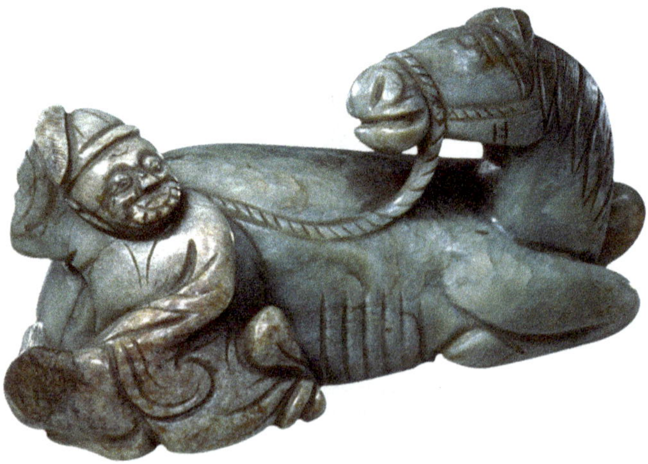

Porcelain

The Yuan Dynasty is an important period in China's development history of pottery and porcelain. On the basis of techniques of the Tang and Song Dynasties, the craftsman created underglazed blue and white porcelain, underglazed copper red porcelain, high-temperature blue glazed and red glazed porcelains, which meant a shift and progression from color glazed porcelain to multi-color porcelain in only one century and laid a foundation for the emergence of a large variety of colored porcelain in Ming and Qing Dynasties.

The biggest progress in Yuan's porcelain industry was the maturing of blue and white porcelain. At the time, there were only three kilns, Yuxi in Yunnan, Jiangshan in Zhejiang and Jingdezhen in Jiangxi. Development went through three main stages: blue and white and drawing, green and white glaze and blue and white, and blue and white porcelain. The later period of the 13th century was the first stage when blue and white were supplementary colors in the colored drawing. The representative was three Kwan-yin Figures of blue and white porcelain discovered in 1276 in Hangzhou, Zhejiang. The second stage started from the beginning of the 14th century to the 1330s. At this time, underglazed blue was the main decoration means. But the blue and white glaze, rather than the typical blue and white porcelain which was crystal, had obvious traces from the green and white glaze. The representative was the Peony-Patterned Jar with Beast-Ear-Shaped Lid Unearthed from Huangmei, Hubei in 1319. In the mid-term of the 14th century, the large blue and white porcelain produced in Jingdezhen was called Zhizheng blue and white porcelain. The fined material, thick body, glazed colors combined to make a mature porcelain work. It helped change the situation of Jingdezhen and was

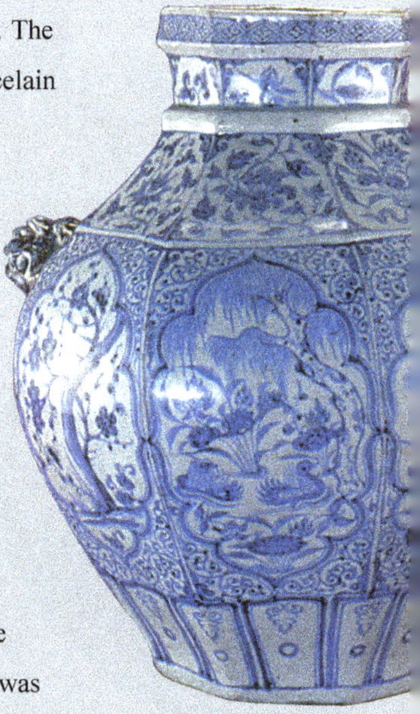

developed quickly and so popular that it became the major porcelain in the later period of the Yuan Dynasty. Cizhou and Jizhou Kilns also saw great development in this aspect.

In Yuan's pottery and porcelain industry, underglazed copper red was an important kind. It became mature in the early 14th century, almost at the same time when white and blue appeared, but its development fell behind the latter because of limits of technique and market, thus there was few left and were only dozens of intact ones. One of the representatives is the "Underglazed Copper Red Pagoda-Shaped Jar with Lid" Unearthed from 1974 from the tomb of the fourth year (1338) of the reign of Zhiyuan in Jingdezhen. There were a lot of kilns producing black colored and brown colored porcelain with iron as the photographic coupler. Typical ones include Cizhou Kiln in the north and Jizhou Kiln in the south.

During this period, color-glazed porcelain also developed greatly. To name a few for examples, the gray glazed porcelain in Longquan Kiln, porcelain with the basic blue color in Jun Kiln and green and white glazed porcelain in Jingdezhen Kiln. New techniques were introduced to Jingdezhen Kiln, helping the manufacture of high-temperature white glaze, blue glaze and red glaze, making a firm body for development of color glazed porcelain in Ming and Qing Dynasties.

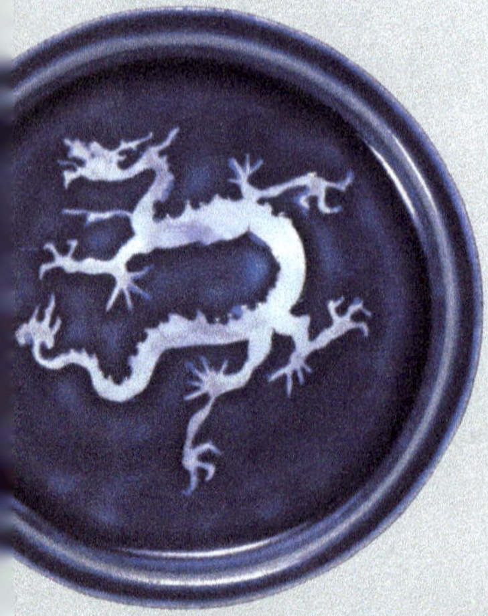

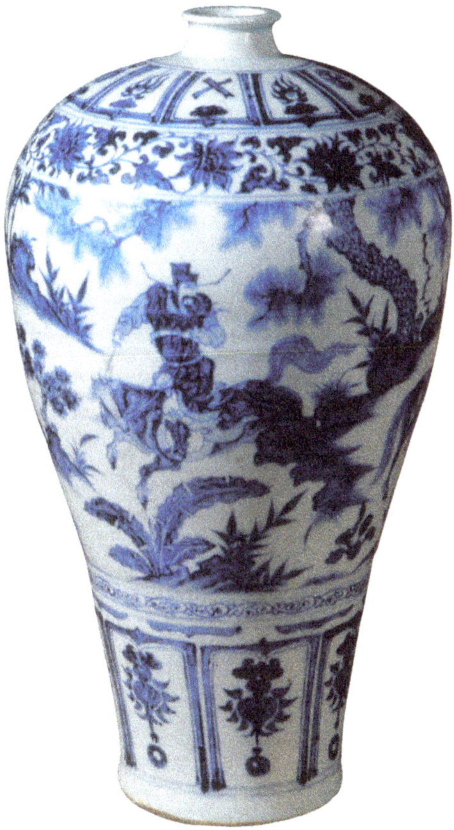

11. Plum Vase with Xiao He and Han Xin's Story, Jingdezhen Kiln
Yuan
Height: 44.1 cm Mouth Diameter: 5.5 cm Bottom Diameter: 13 cm
Unearthed from Tomb of Mu Ying in Jiangning, Jiangsu in 1950
Preserved in the Nanjing Museum
The vase has a white body and heavy glaze with gray luster. It has a small mouth, short "neck" and plump "shoulder". The body of the vase has pine, bamboo, plum, plantain, mountain and rock as the background, with the drawing of "Xiao He Chases Han Xin at Night". The space is filled with patterns of lotus petal and intertwined leaves.
The story of "Xiao He Chases Han Xin at Night" took place during the uprising at the end of Qin Dynasty. The talented Han Xin was not appointed to a key position and left the court with disappointment. It was another talented general Xiao He who persuaded him come back and get what he desired.

12. Plum Vase with Cloud and Dragon Patterns, Jingdezhen Kiln

Yuan

Height: 48 cm Mouth Diameter: 3.2 cm Bottom Diameter: 14.1 cm

Unearthed from Gao'an Cellar in Jiangxi in 1980

Preserved in the Gao'an Museum

This is a kind of furnishing with a solid and thick body. The enamel is glowing, and where the gray glaze is heavy, there are dark stains of rust. It has a lid with precious beard and inscribed with the character "Yu", literally imperial. It has a little mouth, folded and full shoulders, a short neck, a belly with the camber lines downward, and the gaskin extending outward. The patterns of peony and two phoenixes are at the top while those of two dragons playing in the clouds are at the bottom.

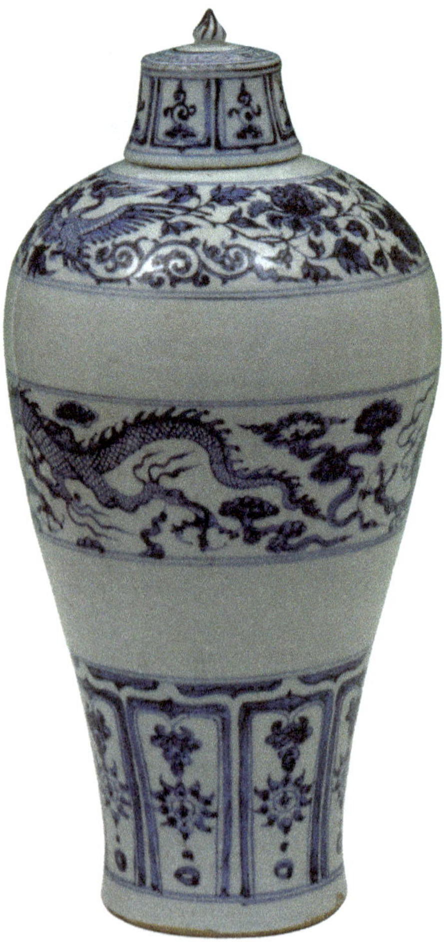

13. Octagonal Pot with Sea and Dragon Patterns, Jingdezhen Kiln

Yuan

Height: 51.5 cm Mouth Diameter: 6.6 cm Bottom Diameter: 14.5 cm

Unearthed from Baoding Cellar in Hebei in 1964

Preserved in the Hebei Museum

This container has a thick and solid body and refined glaze. The mouth is in octagonal shape. On its neck is an octagonal button while the body is also octagonal. It has a plump shoulders and slender bottom. The body is drawn with sea, fire and convexly engraved with four white dragons. There are cloud patterns on the shoulders and bottom parts and four-beasts and flower patterns inside.

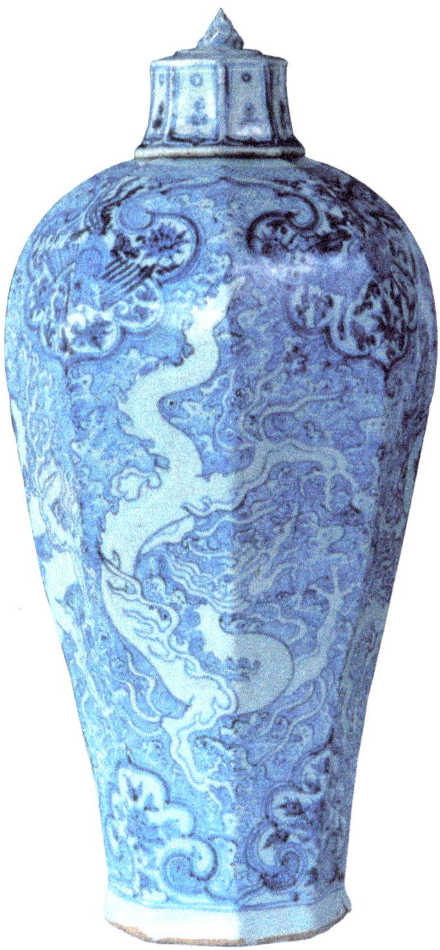

14. Blue and White Porcelain Pot with General Meng Tian's Pattern, Jingdezhen Kiln

Yuan

Height: 30 cm Mouth Diameter: 8.4 cm

Unearthed from Changde, Hunan in 1956

Preserved in the Hunan Museum

This pot is used as a container. The body is white and fined down, white glazed and color drawn with blue and white patterns. The mouth is relatively big and the neck is rather small. It has a round stomach and ring feet. Its big body is drawn with General Meng Tian's figure and over his head is a large banner held by a warrior. The space is filled with patterns of fence, bamboo, leaves, flowers and plantain.

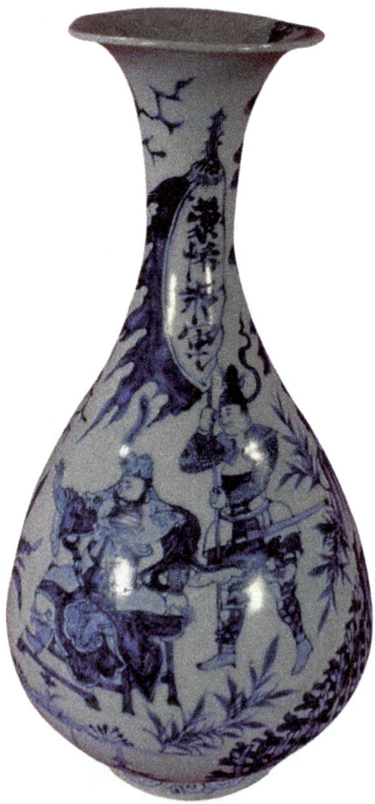

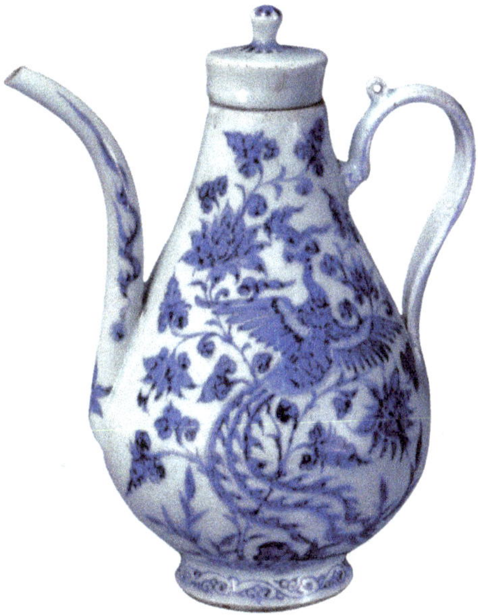

15. Handled Ewer with Phoenix and Peony Patterns, Jingdezhen Kiln

Yuan
Height: 23.5 cm
Mouth Diameter: 4.7 cm
Bottom Diameter: 7.3 cm
Preserved in the Palace Museum in Beijing
This drinking vessel has a mouth, neck and body in balanced proportions. The body is drawn with patterns of phoenix in peony. On one side is a winding spout and on another side is a wide knob.

16. Octagonal Jar with Beast-shaped Knobs, Jingdezhen Kiln

Yuan
Height: 39.3 cm
Mouth Diameter: 15.3 cm
Preserved in the Liaoning Museum
The container has a straight mouth, sloping shoulders and big body. Its shoulder is equipped with beast-shaped knobs. On the outer layer of the mouth are patterns of embroidery. There are patterns of twigs and flowers on the neck and patterns of peony and lotus on the shoulder. On the body are six groups of mandarin ducks playing with lotus, pine, bamboo and plum.

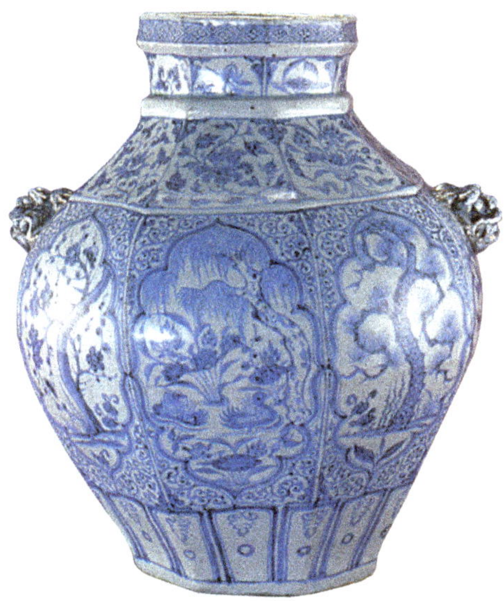

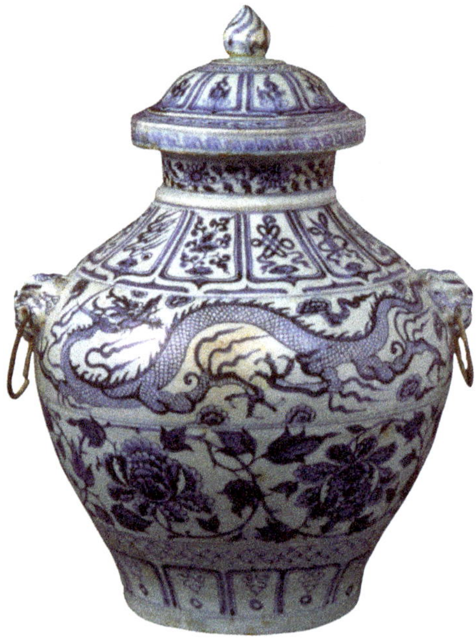

17. Jar with Beast-shaped Knobs and Cloud and Dragon Patterns, Jingdezhen Kiln

Yuan
Height: 47 cm
Mouth Diameter: 14.6 cm
Bottom Diameter: 18.2 cm
Unearthed from Gao'an Cellar in Jiangxi in 1980
Preserved in the Gao'an Museum

The container has solid, white body with red luster. The gray glaze is fined and polished. With a straight mouth, short neck and sloping shoulder, the jar has knobs on both sides of a beast mouth nibbling a loop. Its lid is drawn with lotus petals and leaves patterns in the space while the surroundings are patterns of intertwined twigs. The body of the jar has as many as seven layers of patterns with the theme of two dragons playing with peonies relying on twigs.

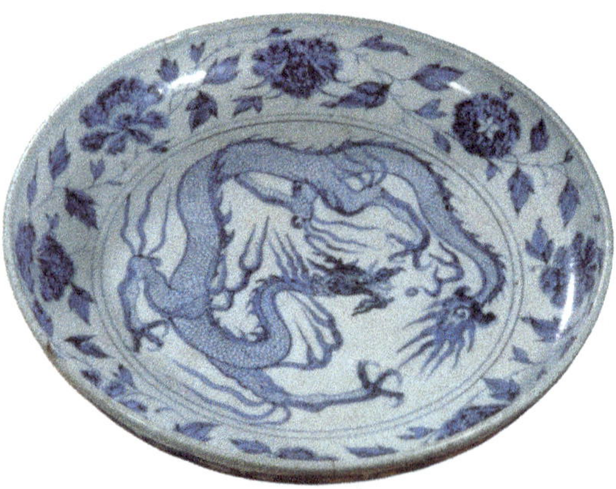

18. Blue and White Porcelain Plate with Dragon Patterns, Jingdezhen Kiln

Yuan
Height: 5.5 cm
Mouth Diameter: 35 cm
Foot Diameter: 21.2 cm
Unearthed from Weichang, Hebei in 1976
Preserved in the Cultural Relics Protection Institute in Weichang Man and Mongol Autonomous County

The plate has a contracted mouth, arc wall, shallow belly, and flat bottom and ring feet. The inner bottom is drawn with the pattern of dragon with three paws. On the inner layer are patterns of flowers intertwined with twigs and on the outer layer there are patterns of lotus petals.

19. Blue and White Porcelain Plate with Kylin Patterns, Jingdezhen Kiln

Yuan

Height: 7.9 cm Mouth Diameter: 46.1 cm Foot Diameter: 26.1 cm

Preserved in the Palace Museum in Beijing

The body is white and blue glazed. The edge has a number of tiny lozenges with folded rim, shallow belly and ring feet. The plate mouth is drawn with a circle of curled grass patterns along the edge. The inner layer is drawn with peony intertwined with twigs. On the inner bottom are a kylin and a phoenix against white background while the space is filled with patterns of lotus and cloud. The outer layer is drawn with a circle of curled grass pattern.

There are two kinds of white and blue porcelain: white background and blue pattern, blue background and white pattern. The former is also called reversed blue and white.

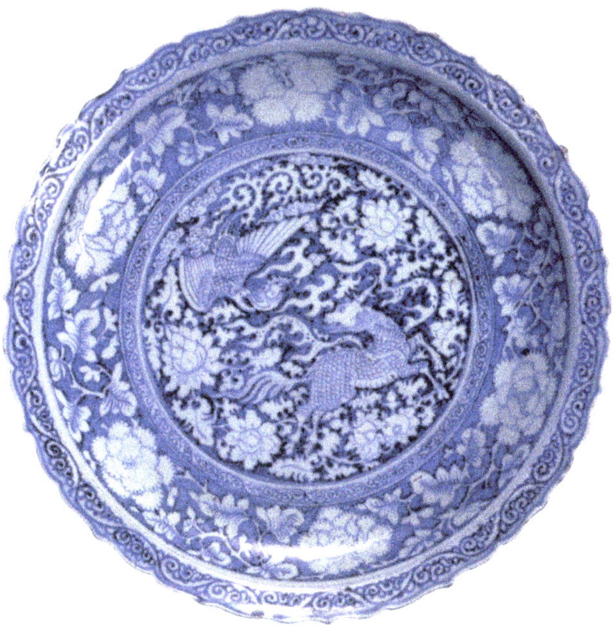

20. Edge-folding Plate with Fish Pattern, Jingdezhen Kiln

Yuan

Height: 7.9 cm Mouth Diameter: 45 cm Foot Diameter: 25 cm

Unearthed from Changde, Hunan

Preserved in the Hunan Museum

This tableware is of refined material and a non-glazed body. The bottom is drawn with patterns of fish in algae. A carp and a grass carp are playing in a blooming lotus pond. The inner layer has patterns of peony intertwined with twigs while the outer layer has patterns of pomegranate flowers.

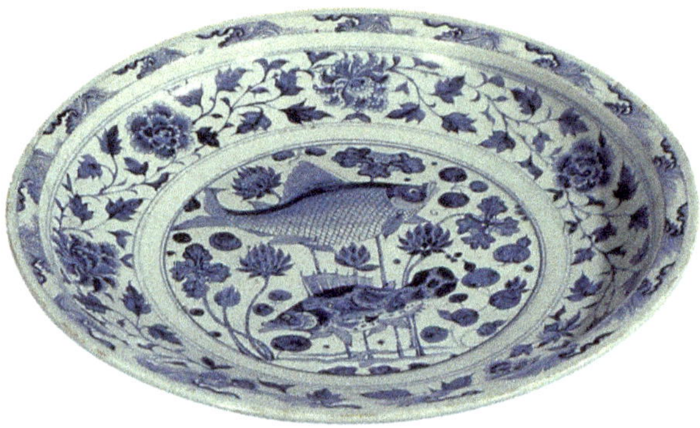

21. Stemcup with Patterns of Plum and Crescent, Jingdezhen Kiln

Yuan

Height: 10 cm

Mouth Diameter: 12.2 cm

Foot Diameter: 4.5 cm

Unearthed from Dingxing Cellar, Hebei in 1972

Preserved in the Hebei Museum

The body material of this drinking vessel is white and fined, while the body is thin. The white glaze is even and smooth. The stemcup is in the shape of a bamboo hat and its inner layer is drawn with plum and a crescent. A stemcup of blue and white porcelain from the Yuan Dynasty is rarely found in West Asia, so its unearthing in China shows it was exclusively used here.

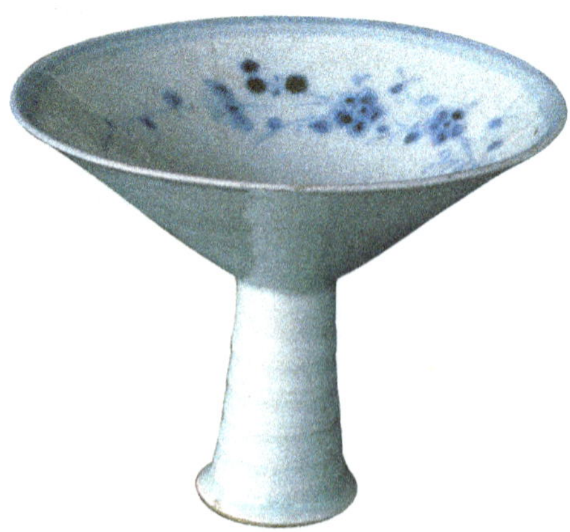

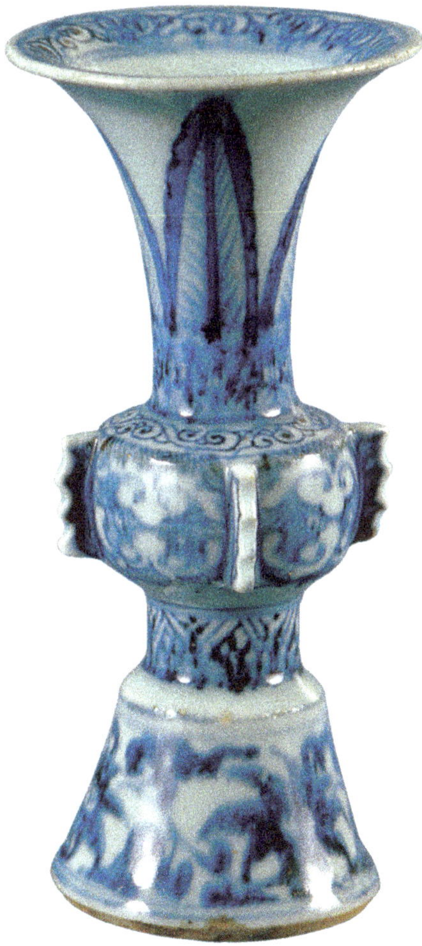

22. Goblet with Patterns of Plantain Leaves, Jingdezhen Kiln
Yuan
Height: 16 cm
Mouth Diameter: 7.5 cm
Foot Diameter: 6 cm
Unearthed from Gao'an Cellar, Jiangxi in 1980
Preserved in the Gao'an Museum

This goblet's shape imitates ancient bronze ware. It has a trumpet-shaped mouth, long neck, folding shoulders and big body. Four ji (lances with two points) emerge from the body. The lower body is in the shape of a taper and the bottom has rectangular pores. The inner mouth has patterns of grass and on the neck are patterns of plantain leaves. On the body, there are patterns of leaves in the shape of a shuttle between the ji and the lower body has patterns of lotus with twigs.

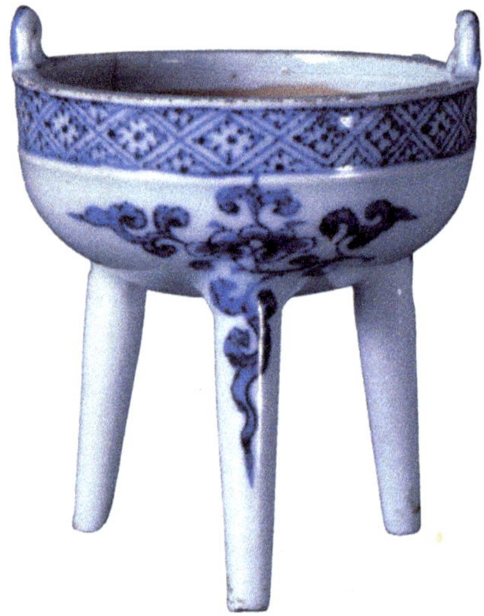

23. Blue and White Porcelain Tripod with Flower Patterns, Jingdezhen Kiln

Yuan
Height: 11 cm
Mouth Diameter: 10.1 cm
Foot Diameter: 7.7 cm
Preserved in the Palace Museum in Beijing
This tripod has a straight mouth and a round bottom. There are three stands as body, which are slender and hollow inside. On both sides of the mouth edge, there are two knobs in the shape of rope in symmetry. The outer layer has a circle of pane patterns and the body has three pairs of twig patterns.

24. Blue and White Porcelain Boat, Jingdezhen Kiln

Yuan
Height: 7.5 cm Length: 15.5 cm Width: 4.2 cm
Preserved in the Guangzhou
This boat is a porcelain sculpture. It is narrow at both ends with a wide beam. There are two cabins. The front one is the larger with a sail, under which sit two women. In the back of front cabin, there stands an old man against the wall looking ahead. The other one is relatively small. At the top of the boat is a sail with pane patterns and the body is dotted with irregular triangle and point patterns.

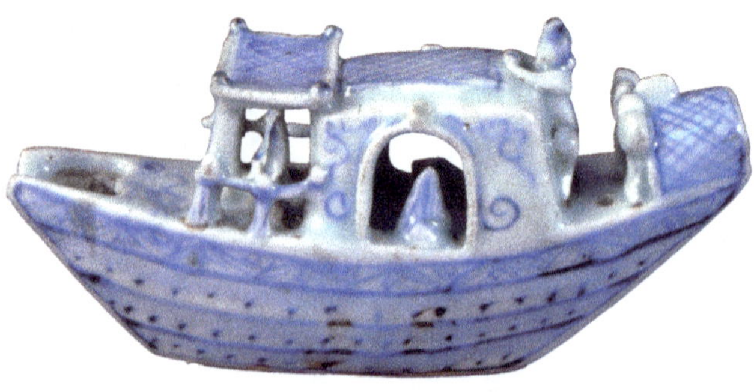

25. Blue and White Porcelain Figure of Kwan-yin, Jingdezhen Kiln

Yuan

Height: 19.5 cm Foot Diameter: 4.8-13.6 cm

Unearthed from Hangzhou, Zhejiang in 1978

Preserved in the Hangzhou Bureau of Garden and Cultural Relics

This porcelain sculpture has an earth-yellow body of rough material. With the blue and white glaze as the background, it has lines of blue and white patterns. Wearing a phoenix coronet and gown with wide sleeves, Kwan-yin is sitting on the pedestal with two hands resting on the stomach. On both sides are her disciples Shancai and Longnu, who hold sacrificial objects in their hands. In front of the body, there are a crane and an immortal deer.

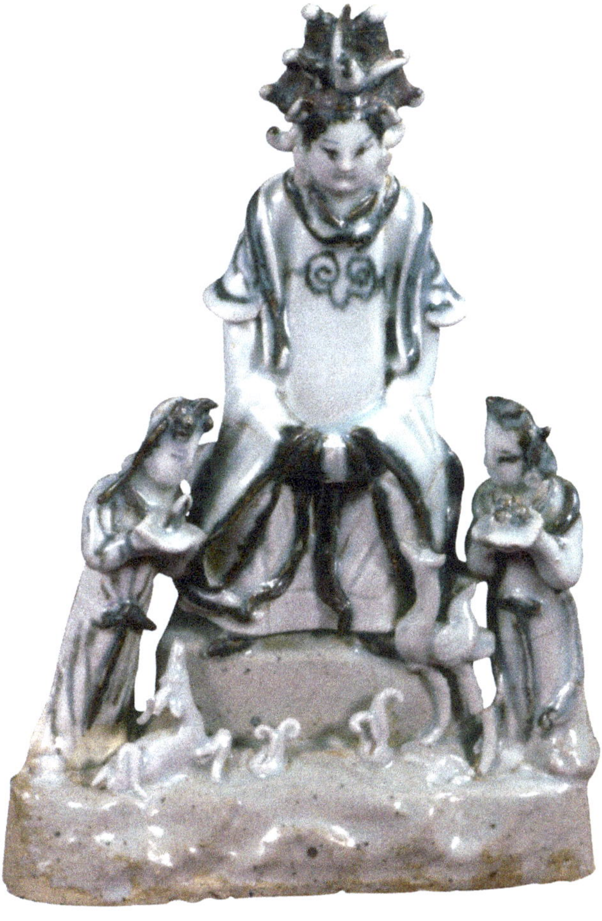

26. Jar with Lid with Figure Patterns, Jingdezhen Kiln

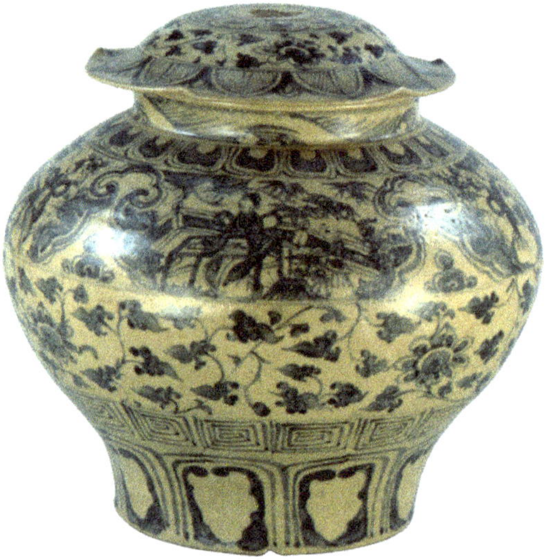

Yuan
Height: 36 cm
Mouth Diameter: 19 cm
Bottom Diameter: 19 cm
Unearthed from tombs in the 26th year (1366) of Zhizheng Reign in Lufeng, Yunnan in 1974
Preserved in the Yunnan Comprehensive Store of Cultural Relics

This container is grey, blue glazed outside. The mouth edge rolls outward. It has a short neck, sloping shoulder and big body, over which is a lid in the shape of a lotus leaf. The body has blue and white patterns all over it. The lid is drawn with patterns of lotus, jasmine and twigs, and plantain leaves. On the neck are seawater patterns, on the shoulders and stomach are lotus petals and figures in four pairs. The lower part is drawn with patterns of jasmine, zigzag and lotus petals.

27. Jar with Pattern of Two Lions Playing with Balls, Jingdezhen Kiln

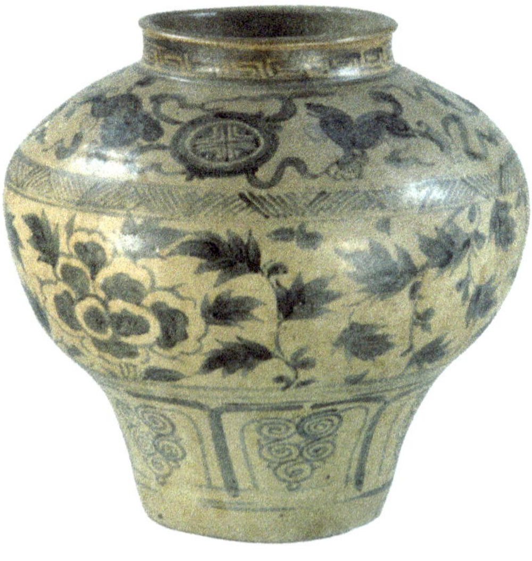

Yuan
Height: 35 cm
Mouth Diameter: 17 cm
Bottom Diameter: 15.5 cm
Unearthed from tombs in the 26th year (1366) of Zhizheng Reign in Lufeng, Yunnan in 1974
Preserved in the Yunnan Museum

This container has a grey body, with the blue and slightly grey glaze. The jar is straight in mouth, short in neck, plump in shoulders and stomach with a flat body. The body is drawn with the patterns of two lions playing with balls, peony intertwined with twigs and lotus petals.

28. Underglazed Copper Red Porcelain Jar with Lid with Flower Patterns, Jingdezhen Kiln

Yuan

Height: 41.2 cm Mouth Diameter: 15.5 cm Bottom Diameter: 18.7 cm

Unearthed from Baoding Cellar in Hebei in 1964

Preserved in the Hebei Museum

This container with fine glaze thin in the upper body and thick in the lower part. The jar has a straight mouth, short neck, sloping shoulder, big stomach and flat bottom. The lid is like an upturned basin with a sculpture of sitting lion as the button. The lid is drawn with lotus petal patterns, the neck with peony and twig patterns, shoulder with honeysuckle patterns with cloud patterns hanging down and peony patterns dotted among them. On the stomach there are two parts of a lozenge, hollowly engraved with four kinds of flowers such as peony and jasmine. The lower part has patterns of lotus and honeysuckle while the bottom has lotus petal patterns. A pair of jars was unearthed; the other one is in the Palace Museum in Beijing.

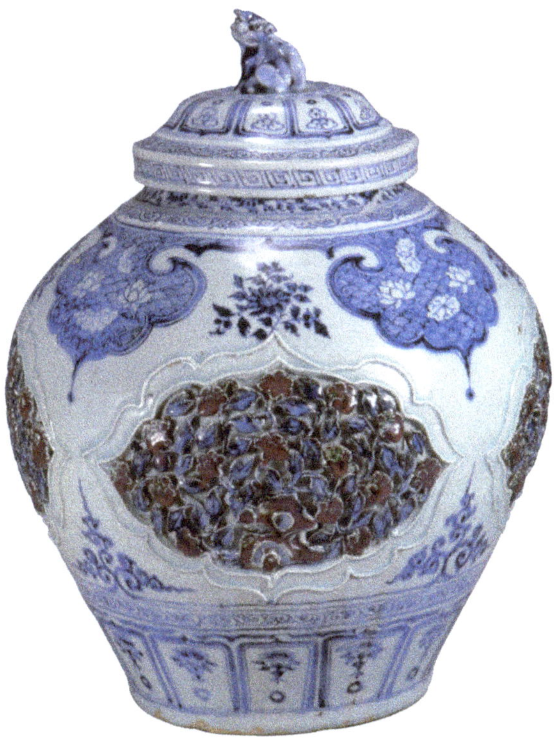

29. Underglazed Copper Red Porcelain Jar with Tower-shaped Lid, Jingdezhen Kiln

Yuan

Height: 22.5 cm Mouth Diameter: 7.7 cm Bottom Diameter: 6.6 cm

Unearthed from Tomb of Ling Family in Jingdezhen, Jiangxi in 1974

Preserved in the Jiangxi Museum

This burial object has a fined body glazed blue and white. The lid is in the shape of a hat and the top button is in tower shape with the eight treasures drawn underneath. The jar has a flat mouth, short neck, sloping shoulder, stomach large in the upper part and narrow in the lower. On the shoulder are sculptures of blue dragon and white tiger, forming the knobs. On the stomach are relief sculptures of Zhuque, an immortal bird and of Xuanwu, an immortal beast part snake and part turtle. There are also lotus petal patterns with blue and white lines while the convex part is underglazed copper red. There are tens of characters inscribed on the shoulder in running script.

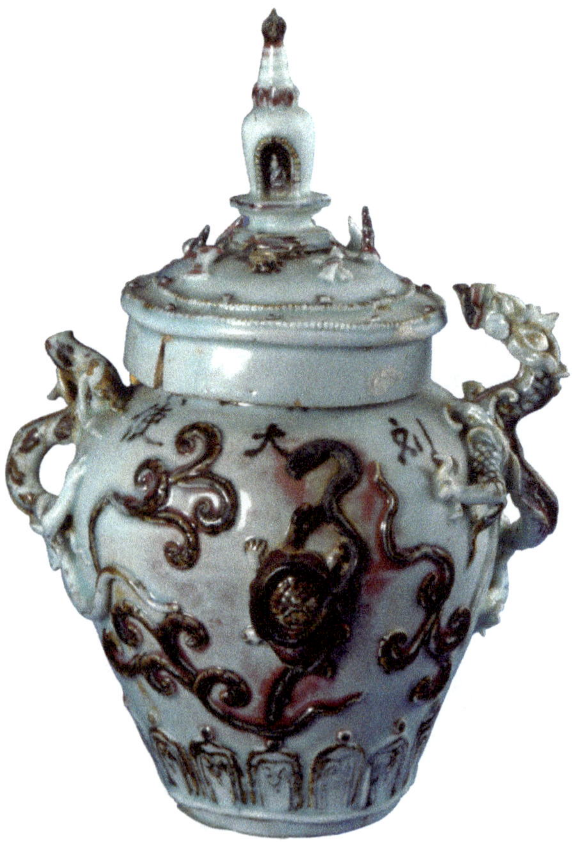

30. Underglazed Copper Red Porcelain Barn in Pavilion Shape, Jingdezhen Kiln

Yuan

Height: 29.5 cm Width: 20.5 cm Depth: 10 cm

Unearthed from Tomb of Ling Family in Jingdezhen, Jiangxi in 1974

Preserved in the Jiangxi Museum

This is a burial object in the shape of pavilion. It consists of a main two-storey tower and towers on both sides. The tower has a double-hipped roof and glazed tiles, red columns, with body surrounded by banisters. There are altogether 18 people, seeming to be playing music. The front door of the barn is red with a couplet in regular script with blue and white patterns on both sides. On the walls of west side and east side, there are inscriptions meaning the barn was used in Ling Min's tomb. On the other side is an epitaph in the same style including the Yuan calendar year (1338).

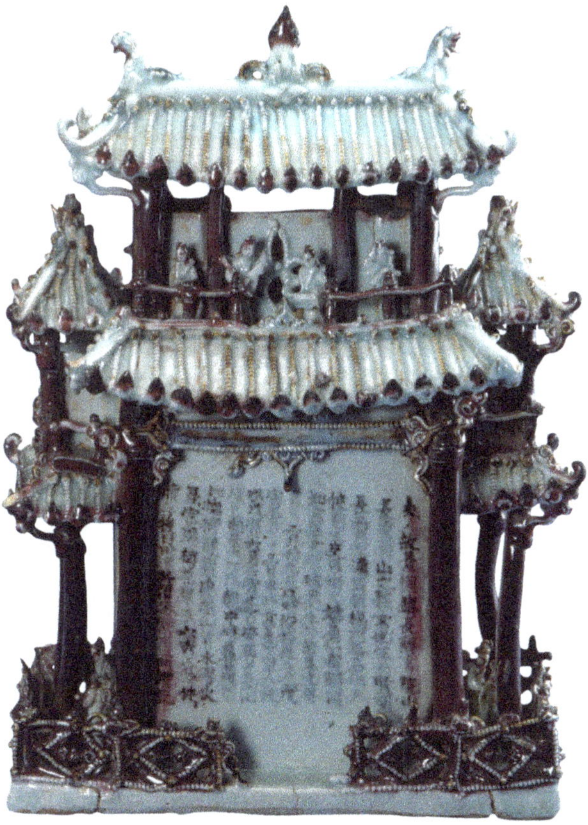

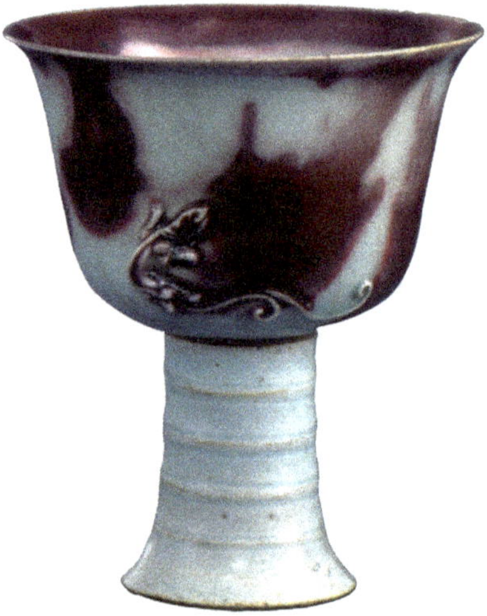

31. Underglazed Copper Red Porcelain Rolling Stemcup, Jingdezhen Kiln

Yuan
Height: 12.8 cm
Mouth Diameter: 10.4 cm
Unearthed from Gao'an Cellar, Jiangxi in 1980
Preserved in the Gao'an Museum

This drinking vessel has a fined body and is glazed blue and white, with underglazed copper red spots. The cup has a big mouth and stomach. The bottom is like a bamboo joint. There is a tenon and mortise between the cup and the bottom, hence the name rolling stemcup. The inner layer has patterns of plum and jasmine. The stomach has underglazed copper red spots, with convex carvings of dragon patterns.

32. Underglazed Copper Red Jar with Flowers and Birds in Openwork, Jingdezhen Kiln

Yuan
Height: 24.8 cm
Mouth Diameter: 13.3 cm
Bottom Diameter: 15.4 cm
Unearthed from Gao'an Cellar, Jiangxi in 1980
Preserved in the Gao'an Museum

This container has a refined body and is glazed blue and white with grey luster. It has a straight mouth, sloping shoulder, and a big stomach becoming smaller in the lower part. There are three line patterns on the outer layer of the neck, and a circle of lotuses on the shoulder, with patterns between two lotuses. On the body are four parts in lozenge with openwork with patterns of crane in jasmine, peacock and peony, and glossy Ganoderma-shaped cloud patterns in the space.

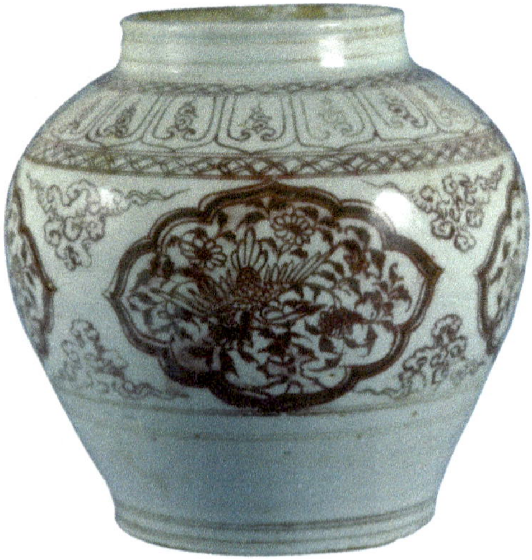

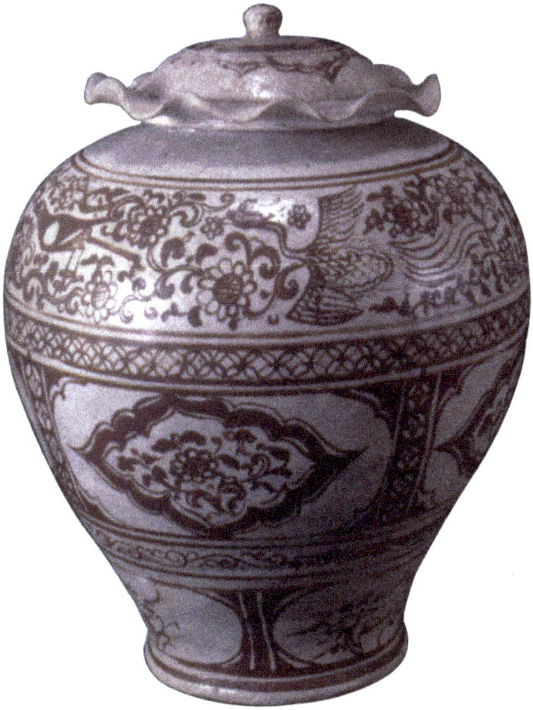

33. Underglazed Ocher Porcelain Jar with Lotus Leaf-shaped Lid, Jingdezhen Kiln

Yuan

Height: 31.4 cm Mouth Diameter: 9.6 cm Bottom Diameter: 13.7 cm

Preserved in the Guangdong Museum

This container has a grey and solid body. The jar has a straight mouth, wide shoulder, big stomach and flat bottom, with a lotus leaf-shaped lid. The jar has brown patterns against the white background. There are patterns of two phoenix, four magpies and jasmine in symmetry in the shoulder. In the center of the stomach are four lozenges in openwork, with a jasmine inside, and the lower part has sectors in openwork with flowers drawn inside. The three layers of patterns are separated by grass patterns.

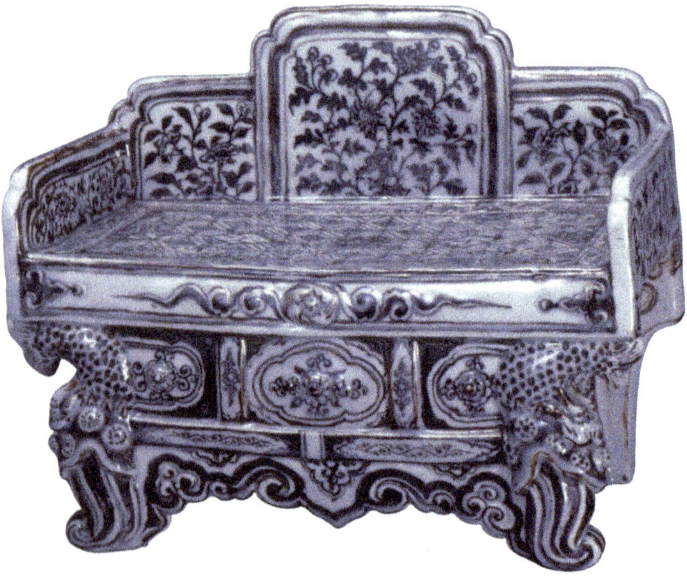

34. Underglazed Red God's Seat with Flower Patterns, Jingdezhen Kiln

Yuan

Height: 24.1 cm Length: 29.3 cm Width: 15.3 cm

Preserved in the Palace Museum in Beijing

This is a furnishing. The seat back and handrail are sculptured like screens. The seat is in rectangle shape, under which is a Sumeru Seat. The four feet are in the shape of Capricorn fish which are standing on their heads and spouting water flows. With underglazed red patterns in the body, the back and handrail are drawn with flower patterns and the seat surface is drawn with brocade patterns.

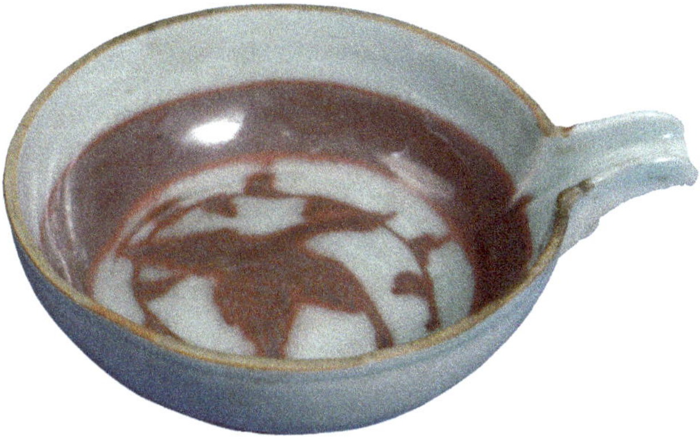

35. Underglazed Red Ladle with Reed-Goose Patterns, Jingdezhen Kiln

Yuan
Height: 5.5 cm
Mouth Diameter: 14.3 cm
Bottom Diameter: 8.7 cm
Unearthed from Gao'an Cellar, Jiangxi in 1980
Preserved in the Gao'an Museum

This is a water container. It has fined body and glazed blue and slightly white. It has a wide mouth, convex bottom and square rebate-shaped opening slightly higher than the mouth. On the inner layer, the center is drawn with the wild goose in the reed. The inner wall has ripple patterns which are firstly carved and then dyed. The red under glaze is bright with the slight diffusion.

36. Blue and Underglazed Ocher Porcelain Pot with Rabbit Patterns, Jingdezhen Kiln

Yuan
Height: 20.5 cm
Mouth Diameter: 6.3 cm
Bottom Diameter: 6.8 cm
Preserved in the Palace Museum in Beijing

This is a container with the blue and white glaze. The pot has a wide mouth, slender neck, big stomach, with elegant shape. In the stomach, there is a rabbit running in flowers with the underglazed ocher as the background which is very bright.

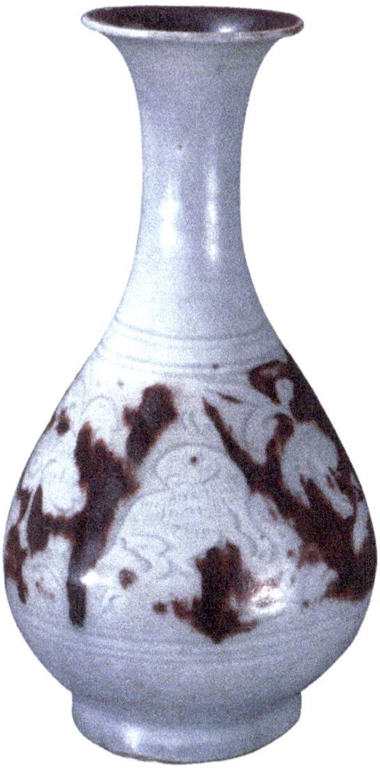

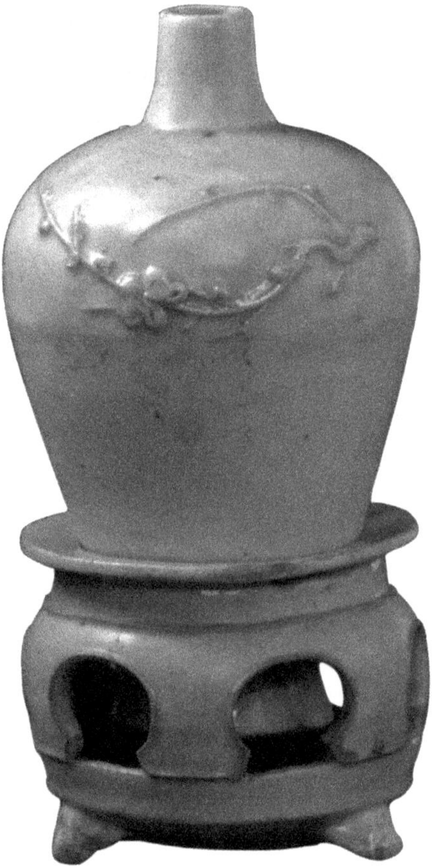

37. Blue and Underglazed Ocher Porcelain Plum Vase with Pedestal, Jingdezhen Kiln

Yuan

Height: 24.7 cm Mouth Diameter: 2.6 cm Bottom Diameter: 6.8 cm

Collected from Wannian, Jiangxi in 1978

Preserved in the Jiangxi Museum

This is a furnishing glazed blue and white with the pedestal and body connected. The pot has a flat mouth, short neck, plump shoulder, with the stomach big in the upper part and narrowing in the lower part. The flat bottom is connected to the pedestal, where there are three feet in the shape of beast face. The pedestal body is hollowly engraved on six sides, with beard patterns along the edge. On the shoulders and upper stomach, is a sculpture of a raspberry.

38. Blue and White Glazed Porcelain Vase with Sculptures of Chinese Zodiac, Jingdezhen Kiln

Yuan

Height: 49.5 cm

Mouth Diameter: 9.5 cm

Bottom Diameter: 11.9 cm

Delivered by the Military Affairs Office of Jingdezhen, Jiangxi in 1979.

Preserved in the Jingdezhen Ceramics House

This burial object has a straight mouth, short neck, sloping shoulder, long and round stomach, with ring feet tilting outward. At the top is a bamboo rain-hat-shaped lid, the center of which is convex, seeming like a tower and the top of which is a sculpture of a little bird. The joint between the shoulders and the neck has a sculpture of four immortal animals, blue dragon, white tiger, Zhuque the immortal bird, and Xuanwu, the immortal beast of snake and turtle. In the stomach there are 12 gods each cradling a zodiac animal. They are drawn with various flowers in the part close to the bottom.

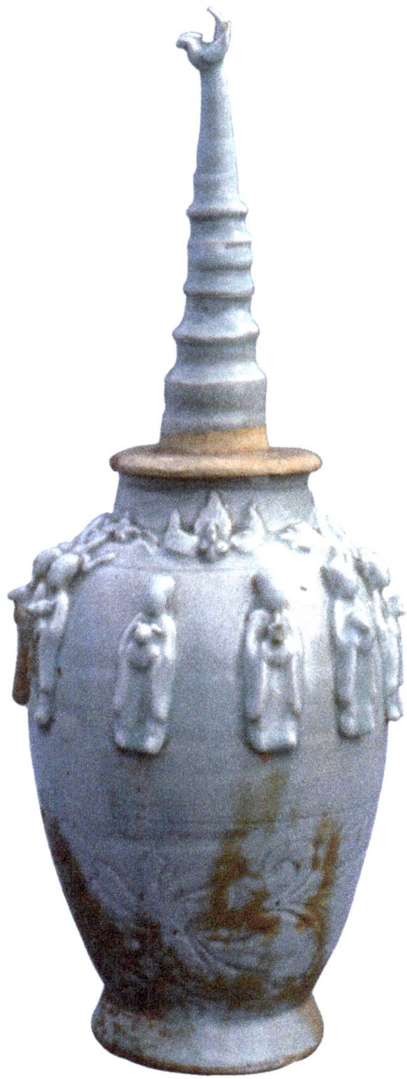

39. Blue and White Glazed Porcelain Jar with Tower-shaped Lid , Jingdezhen Kiln

Yuan

Height: 25.6 cm Mouth Diameter: 8.3 cm Bottom Diameter: 9.6 cm

Unearthed from Boyang, Jiangxi in 1975

Preserved in the Jiangxi Museum

This container has a flat mouth, short neck and sloping shoulder, the stomach big in the upper part and small in the lower, with ring feet tilting outward. There is a bamboo rain-hat-shaped lid with a tower-shaped button and on its top is a sculpture of a standing bird. There are patterns, each with a human body and beast face, under which are four concave lines, giving the patterns a drifting cloud background. The lower part of the stomach is engraved with a circle of double-hipped lotus.

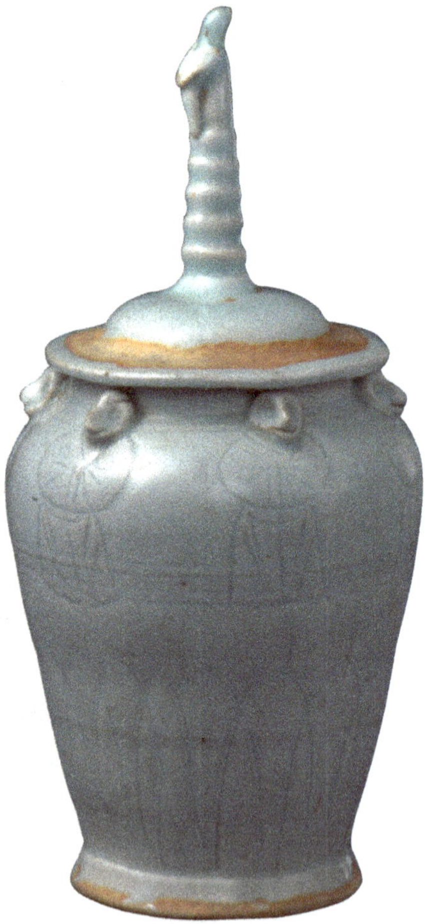

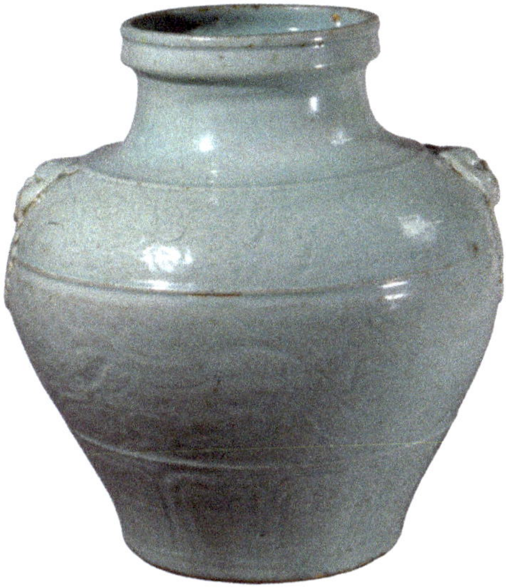

40. Blue and White Glazed Porcelain Jar Carved with Cloud and Dragon Patterns, Jingdezhen Kiln

Yuan
Height: 33.8 cm
Mouth Diameter: 16.3 cm
Bottom Diameter: 18.6 cm
Preserved in the Shanghai Museum

This container is glazed blue and white smoothly. It has a winding mouth, short neck, wide shoulder, big stomach and short ring feet. With a large body, the jar has a shape ancient and simple. The patterns are all carved. On the shoulder are patterns of flower and twig, with the two-dragon patterns on the stomach, and the lotus petal patterns on its lower part. There are two animal head appliqué for knockers in symmetry in the shoulder part.

41. Blue and White Glazed Porcelain Pot in Buddhist Monk's Hat Shape, Jingdezhen Kiln

Yuan
Height: 19.7 cm
Mouth Diameter: 12.7 cm
Bottom Diameter: 9 cm
Unearthed from Beijing in 1965
Preserved in the Capital Museum

This drinking vessel has a fine and white body and is glazed evenly and smoothly blue and white. The mouth of the pot is like a Buddhist monk's hat. The pot has a short neck, big stomach and ring feet. The mouth is in duckbilled shape and the knob is in the shape of a shuttle. This kind of pot was mainly made in Ming and Qing Dynasties and this one is the only known piece which was made in the Yuan Dynasty.

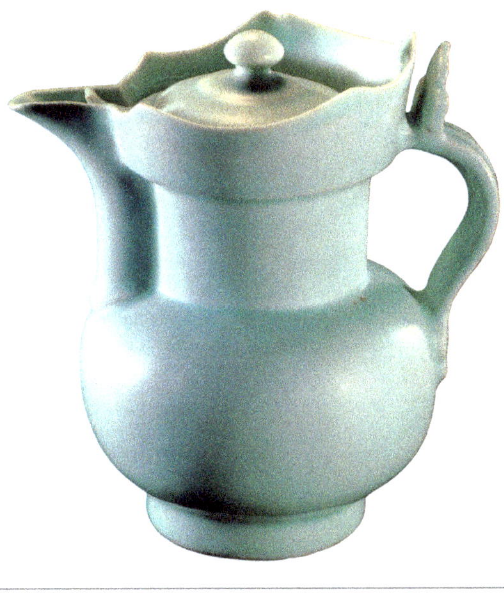

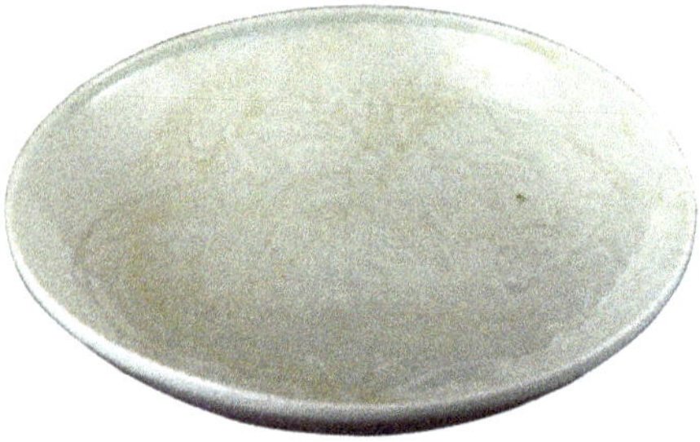

42. Blue and White Glazed Porcelain Bowl with Dragon Patterns, Jingdezhen Kiln

Yuan

Height: 6.5 cm   Mouth Diameter: 21.5 cm   Bottom Diameter: 7.5 cm

Unearthed from Yongxin Cellar, Jiangxi in 1980

Preserved in the Jiangxi Museum

This tableware has a white body and it is glazed blue and white evenly and smoothly. The bowl has a wide mouth, arched wall and short ring feet. There are no patterns on the outer wall while there are patterns of dragons playing with beards and patterns of cloud in the inner wall.

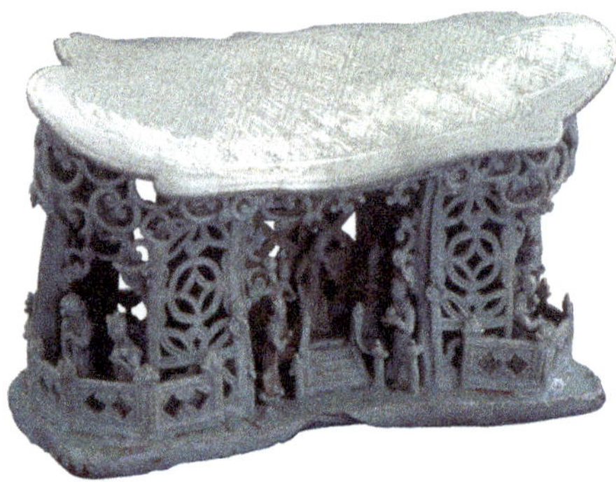

43. Blue and White Glazed Porcelain Pillow Hollowly Carved with Figures, Jingdezhen Kiln

Yuan

Height: 18.2 cm   Length: 32 cm   Width: 15 cm

Unearthed from Yuexi, Anhui in 1982

Preserved in the Yuexi Institute of Cultural Relics Management

This pillow is glazed blue and white evenly and smoothly. Its slightly grey body can be seen. The pillow, hollowly carved, is in the shape of a hall. The top of the pillow is the top of the hall, with one side higher than the other with the pattern of "卍". There are corridors surrounding the main house. In the houses and corridors, there are as many as 18 female and male figures sitting or standing solemnly, or holding fruits for sacrifice or talking to each other.

44. Blue and White Glazed Porcelain Pillow Hollowly Carved with Figures, Jingdezhen Kiln

Yuan

Height: 15.3 cm Length: 32 cm Width: 16 cm

Unearthed from Datong, Shanxi in 1973

Preserved in the Datong Museum

This pillow is glazed blue and white smoothly and brightly with fined body. The top of the pillow is in the shape of petal, and is carved with patterns of "卍". The four sides of the body have figures and stories. The front surface is the mythical story about Guanghan Palace on the moon. On both sides are stories of "Zhuge Liang Enquiring for the Beidou, the Great Dipper" and "Disciples Kneeling and Showing Respect to Kwan-yin".

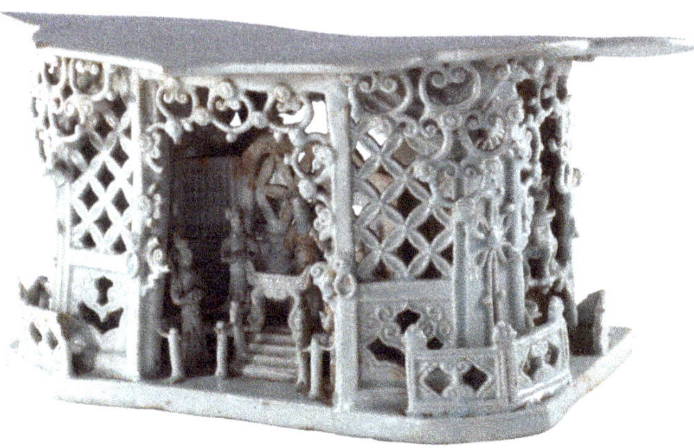

45. Blue and White Glazed Porcelain Figure of Kwan-yin, Jingdezhen Kiln

Yuan
Height: 67 cm
Unearthed from Xicheng, Beijing in 1955
Preserved in the Capital Museum

This porcelain sculpture is glazed yinqing (blue with white luster). She wears a flower coronet, with her long hair on the shoulders and bead earrings. With a cassock, her left hand hangs down and supports her, while the right hand lies on the right knee.

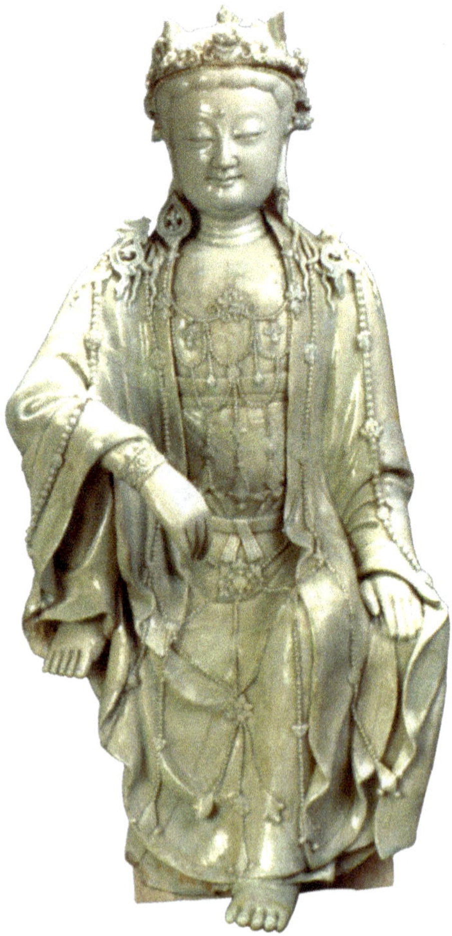

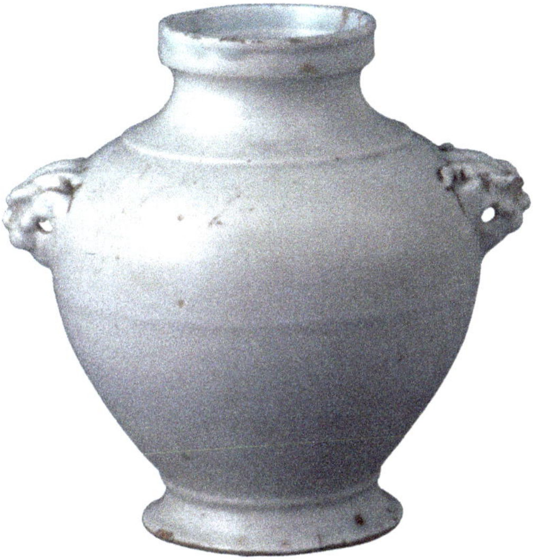

46. Egg White Glazed Porcelain Jar with Lion-shaped Knobs, Jingdezhen Kiln

Yuan
Height: 21 cm
Mouth Diameter: 8.1 cm
Bottom Diameter: 9.5 cm
Collected from Jingdezhen, Jiangxi in 1975
Preserved in the Jingdezhen Ceramics House

This jar has a white body and thick body, glazed gray like a duck egg, with joint traces. The jar has a winding mouth, little neck and plump shoulder. Its big stomach is bigger in the upper part and smaller in the lower. It has a high ring feet tilting outward. There is a convex line pattern. On both sides are lion-shaped knobs. There are holes in lions' mouth for nibbling rings.

In the Yuan Dynasty, southern white glazed porcelain was mainly made in Jingdezhen. The glaze was cloudy and the color resembled that of duck egg, hence the name "Egg White Glazed Porcelain".

47. Egg White Glazed Porcelain Bowl with Two-phoenix Patterns, Jingdezhen Kiln

Yuan
Height: 5.5 cm
Mouth Diameter: 13.6 cm
Bottom Diameter: 3.2 cm
Unearthed from Le'an Cellar, Jiangxi in 1984
Preserved in the Jiangxi Museum

This tableware is glazed from inner layer to the outer layer and at the bottom the body can be seen. It has a wide mouth, sloping stomach and short ring feet. The inner layer is drawn with lines, and center with a pair of phoenix ready to soar. The space is filled with flying bees.

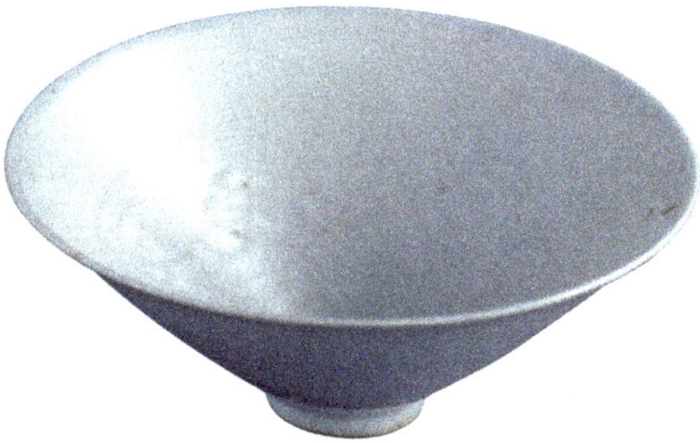

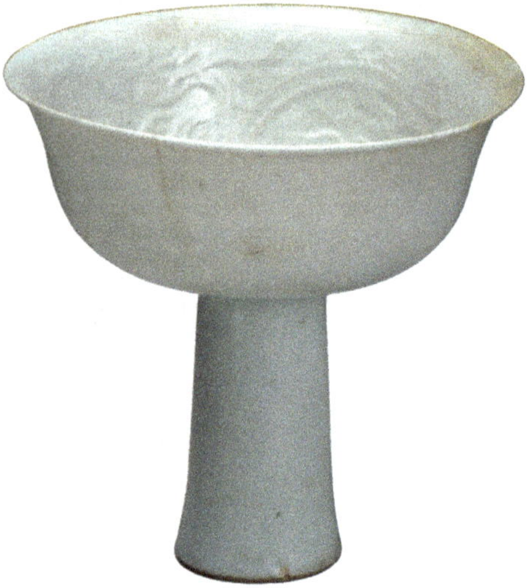

48. Egg White Glazed Porcelain Stem-bowl with Cloud and Dragon Patterns, Jingdezhen Kiln

Yuan
Height: 13.3 cm
Mouth Diameter: 13.8 cm
Feet Diameter: 5.6 cm
Unearthed from Tomb of Ren Family in Qingpu,Jiangsu in 1952
Preserved in the Shanghai Museum

This bowl has a heavy and thick body, evenly and smoothly glazed white with blue luster. It has a wide mouth with its edge tilting outward, with a big stomach, and non-glazed high feet. The inner layer is drawn with two five-paw dragons and the bottom has patterns of flowers and lotus petals.

49. Egg White Glazed Porcelain Stemcup with Jijin Technique, Jingdezhen Kiln

Yuan
Height: 8.9 cm Mouth Diameter: 9.1 cm
Unearthed the Shexian Cellar, Anhui in 1982
Preserved in the Shexian Museum

This stemcup is glazed white with blue luster, thickly yet evenly. The mouth tilts outward. It is plum at the bottom. The stem is big in the lower part and small in the upper, exquisite in shape. The outer layer has openwork with gold line patterns.

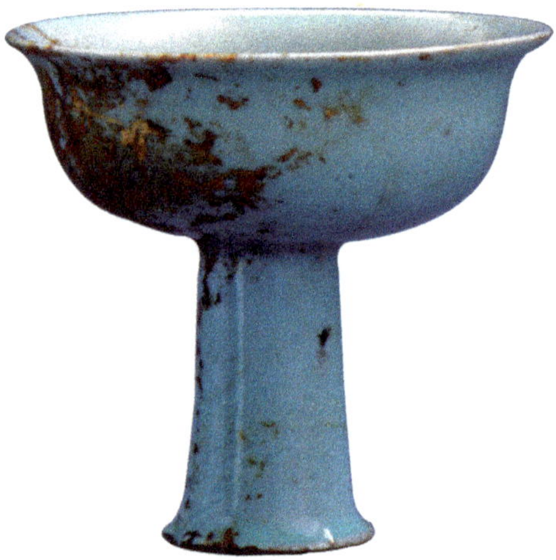

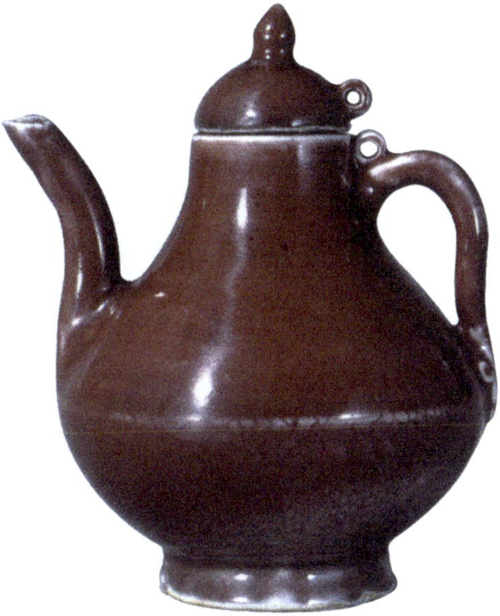

50. Red Glazed Porcelain Pear-shaped Pot with Cloud and Dragon Carvings, Jingdezhen Kiln

Yuan

Height: 12.5 cm

Mouth Diameter: 3.5 cm

Feet Diameter: 5.3 cm

Preserved in the Palace Museum in Beijing

This pot is glazed red all over. This relatively small pot has a wide mouth, round stomach and ring feet. Patterns of cloud and dragons can be seen on the stomach. The pear-shaped pot is created by Jingdezhen.

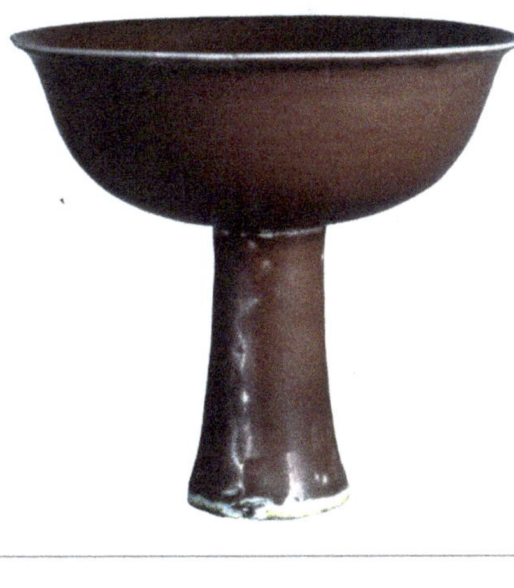

51. Red Glazed Porcelain Stembowl with Cloud and Dragon Patterns, Jingdezhen Kiln

Yuan

Height: 14 cm

Mouth Diameter: 14.6 cm

Feet Diameter: 4.8 cm

Preserved in the Palace Museum in Beijing

This stembowl has a wide mouth and high feet, and is plump at the bottom. There are stamp patterns of two dragons in clouds. The glazed color is relatively dark, which is the feature of red glaze in the early period.

52. Red Glazed Porcelain Male Figures in Burial, Jingdezhen Kiln
Yuan
Height: 20.5 cm
Unearthed from Tomb of Ling Family in Jingdezhen, Jiangxi in 1974
Preserved in the Jiangxi Museum
This burial object is molded and solid, glazed red all over, yet not evenly. The figure has a high hat and wears a vestment, standing with a tablet, with a kind and peaceful appearance.

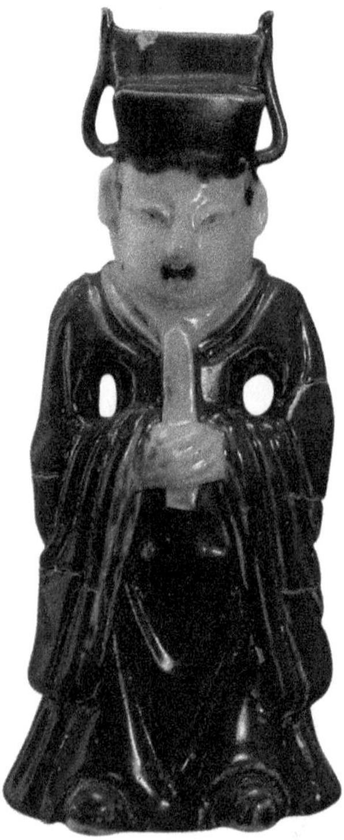

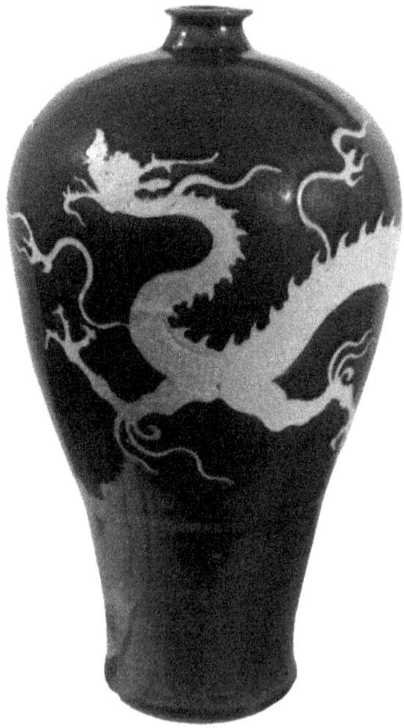

53 .Blue Glazed Porcelain Plum Vase with White Dragon Patterns, Jingdezhen Kiln
Yuan
Height: 43.8 cm Mouth Diameter: 5.5 cm Bottom Diameter: 14 cm
Preserved in the Yangzhou Museum
This vase is glazed blue all over. The body is thick, bright and smooth, with luster of precious stones. The vase has a little mouth, short neck, plump shoulder, big stomach, short neck and the bottom edge tilting outward. On the stomach are three-paw dragon patterns, covered with white glaze. The white dragons have heads connected with neighboring dragon's tails. Their bodies are dotted with fire beards and cloud and their eyes are highlighted by blue glaze.

54. Blue Glazed Porcelain Plate with White Dragon Patterns, Jingdezhen Kiln

Yuan

Height: 1.1 cm Mouth Diameter: 16 cm Bottom Diameter: 14 cm

Preserved in the Palace Museum in Beijing

This container is high-temperature glazed blue all over. The plate edge has folded rim. The center is carved with dragon patterns. The body between pattern lines is winkled and replaced by a white pug.

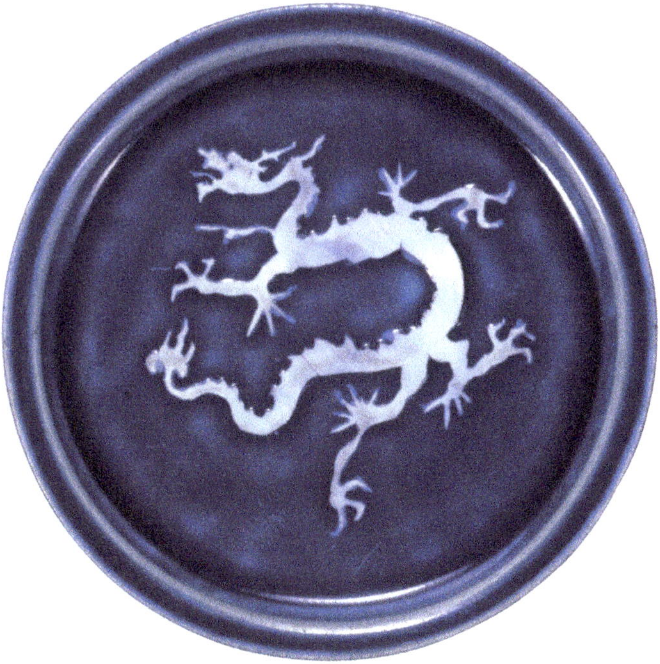

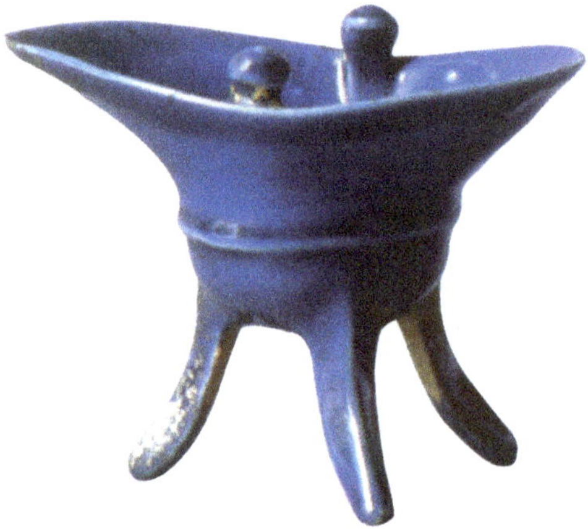

55. Blue Glazed Jue-shaped Cup with Gold Outlines, Jingdezhen Kiln

Yuan
Height: 9 cm Mouth Length: 11.5 cm
Width: 7 cm
Unearthed from Shexian Cellar, Anhui in 1982
Preserved in the Shexian Museum
This drinking vessel has a shape similar to jue (bronze ware). With a thin body, it is glazed cobalt blue all over with gold outlines. It has a wide mouth in leaf shape, with one end round and other pointed. There are convex lines in the stomach; three feet are in lozenge shape.

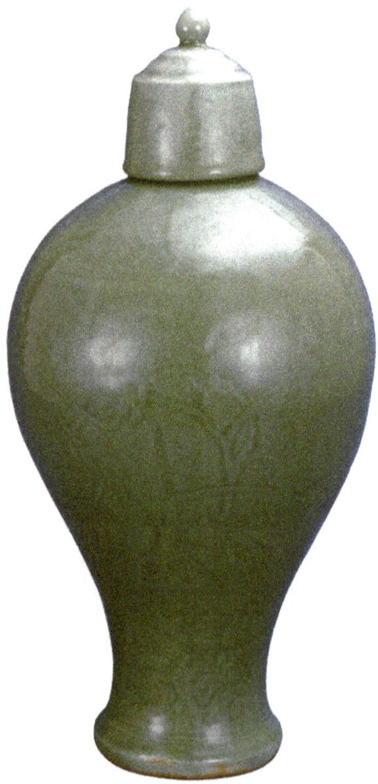

56. Blue Glazed Porcelain Plum Vase with Lid, Jingdezhen Kiln

Yuan
Height: 44.4 cm
Mouth Diameter: 6.1 cm
Bottom Diameter: 11.4 cm
Preserved in the Palace Museum in Beijing
This vase is glazed blue and green, smooth and bright. The vase has a straight mouth, short neck, round shoulders and big stomach, bigger in the upper and smaller in the lower part, and ring feet tilting outward. On the shoulder are five pairs of cloud patterns and on the stomach are patterns of peach, bamboo and at the bottom is a circle of glossy Ganoderma.

57. Vase with Figures of Eight Immortals, Longquan Kiln

Yuan

Height: 19.9 cm Mouth Diameter: 4.1 cm Foot Diameter: 6.8 cm

Preserved in the Palace Museum in Beijing

As a furnishing, the vase is glazed gray with dark brown luster. The body can be seen in the central part of the stomach which is reddish brown. The octagonal vase has a little mouth, short neck and ring feet tilting outward. On the shoulder are convex patterns of eight diagrams in openwork. In the rectangle openwork, there are figures of eight immortals and at the bottom are eight pairs of flower patterns.

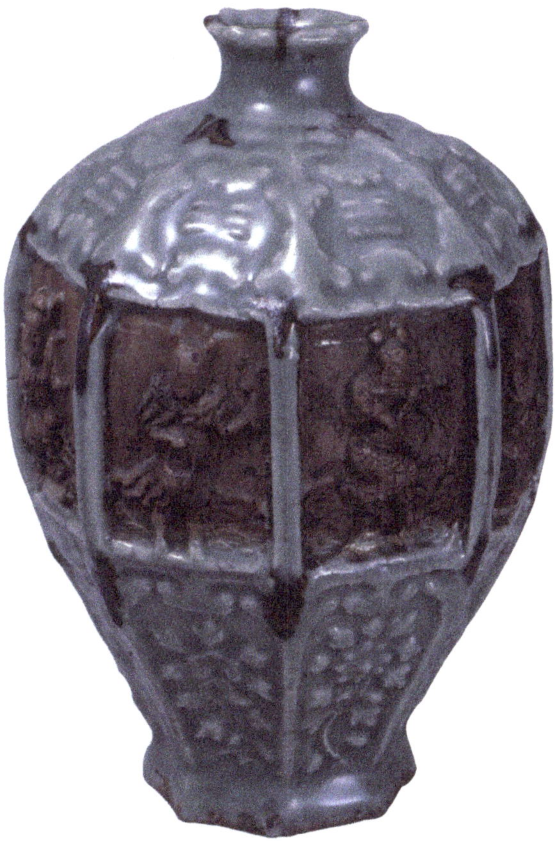

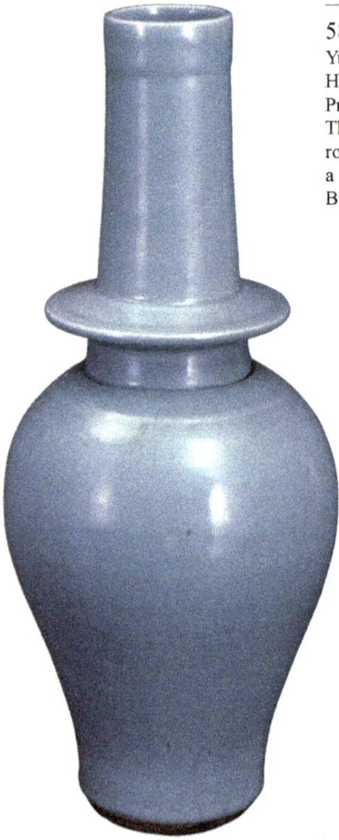

58. Long-neck Vase, Longquan Kiln

Yuan

Height: 48.2 cm Mouth Diameter: 7.4 cm Bottom Diameter: 10.4 cm

Preserved in the Palace Museum in Beijing

This vase is glazed blue all over without spots. It has a straight mouth, long neck, round stomach and ring feet. The neck is as long as a half of the vase and there is a convex joint separating the neck into two parts, like the Tibet grass vase used in Buddhist temples.

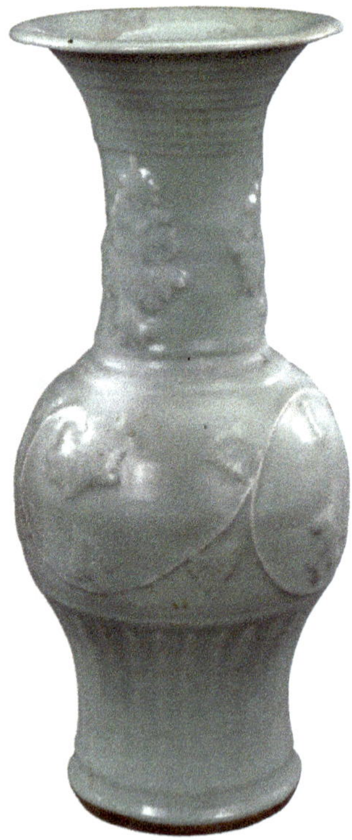

59. Vase with Peony and Twig Patterns, Longquan Kiln

Yuan

Height: 50.4 cm Mouth Diameter: 26 cm Bottom Diameter: 15 cm

Unearthed from Hohhot, Inner Mongolia in 1970

Preserved in the Inner Mongolia Museum

This vase is glazed bright green. It has a wide mouth, long neck, big stomach and concave bottom. Both ends of the neck are carved with line and the middle part has four pairs of paste-on-paste. There are patterns of peony and twigs in the stomach and patterns of plantain leaves at the bottom.

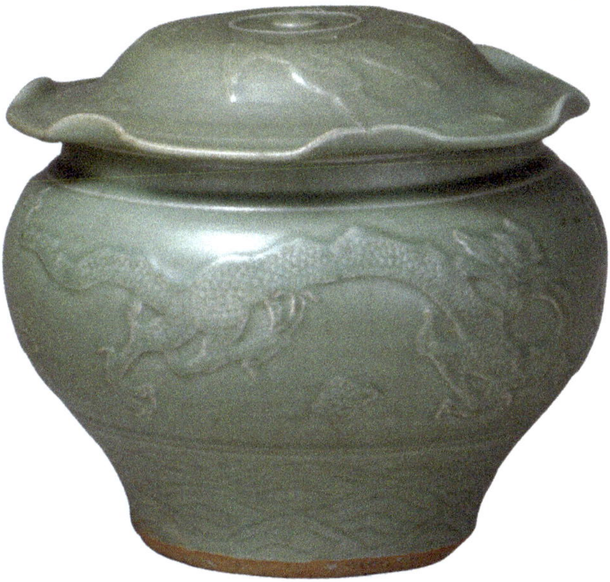

60. Dragon and Phoenix-patterned Jar with Lid, Longquan Kiln
Yuan
Height: 28.6 cm Mouth Diameter: 24.8 cm Bottom Diameter: 18 cm
Unearthed from Nanhui, Shanghai in 1975
Preserved in the Shanghai Museum

As a container, this vase has a heavy and thick body. It is glazed bright blue smoothly and heavily. The jar has a straight mouth, short neck, big stomach and ring feet. The lid is in the shape of a lotus leaf and has patterns of cloud and phoenix paste-on-paste. There are also patterns of dragons playing with beards paste-on-paste on the body.

61. Lotus-shape Bowl with Mountain and Water Carvings, Longquan Kiln

Yuan

Height: 12.3 cm Mouth Diameter: 22.8 cm Bottom Diameter: 9.9 cm

Preserved in the Palace Museum in Beijing

This bowl has a fine body, glazed blue, bright and smooth. The bowl is in the shape of eight-petal lotus, with wide mouth and ring feet. On the inner layer are patterns of the eight treasures and on outer layer are patterns of mountain and water by which an old man is fishing.

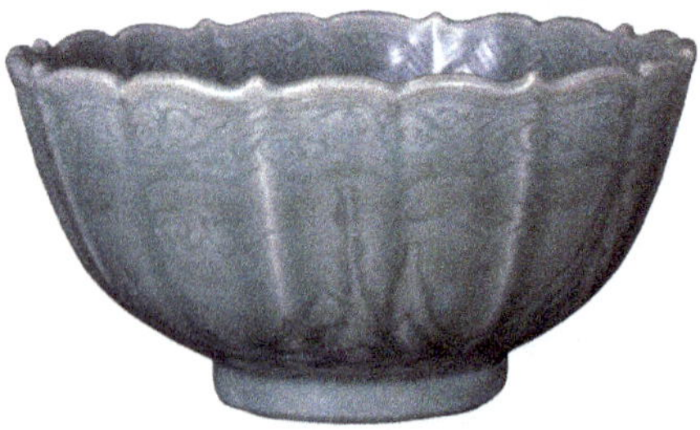

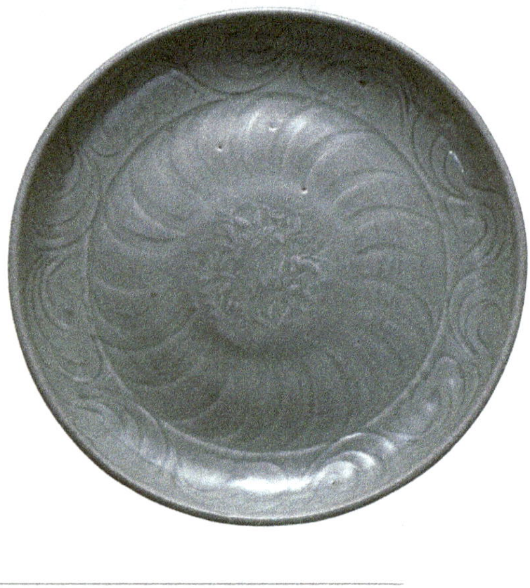

62. Plate Printed with Pagba Script, Longquan Kiln

Yuan

Height: 5.3 cm Mouth Diameter: 33.7 cm Bottom Diameter: 22.1 cm

Preserved in the Palace Museum in Beijing

This plate is glazed blue. It has wide mouth, flat bottom and ring feet. The three methods of carving, outlining and printing are used. Along the edge is carved with cloud. In the center there is a large sunflower and in its center there is printed with lotus and a character in Pagba script.

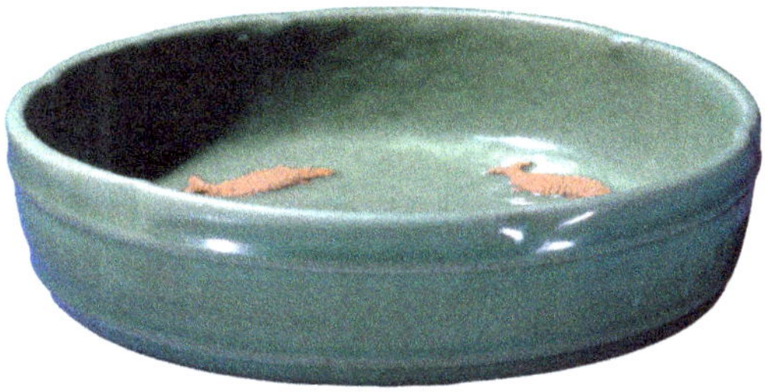

63. Blue Glazed Porcelain Washer with Four-fish Patterns, Longquan Kiln

Yuan

Height: 7.3 cm Mouth Diameter: 28 cm Bottom Diameter: 23.5 cm

Preserved in the Palace Museum in Beijing

As a writing material, the wash has a heavy and thick body. It is glazed smoothly and brightly from inside to outside. The mouth is in the shape of a hexapetalous flower. It has straight walls and flat bottom. On the outer layer are two convex lines while on the inner layer are weaved patterns. The center of the wash is carved with persimmon and calyx patterns in openwork, with lotus patterns inside. The center is stamped with a circle of red fish.

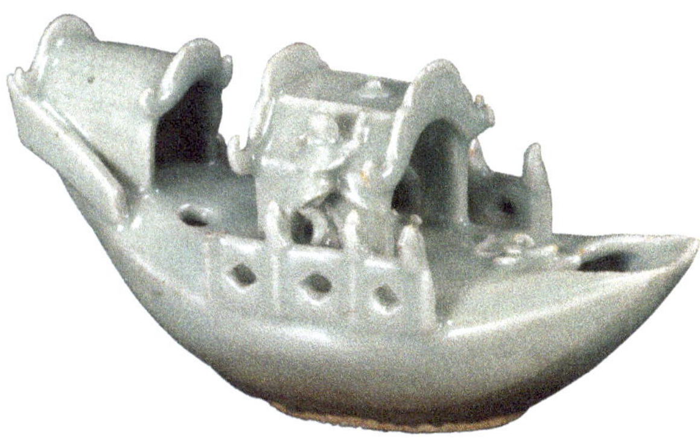

64. Boat-shaped Yandi, Longquan Kiln

Yuan

Height: 9.1 cm Length: 16.2 cm Width: 6.5 cm

Unearthed from Longquan, Zhejiang in 1956

Preserved in the Zhejiang Museum

As a writing material, this has grey and white body seen at the bottom. It is glazed bright blue all over it. The Yandi is in the shape of a boat with a flat bottom. In the boat there are two figures sitting and talking. The boat has a cabin cover and a stern cover. On both sides of the cabin cover, there are banisters. On the left is a wood pulp. At the top of the cover is a bamboo rain-hat, at which a boatman is trying to get. There is a tiny hole in the boat head for dipping water or ink.

65. Jar with Dragon and Phoenix Patterns, Cizhou Kiln

Yuan

Height: 36.3 cm Mouth Diameter: 21.5 cm Bottom Diameter: 14.5 cm

Unearthed from Pengcheng, Fengfeng Mining Area, Handan, Hebei

Preserved in the Handan Museum

This jar has a straight mouth, thick edges, wide shoulders and big stomach big in the upper and narrowing till the bottom. Glazed white, it is drawn with black patterns. The lines clearly separate the jar into three parts: shoulder, stomach and bottom. The shoulder is drawn with vines and flowers. On one side of the stomach is openwork with a dragon, the opposite side is drawn with phoenix and other birds, while the other two sides are decorated with patterns of flowers and curled grass. The bottom is decorated with lines and arch patterns.

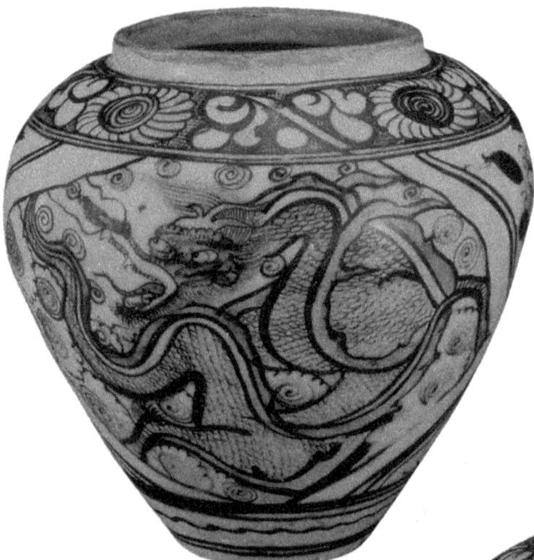

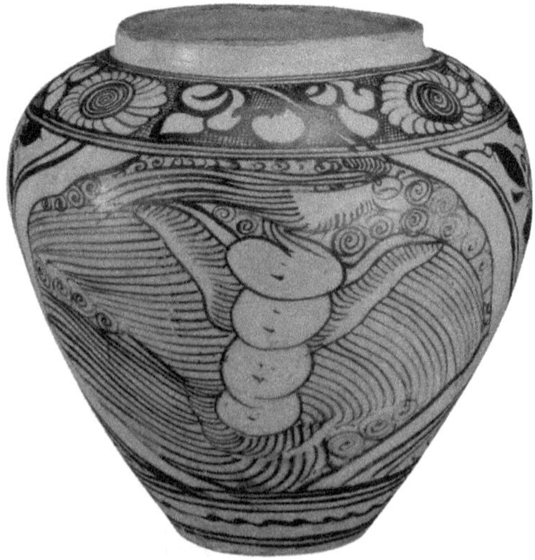

66. Vase with Two-phoenix Pattern with Four Knobs, Cizhou Kiln

Yuan
Height: 57.5 cm
Mouth Diameter: 13 cm
Bottom Diameter: 16.5 cm
Preserved in the Cixian Institute of Cultural Relics Protection and Management
This vase is glazed white in the upper part and black in the lower. It has a lip-like opening, straight neck, ring feet and a big stomach narrowing in the lower. On the neck, there are four knobs in the shape of leaves with veins. On the joints between neck and shoulder are tufts of grass. The shoulders are drawn with three circles in black glaze. On the stomach, openwork is seen with patterns of two phoenixes flying high.

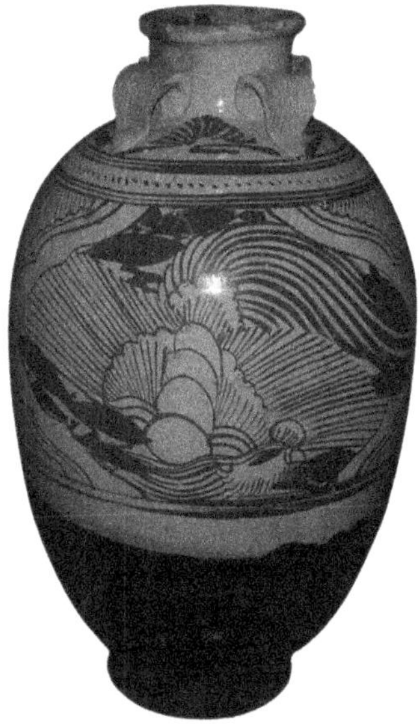

67. Pillow with Eagle-Chasing-Rabbit Pattern, Cizhou Kiln

Yuan
Height: 10.6-13 cm Length: 30.3 cm Width: 16.5 cm
Unearthed from Nanguan, Cixian, Handan, Hebei in 1993
Preserved in the Cixian Institute of Cultural Relics Protection and Management
This pillow is rectangle. With two tilting ends at the top, the pillow has straight walls and flat bottom. It is glazed white and drawn black and dark brown. There are outlines at the top and walls for the four sides. In the outline, there are flower patterns in the four corners and openwork with lozenge in the center, depicting an eagle chasing a rabbit. The front wall has openwork with bamboo and twig patterns while the back wall is drawn with peonies. The other two side walls are drawn with the lotus.

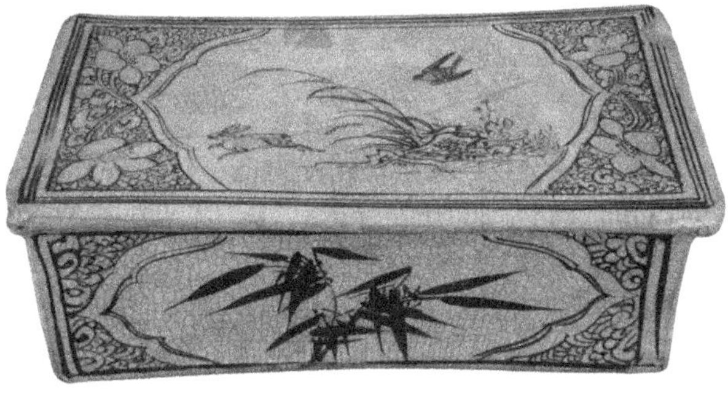

68. Plum Vase, Jun Kiln

Yuan

Height: 37 cm Mouth Diameter: 4.2 cm Bottom Diameter: 7 cm

Preserved in the Hebei Museum

This vase has a grey and white body, fined and thick. It is heavily glazed moon-white, simple yet elegant. The vase has a little mouth, short neck, sloping shoulder, long and round stomach and red and non-glazed ring feet. Its body is decorated with five mauve spots.

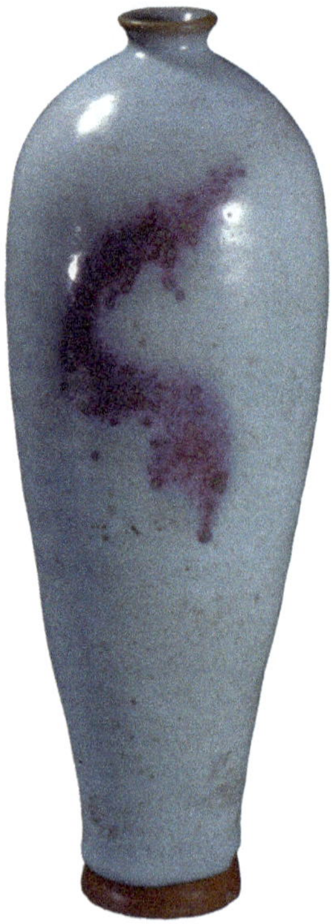

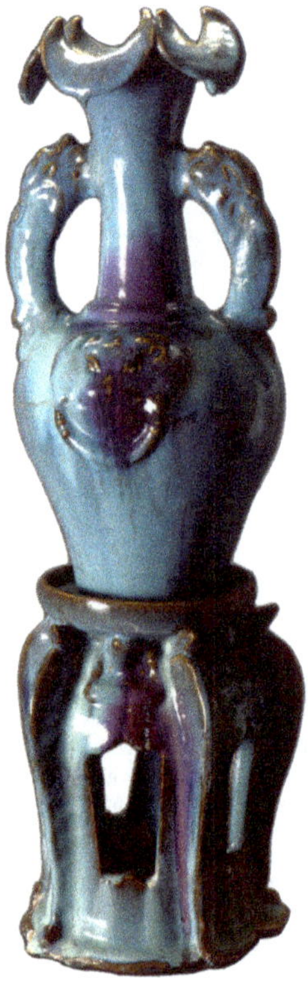

69. Vase with Two Knobs and Pedestal, Jun Kiln

Yuan

Height: 64 cm Mouth Diameter: 15 cm Bottom Diameter: 17 cm

Unearthed from Xinjiekou, Xicheng, Beijing in 1971

Preserved in the Capital Museum

This vase is heavily glazed sky-blue, with a number of irregular mauve and blue and dark brown spots. It consists of vase and pedestal. With a petal-shaped mouth, it has a slender neck, plump shoulder, big stomach and narrowed bottom. On the joints between neck and shoulder are two knobs in the shape of the Capricorn. On the stomach, there are two tiger-head-shaped knockers. The pedestal is hollowly carved with five columns in beast shape. At the top of each column is a guardian.

70. Incense Burner with Convex Dragon Carvings, Jun Kiln

Yuan

Height: 42.7 cm Mouth Diameter: 25.5 cm

Unearthed from Hohhot, Inner Mongolia in 1970

Preserved in the Inner Mongolia Museum

This incense burner is glazed heavily sky-blue. The glaze flow traces are seen on the burner. It has the straight mouth and tilting edge, straight neck, big stomach, and round bottom connected to the three feet in beast shape. At the mouth, there are two rectangular knobs in symmetry. The part between neck and stomach has a pair of knobs in beast shape. On the neck are paste-on-paste dragon patterns and an inscription in square shape, with 15 Chinese characters in regular script stating that "On the15 day of the Jiyou Year (1309), Xiaosong built a censer by himself". On the stomach, there are patterns of beast face and knocker with loop.

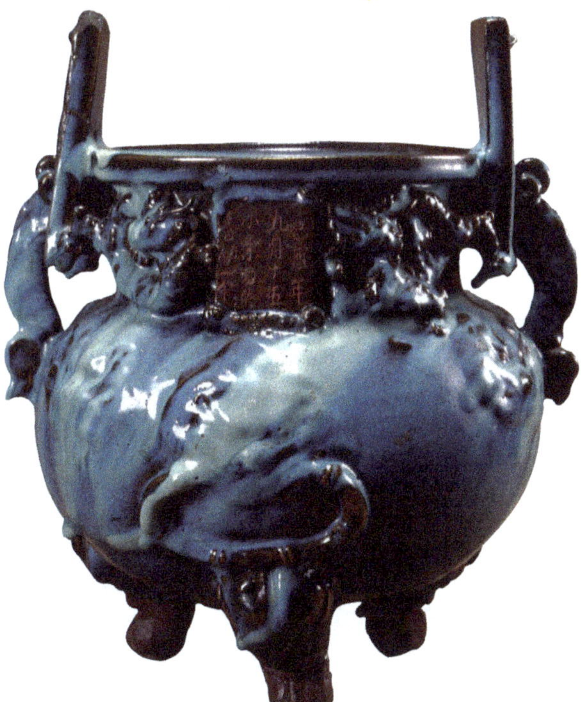

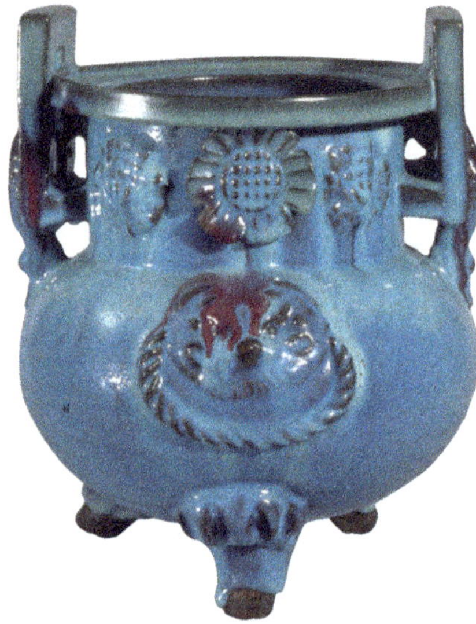

71. Incense Burner with Three Feet, Jun Kiln

Yuan
Height: 35.8 cm
Mouth Diameter: 23.9 cm
Preserved in the Shanghai Museum
This incense burner has a grey body, thick and heavy. It is glazed sky-blue and the foot bottom is not glazed. It has a wide mouth, straight neck, big stomach and three feet tilting outward as support. There are two beast-shaped rings on the stomach and paste-on-paste of sunflower in the neck.

72. Big Basin with Violet Spots, Jun Kiln

Yuan
Height: 10.9 cm Mouth Diameter: 45.5 cm Bottom Diameter: 18 cm
Unearthed from Baoding, Hebei in 1955
Preserved in the Hebei Museum
This toiletry set has a heavy and rough body, grey and white. It is glazed moon-white but the flat bottom is not glazed. The basin is wide in mouth with the folded rim. Along the edge of the mouth, there is a circle of violet patterns inside and outside.

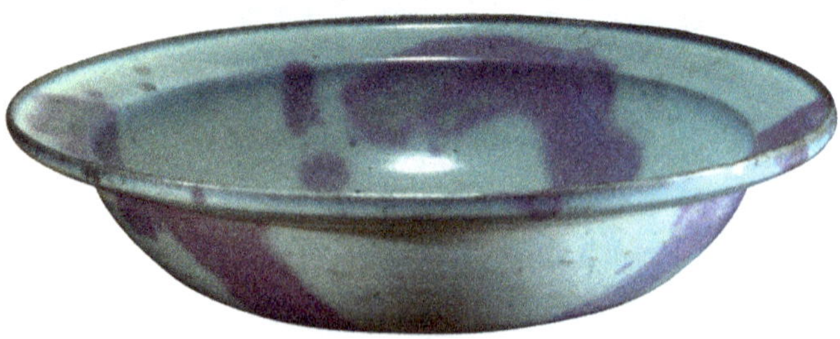

Painting

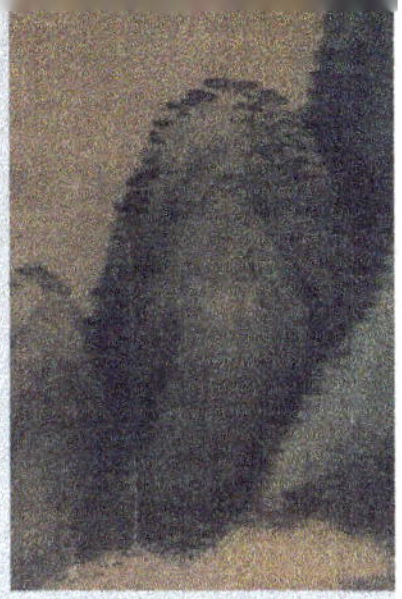

In the Yuan Dynasty, there was nothing like the Imperial Painting Academy that emerged in the Five Dynasties and continued during the Northern and Southern Song Dynasties. Although some painters were recruited to serve the imperial court, the number was small and their status humble. What's more, the system was far less inclusive than that of Song Dynasty. Therefore, the imperial paintings in the Yuan Dynasty were less creative and mainly inherited the style of the Tang and Song Dynasties with few innovations. Literati paintings were rooted among the people and gradually occupied the mainstream.

Art of the Yuan Dynasty featured landscape painting. At the outset, Qian Xuan, Zhao Mengfu and Gao Kegong were the three main representatives of landscape painting and became known as the "Three Outstanding Painters" of the period. Their styles differed but they all renounced the Palace Style of the Song Dynasty and instead carried forward the style of the Blue and Green landscape or 'The Misty Mountain' ascribed to Mi Fu (1051-1107), one of the great Song calligraphers. They also created a new atmosphere combines the Hang and Li styles. In the middle and at the end of Yuan Dynasty there appeared Huang Gongwang, Wu Zhen, Wang Meng, Ni Zan, who were named the "Four Great Painters of the Yuan Dynasty" who greatly admired the Southern School style developed by Dong Yuan and Ju Ran in the Five Dynasties to Mi Fu and Mi Youren in the Northern Song Dynasty, and introduced many innovations based on the earlier work to become models of later ages. Based on the teachings of different masters, other painters can be divided into following groups: Cao Zhibai，Tang Di and Zhu Derun who were influenced by Li Cheng and Guo Xi in the earlier period and taught by Zhao Mengfu; Sheng Mao，Lu Guang，Ma Wan and Fang Congyi, who cherished the work of Dong Yuan and Ju Ran in the Five-dynasty period and were influenced by the Zhao Mengfu，Huang Gongwang and Gao Kegong in the same Dynasty; Sun Junze who learned from the style of Ma Yuan and Xia Gui in the Southern Song Dynasty; Wang Zhenpeng, Li Rongjin, Xia Yong, and so on, who excelled at Pavilion Jiehua (drawing lines with the aid of a ruler in the drawing of palatial buildings). The main change in Yuan landscape painting was a rendering from emphasizing the geomorphic features of landscape and inner structure before to taking landscape as a means of creating empathy and thus greatly showing painters' personalities and character. With the painting skill transferring from painting realistically to painting abstractly and from painting with great delicacy to painting simply, landscape paintings in the Yuan Dynasty opened a new style of far-reaching influence in the Ming and Qing Dynasties.

Flower-and-bird paintings also witnessed new development. Painters, like Qian Xuan, Chen Lin, Wang Yuan etc., changed the palace style of painting these with great colors and delicacy into the technique of using ink and wash or in light colors with freshness and elegance. More masters painted plum blossoms, orchids, bamboos and stones, among whom the most famous bamboo and stone painters were Li Kan, Ke Jiusi, Gu An, Zhao Mengfu, Gao Kegong, Wu Zhen; the masters of ink-plum-blossom paintings were Zou Fulei and Wang Mian. The reasons for the appearance of flower-and-bird paintings in ink and wash and paintings of plum blossoms, orchids, bamboos and stones were as follows: first, aesthetic ideas changed at that time; second, it was suitable for literati painters to express feelings with ink and brush. These painters strived for techniques that would be natural and unpolished, taking quiet color as the best option along with elegant couplets that together made had much impact on later generations.

Figure paintings in the Yuan Dynasty were few and far between. The main reason was that most painters hold an indifferent attitude towards life. However, there appeared some painters of unique style or reaching high levels. Except for Qian Xuan and Zhao Mengfu of the "Three Outstanding Painters in Early Yuan Dynasty", there were the likes of He Cheng, Liu Guandao and etc. in this period, and Ren Renfa, Zhang Wo, Yan Hui, Wang Jiang and etc. in the middle and later Yuan Dynasty.

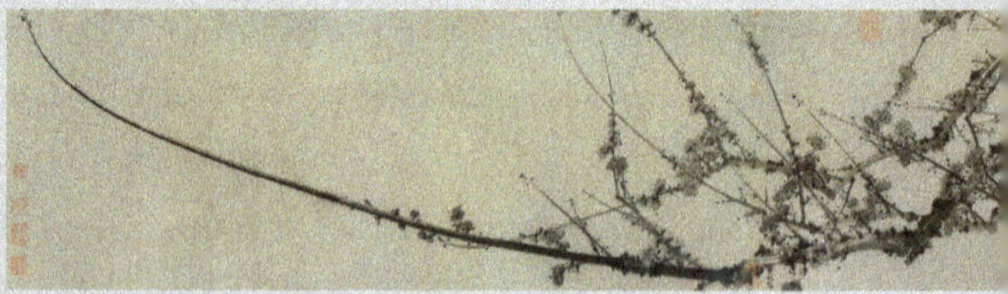

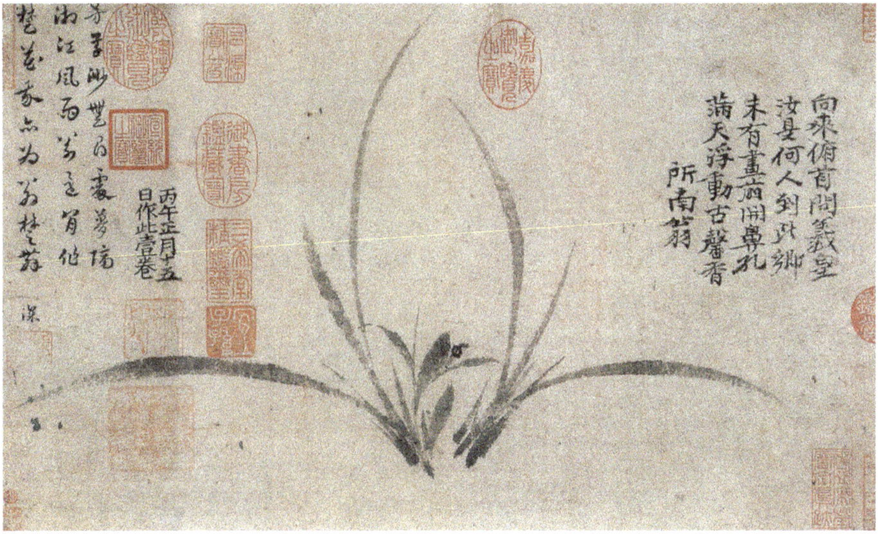

73. Zheng Sixiao: Ink Orchid

Yuan

Length: 25.7 cm   Width: 42.4 cm

Preserved in the Osaka Art Museum in Japan

Paper, ink. It paints a bunch of ink orchid consisting of several leaves and two orchids. The composition is neat with the orchids full and the leaves uncrossed. Every brushstroke is smooth and vigorous, indirect but changeable. There is a poem in the painting which bears the mark "Father Suonan" (his style name) and the year of 1306 and has two official seals. Chen Shen and Wang Mian were among those writing the preface. It also carries the seals of the collectors Song Luo in the Qing Dynasty and the Imperial Palace of the Qing Dynasty and recorded by the *Precious Collection of the Stone Moat Squel: First Edition*.

Zheng Sixiao (1241-1318 or 1239-1316): courtesy name Yi Weng, style name Suo Nan and San Waiyeren, a native of Lianjiang County (present-day part of Fujian). After the Song Dynasty was overthrown, he remained secluded to Pingjiang (present-day Suzhou City in Jiangsu). He excelled at ink orchid and bamboo.

74. Qian Xuan: Eight Flowers Painting Scroll

Yuan

Length: 29.4 cm Width: 333.9 cm

Preserved in the Palace Museum in Beijing

Paper, tint. There are eight kinds of flowers. Before color filling, the petals and leaves were delineated with thin lines while the calyx was tinted with thick ink. The picture is vivid with an elegant writing technique and delicate coloring best showing the tenderness of flowers and the freshness of the leaves. It is sealed with "Shun Ju". At the end of the volume, there is the preface and postscript and seal of Zhao Mengfu in the Yuan Dynasty.

Qian Xuan (1239-1299): courtesy name Sun Ju, style name Yu Tan, Xun Feng, Old Man Qing Qu, Father Xi Lan, Father Zhaxi and etc., a native of Wuxing district in Zhejiang. He is renowned as one of the “Eight Outstanding Literati in Wuxing” with Zhao Mengfu and etc. by his poems, paintings and calligraphy. He excelled at paintings of landscape, flower-and-bird, figure and other domains.

75. Qian Xuan: Fuyun Mountain

Yuan

Length: 29.6 cm Width: 98.7 cm

Preserved in the Shanghai Museum

Paper, light tint. This depicts Fuyun Mountain in Zhachuan (in the Wuxing district of Zhejiang) where the author once lived in seclusion. He used straight lines to delineate the stones so that the sunny side and the shadowy side and the grain of the stone can be clearly shown. Among the trees are light-green water weeds. This is his magnum opus among landscape paintings. There is a poem and a mark in the painting. At the end of the scroll, there are the postscripts by Chou Yuan, Zhang Yu, Huang Gongwang, Ni Zan in the Yuan Dynasty and by people in the Qing Dynasty. It was collected by people in the Yuan Dynasty, Ming Dynasty, Qing Dynasty and by the Imperial Palace of the Qing Dynasty and recorded in the *Shan Hu Wang, Category of Ancient Famous Paintings, Collective Study on Shigutang Calligraphy and Paintings, Pei Wen Zhai Painting and Calligraphy, Spectacular Life, List of Grand View* and *Moyuan Huiguan*.

76. Qian Xuan:Life at West Lake

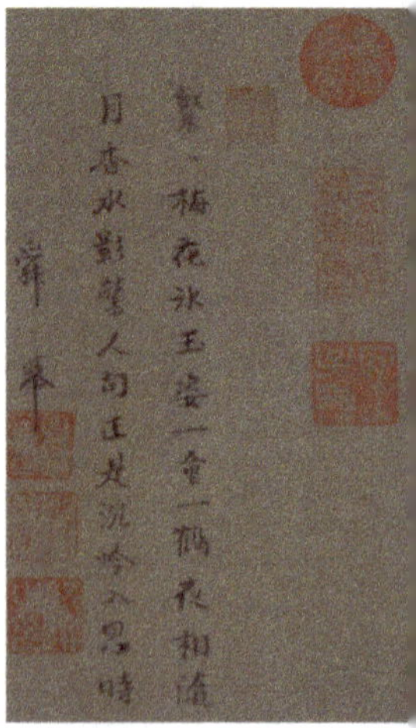

Yuan

Length: 25 cm Width: 72.5 cm

Preserved in the Palace Museum in Beijing

Paper, tint. The painting draws material from the poet Lin Hejing who secluded himself in the Gushan Mountain by the Hangzhou West Lake and lived his whole life with the plum tree as his wife and cranes as his children. The painting is simple and quiet with no background and fine line drawing technique, which is the magnum opus among the painter’s figure paintings. There is a poem, a mark and a seal in the painting. The Imperial Palace of the Qing Dynasty added seals several times. The preface bears Zheng Yongyan’s inscription and the postscript carries the signatures of the Xizhai Study, Shi Hongdao, and so on.

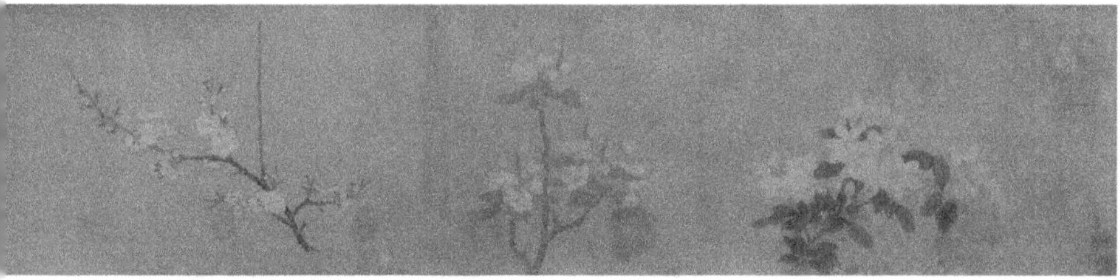

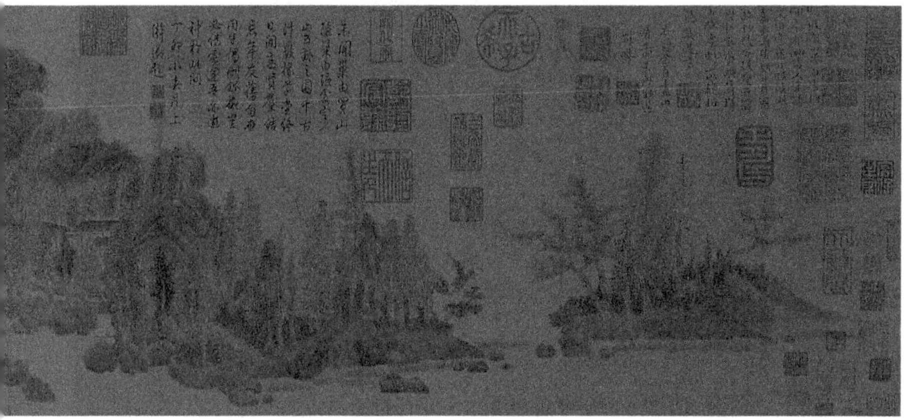

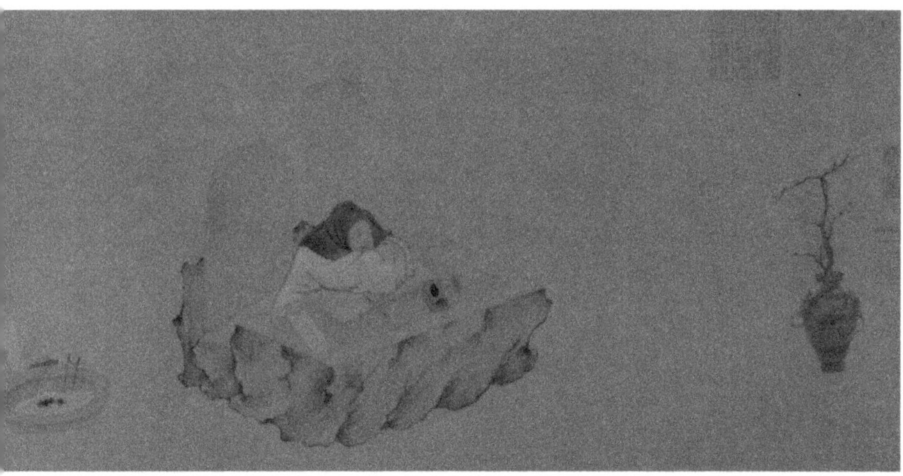

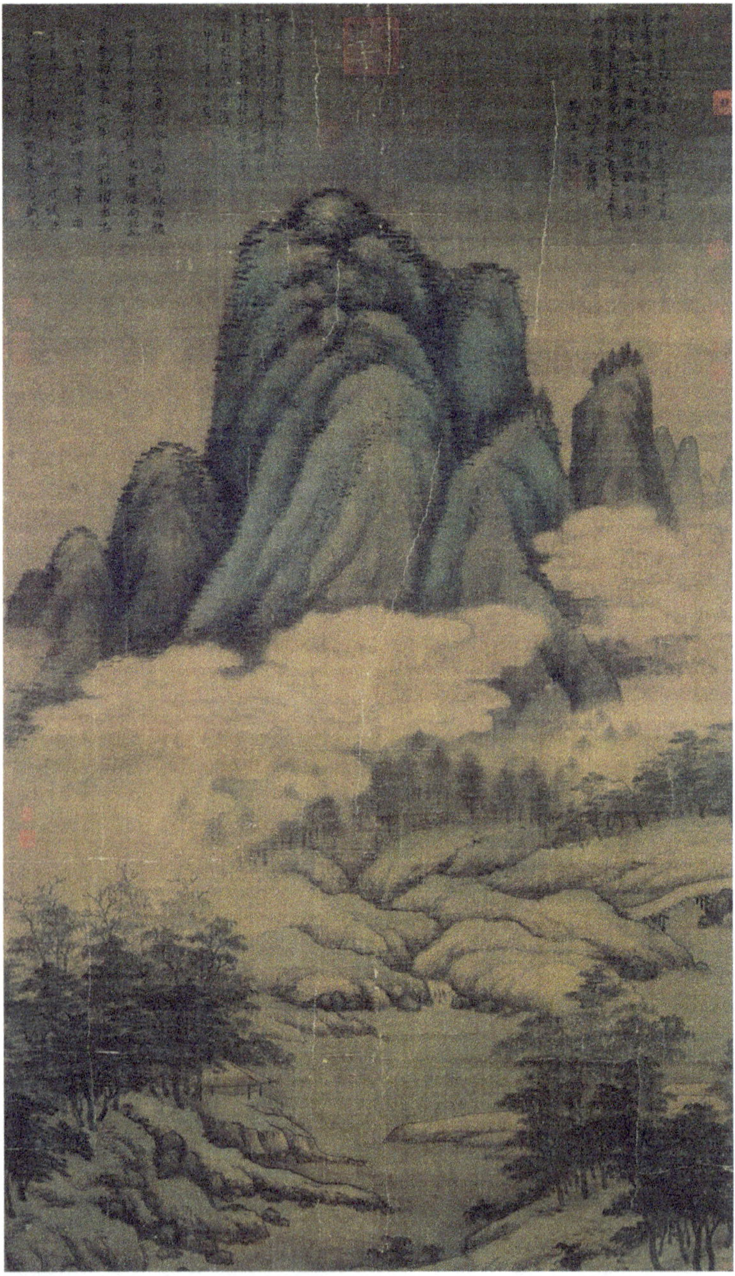

77. Gao Kegong: Yunheng Ridge

Yuan

Length: 182.3 cm Width: 106.7 cm

Preserved in the Palace Museum in Taipei

Silk scroll, tint. It shows the ridge and trees in the clouds, the stream, the bridge, the pavilion and the hut -. mountains aloft, ridges in the clouds, and verdant trees. The ridge is painted with a dry brush and the top is dotted with green color. The draping linen brushstroke is used to paint the stones and angles of the slope before they are colored. The drawing technique is clear and imposing, with the ink dripping and the painting style vigorous and elegant. It is the masterpiece of Gao's later life, which bears the preface and postscript of Li Kan, Deng Wenyuan, Wang Duo and the seals of Liang Qingbiao and An Qi in the Qing Dynasty and of the Imperial Palace of the Qing Dynasty. It is recorded in the *Moyuan Huiguan Study's Paintings* and the *Precious Collection of the Stone Moat Sequel*.

78. Gao Kegong: Ink Bamboo and Stones

Yuan

Length: 122 cm Width: 42.3 cm

Preserved in the Palace Museum in Beijing

Paper, ink. It depicts two bamboo plants. The bamboo branches echo each other and the bamboo leaves divide themseLues by color with the lighter ones at the front and the darker behind. At the foot of the bamboo, there are stones that are delineated. This painting is Gao's only extant bamboo painting. It bears the mark "Made for Zijing by Kegong"and seal "Yanjing". On the right side, there is a poem by Zhao Mengfu, his seal and six seals of the collectors. This painting is recorded in the *List of Grand View* and the *Records of Jiangcun Xiaoxia*.

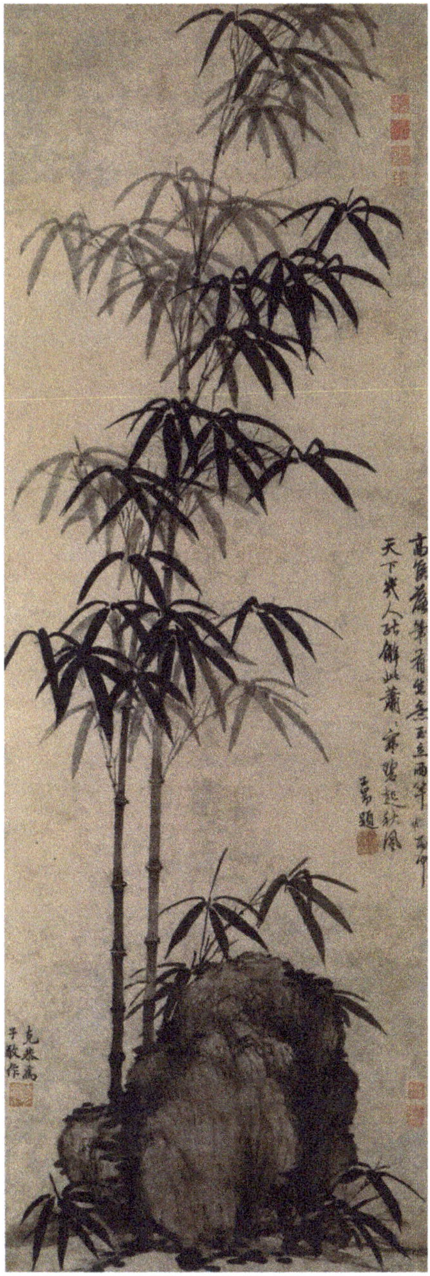

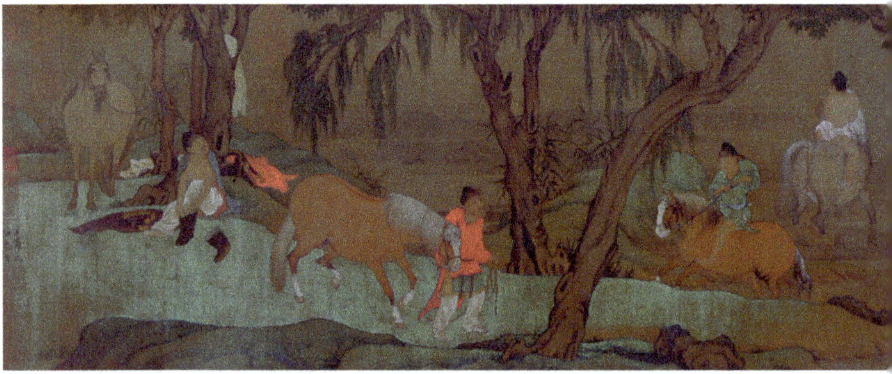

79. Zhao Mengfu: Bathing Horses

Yuan

Length: 28.1 cm Width: 155.5 cm

Preserved in the Palace Museum in Beijing

Silk scroll, tint. It presents a view of trees and a stream in autumn where hostlers are bathing their horses, whch are either standing or crouching, each with a different pose. The grain of the hostlers'clothes is clear and smooth and the outline of the trees and slopes are simple with the color fresh and elegant. It bears the mark "made for He Zhi by Zi Ang"and the poem and seal of Emperor Qianlong. At the end of the scroll are the seals of Wang Zhicheng and others in the Ming Dynasty. It is recorded in the Precious Collection of the Stone Moat Sequel.

Zhao Mengfu (1254-1322): courtesy name Zi Ang, style name Song Xue, Oubo, Shuijinggong Daoren, a native of Wuxing County (present-day Huzhou City in Zhejiang). He was a descendant of the Song Dynasty's imperial family and the eleventh descendant of Emperor Song Taizu. He was a profound scholar, who excelled at poetry, calligraphy, painting, music, among which painting and calligraphy were the best.

80. Zhao Mengfu: Pasturing Horses at the Autumn Dusk

Yuan

Length: 23.6 cm Width: 59 cm

Preserved in the Palace Museum in Beijing

Silk scroll, tint. It depicts a view of early autumn south of the Yangtze River, when the trees are withering away. A hostler in red is washing a horse by the river. There are ten horses in the picture, which are strong and with different bearings. This painting is gaudy and the line of horses are full and vigorous more in the style of calligraphy, an inheritance from the Tang Dynasty. As the masterpiece among the horse and figure paintings in Zhao's later life, it is named as Pasturing Horses at Autumn Dusk with the date November in 1312, the signature "Zi Ang"and the seal "Zhaoshi Zi Ang". In the foreword, there are the note and seal from Emperor Qianlong. There is a preface and postscript and seals by Ke Jiusi in the Yuan Dynasty, Emperor Qianlong, and Wang Youdun. It is recorded in Wang's Coral Net, Peiwen Study's Paintings, Shigu Study's Collection of Paintings, Da Guanlu (Wu Sheng's Review of Paintings), and so on.

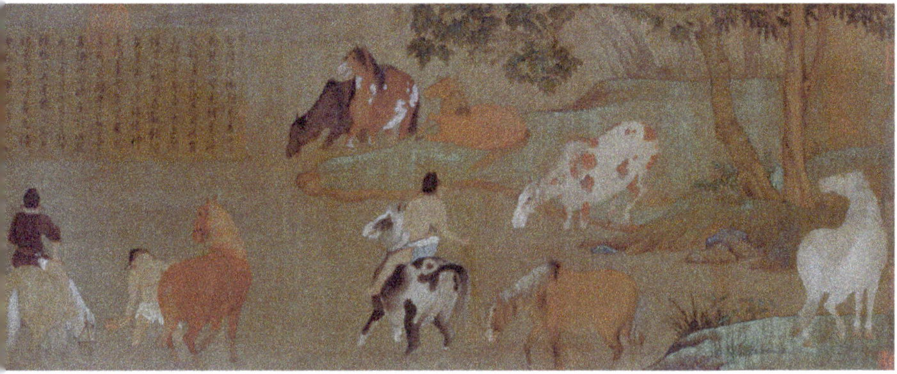

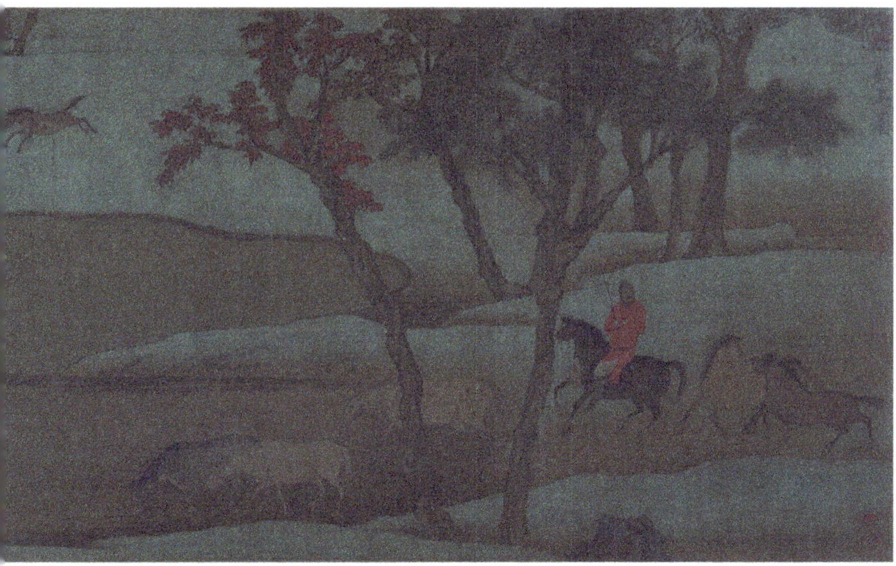

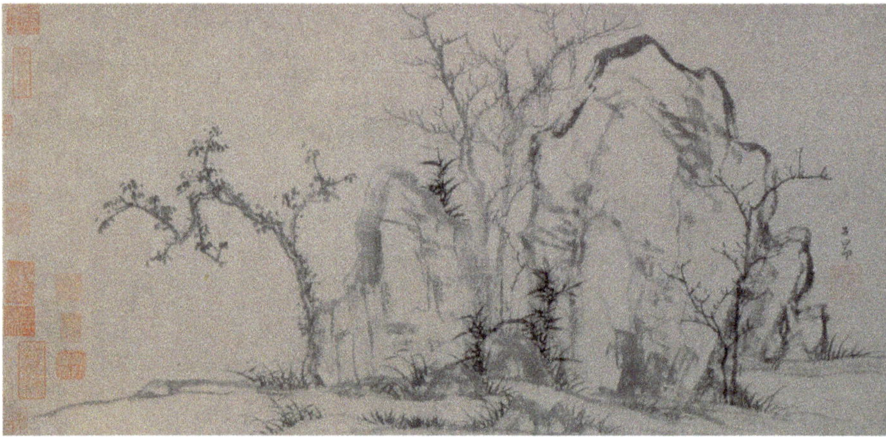

81. Zhao Mengfu: Stones and Trees

Yuan

Length: 27.5 cm Width: 62.8 cm

Preserved in the Palace Museum in Beijing

Paper, ink. It paints a huge smooth slope stone with old trees on the two sides. It employs the calligraphy style characterized by hollow strokes, cracks the surface of the stones and draws the brunches and twigs with seal character and character in the Zhou Dynasty, which is the masterpiece of Zhao's bamboo-and-stone paintings. It bears the signature "Zi Ang" and his seal. At the end of the scroll, there is a poem, short remarks by Ke Jiusi and Wei Su in the Yuan Dynasty and 34 collectors' seals. It is recorded in the *Sequel of Paintings of Xuzhai Studio* and the *Precious Collection of the Stone Moat Sequel: First Edition*.

82. Zhao Mengfu: Village by the River

Yuan

Length: 24.9 cm Width:120.5 cm

Preserved in the Palace Museum in Beijing

Paper, tint. It depicts a village by the river. A draping linen brushstroke is used to paint the hills with light ink and changeable strokes. The moss is dotted with light ink and the trees with dark color. The river is delicate and vivid. This is a masterpiece among Zhao's ink landscape paintings. The scroll bears the date "November of the sixth year (1302) of Da De", the note "painting for Qian Dejun" and the signature "Zi Ang". At the end of the scroll, there are notes from 48 people, Deng Chun and Jue Feisou in the Yuan Dynasty, Dong Qichang, Chen Jiru in the Ming Dynasty and so on. It is recorded in the *Fencing Coral, Calligraphy and Painting Boat on the Qinghe River, Preface to Shan Hu Wang, Collective Study on Shigutang Calligraphy and Paintings*, and *Precious Collection of the Stone Moat Sequel: First Edition*.

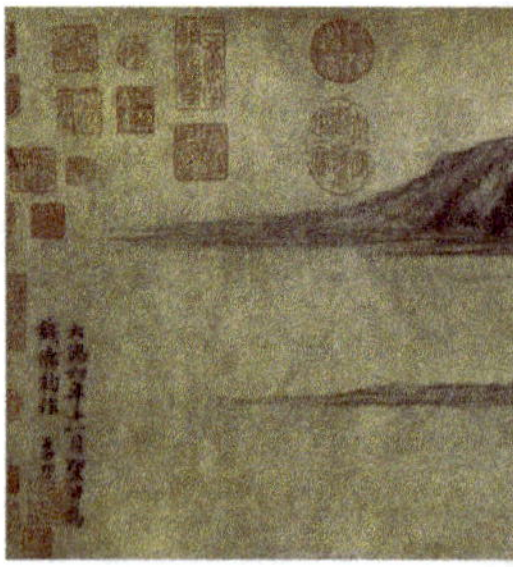

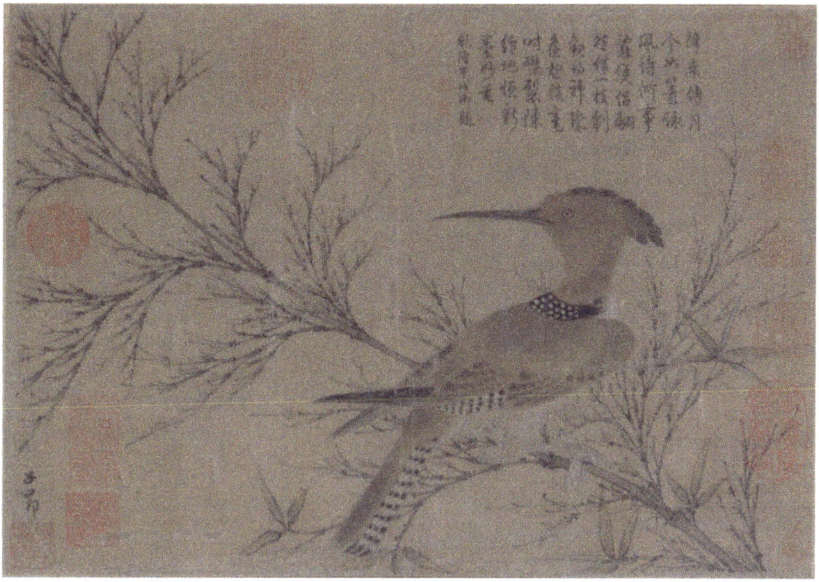

83. Zhao Mengfu: A Hoopoe in a Secluded Bamboo Grove
Yuan
Length: 25.4 cm Width: 36.2 cm
Preserved in the Palace Museum in Beijing
Silk scroll, light tint. It shows a hoopoe on a bamboo pole. The bamboo is drawn by tracing the contour of the strokes and the hoopoe by coloring directly without using the brush to delineate its bone sructure first. It is tinted with the hoopoe with light ochre yellow, clean and bright, which is the masterpiece of Zhao's flower-and-bird paintings. The scroll bears the signature "Zi Ang" and the seal "Zhaoshi Zi Ang". Emperor Qianlong wrote a poem on it with his own seal and the seal of the Imperial Palace of the Qing Dynasty. In the foreword, there are a note and seal from the Emperor Qianlong and seven seals from other collectors. At the end of the scroll are poems by Ni Zan, Hu Yan, and so on. This painting is recorded in the Precious Collection of the Stone Moat Sequel.

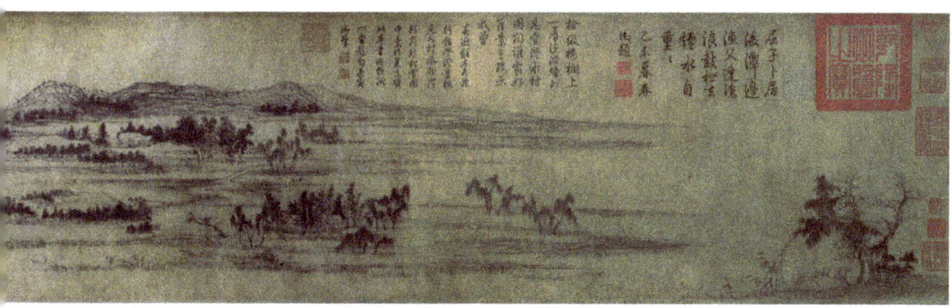

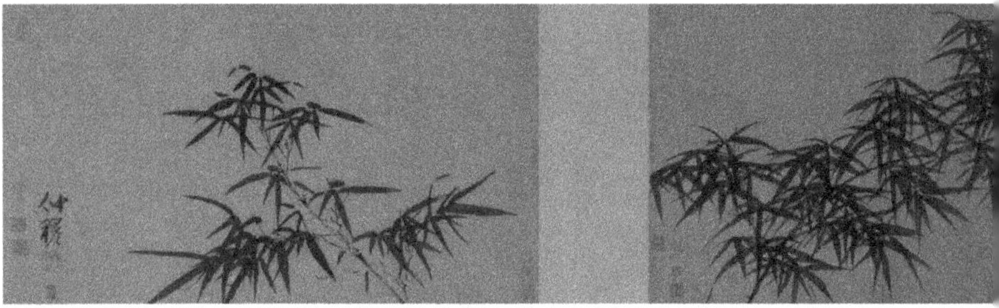

84. Zhao's Family: Three Bamboo Twigs

Yuan
Length: 34 cm   Width: 108 cm
Preserved in the Palace Museum in Beijing

Silk scroll, ink. Three twigs are painted by Zhao Mengfu, his wife Guan Daosheng, and their son Zhao Yong respectively. The first twig is painted by Zhao Mengfu in calligraphy style, vigorous, full and smooth, which bears the date "the first year (1321) of Zhi Zhi"and his seal. The second twig is painted by Guan Daosheng and bears her signature and seal. The strokes are powerful and the leaves intensive. The third twig is painted by Zhao Yong, bearing his signature and seal. The strokes are smooth and show clearly the family style. At the end of the scroll, there is a preface and postscript by Du Mu, Zhou Tianqiu, Wang Zhideng and several collectors' seals.

Guan Daosheng (1262-1319), courtesy name Zhong Ji, a native of Huzhou City in Zhejiang, wife of Zhao Mengfu, titled as Lady of Wei State. She excelled at painting ink bamboo, plum blossom and orchid, and was also the first to create the technique of painting bamboo shoots.

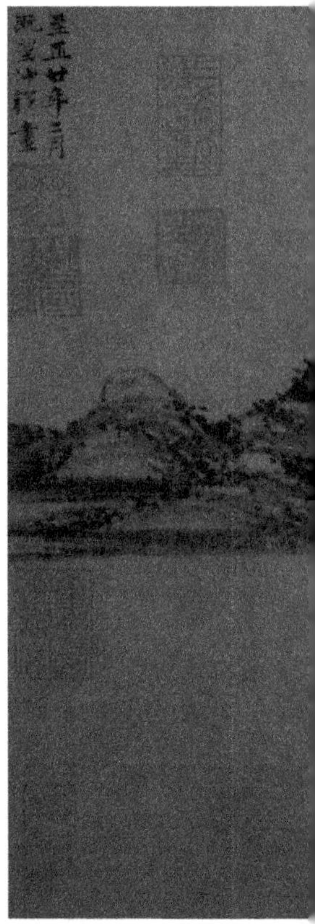

85. Zhao Yong: An Old Pine Tree and Fisherman

Yuan
Length: 30 cm   Width: 52.8 cm
Preserved in the Palace Museum in Beijing

Paper, ink. It depicts an old pine tree by a stone with its twig wound in the shape of the dragon. The pine tree is alone with grass's company. On the lake, there is an old man who is fishing with rolling mountains as the background. The pine tree is painted with the tip of a writing brush, powerful and simple. The stone is painted with the dripping strokes, mild and clear. The old man is drawn with the line drawing. It is the masterpiece of Zhao's landscape paintings, which bears the date "the twentieth year (1360) of Zhi Zheng", his seal, a poem from Emperor Qianlong and seals from collectors. It was collected by the Imperial Palace of the Qing Dynasty, Li Zhaoheng, An Qi and etc.

Zhao Yong (1289-about 1361), courtesy name Zhong Mu, a native of Huzhou City (present-day belongs to Zhejiang), son of Zhao Mengfu. He is a poet good at appreciation. He learned painting from his father, excelling at landscape painting and horse paintings.

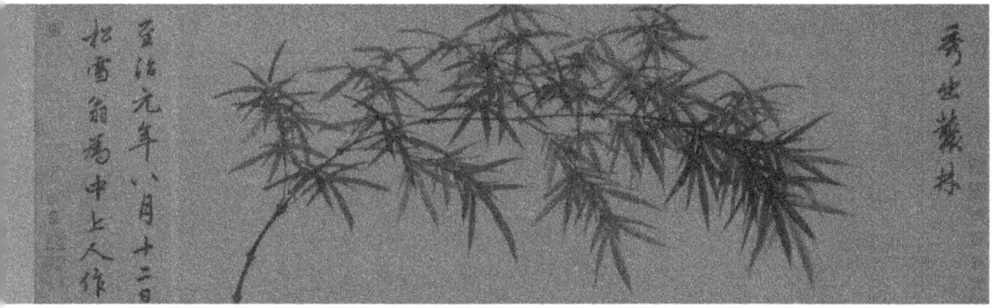
秀出叢林
至治元年八月十二
松雪翁為中上人作

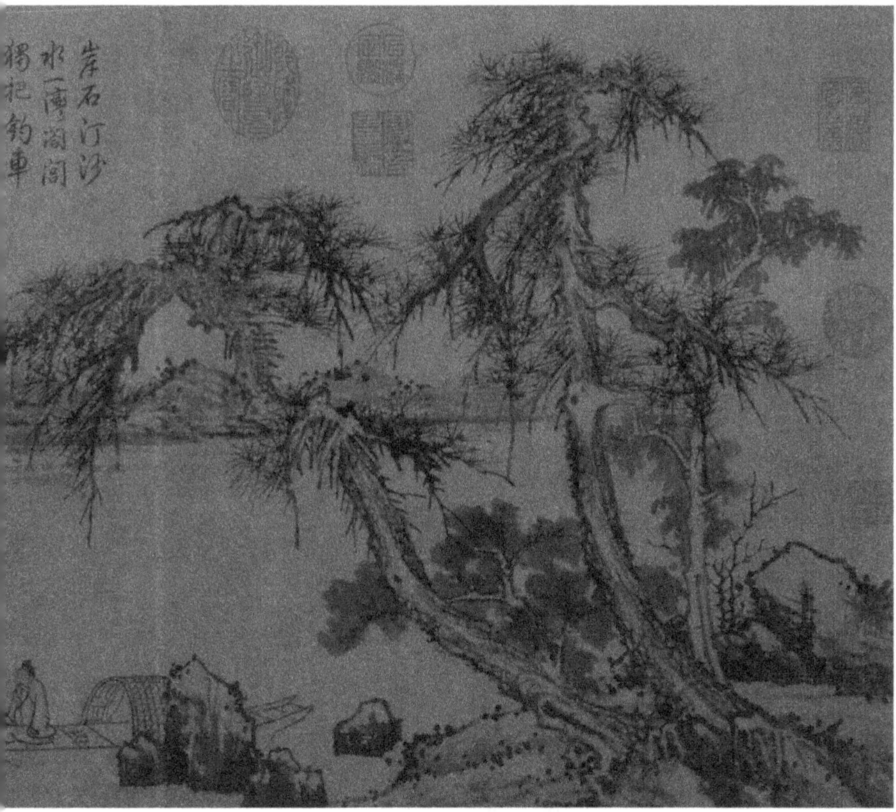
岸石汀沙

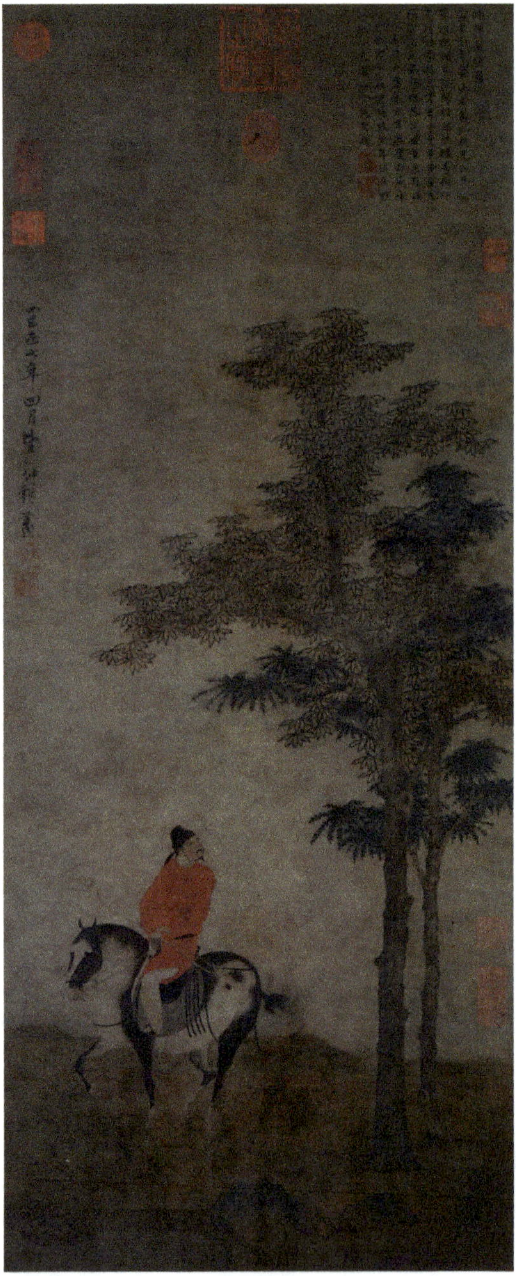

86. Zhao Yong: Shooting from Horseback

Yuan

Length: 109 cm Width: 46.3 cm

Preserved in the Palace Museum in Beijing

Paper, tint. It depicts a man on a horse in a red robe and a black hat carrying a bow in his left hand against a background of tall trees. The man and the horse are painted with thin strokes and light ink, which are tinted with bright colors. The leaves are drawn by tracing the contour of the strokes or dotted with ink. It is the masterpiece among Zhao Yong's figure-and-horse paintings, which bears the date "the fourth month of the seventh year (1347) of Zhi Zheng"and the note "painted by Zhong Mu". Nai Xian in the Yuan Dynasty wrote a poem and placed his seal on it. Also, there are nine seals of the Imperial Palace of the Qing Dynasty. This painting is recorded in the *Precious Collection of the Stone Moat Sequel: Third Edition*.

87. Huang Gongwang: Heaven Pool and Steep Rock

Yuan

Length: 139.4 cm Width: 57.3 cm

Preserved in the Palace Museum in Beijing

Silk scroll, light purple tint. It depicts Tianchi Mountain in Wu County of West Suzhou. Lofty and far-reaching perspectives are adopted in its composition. It portrays the shades and texture of rocks and mountains by pi ma cun (wrinkling technique). It often tints with the mixture of ocher, ink and green. This painting is signed "October, Zhiyuan the first year (1341). Painting of Heaven Pool and Steep Rock - painted by the Dachi Daoren (A Silly Taoist) at will, aged 73". It is inscribed by Liu Guanchang, and stamped by five people who possessed it at some time. It is recorded in *List of Grand View* and *Moral*, etc.

Huang Gongwang, (1269-1354), original name Lu Jian, native of Changshu, Jiangsu. He was orphaned by Huang Le of Yongjia, Zhejiang, and then changed his surname to Huang, with the style name Zijiu and sobriquets Yifeng (One Peak) and Dachi Daoren (A Silly Taoist). He was versed in calligraphy and poetry, good at Sanqu and proficient in rhyme. He was adept in painting landscapes, emulated the calligraphy of the Five Dynasties, and imitated the painting style of Song Dynasty. In his later years, he changed his technique of painting and developed a style of his own. He is known as the greatest of the "Four Great Masters of the Yuan".

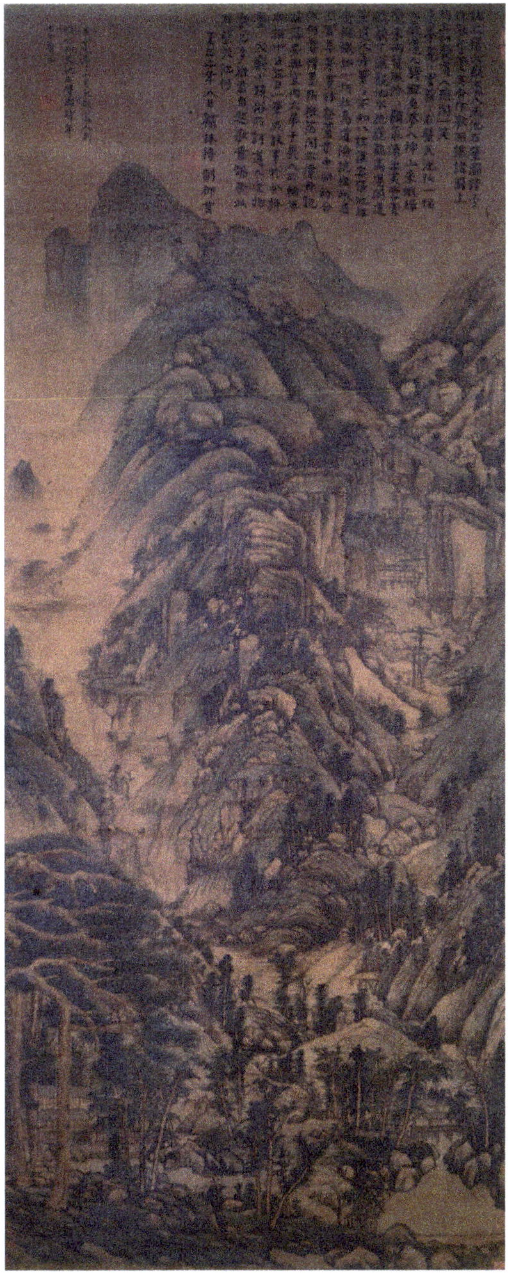

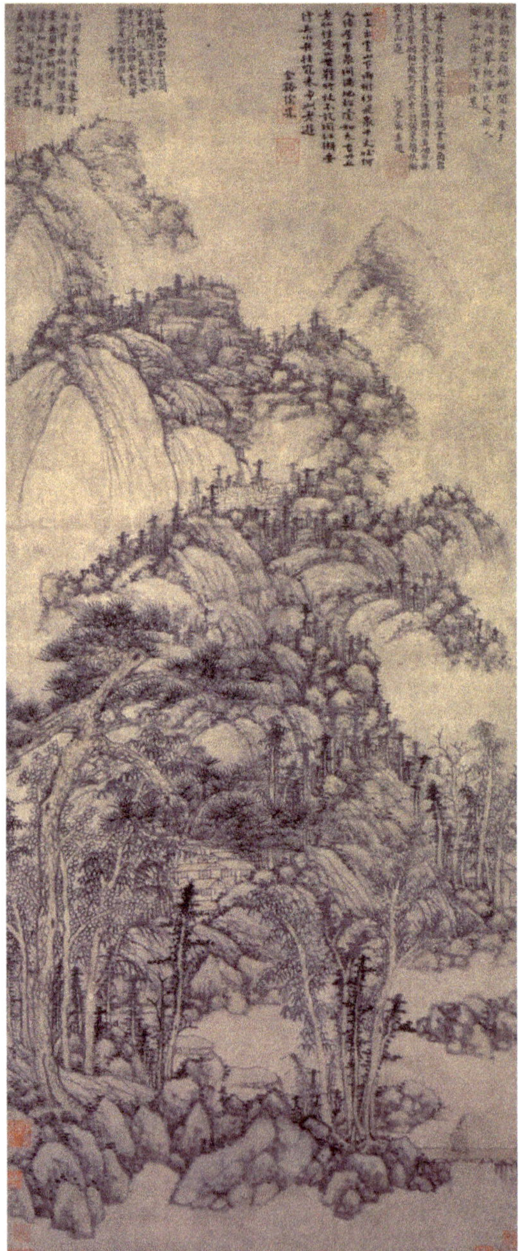

88. Huang Gongwang: Gorgeous Cliff and Beautiful Trees

Yuan

Length: 101.3 cm Width: 43.8 cm

Preserved in the Palace Museum in Beijing

Paper scroll, light purple tint. It depicts a distant circumstance of overlapping mountains and lush trees. The rocks and mountains are portrayed by pi ma cun (wrinkling technique), and the tree roots and the roofs are tinted with light ocher. Huang Gongwang created the technique of painting landscape with light ocher. Firstly, he made use of light and dark ink tonalities, an assortment of wet and dry brushwork to sketch contour and crack structure; then he tinted rocks, mountains and trees with light ocher; finally, he applied light cyanin to his drawing and then the painting was completed. It contains prefaces and postscripts from Zhang Zhu of Yuan Dynasty, Dong Qichang of Ming Dynasty, etc. It is recorded in Guoyunlou Shuhua Record.

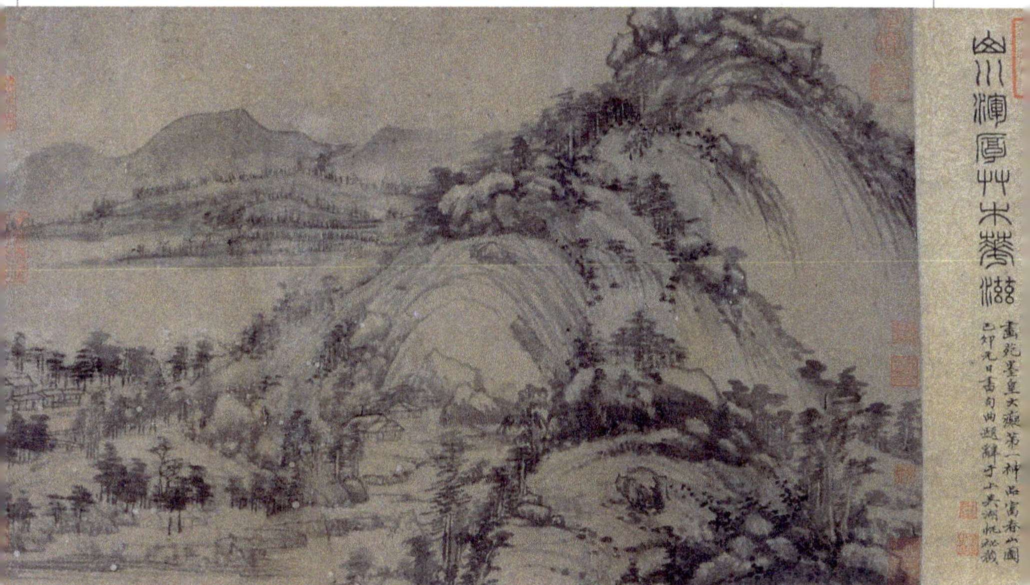

89. Huang Gongwang: Dwelling in the Fuchun Mountain—The Remaining Mountain

Yuan

Length: 31.8 cm   Width: 51.4 cm

Preserved in the Zhejing Provincial Museum

Paper scroll, ink painting. It is a part of the scroll-Dwelling in Fuchun Mountain. It depicts the scenery of hill, river, marsh and mountain. Painting of mountains and rocks often uses dry brush to chap and rub, and by the technique of pi ma cun produces a unique rendering. Trees and forests are often painted with brush dots and scattered ink. The magnificently beautiful forests seem ordinary while in essence it is magic. The simplest form, vigorous strokes and the vivid depiction of close shot and distant view, make it a masterpiece of landscape painting in the Yuan Dynasty.

Dwelling in the Fuchun Mountain took Huang Gongwang several years to complete it and it is presented to Master Wu Yong as a gift. In the early Qing Dynasty, it was collected by Wu Hongyu (Yongqing), who treasured it. Before he died, he asked for it to be burned; fortunately, it was rescued by his nephew Wu Zhendu, although the first section had been destroyed. The surviving part of the first section was renamed *The Remaining Mountain*; the second and longer section was renamed *The Master Wuyong Scroll*; and they are kept at two different places.

90. Huang Gongwang: Scroll Painting of Dwelling in the Fuchun Mountain—The Master Wuyong Scroll

Yuan

Length: 34.1 cm Width: 1088.5 cm

Preserved in the Palace Museum in Taipei

Paper scroll, ink painting. It depicts the idealized panorama on both sides of Fuchun Mountain in early autumn in the form of a handscroll. The composition changes endlessly in proper density. With humid ink, simple but profound scene, the vast stretches of Jiangnan landscape is perfectly presented. This painting is Huang Gongwang's greatest masterpiece of landscape painting. It was prefaced by Dong Qichang and Emperor Qianlong. And it was postscripted by Huang Gongwang himself, signing "Dachi Xueren wrote in Xia's Zhizhi hall", stamped. At the end of this paper scroll is a postscript by Shenzhou, Wenpeng, Wang Zhideng and Zhou Tianqiu of the Ming Dynasty, etc. It passed through the hands of Anqi of Qing Dynasty, Neifu (The imperial storehouse in the Qing Dynasty), etc. It is recorded in the *Precious Collection of the Stone Moat Sequel: Third Edition*.

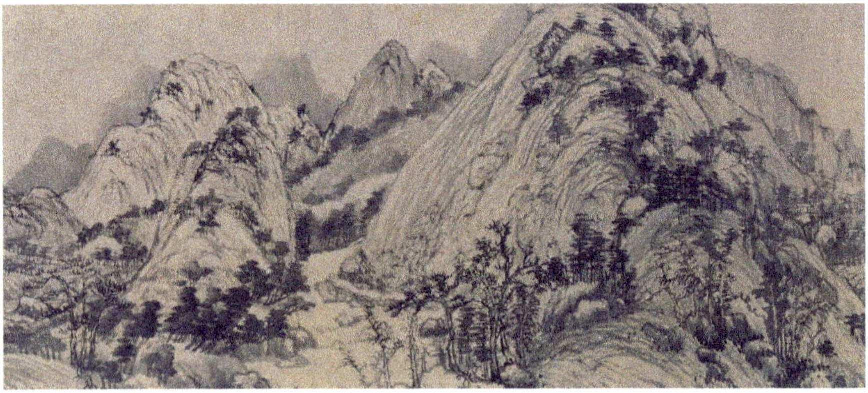

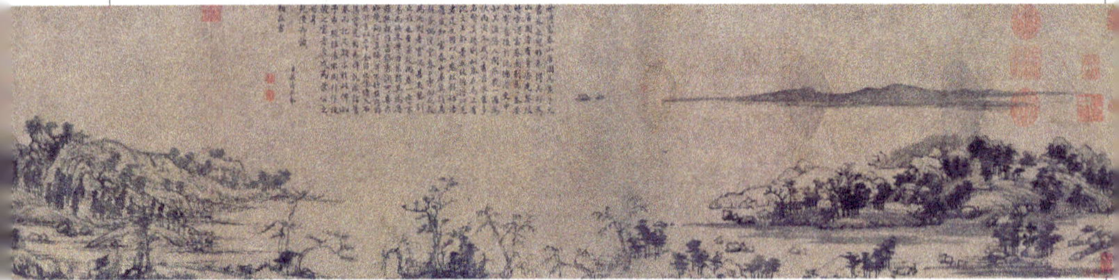

91. Wu Zhen Scroll Painting of a Fisherman

Yuan

Length: 84.7 cm Width: 29.7 cm

Preserved in the Palace Museum in Beijing

Silk scroll, ink painting. It depicts distant hills, flat ridges, mist, thick woods, streams, shoals, waterweeds, fishing boats and fishermen. Round strokes and gloomy ink of it present a significance of leisure and comfort. This painting is prefaced with a Yufu Ci, "August, Zhiyuan the second year (1336), autumn. Meihua Daoren painted four pictures of "The Fisherman: and wrote the inscription sealed with two stamps. It also contains eight stamps from its collectors. A Blank Page for Prefaces and Postscript has the inscription from Wang Duo of Qing Dynasty, stamped. It is recorded in the *Recording in Passing the Xinchou Summer*.

Wu Zhen (1280-354), with the style name Zhonggui and sobriquet Meihua Daoren, a native of Jiaxing in Zhejiang. He was versed in poetry and calligraphy, good at landscape, plum blossom, bamboo and rock. He is one of the "Four Great Masters of the Yuan".

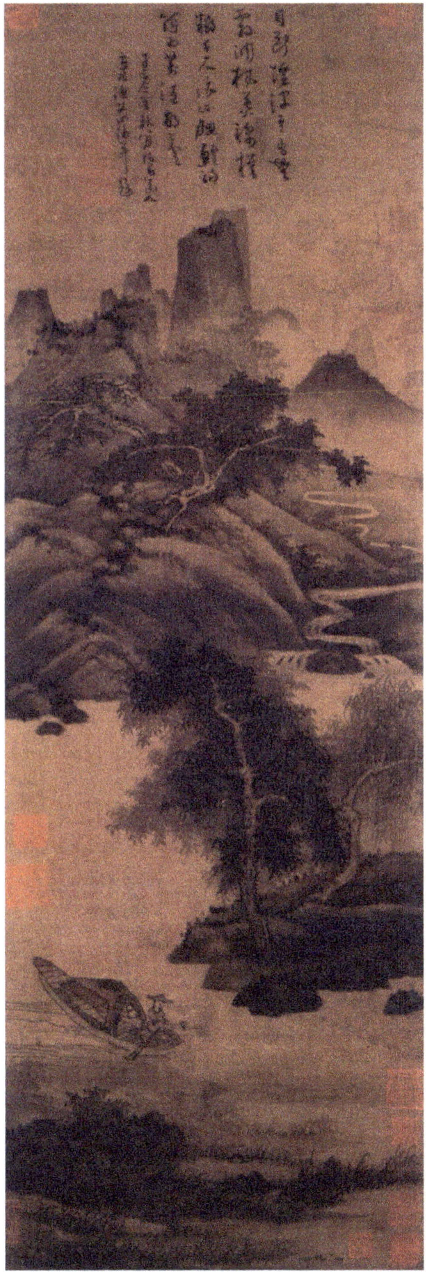

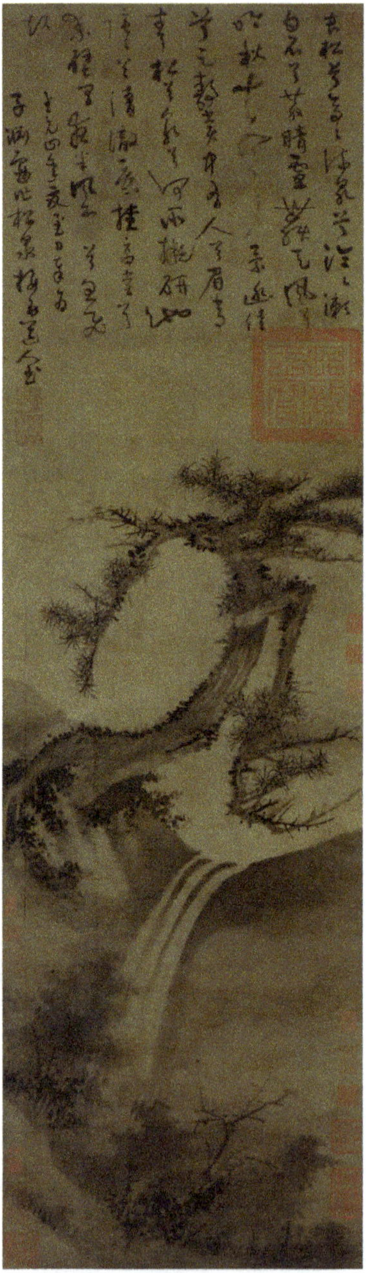

92.Wu Zhen Scroll Painting of Pipe Trees and Springs

Yuan

Length: 105.6 cm Width: 31.7 cm

Preserved in the Nanjing Museum

Paper scroll, ink painting. It depicts pine trees covering the hillside with a spring flowing down between them. The pipe tree trunks, sketched with bald writing brush, chapped and rubbed with dry ink, are both twisted and standing upright. Pine needles are portrayed with fine strokes. This painting has its own prefaced poem and signed: " at the summer solstice of Zhiyuan the fourth year(1338), painted pine trees and Springs for Ziyuan for fun, written by Meihua Daoren", stamped downside with "Meihua'an" and "Calligraphy and Painting Records." And it was stamped by many other collectors. The back of the scroll has a postscript by Sun Chengze, Gao Shiqi, Fan Zengxiang and Luo Zhenyu of the Qing Dynasty, etc.

93. Wu Zhen Volume of Ink Bamboo

Yuan

Volume size: 22 MO

Length: 53 cm Width: 68.5 cm

Preserved in the Palace Museum in Taipei

Paper scroll, ink brush. The first two papers are written with "The inscription of Sushi and Record of the relentless bamboo at tall bamboo valley by Yuke", and the remaining 20 papers depict new shoots, twigs, old poles, bamboos in rain, wind and snow, bamboo forest on sloping land, drooping bamboos on precipice. It is said that his drawing imitates Wen Tong, Su Shi, and Li Kan; however, this painting lays less emphasis on the accurate gestures of bamboos, it pays more attention to depicting artistic conception. Strokes of this painting are full of strength, creating a very free and easy implication. Each paper of this painting was signed by Wu Zhen, and in Zhizheng the tenth year (1350) when he was aged 71, and addressed to his son Fonu.

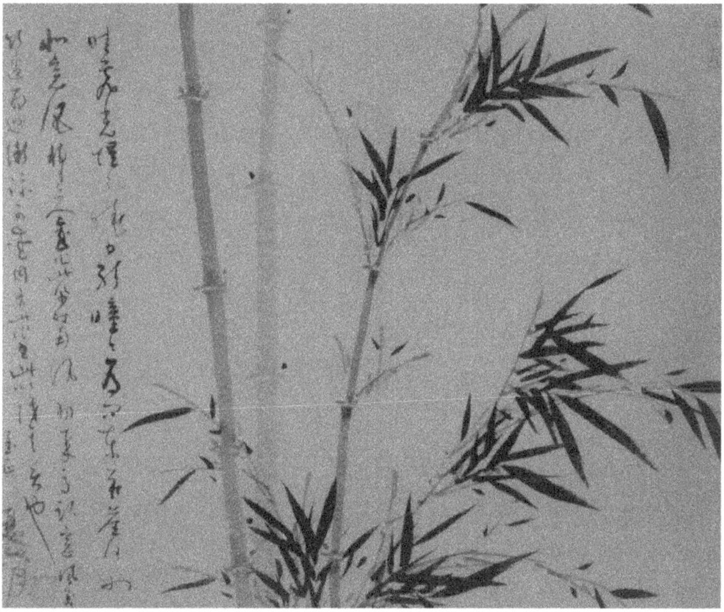

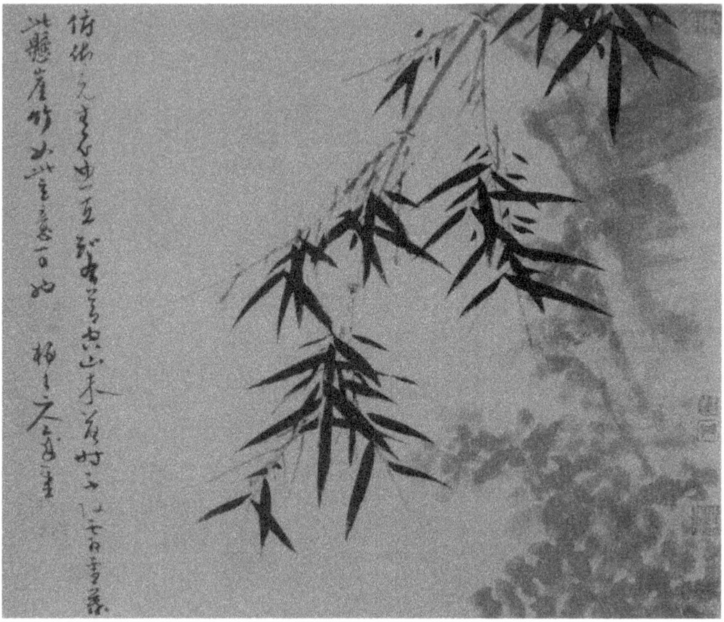

94. Ni Zan: Bamboo Branches

Yuan

Length: 34 cm Width: 76.4 cm

Preserved in the Palace Museum in Beijing

Paper scroll, ink. It depicts a thin and long bamboo, with upright and flexible bamboo branches, properly pitched and dense bamboo leaves. Among the thick and moist strokes of this painting, flying white can be seen occasionally. The bold and smart brushwork makes it a master work of Ni Zan's ink bamboos. This painting is prefaced by Ni Zan himself, signing as “Lan Zan”. It carries a poem as a preface by Emperor Qianlong, and is stamped with more than 10 seals of its collectors such as the Neifu (Imperial storehouse) of the Qing Dynasty, etc. It is recorded in the *Precious Collection of the Stone Moat Sequel*, and *Moyuan Huiguan*.

Ni Zan (1301-1374), original name Ting, with the style name Yuanzhen and sobriquets Yunlin, Youxia, was a native of Wuxi. His family was powerful in Jiangnan region and the members liked to communicate with famous people. At the end of Yuan Dynasty, people lived in a turbulent society. The Ni family scattered their fortune and dwelled in cottages or temples, so he was also named "Ni Yu ". He was good at drawing landscapes, bamboos and rocks, and he painted most of them with ink. He is one of the “Four Great Masters of the Yuan”.

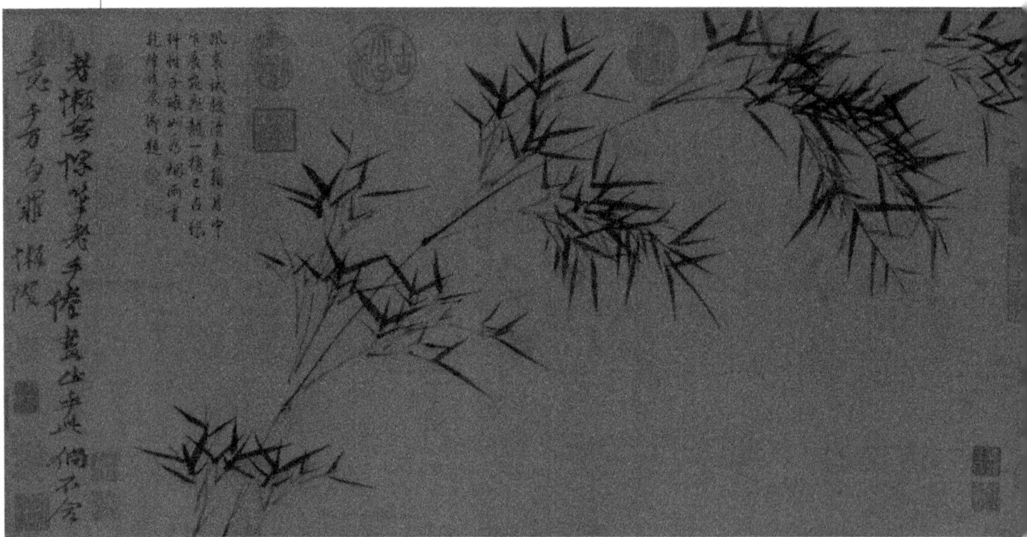

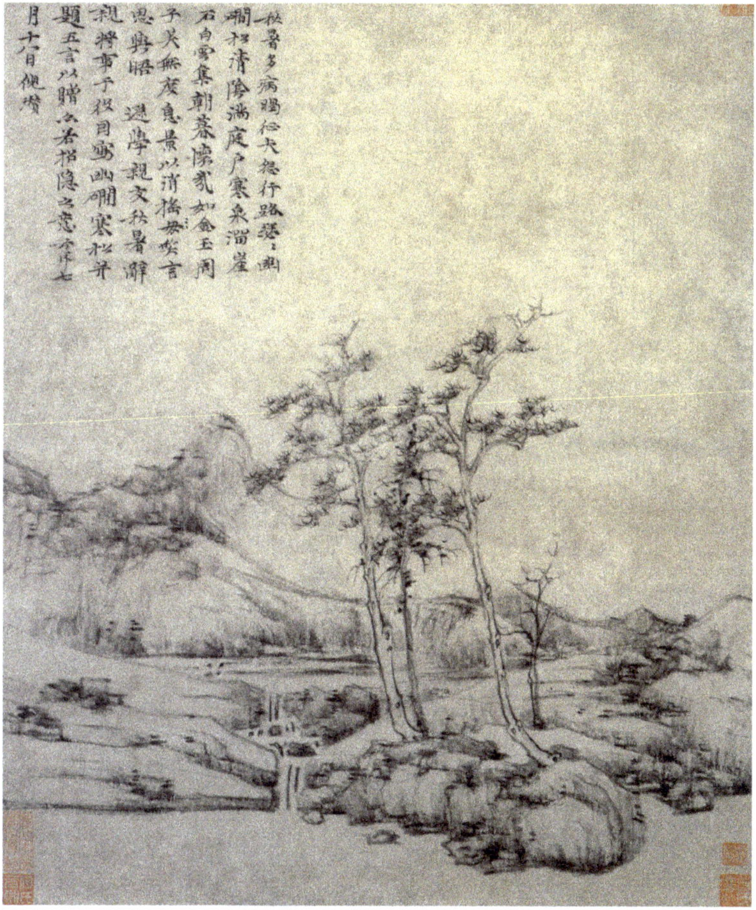

95. Ni Zan: Distant Cold Flow Pine

Yuan

Length: 59.7 cm Width: 50.4 cm

Preserved in the Palace Museum in Beijing

Paper scroll, ink. It depicts a flat slope and low hill, sparse woods and distant mountains, cold spring and slow stream. The strokes are simple and quiet. The mountains and rocks are sketched with dry and pale brush, chapped and rubbed slightly. The pine trunks are contoured by two strokes, neither chapped nor tinted, only dotted with some scars. The pine needles are scattered. This painting is prefaced by Ni Zan himself with a five-character poem, and signed "18th day of the 7th month by Ni Zan". It is also stamped with four seals of its collectors, and a Banyin (a kind of seal). It is recorded in the *Calligraphy and Painting Boat on the Qinghe River, Table of Calligraphy and Paintings*, and *Collective Study on Shigutang Calligraphy and Paintings*, etc.

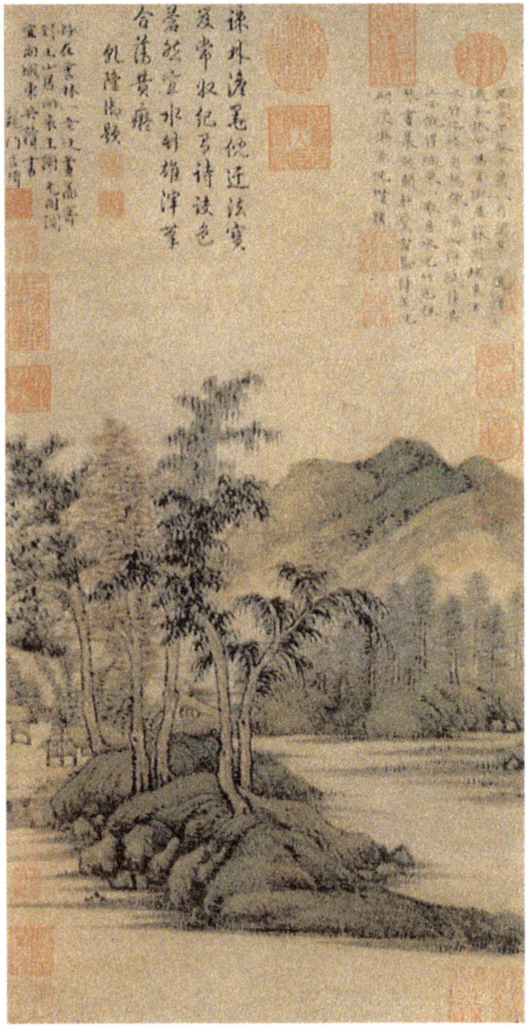

96. Ni Zan: Water and Bamboo Dwelling

Yuan

Length: 53.5 cm Width: 28.2 cm

Preserved in the National Museum of China

Paper scroll, tint. It depicts the wonderful scenery of water and bamboo in the eastern part of Suzhou City. The rocks and mountains are portrayed by pi ma cun. This painting inherited most of Dong Yuan and Ju Ran's technique of drawing, and was tinted with two tones of cyan and green. This painting is inscribed by Ni Zan himself, noting that it was painted in "Wangri (the 15th day of a lunar month), eighth month, Zhizheng the Guiwei year (1343)", it is the earliest landscape drawing in his works so marked. There is also a poem on it, which was signed "Ni Zan wrote", and stamped with "Ni (Surname) Zhen (Family name)". It is also has a postscript by Emperor Qianlong (Qing Dynasty), and stamped with seals of more than 10 collectors.

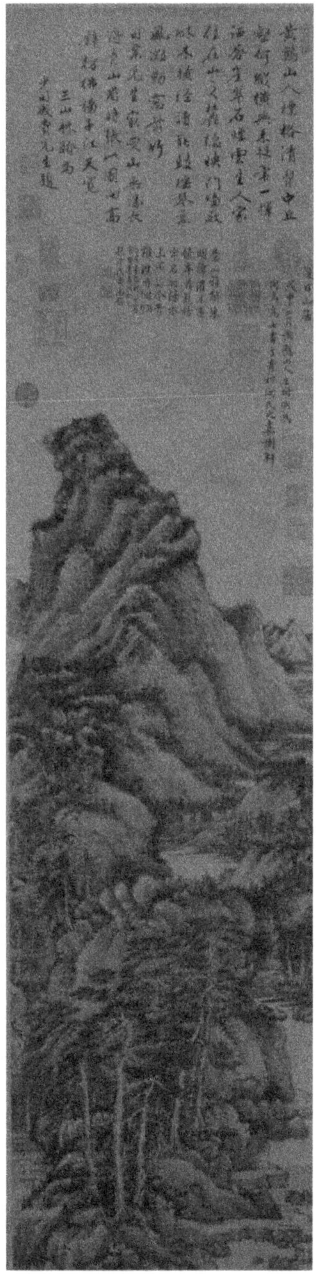

97. Wang Meng: Mountain Dwelling on a Summer Day

Yuan

Length: 118.4 cm Width: 36.5 cm

Preserved in the Palace Museum in Beijing

Paper scroll, ink. It depicts the green mountains on summer days, Changsong and steep mountains, col and dwellings, a woman carries a baby in her arms in a half exposed cottage. The contour of this painting is complex, with a large blank space on top of the mountain peaks. Mountains and rocks are portrayed by Pi Ma and Cabled Cun. The pine trees are contoured with light ink, occasionally applied with dark ink. The woods on hills are tinted by coke ink through Cefeng (side tip of the writing brush). This painting is prefaced by Wang Meng himself with "Dwelling on mountains on a summer day, the second month of Wushen (1368) Year, Huanghe Shanren Wang Xuming painted this picture for a goldsmith with the same surname as me at Tao's Jiashu varanda, Qing village". It is prefaced and stamped by Lin Han of the Ming Dynasty, and Emperor Qianlong. It is recorded in the *Precious Collection of the Stone Moat Sequel* and *List of Grand View*.

Wang Meng (1308-1385), with the style name Shuming and sobriquet Huanghe Shan Qiao, grandson of Zhao Mengfu. He served in a minor government capacity. At the end of the Yuan Dynasty, he abandoned official life and retired to Huanghe Mountain (present-day northeast Hangxian County, Zhejiang). He was good at painting, and versed in poem and calligraphy. He is one of the "Four Great Masters of the Yuan".

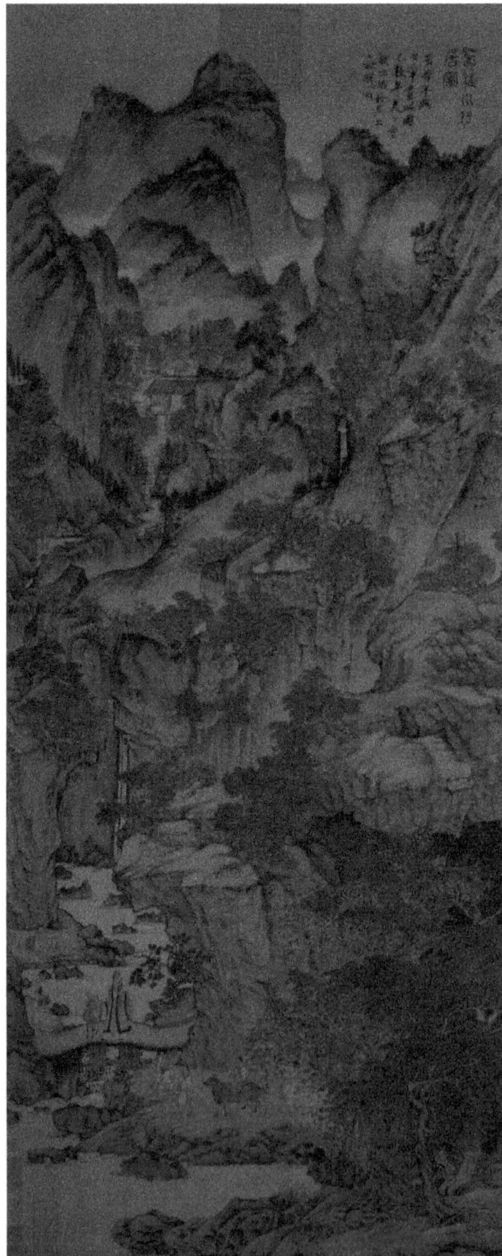

98. Wang Meng: Ge Zhichuan Resettlement

Yuan

Length: 139 cm Width: 58 cm

Preserved in the Palace Museum in Beijing

Paper scroll, tint. It depicts the scene of Ge Hong (Zhichuan)'s resettlement on Luofu Mountain. The leaves are drawn by Shuanggou and colored; the mountains and rocks are painted with gamboge slightly added with ink. The painting is not dotted, the ink used is light, and it is a masterly work of Wang Meng's fine brush in landscapes. This painting is prefaced by Wang Meng himself, signing "Wang Shuming mark". It is also stamped with 14 seals of its collectors. It is recorded in *Wangshi ShanHu Wang, Moyuan Huiguan*, and *Paintings of Xuzhai Studio Sequel*.

Ge Hong, with the style name Zhichuan, sobriquet Bao Puzi. He lived in the Eastern Jin Dynasty, born in a big family of Jiangnan. When he was young, he liked soothsaying, was addicted to alchemy, and mastered medicine and pharmacology. He later secluded himself on Luofu Mountain to make pills of immortality.

99 .Wang Meng: Taibai Mountains

Yuan

Length: 27.6 cm Width: 238 cm

Preserved in the Liaoning Provincial Museum

Paper scroll, tint. It depicts Tiantong temple of Taibai Mountain and its environment, especially the pipe woods on both sides of the 20-mile narrow path leading to the temple. The composition is rigorous and the structure is profound. The strokes are sharp and slender, tinted with cinnabar and cyanin. Some separated trees are applied with dark ink, creating a different style. The head of this volume is sealed with "Picture of Taibai Mountain". This painting is prefaced by Emperor Qianlong with a long inscription, and a postscript by people of the Yuan and Ming Dynasty. It used to be collected by Tiantong temple as well as Shen Zhou, Xiang Yuanbian, Neifu (Imperial storehouse) of Qing Dynasty, etc, but was later lost. It is recorded in the *Calligraphy and Painting Boat on the Qinghe River, Table of Collection of Calligraphy and Paintings, Moyuan Huiguan Sequel* and *Precious Collection of the Stone Moat Sequel: First Edition*.

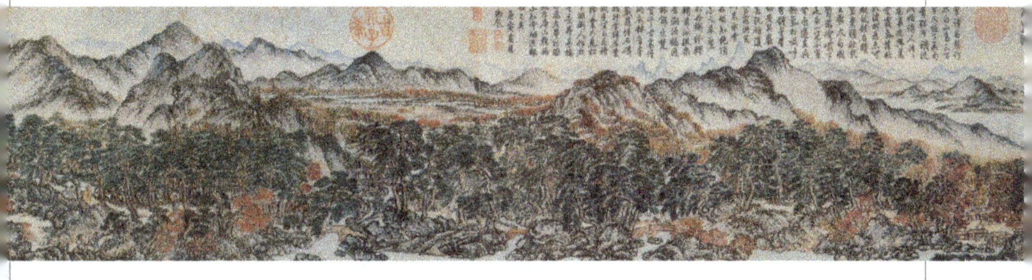

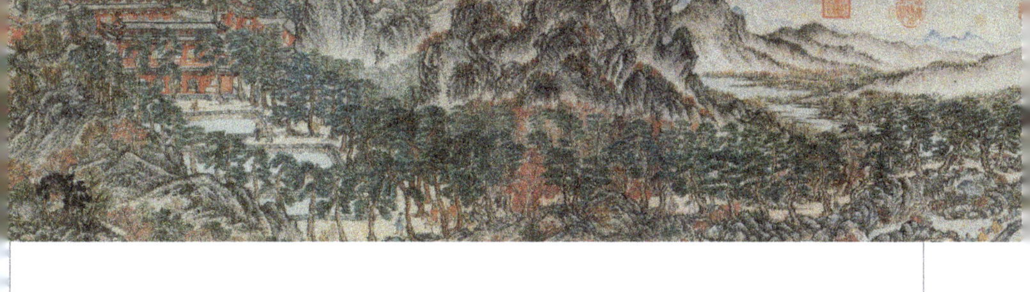

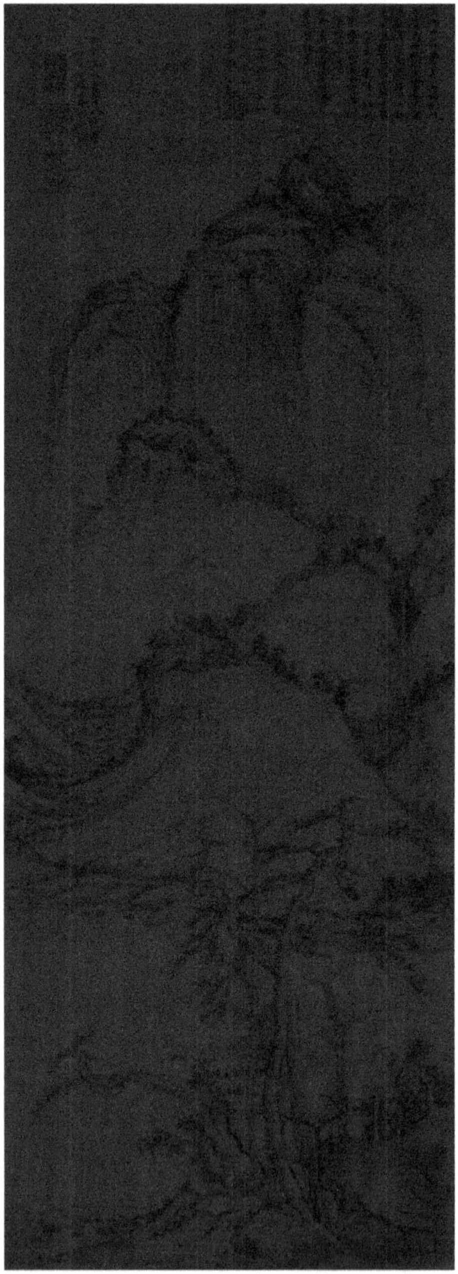

100. Cao Zhibai Scroll Painting of Sparse Pine and Secluded Cave

Yuan

Length: 74.5 cm Width: 27.8 cm

Preserved in the Palace Museum in Beijing

Paper scroll, ink. It depicts the overlapping mountains receding ever higher. The woods are luxuriantly green, the flying springs are suspended among the mountains and there are cottages appear indistinctly in the cols. In the vicinity, there is a tortuous creek and shoreside islet. Cottages on shore are set off by the woods. And there are tall pines and miscellaneous trees on the sloping land. The strokes are dry, tinted with light ink. This painting is prefaced by Cao Zhibai himself: "Born in Renshen, aged eighty, middle spring, Zhizheng Xinmao (1351), signed by Yunxi", stamped by three seals. It is also inscribed with two poems by two people of Yuan Dynasty. It is recorded in the *Paintings of Xuzhai Studio Sequel*.

Cao Zhibai (1272-1355), with the style name Youxuan, and anther style name Zhensu, sobriquet Yunxi. He is a native of Huating (Modern Songjiang, Shanghai). He was good at painting landscapes, and in his later years often chapped and rubbed his paintings with a dry brush.

101. Cao Zhibai: Snow Mountain

Yuan

Length: 97.1 cm Width: 55.3 cm

Preserved in the Palace Museum in Beijing

Silk scroll, ink. It depicts the cold forest after snow, a grass hut; a wineshop built by the hill, a man in straw rain cape carrying a load, walking on a wooden bridge, and a fishing boat docking. The sky is tinted with light ink to set off the snowy hill. The mountains and rocks are contoured by ink lines, slightly chapped and rubbed. There are no leaves on the trees, and the branches look like crab claws. This painting is signed with "Yunxi depicted this for Guquan", and stamped with two seals. "Guquan" is Lin Mengzheng, a native of Huangyan (present-day Zhejiang) in the Yuan Dynasty.

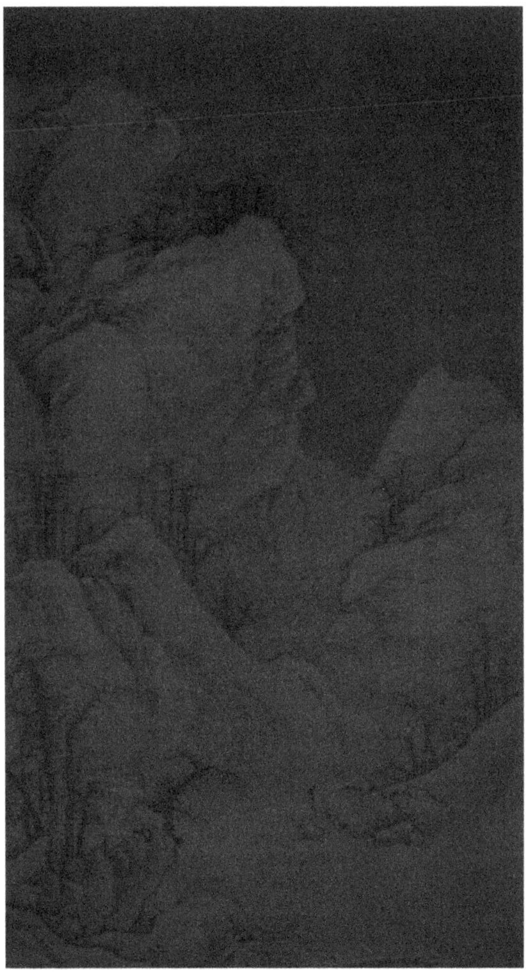

102. Zhu Derun: Xiuye Pavilion

Yuan

Length: 28.3 cm Width: 210 cm

Preserved in the Palace Museum in Beijing

Paper scroll, light tinted. It depicts the scenery of Xiuye Pavilion, where Zhu Derun's friend Zhou Jingan reads his books. The mountains, rocks and trees are tinted with cyanin ink, mostly are wet brushes, alternating with dark and light, dry and wet. It is a masterly work of Zhu Derun's painting of landscapes. This painting is prefaced with "Xiuye Pavilion Record", signed "April 10th, Zhizheng the 24th year (1364), Suiyang Sanren, aged 71, Zhu Derun painted and recorded". It is also prefaced with a poem by Emperor Qianlong, stamped with 45 seals of its collectors. At the beginning of the preface is written "Xiuye Pavilion" by Zhou Boqi of the Yuan Dynasty, stamped. At the end of this scroll is a postscript by 21 people, stamped with 60 seals from its collectors from the Ming and Qing dynasties, and three Banyins (kind of seal). It is recorded in the *Fencing Coral, Pei Wen Zhai Painting and Calligraphy Series, List of Grand View*, and *Precious Collection of the Stone Moat Sequel*.

Zhu Derun (1294-1365), with the style name Zemin and sobriquet Suiyang Sanren. He was a native of Suiyang (modern Shangqiu, Henan), lived in Kunshan (present-day Jiangsu). In his early years, he was appreciated by Gao Kegong for his drawings. He was good at painting landscapes, and learnt from Zhao Mengfu.

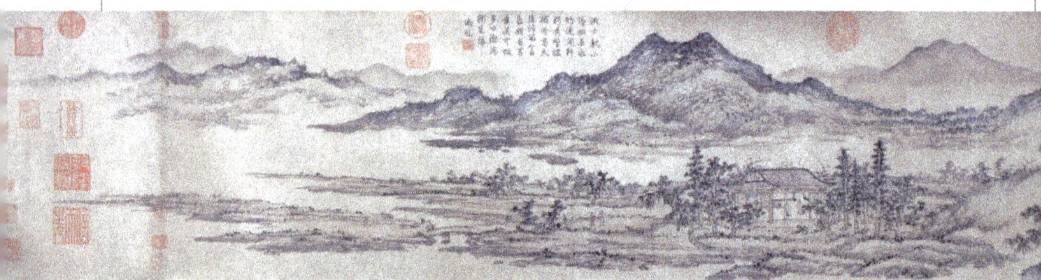

103. Tang Di: Overlooking alongside the Lyre

Yuan

Length: 157.6 cm Width: 111 cm

Preserved in the Sichuan Museum

Silk scroll, tint. A hermit wearing a gown and holding a lyre stands looking out over a lake. Beside the lake are green pines; mountains loom in the distance. The lakes and mountains are spacious and vast. Density is well arranged, and the painting's dynamics well reflect the tranquility. The brushwork style is mellow and full, which represents a change from the group led by Guo Xi. The title is "The First Ten-day Period of Autumn, Zhiyuan Ninth Year (1272) , made by Wuxing Tang Di named Zihua", second side of the sealing style, with seals on the four sides. It was once collected by Liang Qingbiao and Zhang Daqian.

Tang Di (1296-1364), named Zihua and called Dunzhai, was born in Wuxing (present-day Huzhou, Zhejiang). He is good at painting landscape, and learned painting from Zhang Mengfu. Most of his masterpieces describe working scenario of laborers such as farmer, fisherman.

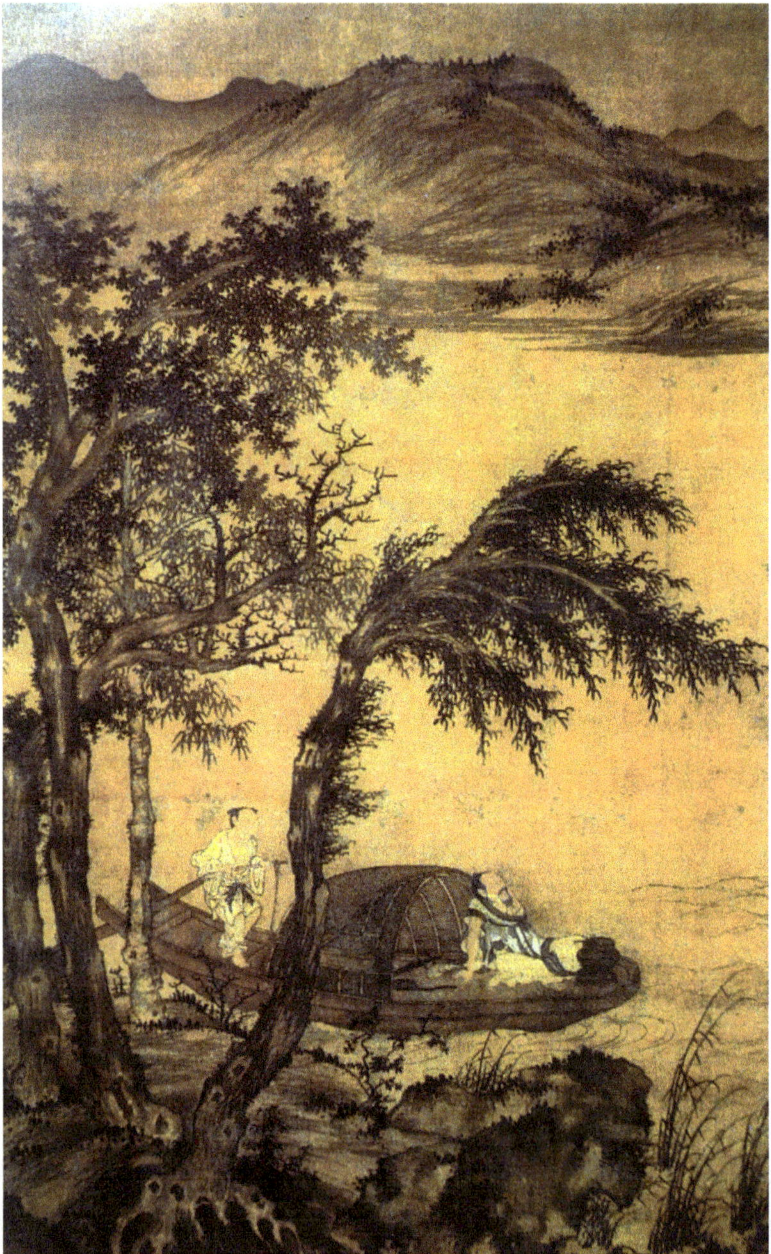

104. Sheng Mao:Painting of Whistling at Autumn Barge

Yuan

Length: 167.5 cm Width: 102.4 cm

Preserved in the Shanghai Museum

Silk scroll, tint. Mountains in the distance, clear lake, luxuriant trees and slopes; a scholar stands in a boat, whistling,while a boy rows at the stern. The techniques of painting mountains, water, trees and stones reflect the influence of Dong Yuan, Ju Ran. The style of painting is deliberate. It was later collected by the Ming government.

Sheng Mao (14th century), named Zizhao. Native of Lin'an (present-day Hangzhou), but lived a long time in Jiaxing. Good at painting figures, landscapes, flowers and birds. At a young age, he was instructed by Chen Lin, but changed his painting style slightly and then was influenced by Zhao Mengfu.

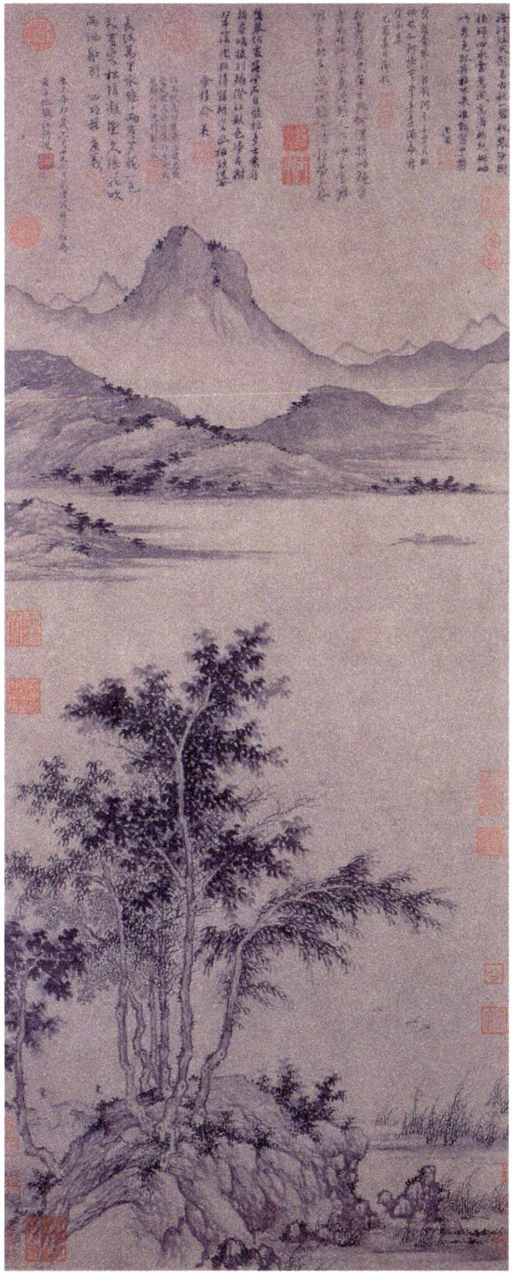

105. Sheng Mao: Waiting for Crossing the River in Autumn

Yuan

Length: 112.5 cm Width: 46.3 cm

Preserved in the Palace Museum in Beijing

Paper, Ink. This depicts scenery of rivers and trees in autumn. Mountains stand in the distance, while the surface of the water is tranquil as a boat crosses the river. On the nearby shore, giant reeds are painted, whiule geese fly overhead. On the bank, an old man waits to cross the river with a young child. The title is "16th day of the third month of the Zhizheng Xinmao Year (1351), Wutang Sheng Mao paints waiting to cross the river", painting "Sheng Mao", "Zi Zhao", and then with the colophon of Lao Pu, Ying Yu'an, Yuying and Emperor Qianlong. Thirty seals are recorded and then one seal is further recorded. It was collected by Geng Zhaozhong, Da Chongguang and the Qing Government. It is recorded in *Record of Ancient Crafts*.

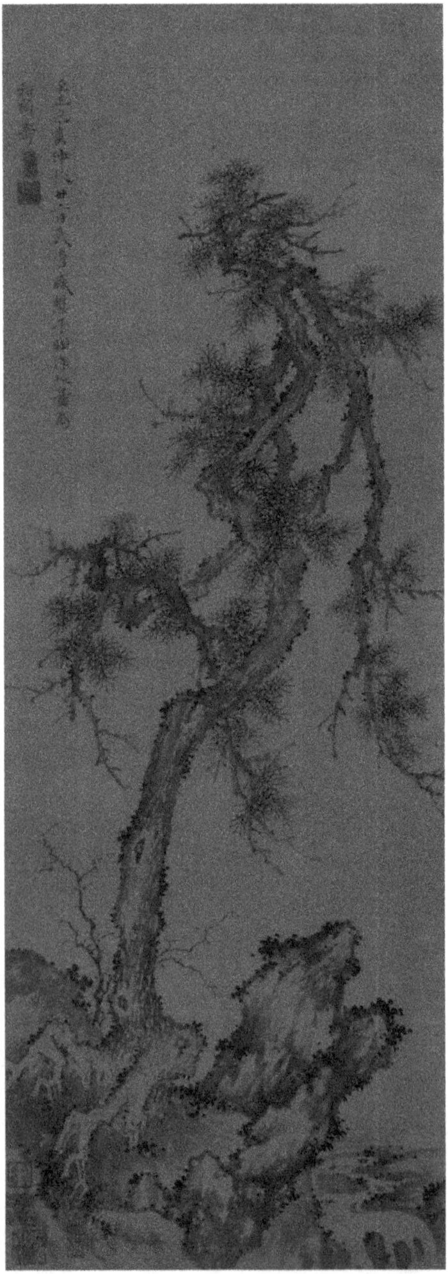

106. Sheng Mao: Tophus

Yuan

Length: 77.4 cm   Width: 27.2 cm

Preserved in the Palace Museum in Beijing

Paper and Chinese writing brush. The painting depicts old pines growing between stones. Their roots are exposed, the branches bend and droop, and the pine needles densely cover the end of the branches. Streams gurgle around the stones. The artist uses light ink to paint the trunks and thick ink to paint the moss. The pine needles are painted with a brisk and neat style, the slopes and stones are colored by ink. The title is "the 22nd day of the second comth of the autumn of the Zhizheng Yihai Year" (1353), Wutang Sheng Mao Zi Zhao made the painting for celebrating a birthday", sealed with "Sheng Mao", "Zi Zhao". Four seals are recorded.

107. Ma Wan: Poetic Couds at Dusk

Yuan

Length: 95.6 cm   Width: 56.3 cm

Preserved in the Shanghai Museum

Silk scroll, tint. The painting depicts various mountain peaks. Trees stand among the mountains wreathed in ethereal clouds. Pavilions can be seen indistinctly. A stream winds down among the mountains. Most of the strokes are made up of cross points, which is from the Yushan system of the Mi family. The title is "Clouds at dusk with poetics, the 15th day of the seventh month of the Zhizheng Yichou Year (1349), painted by Ma Wan named Wen Bi" , and two seals are recorded. It is recorded in the *Spectacular Life*.

Ma Wan (14th century), named Wen Bi, called Lu Dunsheng, born in Guanyuan at the beginning of Yuan Dynasty, native of Jiangning (present-day Nanjing, Jiangsu). He was good at poems, calligraphy and painting, called the "Three Skills". He was good at painting landscapes and learned from Huang Gongwang.

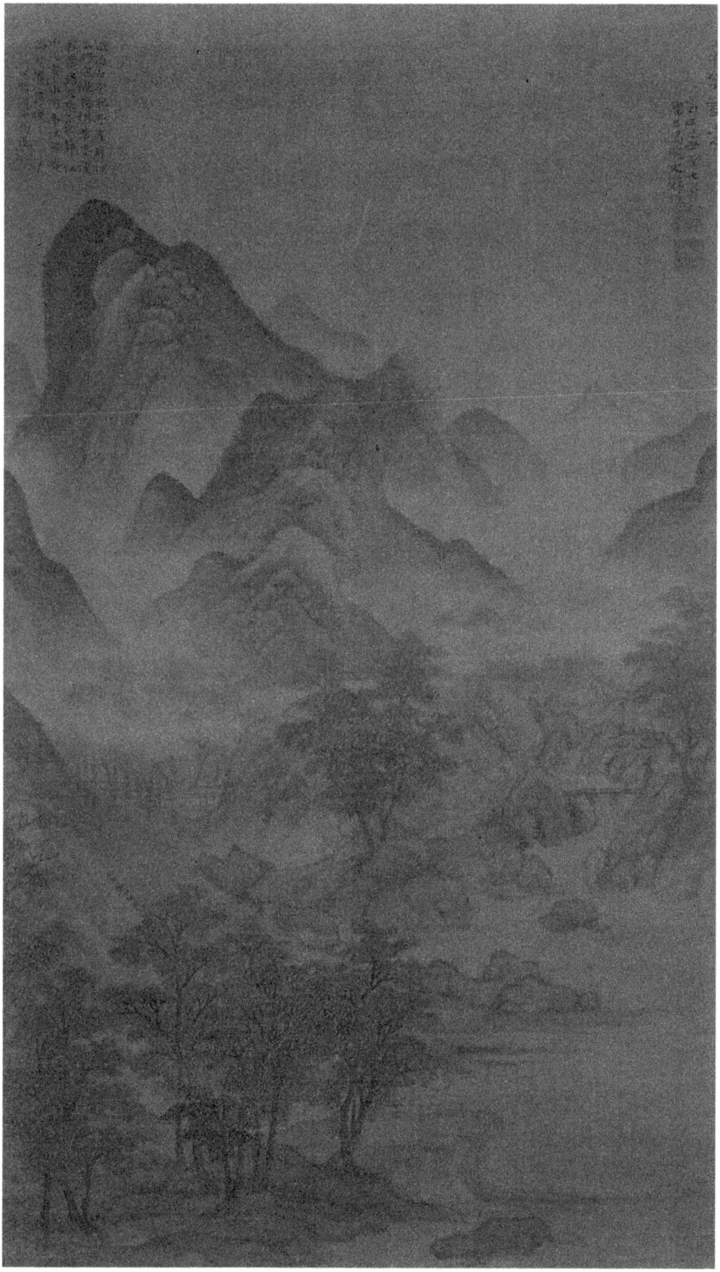

108. Ma Wan: Crossing the Snowy Ridge

Yuan

Length: 125.4 cm Width: 57.2 cm

Preserved in the Palace Museum in Beijing

Silk scroll, ink painting. The picture depicts snow-clad mountains, with spring waterfalls tumbling down. Traces of human presence are rare. A stone staircase and footpaths are shown and houses stand beside the mountains. Mountain stones are split, colored by ink. A blank indicates the snow. The composition of the painting is dense and neat, the pen and ink use is vigorous. The title is "Crossing the Snowy Barge", sealed with "Wen Bi made for Yan Ming", and two seals are recorded. There are two seals of collectors.

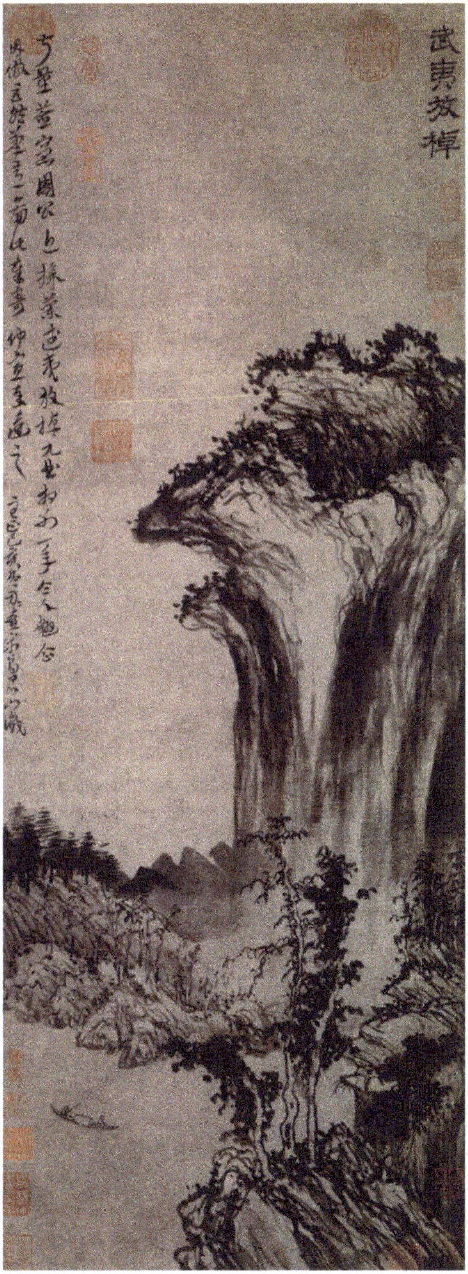

109. Fang Congyi: Boating in Wuyi

Yuan

Length: 74.4 cm Width: 27.8 cm

Preserved in the Palace Museum in Beijing

Paper, Ink. The serpentine scenery of Wuyi Mountain is depicted. The composition of the painting is quite special. A hemp-fiber texture stroke is used through the Jiesuo method, the ink is thick and the style is quick and smooth, free and easy. The title is "Boating In Wuyi", with a colophon sealed with "Winter, Zhizheng Yihai (1359), Fang Fanghu and Yu Wujun". Eighteen seals are recorded. It is collected in the *List of Grand View, Collective Study on Shigutang Calligraphy and Paintings*, Baoyu Studio Calligraphy and Paintings.

Fang Congyi (14th century), named Wuyu, called Fanghu, native of Mangdao, priest of Shangqing Temple, born in Guigu Mountain, native of Guixi(present-day Jiangxi). He was skilled at poems and calligraphy, good at painting landscape and learned from Gao Kegong, etc.

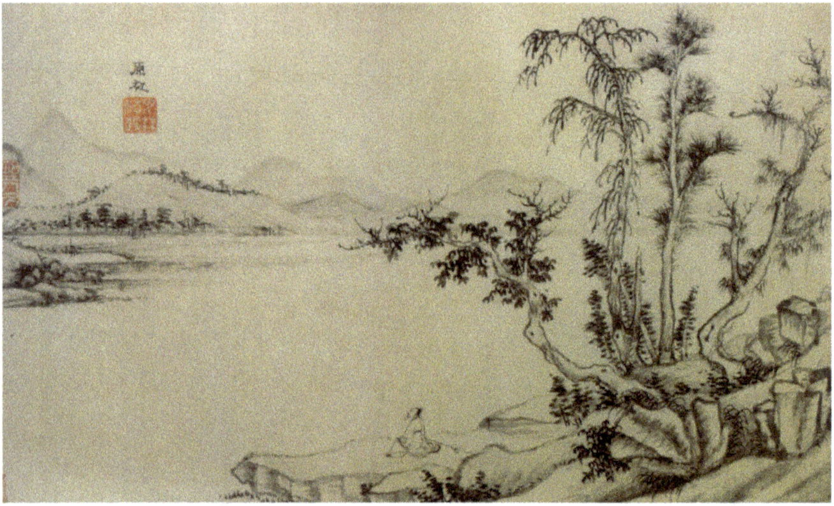

110. Zhao Zhong: Looking at the Mountain across the Strait

Yuan

Length: 30 cm Width: 50.1 cm

Preserved in the Palace Museum in Beijing

Paper, Ink. An old man sits on a stone next to the shore and looks far into the distance. The river is tranquil and the mountains across the river gradually fade into the distance.. Trees and stones are painted by light ink and colored by thick ink, and the characters are painted by line drawing. The painting is sealed with "Yuan Chu", and two seals are recorded. It is recorded in the *Precious Collection of the Stone Moat Sequel*, and *Collective Study on Shigutang Calligraphy and Paintings*.

Zhao Zhong, named Yuan Chu and called Dongwu wildman, was born in Jiaxing (one source suggests Wujiang), and was active in the late period of Yuan Dynasty. He was fond of writing and painting characters, landscapes and flowers.

111. Zhang Guan: Open Forest and Thatched Cottage

Yuan

Length: 25.8 cm Width: 59.6 cm

Preserved in the Palace Museum in Beijing

Paper, Ink. The woods by the river and the bank are upright and sparse, and a number of hatched cottages are shown on the slopes. The river is open and tranquil; there is a boat on it. Mountains in the distance are surrounded by water and extend until they fade away into the edge of the sky. He used wet pens to outline the rocks and then colored them with thick ink. Trees and curled grasses are completed by stippling. The composition is various, near and far, dense and sparse. The painting is sealed with "the eighth month in the Zhizheng Wuxu Year (1358), and made by Zhang Guan". Emperor Qianlong wrote a poem on it along with a seal. It is included in the *Precious Collection of the Stone Moat*.

Zhang Guan, named Ke Guan, born in the Yuan Dynasty, native of Fengjing, Songjiang (present-day Jinshan, Shanghai), but lived in Jiangxing at the end of Yuan Dynasty. He was skilled at painting landscapes and influenced by Wu Zhen, Sheng Mao. His style of painting is natural and poised. He was good at imitating as well as appreciation.

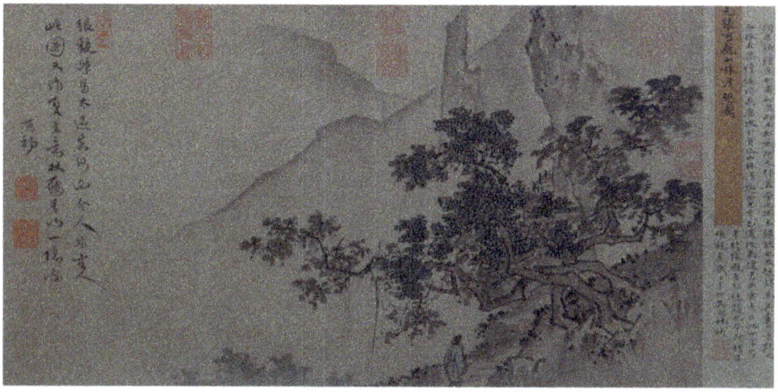

112. Zhang Guan: Having Fun in the Mountains
Yuan
Length: 30 cm Width: 54.7 cm
Preserved in the Palace Museum in Beijing
Paper, tint. Trees grow abundantly along winding roads. An old man, strolling along he road under the trees with a rod while looking sideways. Mountains in the distance gradually fade out. The mountains and stones are colored by thick ink and the trees are highlighted by thick ink. It is the masterly work of Zhang Guang imitating Ma Yuan and Xia Guifeng. Zhao Zhong wrote a poem sealed with "Yuan Chu" on the painting. Two seals are at the lower corner, and five seals are recorded. Wu Hufan wrote a colophon on the front. It is recorded in the *Precious Collection of the Stone Moat*.

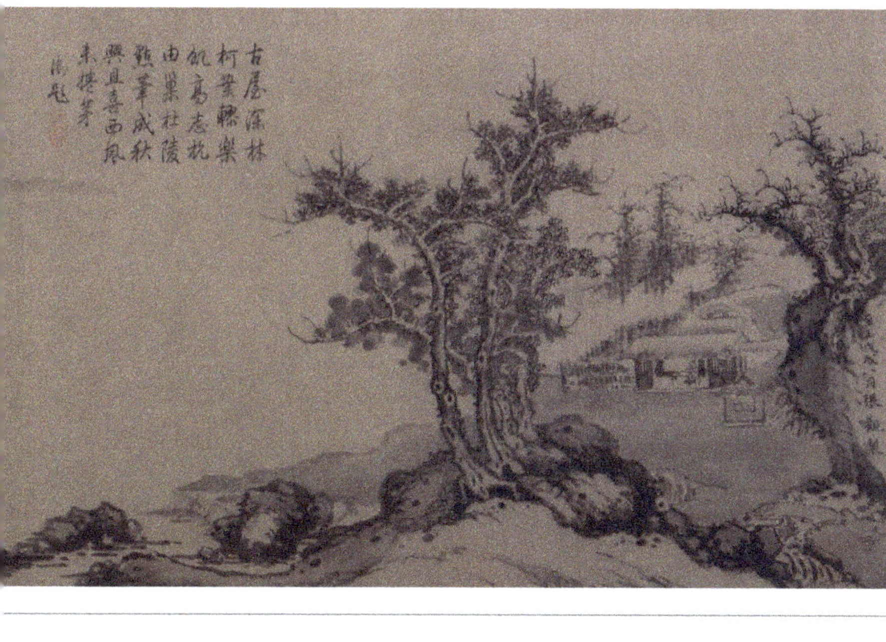

113. Yao Tingmei: Pavilion and Streams

Yuan

Length: 48.7 cm Width: 27.7 cm

Preserved in the Hubei Provincial Museum

Silk scroll, light tint. It depicts burrow stone, level land, high mountains and waterfalls. Pavilions among the mountains appear indistinctly and the streams flow at great speed through bridges. A man walks with a rod. There are two boats on the water. Mountain stones are painted by the cirrus method. The branches pitch up like antlers and droop down just like a crab claw. The pavilion uses ruler painting, which is carefully and neatly done. It is a masterly work of Yao Tingmei. One seal of the painting is recorded.

Yao Tingmei, named Yanqing, native of Wuxing (Huzhou, Zhejiang), active during the Zhizheng period of the Yuan Dynasty. He was skilled at painting landscape, and learned from Guo Xi.

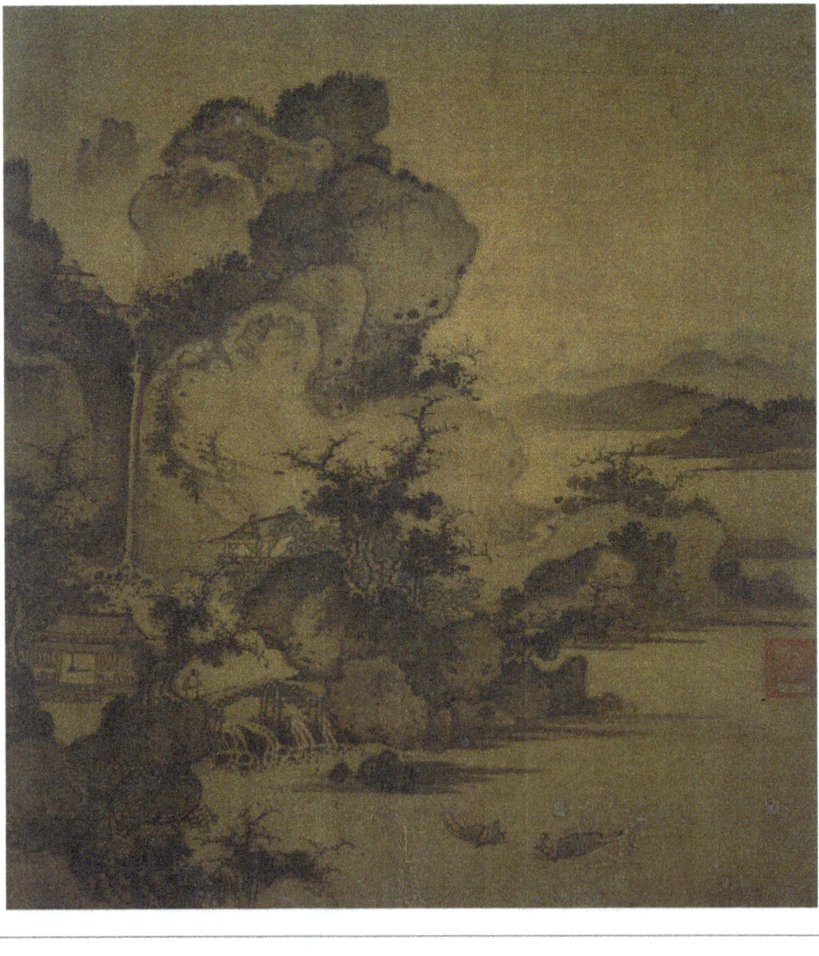

114. Zhao Yuan: Hexi Humble Cottage

Yuan

Length: 84.3 cm Width: 40.8 cm

Preserved in the Shanghai Museum

Paper, tint. Diagonal composition is adopted. A sandbar in the lower right of the painting is the Chengxing sea inlet at Jiaxing. A cottage is built on a sandbar and someone is talking inside. Luxuriant trees are well-spaced across the bank. The fishing boats in the river are busy. The pen and ink is sparse and the color is simple, mostly dry brushing. The title is "ZhaoYuan of Ju City made the painting of Hexi humble cottage for the owner of Yu Mountain". "The owner of Yu Mountain" refers to Gu Aying. Gu's poem and colophon are on the painting. From this, it can be known that the painting depicts the scenery of Jiaxing Hexi Humble Cottage, a private house owned by Gu Aying.

Zhao Yuan, whose exact date of birth towards the end of the Yuan Dynasty or early in the Ming Dynasty is unknown, had the original name of Yuan. At the beginning of Ming Dynasty, in order to avoid offending Zhu Yuanzhang, he changed the character to another Yuan. He was named Shanchang and called Danlin, and lived in Gusu (present-day Suzhou, Jiangsu). He was skilled at painting landscape, especially at painting bamboo. People at that time thought highly of him.

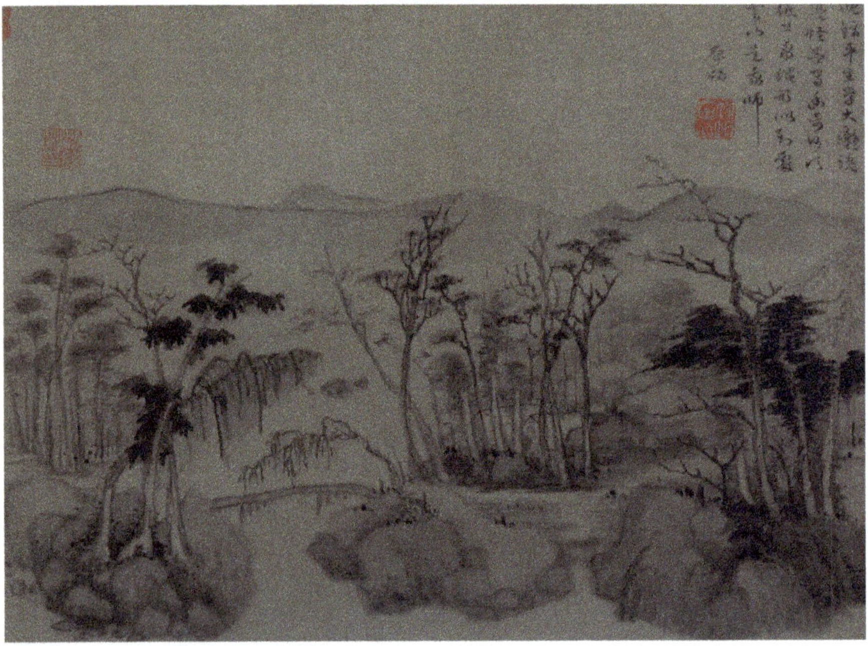

115. Shen Xuan: Plain Forest and Mountains in the Distance
Yuan
Length: 30 cm Width: 40.9 cm
Preserved in the Palace Museum in Beijing
Paper, Ink. The painting depicts trees and slopes; streams crossed by bridges wind through them. The mountains in the distance are outlined with rough lines and colored with light ink. The branches are filled with colors in elaborate style. The leaves are painted by thick ink, with the existing shades. The painting style is simple and sparse, and the artistic conception is quiet and beautiful. It is the existing master work of Shen Xuan. The painting is sealed with "seal of Shen Xuan" and then Zhao Zhong wrote a poem on it and signed. It is recorded in the *Precious Collection of the Stone Moat Sequel*, and *Collective Study on Shigutang Calligraphy and Paintings*.
Shen Xuan is not recorded in the History of Paintings. He was active during the Zhizheng Period of the Yuan Dynasty. He was skilled at painting landscape and the technique of painting was similar to that of Huang Gongwang.

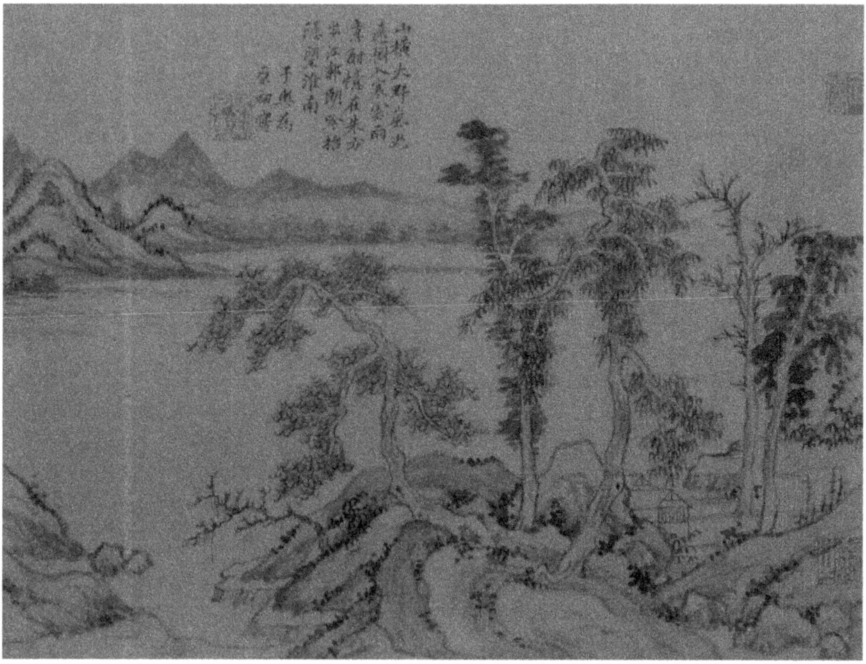

116 .Liu Kan: Sparse Forest and Mountains in the Distance
Yuan
Length: 28.9 cm Width: 38 cm
Preserved in the Palace Museum in Beijing
Paper, Ink. The scenery in regions south of the Yangtze River is painted. Uneven grass is on the nearby bank. The rocks are rugged, with the sparse forest, and the hut. The surface of the river is tranquil and mountains extend into the far distance. The artistic conception is disperse and simple. The painting is along with a poem signed with “Ziyu wrote for Yuanchu”, and sealed with “Liu Ziyu”.
Liu Kan, or Zi Yu, was born in Jiashan, Zhejiang. During Zhizheng reign, he secluded himself to read. He was good at language, especially clerical script. He was also good at painting landscapes. Few works have been handed down.

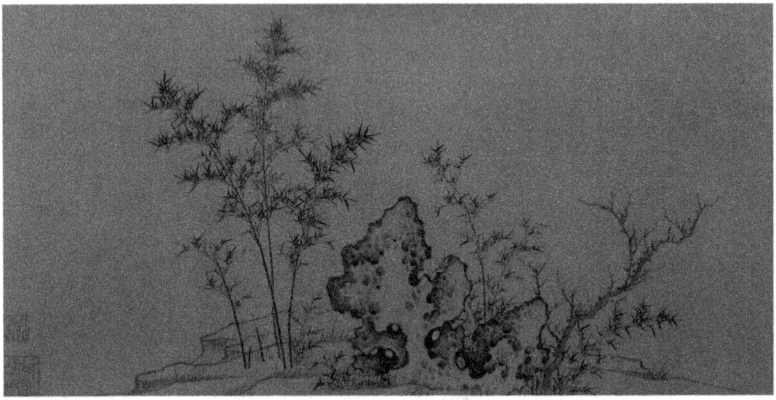

117. Wu Guan: Ancient Woods and Bambusa Stone

Yuan

Length: 30 cm Width: 58.3 cm

Preserved in the Palace Museum in Beijing

Paper, Ink. This depicts a slope, lakes and stones. Bamboos and trees grow luxuriously. He used light and thick ink to paint dead wood and bamboo, and used the free and easy style to outline the lake stones. The composition is balanced, and the painting of stones and bamboos is diligent. The picture is fresh and lovely. The painting is sealed with "Whale". It is recorded in the *Precious Collection of the Stone Moat Sequel* and *Collective Study on Shigutang Calligraphy and Paintings*.

Wu Quan, named Yingzhi and called Old Man of Bamboo Village, was a native of Jiaxing, Zhejiang. He was once president of Jinling County and then went to live in seclusion. He collected many books and painting and was skilled at painting plum, bamboo and landscape.

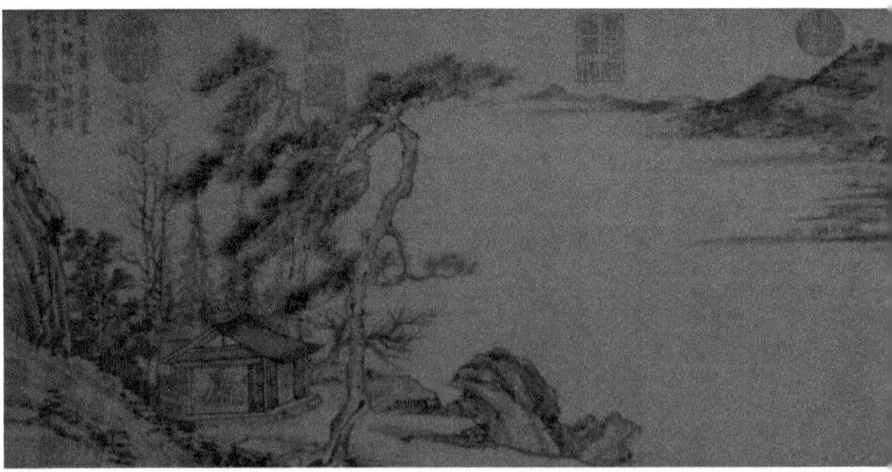

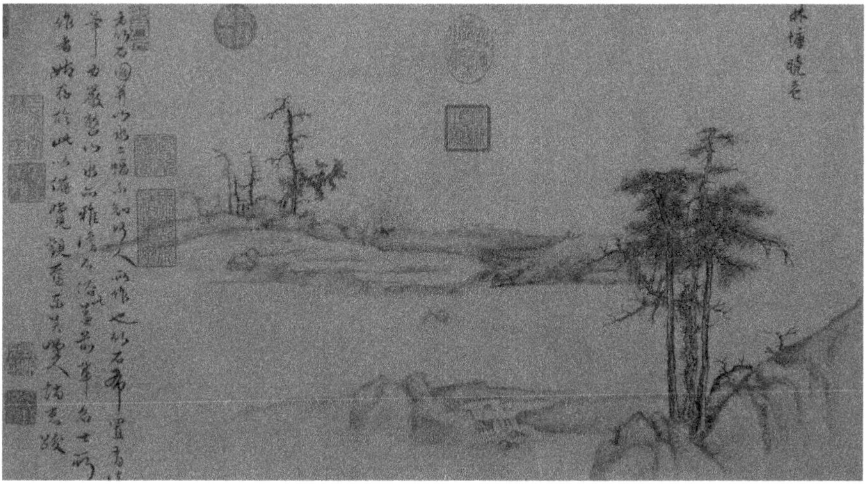

118.Wu Guan: Forests and Ponds at Dawn

Yuan

Length: 30 cm Width: 52 cm

Preserved in the Palace Museum in Beijing

Ink on paper with brush. It depicts scenery of forests and ponds. Taksmatsu near the bank approaches the sky, and the running water in the slopes never ends. Hills and sparse forests stand on the opposite bank. The mist and clouds are filled in. The composition is simple, the artistic conception is quiet and beautiful, and the pen and ink is free. The title is "Scenery of Forests and Ponds at Dawn". Zhao Zhong wrote a colophon and sealed it. It was collected by Qing Government. It is recorded in the *Precious Collection of the Stone Moat Sequel* and *Collective Study on Shigutang Calligraphy and Paintings*.

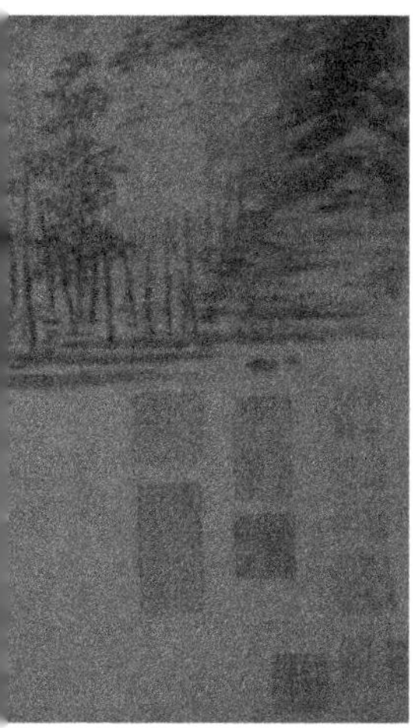

119. Zhang Wo: Bamboo West Cottage

Yuan

Length: 27 cm Width: 81 cm

Preserved in the Liaoning Provincial Museum

Paper, Ink. In the painting, there is a broad river with shochiku and bamboos growing at either side. A cottage hides among the trees, and a person sits inside the house. Yang Yu, the owner of the Bamboo West Cottage wrote a poem for it. In the Yuan Dynasty, Yang Weizhen wrote *Diary of Bamboo West Cottage*, Zhang Yu, Tao Zongyi and Xiang Yuanbian wrote poems and colophons for it. It is recorded in the *Spectacular Life, Record of Jiangcun Xiaoxia* and *Precious Collection of the Stong Moat Sequel*.

Zhang Wo (? - 1356), named Shuhou, called Zhen Qisheng. His ancestral home was Huainan (today's Anhui), but he lived in Hangzhou. He was skilled at painting characters and line drawings after the method of Li Gongling.

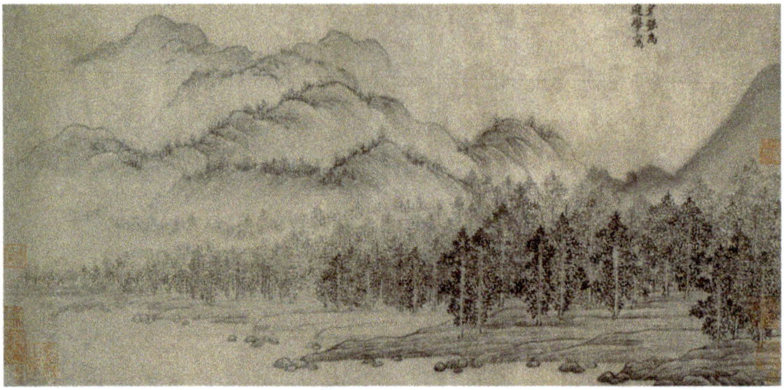

120. Wang Lizhong:Landscape

Yuan

Length: 25.2 cm Width: 53.3 cm

Preserved in the Palace Museum in Beijing

Silk scroll, ink painting. In the painting, a chain of mountains near the river recede in numerous ridges. The trees are luxuriant and the villages built near to the mountains can be seen indistinctly. The mountain rocks are painted by the hemp method, the technique of painting is powerful and meticulous. The forests are outlined by stick drawing and the leaves are completed by thick and light ink. The inscription is "Yan Qiang wrote for Xun Xue", which is a rare masterpiece of Wang Lizhong that has been handed down. Nine seals are recorded.

Wang Lizhong, whose date of birth is unknown, was named Yan Qiang and called Zhong Zhai was a native of Suining (present-day Sichuan). During the Yuanzheng Period of the Yuan Dynasty, he was once an official in Wuxi. At the end of Yuan Dynasty, he worked as a magistrate of Songjiang. He retired in the Ming Dynasty. He was skilled at calligraphy and painting.

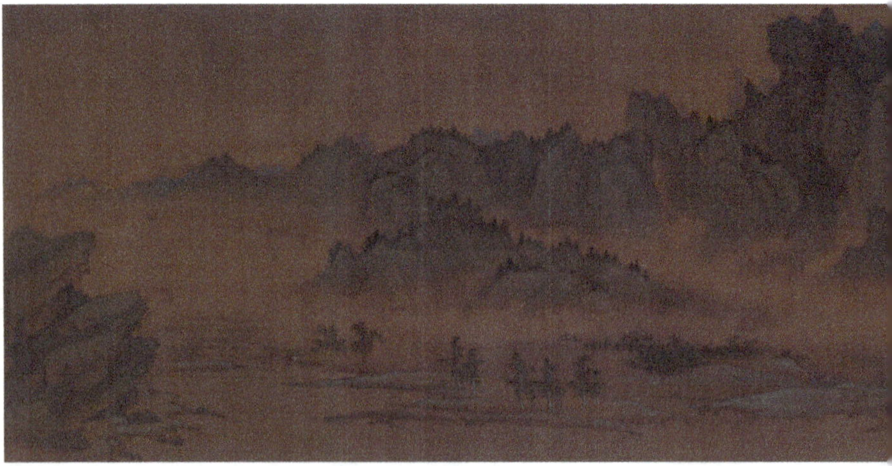

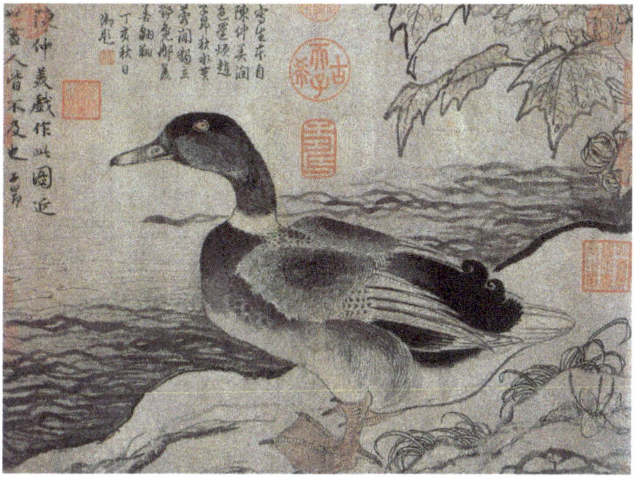

121. Chen Lin: Wild Duck alongside the Stream

Yuan

Length: 30.5 cm Width: 37.2 cm

Preserved in the Taipei National Palace Museum

Paper, tint. The close-up technique is used to paint a green-headed male duck. The background is lined with streams, slopes, stones, lotus and wild flowers. The artist drew the outline diligently, but the drawing is relatively simple and he used ink painting as the major way to color, along with cyanine, ocher pastel shades. Emperor Qianlong wrote a poem for it. It is recorded by the Qing Government. Qiu Yuan wrote a colophon for it. It is recorded in the Precious Collection of the Stone Moat Sequel: First Edition.

Chen Lin, named Zhongmei, was a native of Qiantang (Hangzhou, Zhejiang). He was the son of Chen Yuzi, teacher of a painting school of the Southern Song Dynasty. He inherited the tradition of his family and was skilled at painting landscapes, characters, birds and flowers. He was once instructed by Zhao Mengfu and created a new trend of freehand brushwork of birds and flowers.

122. Shang Qi: Mountains in Spring

Yuan

Length: 39.6 cm Width: 214.5 cm

Preserved in the Palace Museum in Beijing

Silk scroll, tint. The rolling-type scenery of the northern part of China is depicted. The composition inherits the features of landscape painting in the Jin Dynasty, forming the structure of changing and concluding, combining dark green with ink painting and disclosing a slightly literary atmosphere. The painting carries "signed by Shang Qi, Defu" and is acknowledged as his authentic work. It was recorded in Qing Dynasty. It is now recorded in the *Precious Collection of the Stone Moat Sequel: First Edition*.

Shang Qi (? - 1324), named Defu, called Shouyan, born in the Yuan Dynasty, native of Jiyin, Caozhou (present-day Heze, Shandong). Shang Ting, his father, was a famous official in the Yuan Dynasty. Guan Qi associated with scholars. He was good at painting traditional landscapes by using blue and green colors. He once created the landscape murals in the capital.

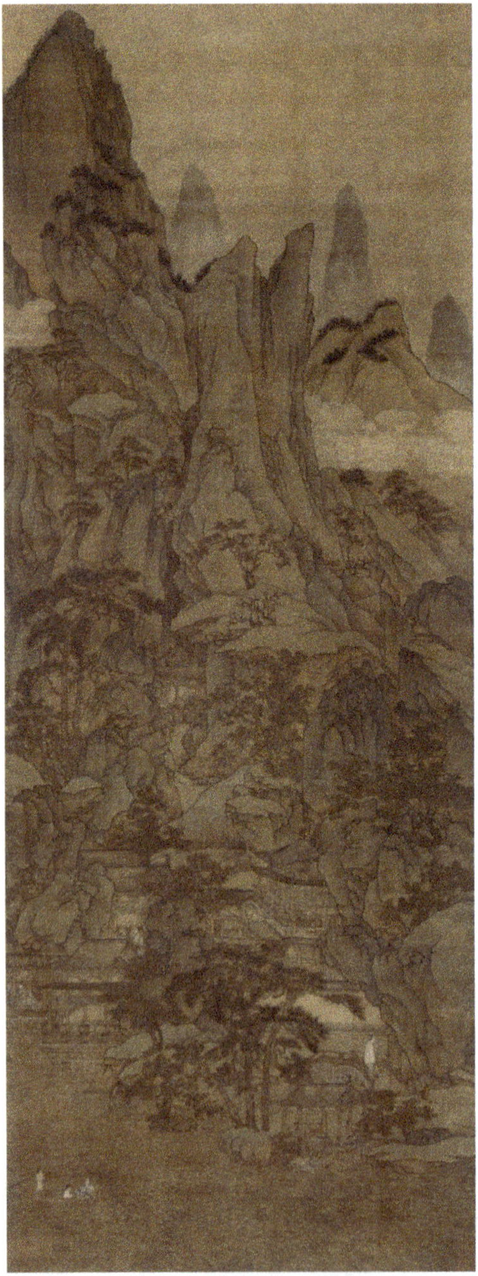

123. Hu Tinghui: Boating Alongside the Spring Mountains

Yuan

Length: 143 cm Width: 55.5 cm

Preserved in the Palace Museum in Beijing

Silk scroll, tint. In the painting, green hills rise the sky, the mist coils up, lush pines, and buildings among the mountains appear indistinctly with a winding porch crossing-a favorite place for scholars. At the foot of the mountain, there are bridges and streams. Someone is boating to enjoy the scenery. The artist uses line drawing to outline and then fills with color, which inherits the technique of painting landscape in the Tang Dynasty. It is sealed with "Tinghui".

Hu Tinghui, born in Wuxing (present-day Huzhou, Zhejiang), was good at painting. He came froim the same county as Zhao Mengfu and was once invited by the latter to complete the Painting of Picking Melon. Then, he wrote a poem depending on his memory that looks genuine.

124. Chen Xuan: Trees on Rocks

Yuan

Length: 66.7 cm Width: 27.6 cm

Preserved in the Tianjin Museum

Paper, Ink. In the painting, ridges and peaks rise higher one behind another with jungle covering, through which streams pour down;, temples appear indistinctly. The streams crossed by bridges and the jungle are well proportioned. The composition is lofty with clear layers. The mountains are painted with the hemp and raindrop methods. The leaves are completed by dotting. The artist wrote a poem by himself and signed the work with "July, Zhizheng Dingyou (1357), made by Chen Xuan". Three seals are recorded. Chen Wen and others wrote poems for it.

Chen Xuan, named Jushan, was born in the region south of the Yangtze River. His date of birth is unknown, but he was active about the end of the Yuan Dynasty and the beginning of the Ming Dynasty. He was skilled at painting landscape and learned from Dong Yuan, Ju Ran. His technique of painting is similar to that of Cao Zhibai. His paintings are almost all about the scenery in Shaoxing, Zhejiang.

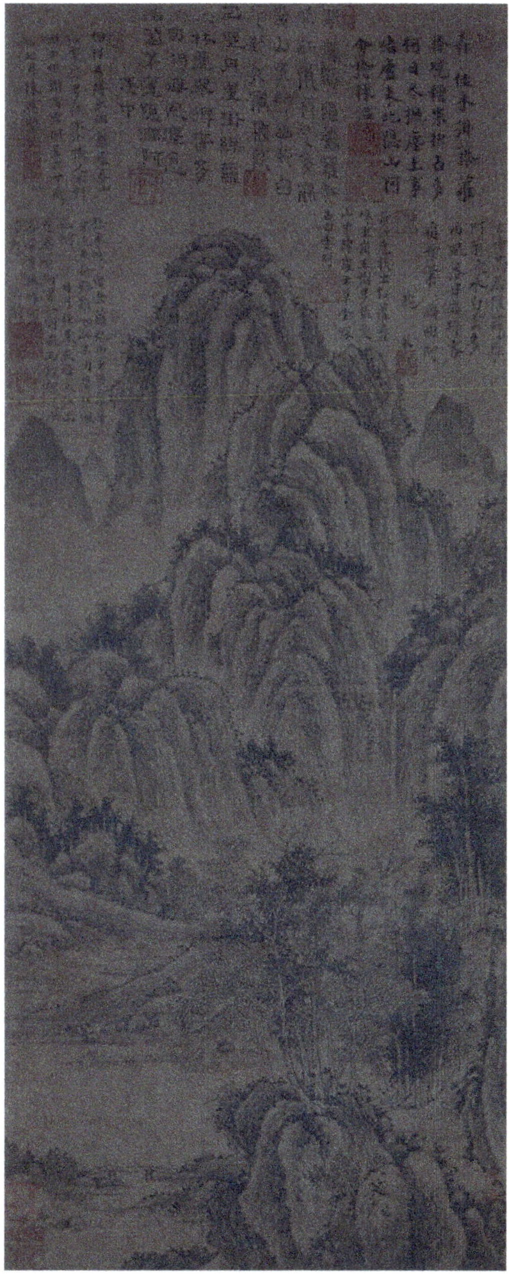

125. Xia Yong: Tower Next to Water

Yuan

Length: 23.9 cm Width: 25.3 cm

Preserved in the Palace Museum in Beijing

Silk scroll, Ink. It is framed by a round silk fan. In the painting, Chong Building stands beside the water stage, rails set on the ridge, and eaves located next to the top of the mountains. A scholar sits inside the building. Pine lanes and stone bridges stand in front of it, surrounded by lakes. The ruler painting is rigorous and the structure is adequate. It is a genuine work of Xia Yong. Emperor Qianlong wrote a poem for it signed with his seal. It is recorded in *Precious Collection of the Stone Moat Sequel: First Edition*.

Xia Yong, whose date of birth and death is unknown, named Minigyuan, was a native of Qiantang in the Yuan Dynasty (Hangzhou, Zhejiang). He was a folk painter, and most of the paintings are from famous buildings in ancient times. He was skilled at small wash painting. His technique of painting is careful and neat, and most of them have regular script with small characters.

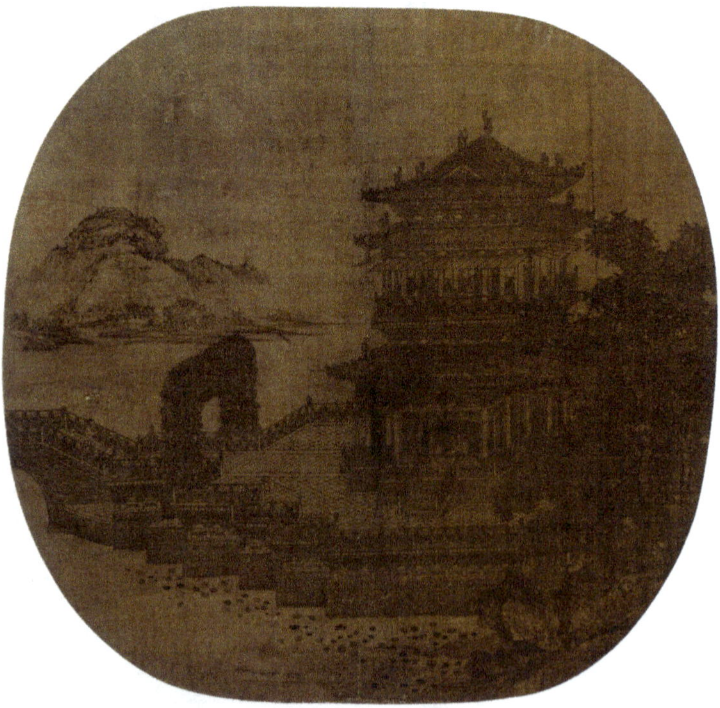

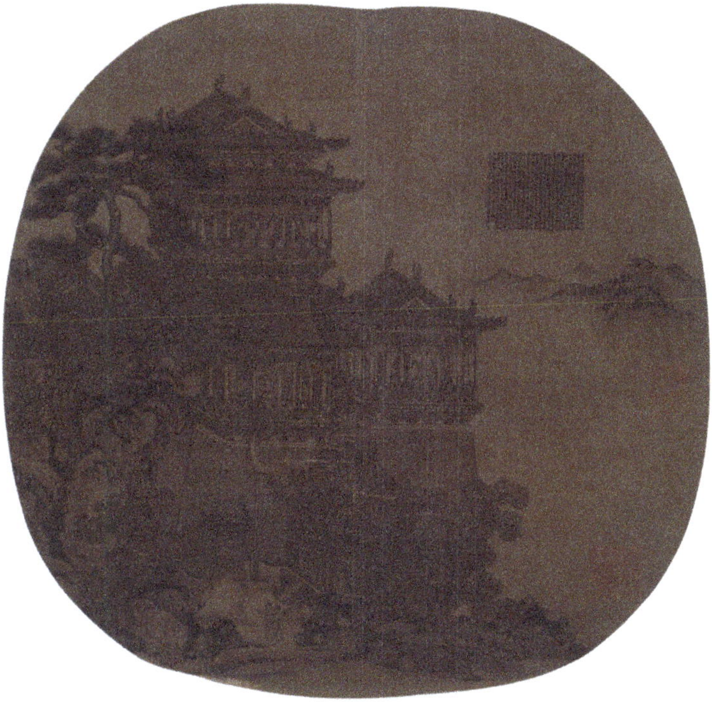

126. Xia Yong: Yueyang Tower

Yuan

Length: 25.2 cm Width: 25.8 cm

Preserved in the Palace Museum in Beijing

Silk scroll, Ink. It is framed by a round silk fan. In the painting, Yueyang Tower is a three-floor building, towering and reaching up to the sky. There are many travelers inside the building. Green pines stand next to the building and the rocks rug under the building. The trees grow and the travelers come and go. There is a boundless gully in front of the building, and mountains are in the distance. His technique of painting is powerful and meticulous, and the structure of the building is dense and taunt, filled with the sense of layering, near and far. The Fan Zhongyan's Diary of Yueyang Tower in regular script with small characters is written on it and a seal is signed. It is recorded in the *Precious Collection of the Stone Moat Sequel*.

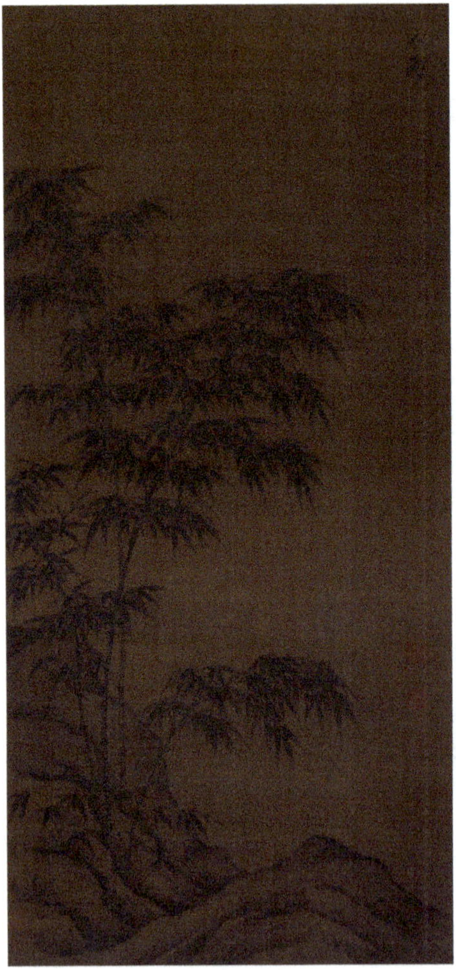

127. Li Kan: Bamboos in the Rain

Yuan

Length: 111.5 cm Width: 55 cm

Preserved in the Palace Museum in Beijing

Silk scroll, tint. In the painting, four bamboos stand on a stony slope; the leaves are luxuriant and drooping, just like washing in the rain. The stems and the leaves are green and the ends of the leaves are bistre, with the ochre stem of the bamboos. The blank represents the drops of water on the leaves of the bamboos. It is the master work of bamboo with elaborate style painted by Li Kan. The title is "Washing In Rains" with a seal. It is recorded in the *Collective Study on Shigutang Calligraphy and Paintings*.

Li Kan (1244-1320), named Zhongbin and called Taoist of Xizhai, was a native of Yan (present-day Beijing) and later lived in Weiyang (present-day Yangzhou). He was once ordered to make mural paintings for palaces and temples. He was good at painting bamboos, weather elaborate style or Chinese pen brushing.

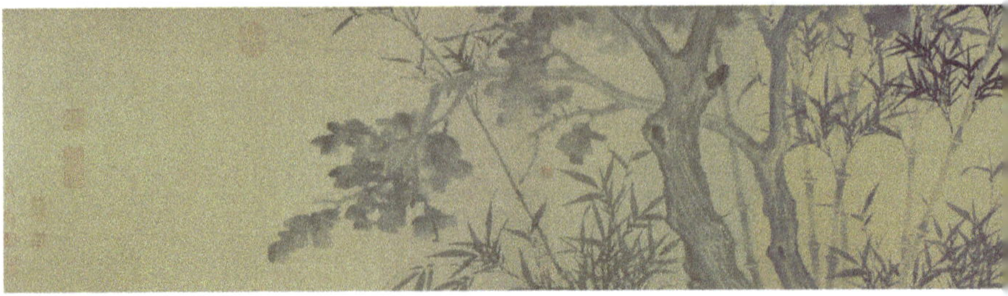

128. Li Kan: Outlining Bamboos and Stones

Yuan

Length: 185.5 cm Width: 153.7 cm

Preserved in the Palace Museum in Beijing

Silk scroll, tint. In the painting, there are several bamboos, tall and luxuriant. Slope stones, newly-born bamboos and curled grasses are painted under the bamboos. The artist used elaborate style to paint the bamboos and uses green color for emphasis. He used thick ink to paint the slope stones as well as light ink to color, which forms a contrast with the bamboos. It is the master work of Li Kan. The seal of the painting is destroyed. Li Dongyang, a man of the Ming Dynasty wrote a colophon for it.

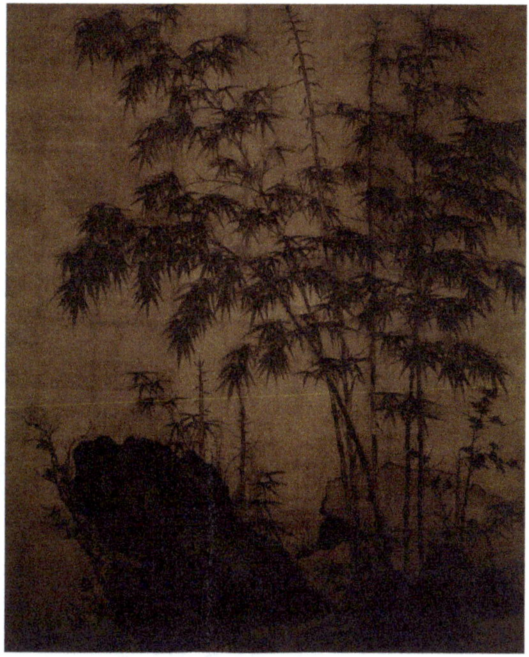

129. Li Kan: Four Objects

Yuan

Length: 35.6 cm Width: 259.8 cm

Preserved in the Palace Museum in Beijing

Ink on paper with brush. Bamboos in the rain, orchid in spring, lake stones and Chinese parasol form the painting's theme. They are well arranged. The artist uses ink entirely for the painting, and the pen and ink use shows aplomb and simplicity. It is signed with the words "write in the Dade Ding Year (1307)". It was collected by Anqi in the Qing Dynasty and Qing Government. It is recorded in the *Moyuan Huiguan*.

The painting is the second half of a longer one, at about the middle to late period of the Ming Dynasty. The longer part is divided into two sections. The first half is collected in the Kansas Nelson and Atkins Art Museum.

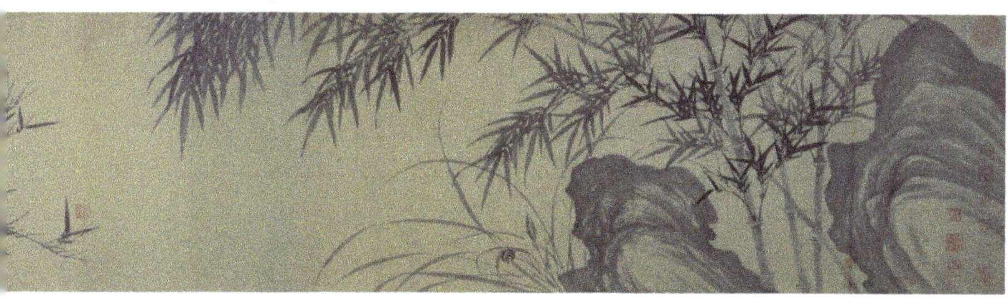

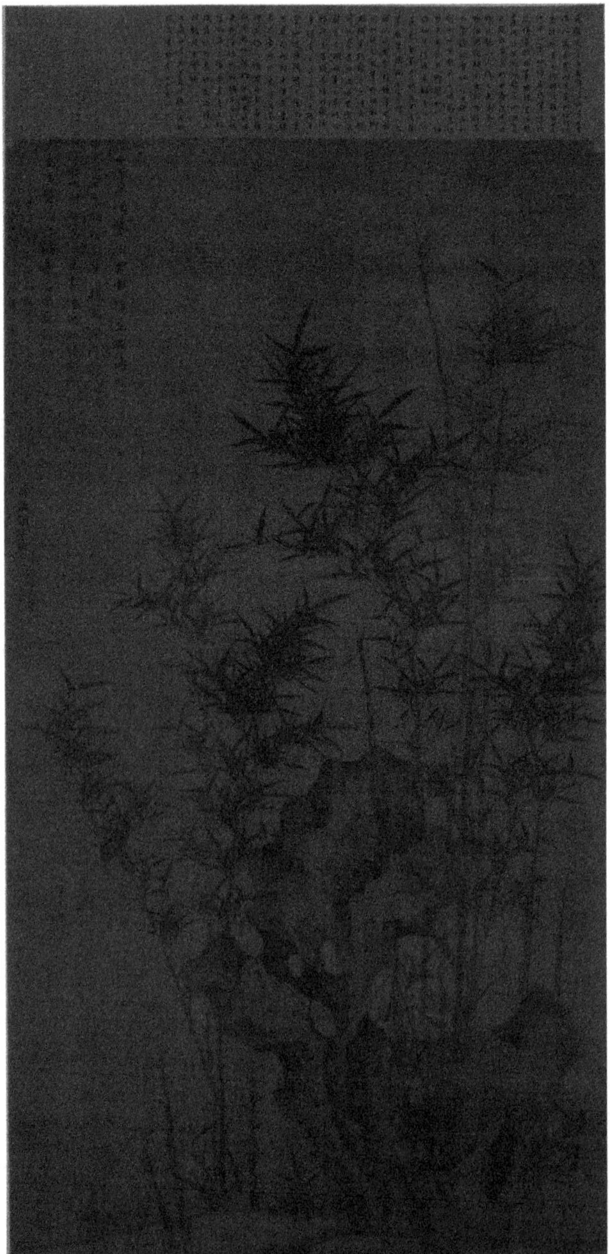

130. Gu An: Bamboos and Stones

Yuan

Length: 184 cm Width: 102 cm

Preserved in the Palace Museum in Beijing

Silk scroll, Ink. This depicts bamboos and stones. New bamboos grow in a sparing way. The technique of painting is powerful and careful. The lake stones are painted by drawing and dying. It is the master work of bamboos painted by Gu An. It is signed with the words "Painted by Donghuai Gu An". Zhang Shen once wrote a poem for it, and Xu Zonghao once wrote a postscript.

Gu An (1289-1365), named Dingzhi and called Pedantic Man, was born in Pingjiang (present-day Suzhou, Jiangsu), and lived in Kunshan (present-day Jiangsu). He was skilled at painting bamboos and learned from Wen Tong and Zhao Mengfu.

131. Gu An: Ink Bamboo & Stone

Yuan

Length: 126.7 cm Width: 41.6 cm

Preserved in the Palace Museum in Beijing

Paper, ink. It depicts a scene of three thin, but tall ink bamboos' standing straight and powerfully and adorned with bamboo shoots; overlaying nest stones under the bamboos are mellow and full. The bamboo poles are painted by dry brush with light ink, while the bamboo leaves are painted by pressing down with the Chinese writing brush. The penmanship is vigorous and free, and both heavy ink and light ink are applied to convey the bamboos' quietness, beauty and elegant spirit. There are inscriptions "Dingzhi painted it for elegant friend Haiyu Liuju", "Seal of Gu Dingzhi" & the seal "the pedantic aged (Yune Laoren)" on the painting and poems by Xu Zonghao and Chen Banding on the mount of the painting.

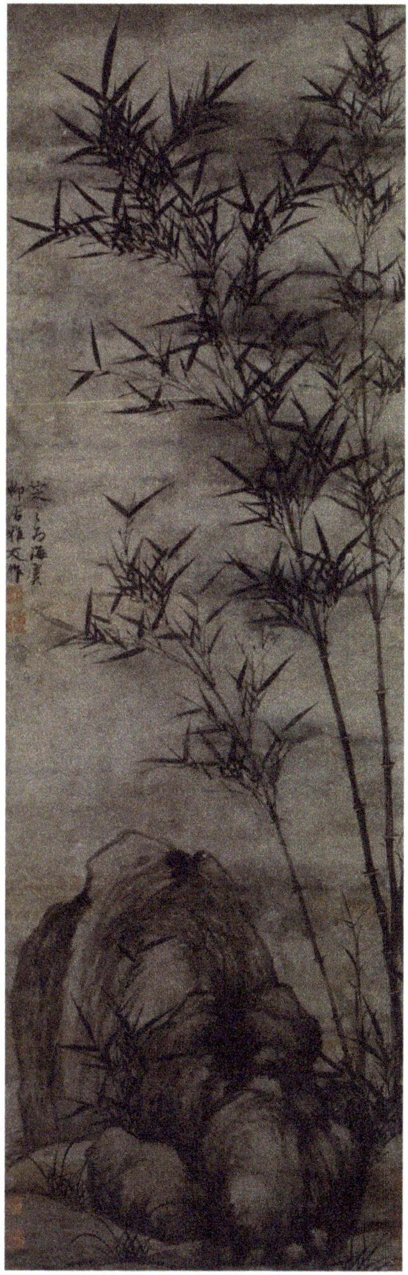

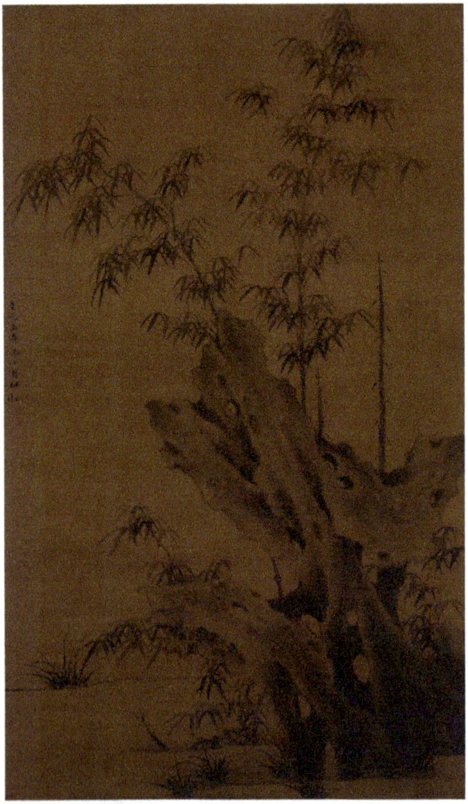

132. Xie Tingzhi:Bamboos and Stones

Yuan

Length: 173.2 cm Width: 105.1 cm

Preserved in the Palace Museum in Beijing

Silk scroll, ink. It depicts a grassy slope and lake stones. Several straight bamboos are scattered behind the stones, while little bamboos and fragrant thoroughworts cluster on the slope and bamboo shoots break through the soil. The lake stones are painted by drawing with wrinkle and rendered by light ink. Casual and elegant drawing paints light colored and dark colored bamboo leaves provide a coherent combination and create a vivid wash painting. The painting carries an inscription "By Zhonghe in the tenth month of the 5th year (1339) of of the reign of Zhiyuan" and two seals. It is the only extant ink bamboo work of the painter.

Xie Tingzhi, also named Zhonghe and known as Xuecun, was born in Kunshan (present-day Jiangsu). He was good at writing poems, painting and calligraphy, especially painting ink bamboo.

133. Zhang Xun: Double Drawing Bamboos and Stones

Yuan

Length: 43.4 cm Width: 668 cm

Preserved in the Palace Museum in Beijing

Paper, ink. It depicts ink bamboos and green pines on sloping low hills. The bamboos are painted by powerful and meticulous double drawing and the pine needles are tinted by heavy ink, showing greenness, while stones on the slope are painted by pima wrinkling. The painting carries a self-preface, an inscription "Painted by Zhang Xun from Wujun in Wu's House on the 30th day of the fouth month of the ninth year (1349) of the reign of Zhizheng", a seal of Zhang Xun, another 63 seals and prefaces & postscripts written by 14 scholars such as Ni Zan and Zhang Shen. The painting, the only existing work of the painter, is recorded in the *Pei Wen Zhai Paintings and Calligraphy, Collective Study on Shigutang Calligraphy and Paintings* and the like.

Zhang Xun (14th Century), also named Zhongmin and known as Xiyun lived in Pingjiang (Suzhou, Jiangsu) in the Yuan Dynasty. He was good at painting double drawing ink bamboos. He learned ink bamboo drawing and later drew it by double drawing that was an extremely clever and ingenious painting method in those times.

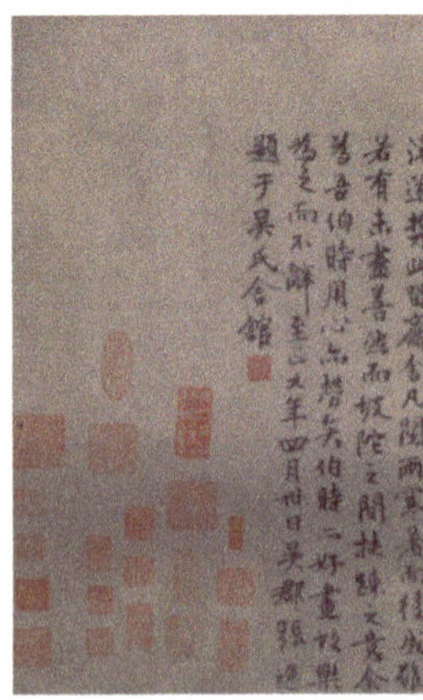

134. Wang Yuan: Flowers, Stones and Golden Pheasants

Yuan

Length: 162.5 cm Width: 133 cm

Preserved in the Shanxi Museum

Silk scroll, ink. It depicts the scene of two golden pheasants' standing opposite on the lake stones, peach blossoms and tall bamboos rising steeply beside the stones and green grass growing thickly. The golden pheasants are painted meticulously and gently, while ink bamboos are painted by powerful double drawing, lake stones wrinkled vigorously and unrestrained and peach blossoms and leaves stippled by ink. There is an inscription "Wang Yuan, also named Ruoshui, painted the Painting: Peach Blossoms, Bamboos and Golden Pheasants for good friend Zhonghua in Qiantang, in the twelfth month of the lunar year of the third year (1343) of the reign of Zhizheng" .

Wang Yuan (14th century), also named Wang Ruoshui and known as Danxuan, lived in Qiantang (Hangzhou in Zhejiang). He was active in the middle and late Yuan Dynasty. He learned painting from childhood and was taught and guided by Zhao Mengfu for painting techniques. He was good at painting mountains, rivers and figures, especially ink flowers, birds, bamboos and stones.

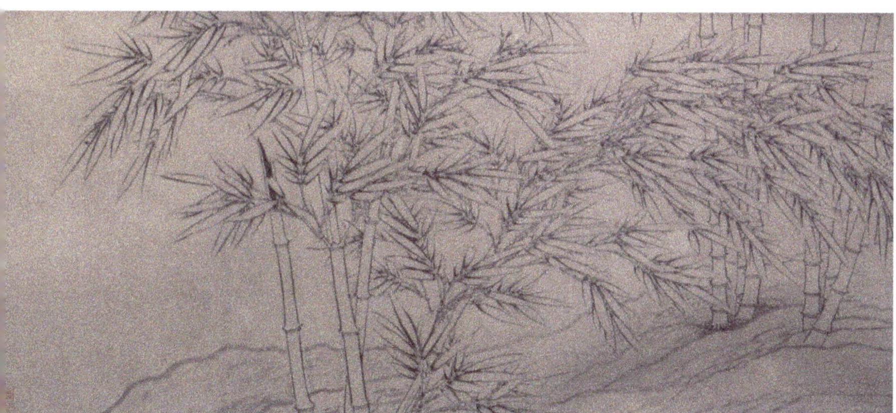

135. Ke Jiusi: Ink Bamboo Painting Scroll Painted in Qingbi Pavilion

Yuan

Length: 132.8 cm Width: 58.5 cm

Preserved in the Palace Museum in Beijing

Paper, ink. It depicts two ink bamboos beside fantastic rocks decorated by a little grass. Bamboo leaves are painted by casting aside the Chinese writing brush, with pima wrinkling for lake rocks. The work carries a self-preface "Staying in Qingbi Pavilion on December 13th of the 15th year (1338) of the reign of Zhiyuan, I paint. Inscribed by Danqiusheng", four seals, a poem and seal of Emperor Qianlong and another 31 seals. The painting is recorded in *Moyuan Huiguan, Precious Collection of the Stone Moat Sequel: First Edition,Collection of Xuzhai Paintings*, and *Collective Study on Shigutang Calligraphy and Paintings*.

Ke Jiusi (1290-1343), also named Jingzhong and known as Danqiusheng, was born in Xianju, Taizhou (a place in Zhejiang currently). He had extensive learning, great capacity and enjoyed high fame in poem, painting and calligraphy. He was good at painting mountains,rivers, flowers and especially ink bamboos.

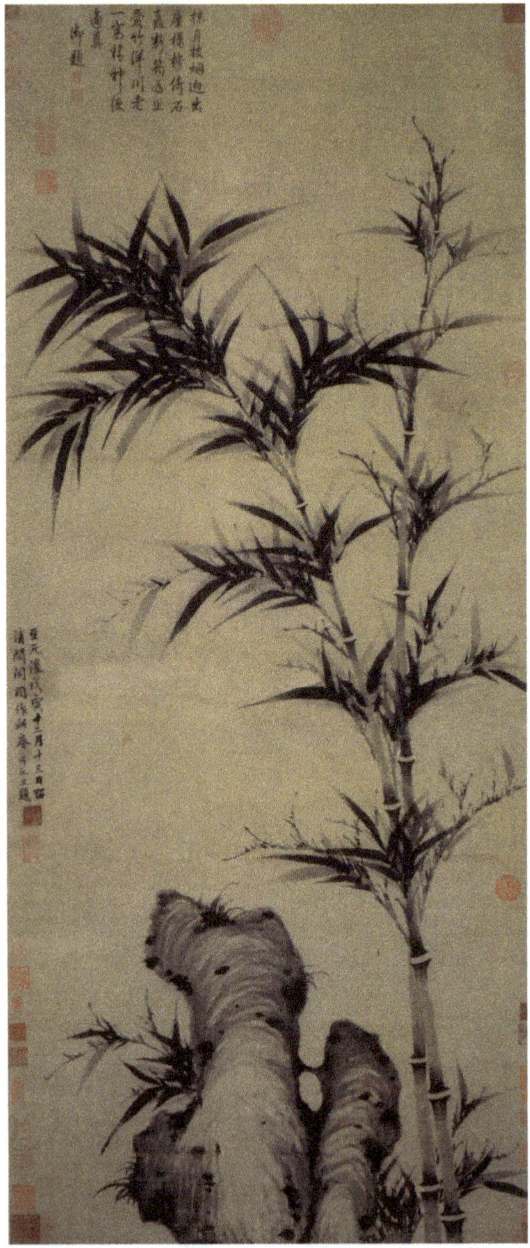

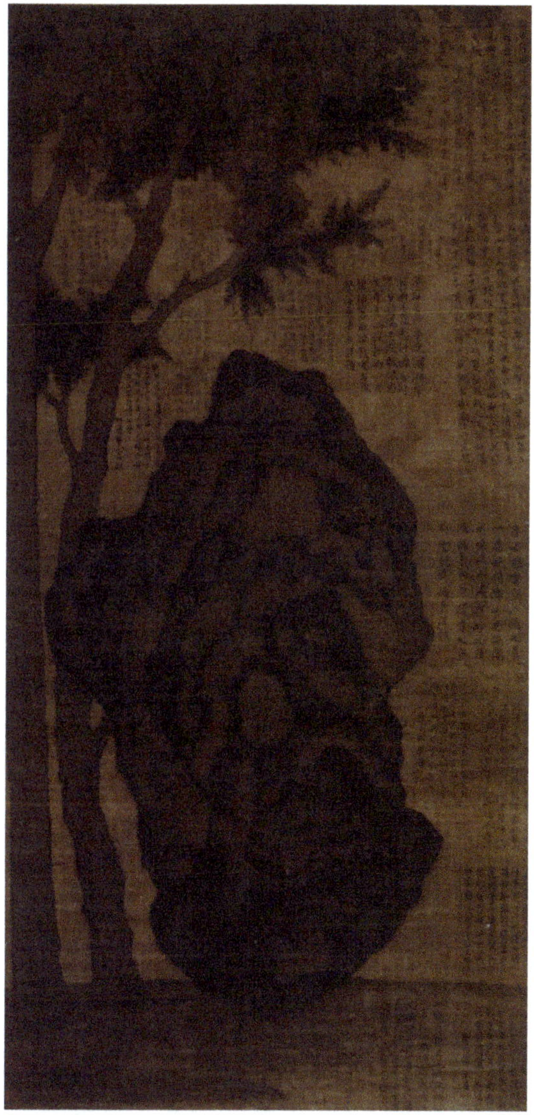

136. Lu Xingzhi: Green Chinese Parasol and Dark Green Stones

Yuan

Length: 107 cm Width: 53.2 cm

Preserved in the Palace Museum in Beijing

Silk scroll, tint. It depicts a huge hill stone with Chinese parasol and tall ancient cypress trees reaching towards the sky beside it. The lake stones are painted by complicated wrinkling and thick tint, while the trees are painted by double drawing and both tiny leaves and multi-leaves are drawn. There are two self-prefaces, an inscription "By Lu Xingzhi", the painter's seal, prefaces of 14 scholars such as Liu Zehai and another 25 seals on the painting. The painting is recorded in the *Wangshi Shan Hu Wang, Pei Wen Zhai Painting and Calligraphy Series,* and *Collective Study on Shigutang Calligraphy and Paintings*.

Lu Xingzhi, also named Lu Jiheng, lived in Wujiang, Jiangsu, in the late Yuan Dynasty and early Ming Dynasty. Early in the latter period, he was given Hanlin ancient books and records. He was good at writing poems, calligraphy and painting trees and stones in the style of clear and powerful painting.

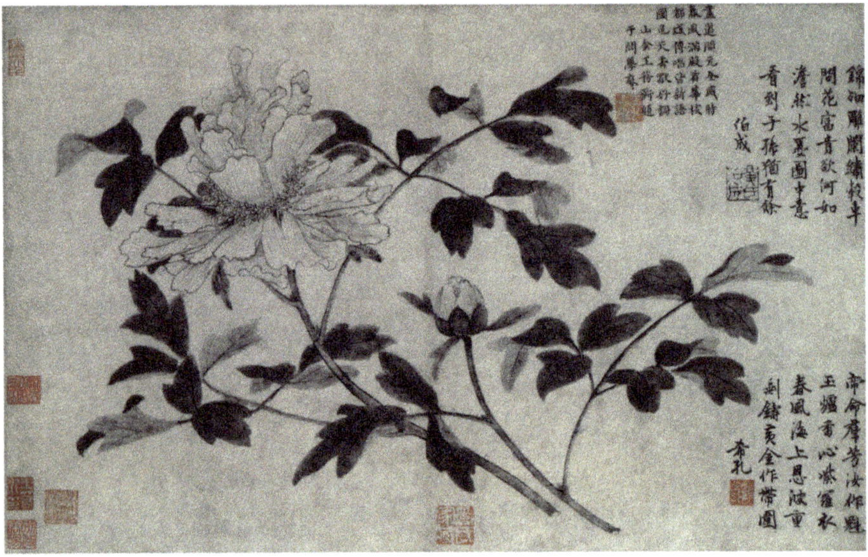

137. Wang Yuan: Peonies

Yuan

Length: 37.7 cm   Width: 61.6 cm

Preserved in the Palace Museum in Beijing

Paper, ink. It depicts the scene of two broken peony branches with one extending golden stamen surrounding by layers of petals and another sprouting. Flowers are painted by thin line drawing; leaves are dyed by ink and heavy ink is applied to outline of stems and the back and turning of the leaves are painted by light ink. There are "Seal of Wang Ruoshui", poems written by Wang Wudao and the like and several other seals on the painting. On the tail of the painting is Peony Ode poetized by Yuanyu and written by Li Sheng.

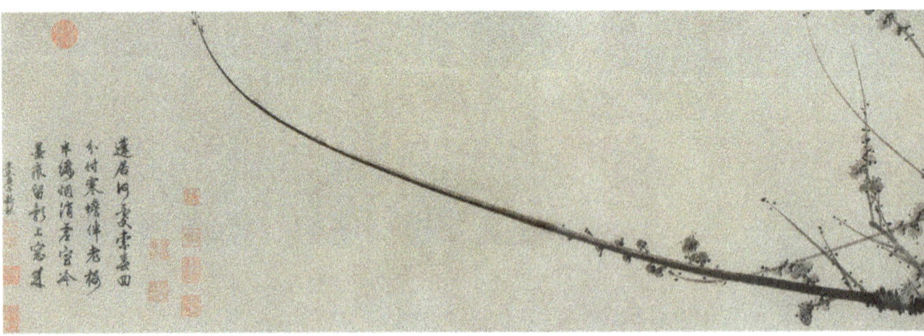

138. Zang Liang: Grass and Insect Painting

Yuan

Length: 18.6 cm   Width: 22.5 cm

Preserved in the Palace Museum in Beijing

Silk scroll, tint. It depicts the blossoming of orchids with two wasps among which one has just landed on a leaf and another is about to land. Drawing comparatively unrestrainedly on some parts and meticulously on others and the quiet and beautiful ink color altogether create a vivid scene. There is a seal "Xiang Qing" on the painting.

Zang Liang, also named Xiang Qing, was born in Qiantang (Hangzhou). He was good at painting flowers, bamboos and feathers.

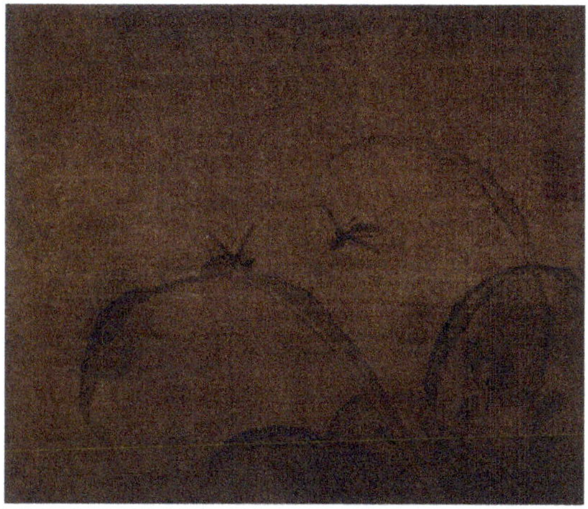

139. Zou Fulei: Spring Information

Yuan

Length: 34.1 cm   Width: 221.5 cm

Preserved in the Freer Gallery of Art in Washington, the U.SA

Paper, ink. It depicts a spray of ancient plum blossoms whose old stems are strong and new ones elegant and beautiful. Petals of the plum blossoms are stippled by light ink and decorated by mosses and stamens stippled by pure ink. Stippled flowers in light color, leave colors embellish each other, and painting rules are still strictly obeyed in this painting. There are a self-preface of a four-line poem with seven characters to each line, an inscription "In new autumn of Gengzi year (1360) of the reign of Zhizheng" and the inscription "Spring information" written by Yang Yu of Yuan Dynasty in clerical script on the painting. On the tail of the scroll are postscripts written by Yang Weizhen of the Yuan Dynasty and Gu Anzhu of the Yuan Dynasty. The painting has been authenticated and recorded by several famous collectors in the Ming Dynasty and the Qing Dynasty.

Zou Fulei, also named Yundong Taoist, is a painter in the Yuan Dynasty. He was active in late Yuan Dynasty and is good at painting plum blossoms.

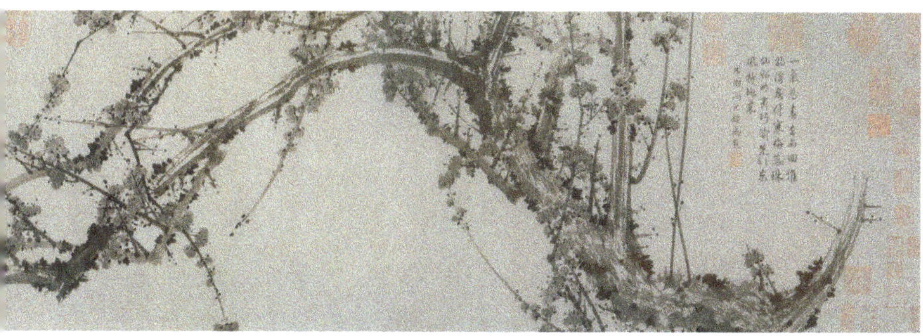

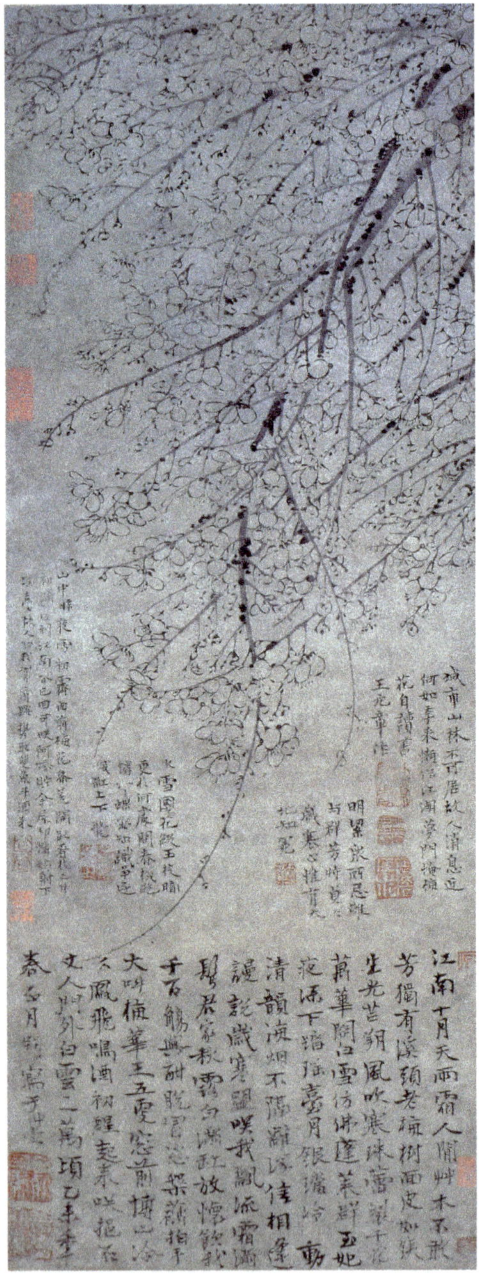

140. Wang Mian: Plum Blossom

Yuan

Length: 67.7 cm Width: 25.9 cm

Preserved in the Shanghai Museum

Paper, ink. It depicts a scene of luxuriant plum branch hanging upside down with plenty of flowers. The new style of ink plum blossom painting is created by drawing flowers and stippling stamen with ink and Chinese writing brush. The whole layout of the painting is well-proportioned and the painting shows power and vigor, with smooth, free and easy lines. There are five poems poetized by the painter, an inscription of "Painted on the first month of the 32nd year (1355) of the reign of Zhizheng in the Humble Cottage" and poems poetized by Zhu Yunming of the Ming Dynasty, Wen Huiming of the Ming Dynasty and Tang Yin of the Ming Dynasty on the painting. Wang Mian (1287-1359), also named Yuanzhang and known as Zhushi Shannong, Fanniuweng, Meihua Wuzhu, Kuaiji Waishi and the like, lived in Zhuji (the current Shaoxing, Zhejiang). He is good at painting bamboos and stones, especially ink plum blossoms. He was taught by Yang Buzhi and Monk Huaguang (Zhongren).

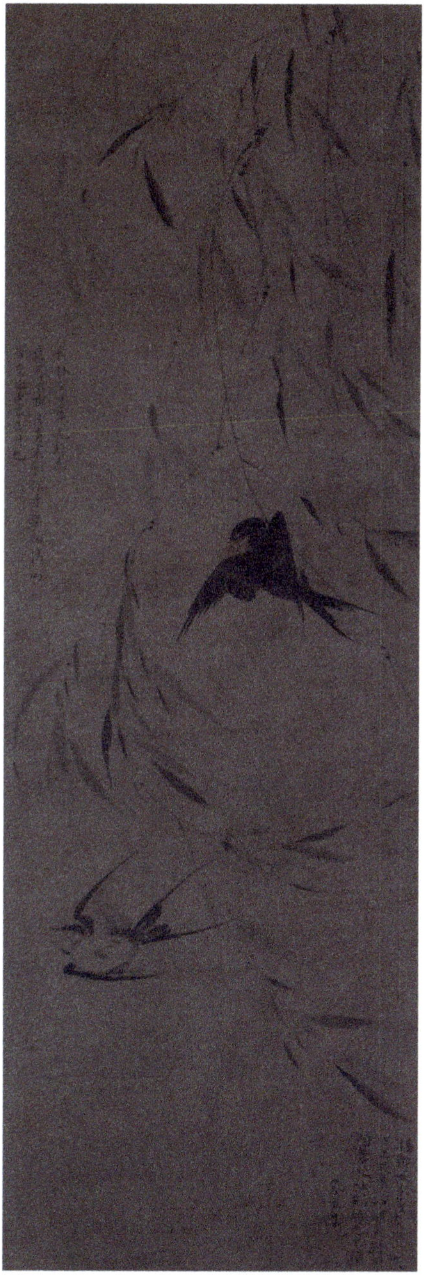

141. Sheng Changnian: Willow and Swallows

Yuan

Length: 75.3 cm Width: 25.5 cm

Preserved in the Palace Museum in Beijing

Ink on paper with brush. It depicts weeping willows whose leaves swirl prettily and charmingly, while a swallow flies against the wind and another is about to land on the willow. The painting style is flexible and the kinetic potential is vividly and meticulously created. A dynamic atmosphere prevails and makes the scroll full of the delights of nature. There is the inscription of "Sheng Changnian (Ling of Yuan Dynasty) from Wulin painted the scroll for Shen Yanshu, a good friend from Wujun, in Liangxi dwelling place in the third month of the 29th year (1352) of Zhizheng Reign". There is another poem inscribed on the painting and signed by "Cai Qiusheng"; the seal is unclear.

Sheng Changnian, whose date of birth and death is unknown, also named Fuling, was born in Wulin (current Hangzhou, Zhejiang) in the Yuan Dynasty. He was active in the reign of Zhizheng and was good at painting flowers, birds in simple, elegant and light painting style and with less embellishment. He was especially good at painting willows and swallows with a new conception.

142. Wang Dijian: Narcissus

Yuan
Length: 31.4 cm
First Section Width: 80.2 cm
Second Section Width: 146 cm
Preserved in the Palace Museum in Beijing

Paper, ink. The painting is not completed and divided into two parts. It depicts the scene of narcissuses' blossoming vigorously in the spring and plenty of flowers with dense leaves. Layout of the painting is complex and dense with flowers and leaves staggering and creating a vivid scene. The painting is drawn by the techniques of double drawing and ink filling. There are remaining seals on the painting and on the tail of the scroll is a poem postscript. The painting is recorded in the Precious Collection of the Stone Moat.

Wang Dijian, also named Tingji or Jiyin, was born in Xinchang (a place in Zhejiang currently). He is good at painting narcissuses and can paint maintains and rivers, too.

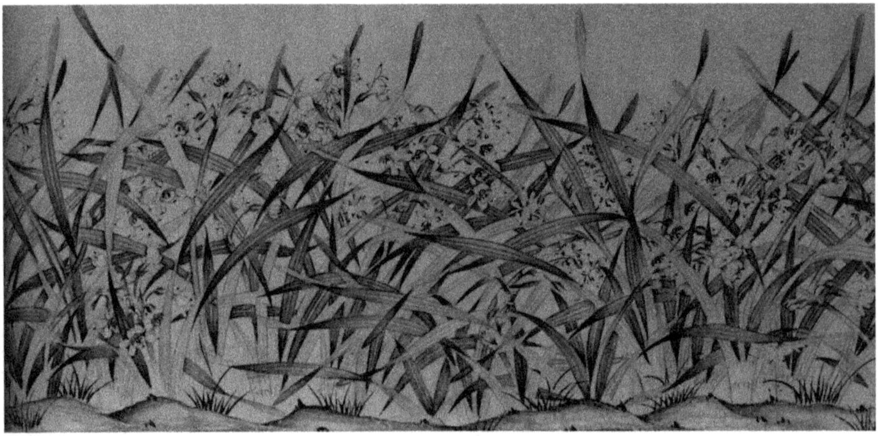

143. Zhang Shunzi: Goshawk, Chinese Parasol and Bamboos

Yuan
Length: 146 cm Width: 93 cm
Preserved in the Shandong Museum

Silk scroll, tint. It depicts the scene of luxuriant Chinese parasols with old stems and new branches surround several tall bamboos. They are well-spaced and stand opposite to each other to form a delightful contrast, while a lanneret stands on the tip of a branch looking sideward. Chinese parasols are painted by double drawing and wrinkling, conveying gentleness and elegance. Branches of the ink bamboos are mellow and full, while their leaves are thick but in order. There is a poem inscribed on the painting and signed with "Zhang Shunzi, or Shikui, inscribes it for Deying" and there are three more poems made by Sadadao of Yuan Dynasty.

Zhang Shunzi, also named Shikui, was a folk painter in the Yuan Dynasty. He was good at painting mountains, rivers, trees and stones.

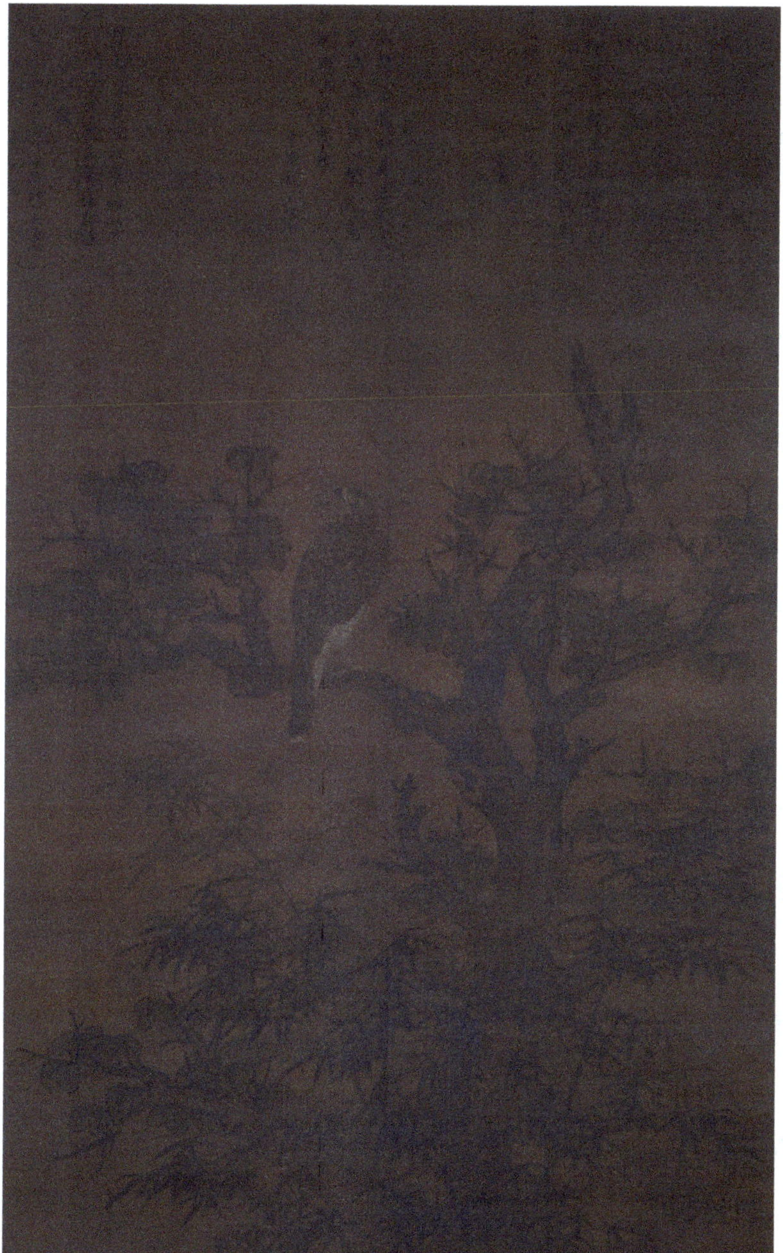

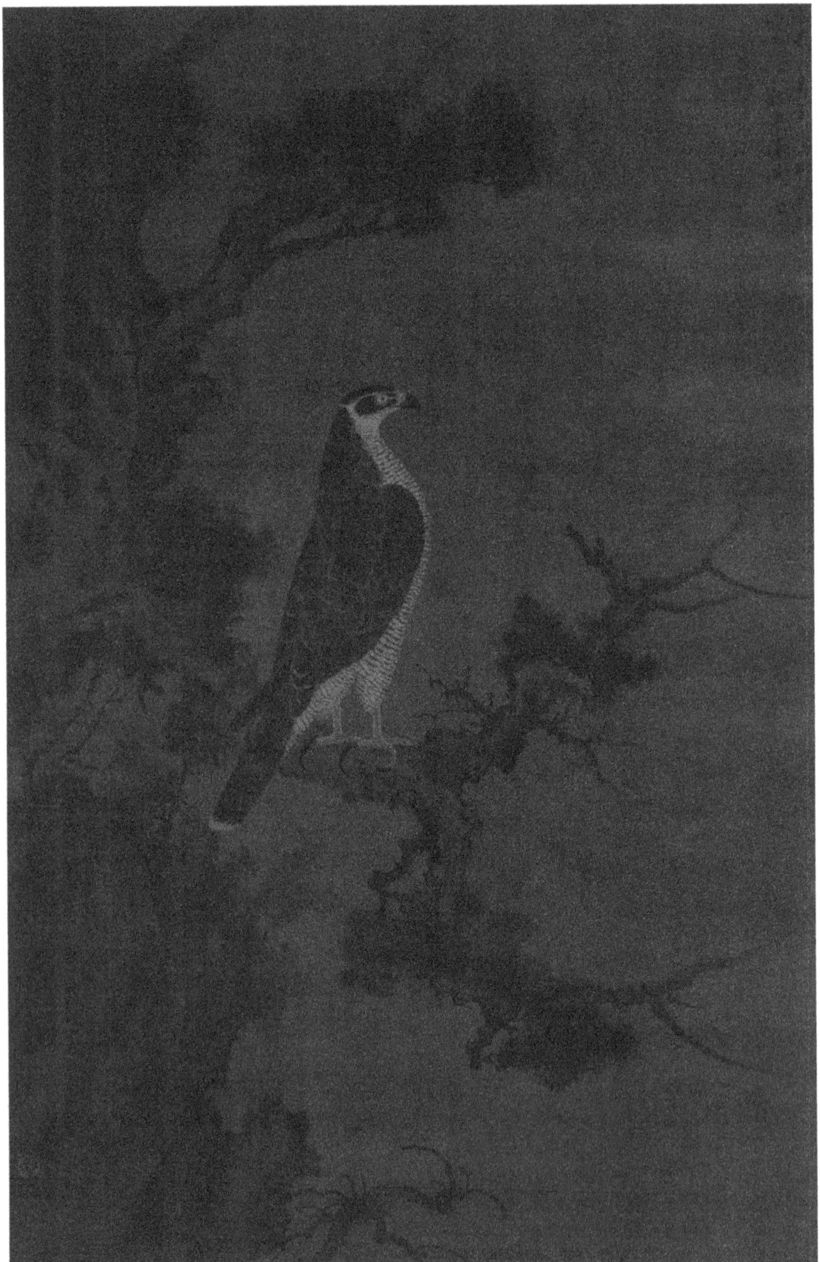

144. Xue Jieweng and Zhang Shunzi: Eagle and Sabina Chinensis

Yuan
Length: 147.3 cm Width: 96.8 cm
Preserved in the Palace Museum in Beijing

Silk scroll, tint. It depicts an ancient sabina chinensis whose dead wood and new leaves contrast with each other. It stands among hills and stones, and its stems and branches are vigorous. Raising its head, an eagle stands proudly on an old branch that has grown wild. The eagle's eyes brim with radiating vigor, while both of its sharp talons clutch the branch tightly. The eagle is created by painting with exact delineation and enriched colors, while the ancient Juniperus chinensis, mountains and stones are created by the freehand brushwork of traditional Chinese painting. There is an inscription indicating the yellow eagle is painted by Xuejieweng and the ancient Juniperus chinensis is painted by Zhang Shunzi. The content of the seal is unclear. Other seals, "Liang" and "Preserved by Huang Zhou", are on the scroll.

Xue Jieweng was a folk painter in the Yuan Dynasty, but his *History of Paintings* is not known.

145. He Cheng: Returning Village

Yuan
Length: 41 cm Width: 723.8 cm
Preserved in the Jilin Museum

Paper, ink. Painted according to Tao Yuanming's Home Coming, the painting depicts the scene of an elegant scholar who appears repeatedly with landscape as the background. The figures are mainly drawn by the technique of line drawing, while slope stones, trees and wood are wrinkled by pure ink and decorated by light ink. The signature on the painting was added later and there are postscripts of Zhao Mengfu, Deng Wenyuan, Yu Ji, Ke Jiusi and some others on the back . The painting is included in the *List of Grand View Spectacular Life*.

He Cheng lived in the late Jin Dynasty and early Yuan Dynasty. He was a Painting Daizhao in the palace in the period of Jin Shizu and became Grand Secretary and Zhongfeng Senior Official in the Zhaowen Studio in the Yuan Dynasty. He was good at painting tales of people, pommel horses and ruler painting as well as painting mountains and rivers.

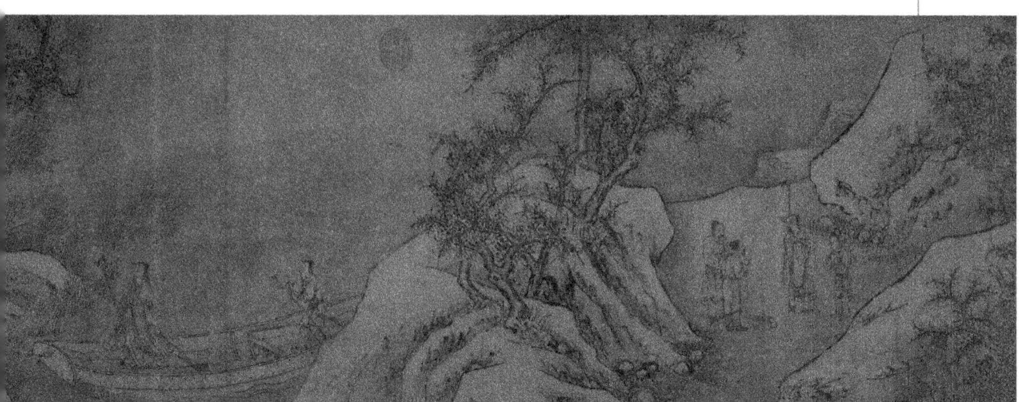

146. Ren Renfa: Zhang Guo Paying His Respects to the Emperor Xuanzong of the Tang Dynasty

Yuan

Length: 41.5 cm Width: 107.3 cm

Preserved in the Palace Museum in Beijing

Silk scroll, tint. It depicts the legend of Lung-Chi Lee, an Emperor in the Tang Dynasty, meeting Zhang Guo, one of the Eight Immortals. The textures of the clothes are thin but powerful and tinted with bright, clear and calm color, while the facial expressions of the people are described even to the most trifling degree. All of these make it the representative figure painting of Ren Renfa. The painted is signed with "By Yunjian Ren Renfa" and the seal of "Ren Ziming"; besides, there is a poem in the handwriting of Emperor Qianlong and 12 preservation seals. There are two poems made by Kangli Naonao and Wei Shu and several seals stamped on the back. The painting is included in the *Pearls of the Mysterious Palace*.

Ren Renfa (1254-1327), originally named Ting and also known as Ziming or Yueshan Daoren, was born in Songjiang (present-day Songjiang, Shanghai). He was good at painting pommel horses, figure stories, flowers, birds and the like. He had imitated Tang people's paintings and those of Li Gonglin of the Song Dynasty and was equally famous with Zhao Mengfu in his time.

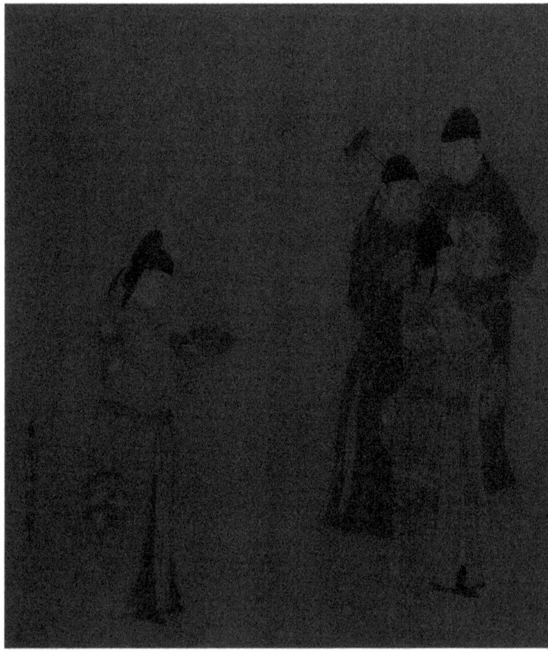

147. Ren Renfa: Two Horses

Yuan

Length: 28.8 cm Width: 142.7 cm

Preserved in the Palace Museum in Beijing

Silk scroll, tint. It depicts one fat horse holding its head high and acting vigorously and one thin horse lowering its head and waking slowly. The two horses create a mighty contrast and indicate the contrast of greediness and rightness. There is a preface by the painter on the painting. The painting is signed "Yueshan Daoren" and stamped by twenty seals. There are prefaces and postscripts and seal of Ke Jiusi on the tail of the scroll. The *Precious Collection of the Stone Moat Sequel* analyzes and records the painting.

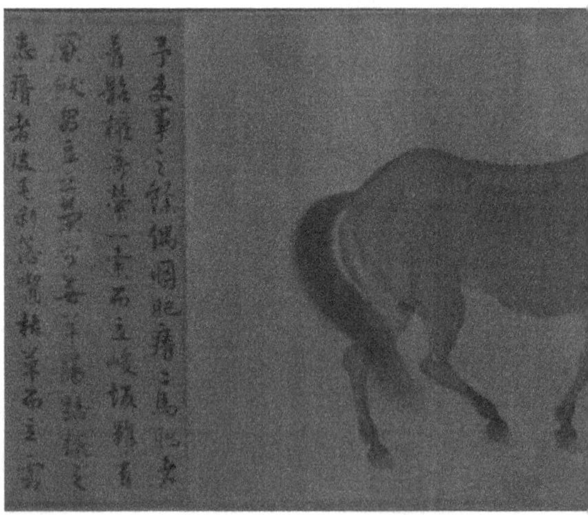

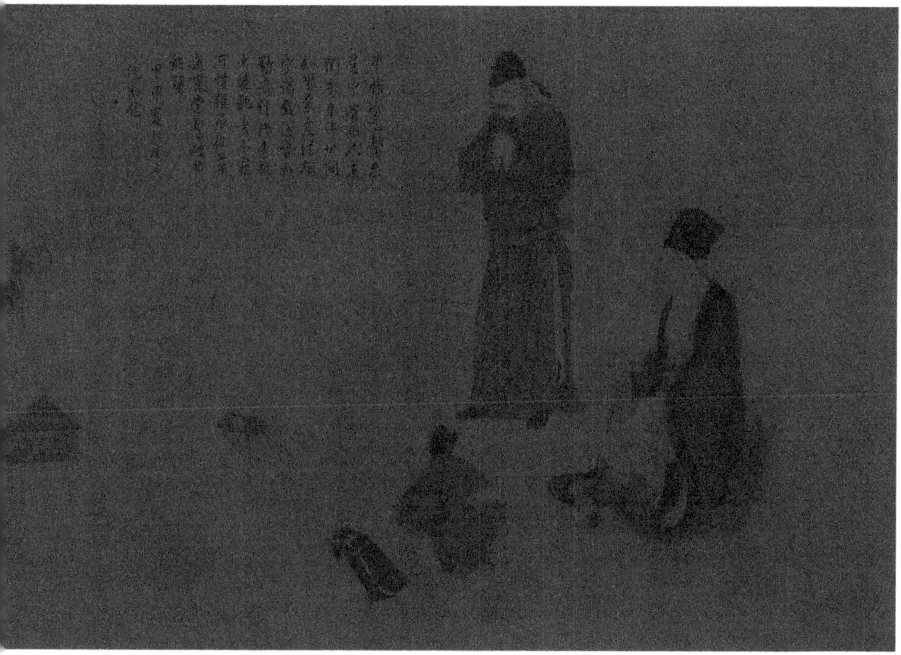

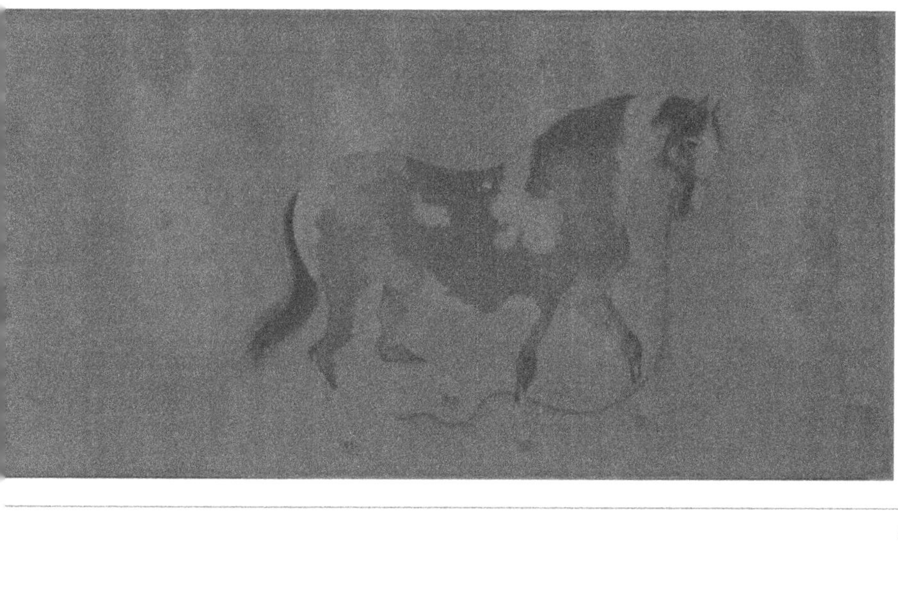

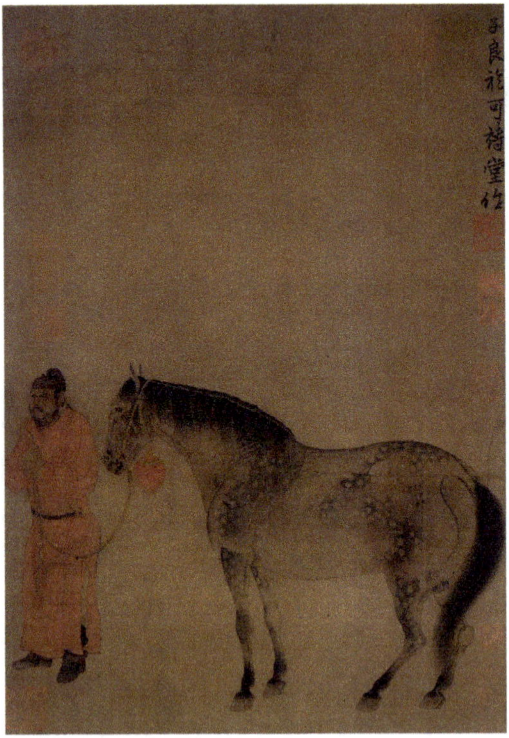

148. Ren Xianzuo: People and Horses

Yuan

Length: 50.6 cm Width: 36 cm

Preserved in the Palace Museum in Beijing

Silk scroll, tint. It depicts an official dressed in red vestment and wearing a black gauze cap on his head leading a horse by the hand. The fine horse is plump and sturdy in high spirits. The painting is succinctly made and the lines of the images are smooth. Texture of horse official's clothes shows the status of the wind, while the horse on the painting is vivid and lively. There is inscription "By Ziliang in Keshi Hall" and the seal "Ren Ziliang". Besides, there are 11 preservation stamps.

Ren Xianzuo, also named Ziliang, was born in Songjiang (a place in Shanghai currently) the son of Ren Renfa. He held office as county administrator, Fengxun senior official and an assistant to the chief local official of Taizhou. He was good at painting figures, horses and follows painting style of the family.

149. Wang Yi and Ni Zan: Yang Zhuxi

Yuan

Length: 27.7 cm Width: 86.8 cm

Preserved in the Palace Museum in Beijing

Paper, ink. It is a small portrait of Yang Qian (also named Zhuxi), a scholar of the Yuan Dynasty. With black scarf on the head and having a thin face with long whiskers, the figure wears long gown and stands with a cane. The painting is drawn by thin lines and lightly decorated by light ink. Ni Zan supplements pines and stones on the painting and the ink and lines briefly demonstrate the beauty of pines. There is an inscription of "The small portrait of Yang Zhuxi is painted by Wang Yi who was born in Yanling, and Ni Zan who was born in Gouwu, supplements with pines and stones in the second month of the 40th year (1363) of the reign" and 48 seals. On the back of the painting are prefaces and postscripts written by people, such as Zheng Yuanyou and Yang Weizhen of the Yuan Dynasty and more than 80 seals. The painting is recorded in the *Wangshi Shan Hu Wang* and *List of Grand View*.

Wang Yi (14th century), also named Sishan or Chijuesheng, whose native place was Muzhou (current Jiande, Zhejiang), lived in Hangzhou. He was a famous portraitist in the Yuan Dynasty.

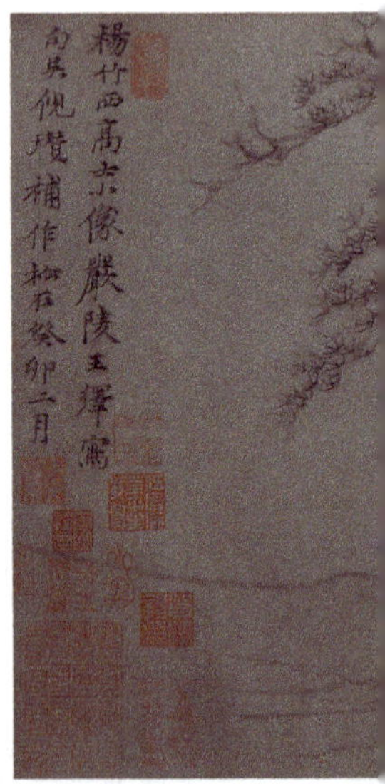

150. Zhu Yu: Uncovering Earthen Bowl

Yuan

Length: 29.7 cm Width: 86.2 cm

Preserved in the Shanghai Museum

Paper, line drawing. The painting is based on the story of the ghost mother in Mahāratnakūa Sūtra. The story advocates the ideas that the powers of the Buddha are unlimited and evil can never prevail over good. Trees and stones are painted by stippling and wrinkling and terse ink and lines are applied to paint them, too. Line drawing, which is used to paint figures, creates vivid and dynamic figures and spirit with accurate structure. The painting carries the wonderful overtones of Wu Daozi's figure paintings - "Clothes Ribbon of Wu's Painted Figure Flies Against the Wind".

Zhu Yu (1293-1365), also named Junbi, was an imperial painter born in Kunshan (present-day Jiangsu). Because of travelling with Wang Zhenpeng, he later became good at ruler painting.

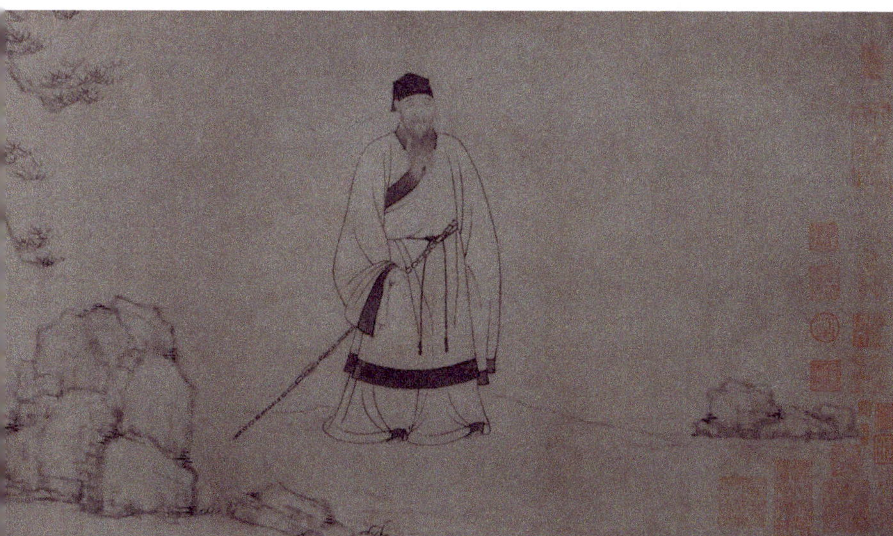

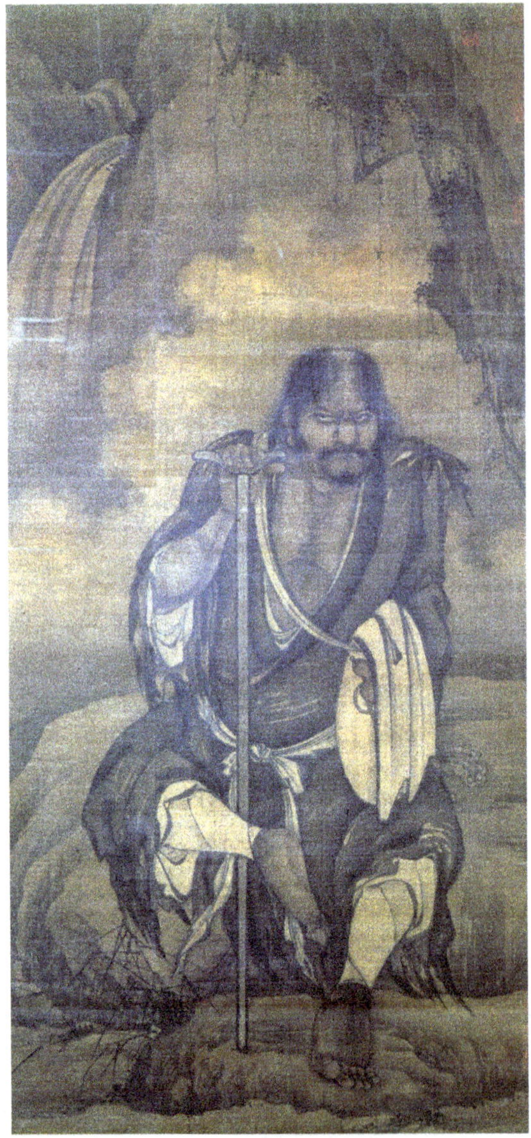

151. Yan Hui: Portrait of Li Tieguai

Yuan

Length: 146.5 cm Width: 72.5 cm

Preserved in the Palace Museum in Beijing

Silk scroll, ink. This depicts Li Tieguai, one of the Eight Immortals in myth and legends, facing frontwards. The clothing texture is painted freely in freehand brushwork with the main lines thick and sub-lines slender; heavy ink is applied for decoration. The earlock of Li Tieguai is demonstrated by thin lines well-distributed and meticulously made. The background is a cliff with cirrus clouds, high mountains and waterfall that creates a rising mist. There is an inscription "Yue, Yan Hui", seal "Qiuyue" and ten preservation seals such as that of Qing Neifu. The painting is analyzed and recorded in the *Pearls of the Mysterious Palace*.

Yan Hui (late 13th century to early 14th century), also named Qiuyue, was born in Jiangshan (present-day Zhejiang). He was good at painting scenes of doctrine preaching, figures and especially ghosts. He used a thick and strange painting technique and most of his works are wash paintings.

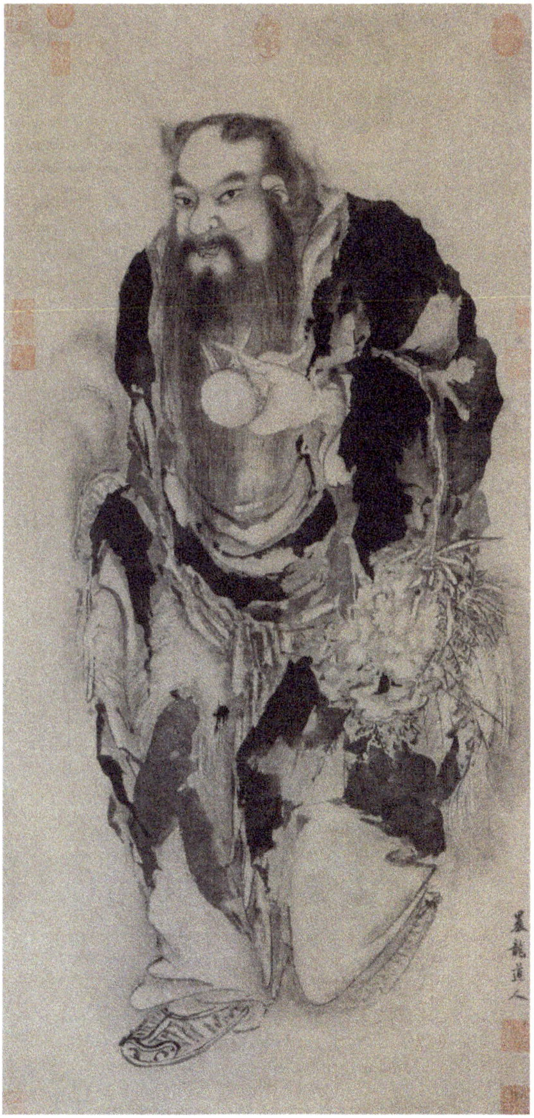

152. Xu Zhen: Zhong Li

Yuan

Length: 113.2 cm Width: 55.6 cm

Preserved in the Palace Museum in Beijing

Paper, ink. It is a portrait of Zhong Liquan, one of the Eight Immortals in myths and legends. Zhong's face, hands and feet are meticulously and finely painted and the scattering tip of the writing brush and heavy ink are used to draw Zhong's clothes. The fine lines and thick heavy ones create great contrast together. There is a signature "Ink Dragon Holy Man", "Seal of Xu Zhen", the seal of "Ink Dragon Holy Man" and several other seals on the painting.

Xu Zhen, also known as Ink Dragon Holy Man, was possibly a Taoist. He was good at painting figures by freehand brushwork. This is his only extant work.

153. Zhou Lang: Du Qiu

Yuan
Length: 32.3 cm Width: 285.5 cm (plus book)
Preserved in the Palace Museum in Beijing
Paper, tint. It depicts a woman clothed in Tang style, with a panpipe in hands and high topknot on the head. With plump and beautiful face, the woman wears a long dress. The painting is drawn by using the technique of "smooth silk drawing" ("yousi"). The clothes texture is smooth and the painting is tinted by light and elegant color. There is a signature "Zhou Lang, also named Zhou Bogao", a seal of "Binghu Huayin", the entire Poem of Du Qiuniang by Du Mu in the cursive handwriting of Kangli Naonao of the Yuan Dynasty, a preface by Song Sui and 20 seals on the painting, which combines painting and calligraphy harmoniously.
Zhou Lang (mid-14th century), also named Bogao or Binghu Huayin, lived of the reign of Emperor Shun of the Yuan Dynasty. He was good at painting horses and figures of ladies. The faces of the painted pretty and charming ladies are plump and dignified, while ribbons on their clothes flutter and the texture of the clothes is natural and unrestrained. His painting style is much like that of painters in the Tang Dynasty.

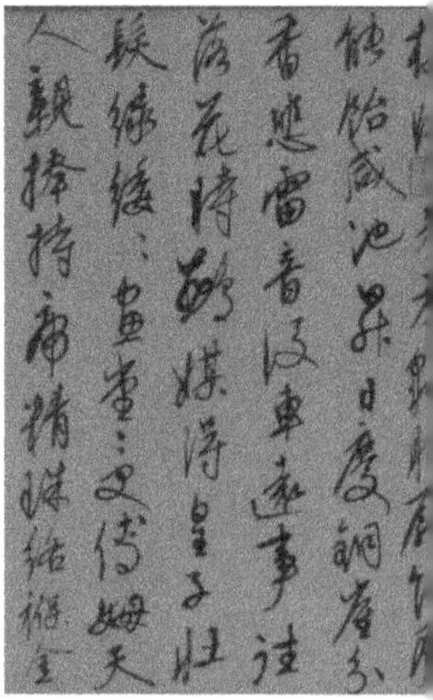

154. Zhou Lang: Folang Steed Presented as a Tribute (France)

Yuan
Length: 30.3 cm Width: 134 cm
Preserved in the Palace Museum in Beijing
Paper, line drawing. It depicts the scene of a translator leading a horse offered in tribute to the emperor of the Yuan Dynasty, and two following envoys of Folang Country. They wear a mix of Western-style clothes and traditional Chinese clothing, along with canes and swords. The Emperor inspects the horse closely while surrounded by maids of honor, officials and horse evaluators. The painting style is delicate, soft and gentle; light ink is applied for tinting. There is an inscription "Painted by Official Zhou Lang in accordance to the imperial order" and a seal with unclear words. The preface of Jie Xisi of the Yuan Dynasty on the front of the painting was imitated by person(s) of the Ming Dynasty.
According to records in *History of the Yuan Dynasty*, the Roman Pope appointed the priest Marignolli to present a horse of Folang Country to Toghun Tiemuer, Emeror of the Yuan Dynasty at that time. The emperor ordered Zhou Lang to draw a picture to record the grand event.

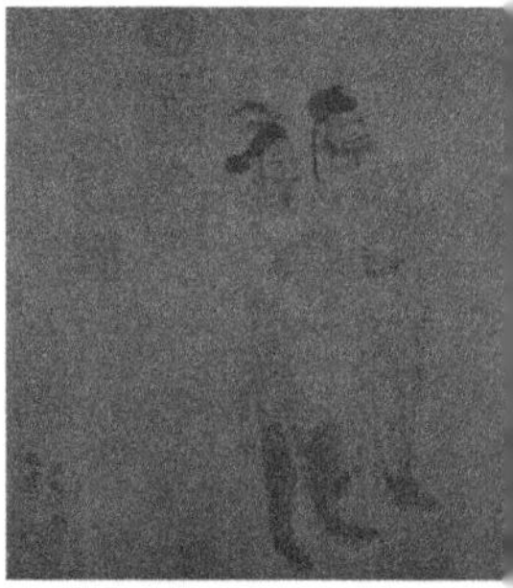

155. Wang Zhenpeng:Yu Boya's Playing the Qin

Yuan
Length: 31.4 cm Width: 92 cm
Preserved in the Palace Museum in Beijing
Silk scroll, ink. It depicts a scene of the story in which Yu Boya plays his qin stringed piano to his bosom friend Zhong Ziqi. The drawing is fine, meticulous, smooth and powerful. Vivid and lifelike figures are carefully and meticulously painted. There is a signature of "Wang Zhenpeng", a seal "Guyun Chushi" and several seals. On the tail of the painting are three inscriptions respectively written by Feng Zizhen, Zhao Yan and Zhang Yuanshi of the Yuan Dynasty, and seven seals. The painting is recorded in the *Precious Collection of the Stone Moat Sequel: First Edition*.
Wang Zhenpeng, also named Pengmei or Guyun Chushi, was born in Yongjia, Zhejiang (present-day Wenzhou, Zhejiang). He was good at ruler painting as well as figure painting. The contents of most of his ruler paintings are imperial constructions and he is recommended as the best ruler painter in the Yuan Dynasty. Li Gonglin taught him figure painting.

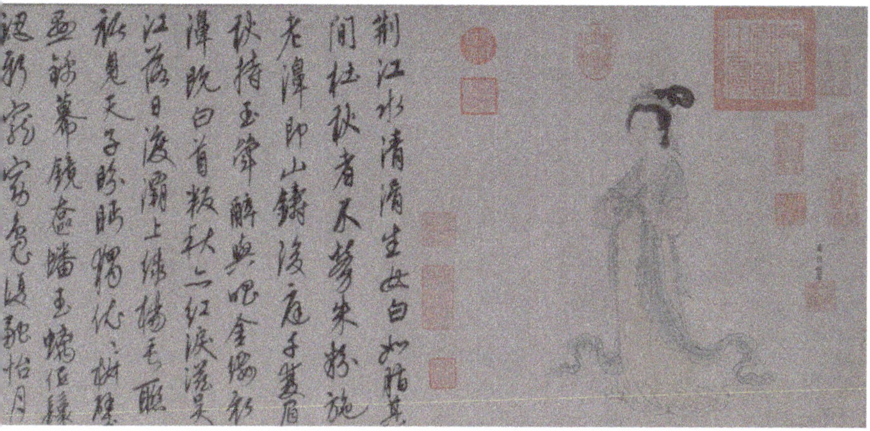

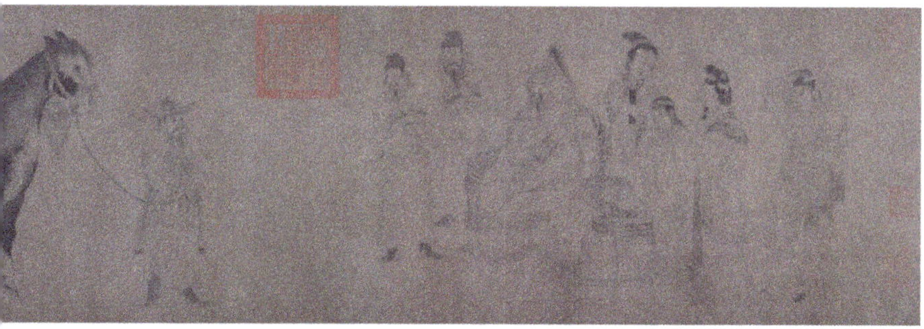

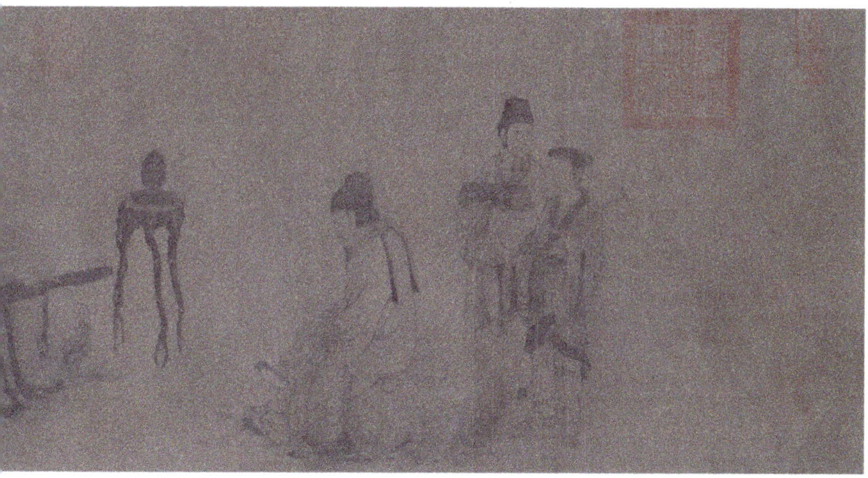

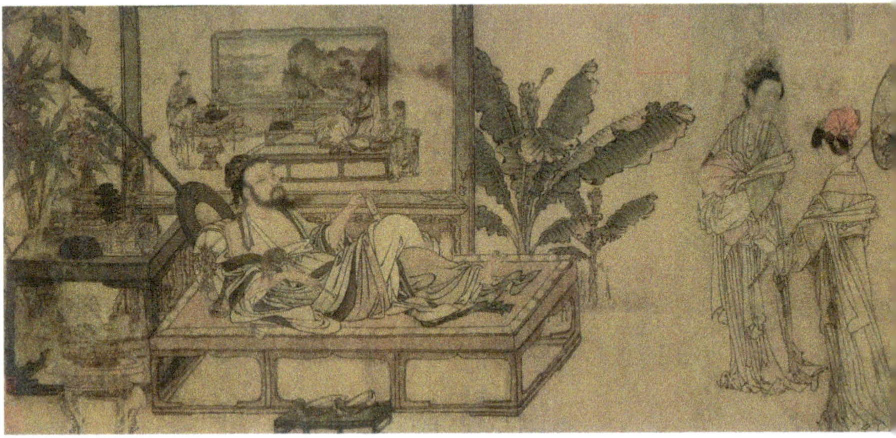

156. Liu Guandao: Spending the Summer at Leisure
Yuan
Length: 29.3 cm Width: 71.2 cm
Preserved in the Nelson-Atkins Museum of Art in Kansas, the U.S.
Silk scroll, tint by light ink. It depicts the leisured lifestyle of scholars. The layout of the whole painting shows tight arrangement on the left side and loose on the right to form a contrast. The signature of the painting "Guan" is signed in the interspace between broadleaf plants and bamboos and the word "dao" is incomplete. Jiangcun Shuhua lu wrongly regards it as a painting of Liu Songnian.
Liu Guandao, also named Zhongxian, was born in Zhongshan (current Dingzhou, Hebei). In the 16th year (1279) of the reign of Zhiyuan, he painted Portrait of Yuzhong and was granted supplementarily as Yuyijushi. He was good at painting pictures with Buddhism and Taoism features, figures, birds & beasts, flowers & bamboos as well as mountains and rivers.

157. Unknown Artist: Lao Tze's Introducing the Tao Te Ching
Yuan
Length: 24.8 cm Width: 117.7 cm
Preserved in the Palace Museum in Beijing
Paper, ink. It depicts the scene of Lao Tze with long beard and hair disheveled sitting on a couch, while a child stands behind him, while another person kneels in front of the couch. The mellow, full, free and easy lines create vivid and lively figures. The words "By Cheng Mao, also named Zizhao)" were added later. There are over 20 seals on the painting and on the tail of the painting is the entire Tao Te Ching in the clerical script of Wu Rui, an inscription of Hu Zi'ang and over 40 seals of the Ming Dynasty or the Qing Dynasty. The painting is recorded in the *Pearls Forest of the Mysterious Palace*.

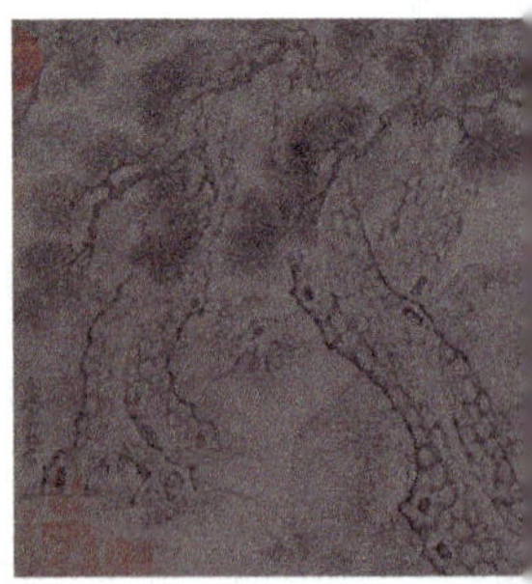

158. Unknown Artist: Four Doctors of Shangshan

Yuan

Length: 155.3 cm Width: 77.2 cm

Preserved in the Palace Museum in Beijing

Silk scroll, tint with dark green. It depicts four hermits, namely Dongyuangong, Luli, Qiliji and Xiahuanggong, living in seclusion in Shangshan (current Shangzhou, Shaanxi) to avoid disturbances of the late Qin Dynasty and early Western Han Dynasty. Mountains and stones on the painting are painted by "jiesuo wrinkling" and "pima wrinkling" and the dense trees and leaves are well-distributed with distinctive gradation. The painting is orderly but not rigid and the style is similar to that of the school represented by Cheng Mao. There is no signature and the seal is incomplete.

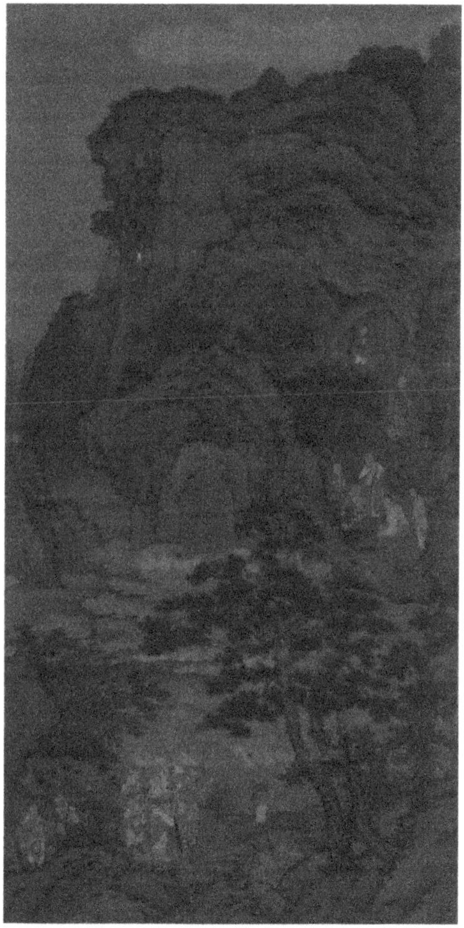

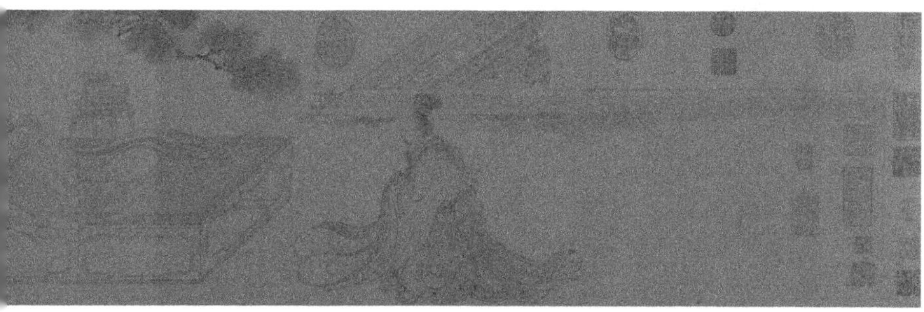

159. Unknown Artist: Carrying Rafts under Lugou Bridge

Yuan

Length: 143.6 cm Width: 105 cm

Preserved in the National Museum of China

Silk scroll, tint. It depicts the scene of Lugou Bridge of Wanping County in the Yuan Dynasty and the landscape around the bridge. There are eleven arches with a stone lion on the top of each pillar. At each end of the bridge stand a pair of stone lions or stone elephants as well as stone ornamental pillars. People and horses come and go on the bridge and several boats and rafts are on the river, while timbers are stacked on both banks. Winehouses, guest houses and shops stand in great numbers and envoys and travellers come and go ceaselessly. A chain of rugged mountains stand in the distance, while temples and large houses appear indistinctly and plenty of pedestrians and travelers are on the roads. The painting is of great historical value.

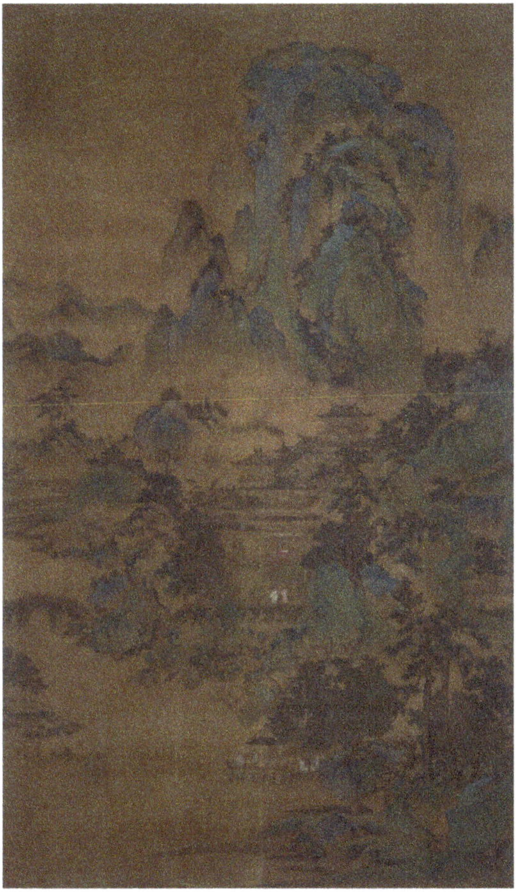

160. Unknown Artist: Green Hills and Pavilions

Yuan

Length: 170 cm Width: 103 cm

Preserved in the Duoyun Pavilion of Shanghai

Silk scroll, tint with dark green. It depicts a great mountain towering in the upper side of the painting embraced by other mountains all around with forests of luxuriant green and flourishing grass; pavilions on the mountainsides stand in great numbers, while pines at the foot of the mountains are tall and straight; streams run calmly beside the pavilions and an arched bridge crosses the streams. Each of the two boatmen on the painting takes a boat and cleaves the water and several people in front of the pavilions are leisurely looking far into the distance beside the streams or take their ease. Thin lines are applied to draw the outlines and veins of mountains and stones and after lining, and light grey green and mineral green are used to tint the mountains and stones. Pavilions on the painting are strictly drawn by ruler painting and pines are drawn by double drawing and color filling.

161. Dong Wanggong and Xi Wangmu

Yuan

Length: 440 cm Width: 1556 cm

Unearthed from western wall of Sanqing Temple, Yongle Taoist Temple, Ruicheng, Shanxi

Mural painting in Taoist temple. It depicts the scene of Dong Wanggong and Xi Wangmu with many immortals attending upon on both sides. Dong Wanggong is dressed in imperial robes, while Xi Wangmu wears the robes of the empress. Traditional heavy colored drawing and filling techniques are applied to tint, ink lines are the mainstays and colors such as gold, light red, dark green are used to tint and the supplement is quite harmonious. Some parts of the mural painting show painting powder and gold foil.

Yongle Taoist Temple is a magnificent Taoist Palace-like architectural complex first built in the Yuan Dynasty. The western, northern and eastern walls of Sanqing Hall are covered with plenty of images of immortals.

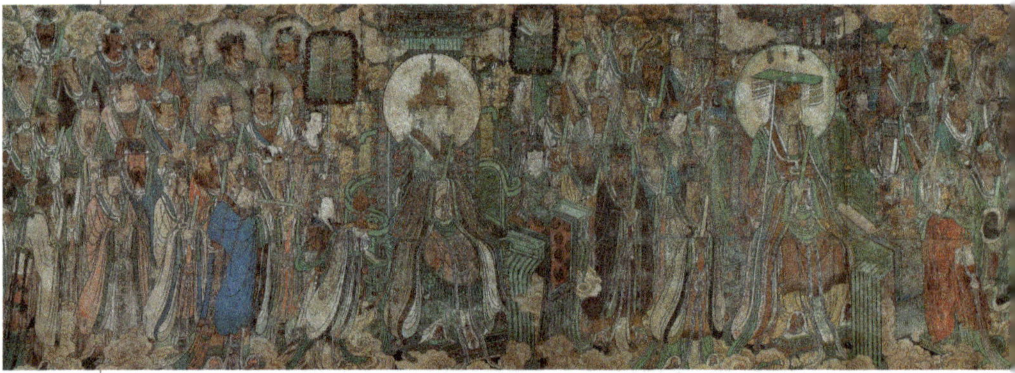

162. Two Immortals Discussing Ethics

Yuan

Unearthed from back of the sector wall, Chunyang Hall, Yongle Taoist Temple, Ruicheng, Shanxi

Mural painting in Taoist temple. The mural painting depicts the scene of Zhong Liquan's preaching before immortalizing Lu Dongbin, and Zhong Liquan teaching while Lu Dongbin listens with respectful attention.

Chunyang Hall of Yongle Taoist Temple spans five rooms and has a depth of three rooms. There are mural paintings on the four walls and sector walls. The whole area of the mural painting is 212.62 square meters and was painted in the 18th year of the reign of Zhizheng (1358). The length of the paintings on the eastern, northern and western sides is 3.5 meters and the area of the paintings is 203 square meters. A total of 52 paintings form a large work describing the inner journey of Lu Dongbin and displaying his whole life in the form of serial paintings.

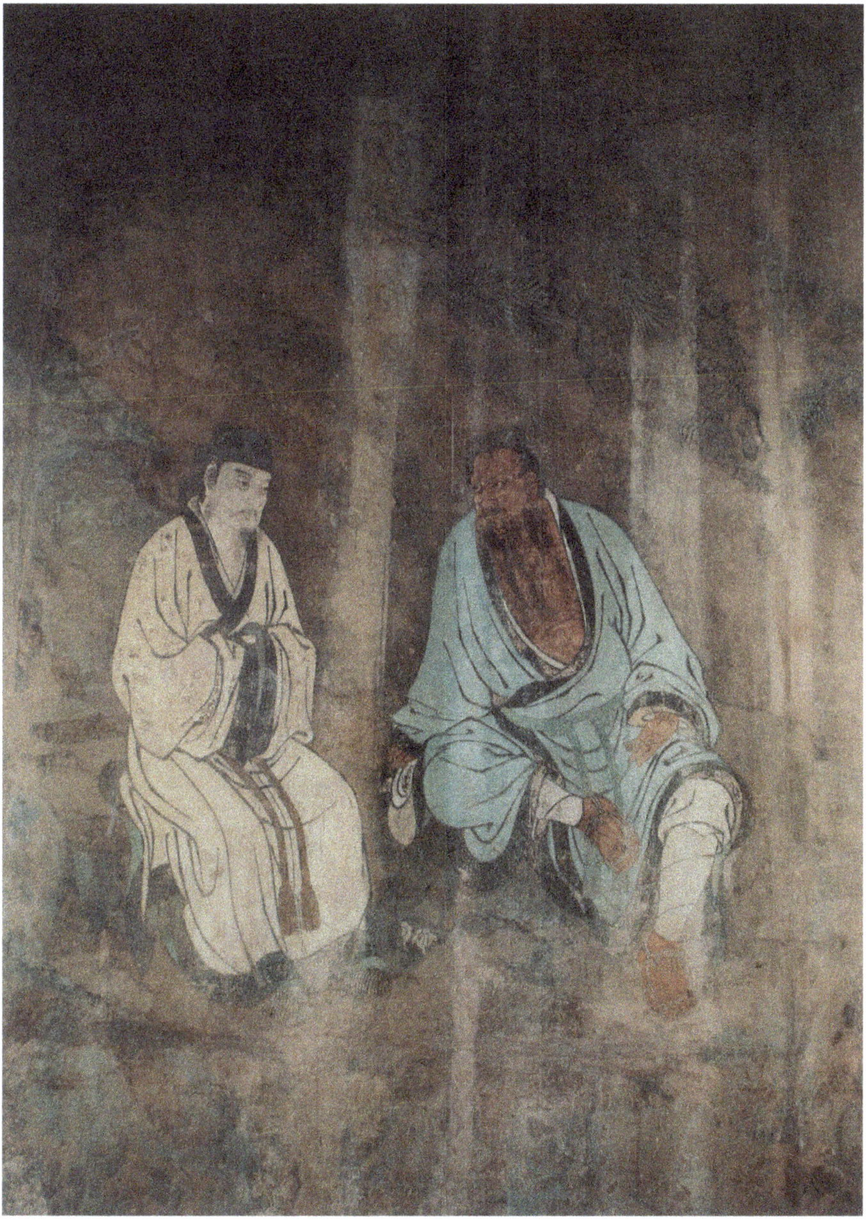

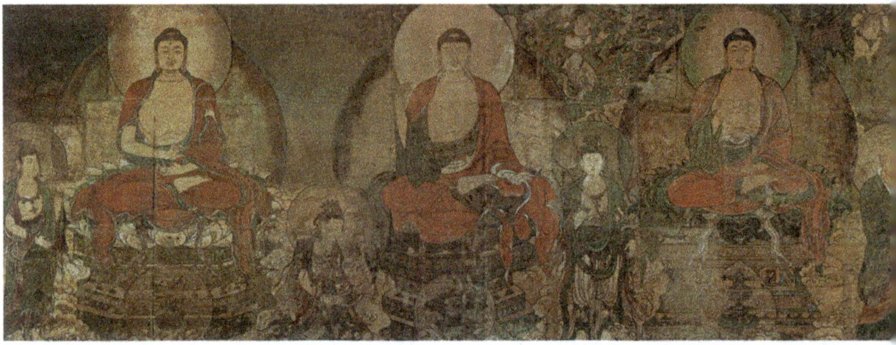

163. Seven Buddhist Patriarchs' Preaching Buddhism

Yuan

Length: 320 cm Width: 1810 cm

Unearthed from southern wall of the nave of Xinghua Temple, Jishan County, Shanxi

Preserved in the Palace Museum in Beijing

Mural painting in Taoist temple. It depicts seven Buddhist patriarchs sitting in meditation with spiral hair and outthrusts on the heads. Wearing red cassocks, they bare their chests, and reveal green monk robe. The drawing line of the painting is powerful and the color used demonstrates profundity and dignity. Parts of the painting are decorated by painting powder and gold foils. The seven figures depict Sakyamuni and six Buddhists acquiring true consciousness before his appearance. The painting was originally on the southern wall of the nave of Xinghua Temple, Jishan, Shanxi and completed in the seventh year (1320) of the reign of Yanyou. In 1926, the paintings in the temple were cut and carried away secretly by antique dealers, but, fortunately, were bought later by Peking University.

164. Avalokiteshvara with Thousand Hands and Thousand Eyes

Yuan

Unearthed from north wall of the 3rd grottoes of Mogao grottoes at Dunhuang, Gansu

Mural painting of a grottoes. Avalokiteshvara with eleven stacking heads in the shape of a Buddhist pagoda standing on a lotus flower bare-footed. Her thousand hands are in order like wheels and there are eyes in the hands. Among the hands, there are 42 big ones holding Buddhist instruments or treasures and hand gestures showing several meanings, such as treasure bottles, willow branches, Buddha on the top, Sumeru, hand-cupping and the like. Avalokiteshvara has eight bodies.

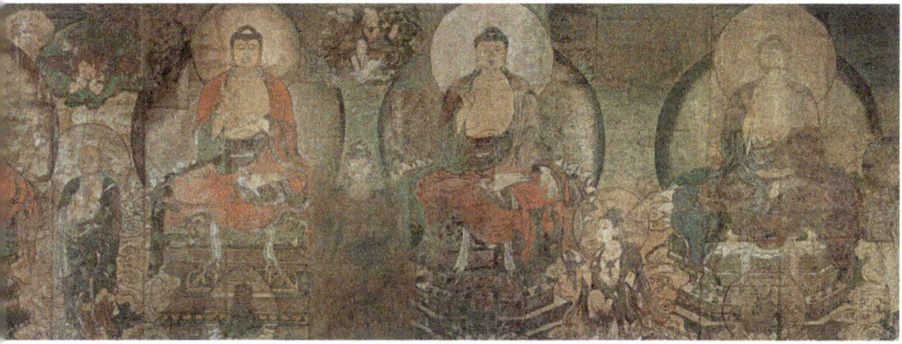

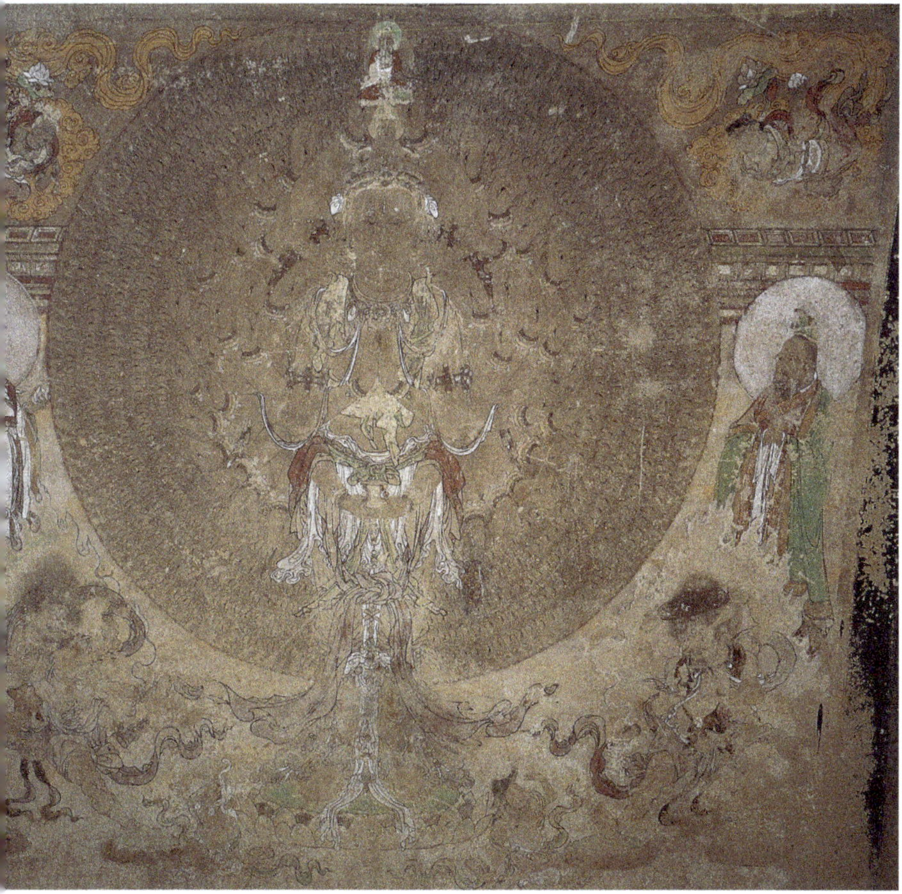

165. Palden Lhamo

Yuan

Unearthed from southern side of the gate, the eastern wall of the 465th grottoes of Mogao grottoes at Dunhuang, Gansu

Mural painting of grottoes. With five-human-skull-crown and hair of light red color like fire on the head and large human skull chaplet hanging around the neck, the Palden Lhamo on the painting seems angry. Its two front hands hold a King Kong cane and blood bowl and two back hands are lifting a trident and King Kong sword. The Palden Lhamo sits on a mule covered with human skin running in a sea of blood. Palden Lhamo, also named the Goddess Lakshmi or Heavenly King of Mule, is an important female Dharma protector of Esoteric Buddhism. She is responsible for affairs related to birth and death, diseases and acute communicable diseases and good and evil.

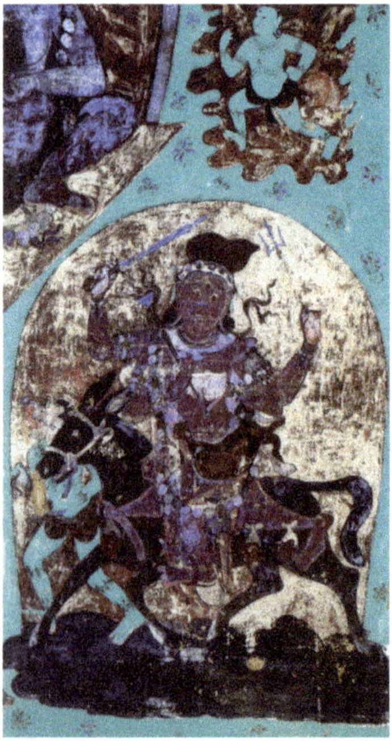

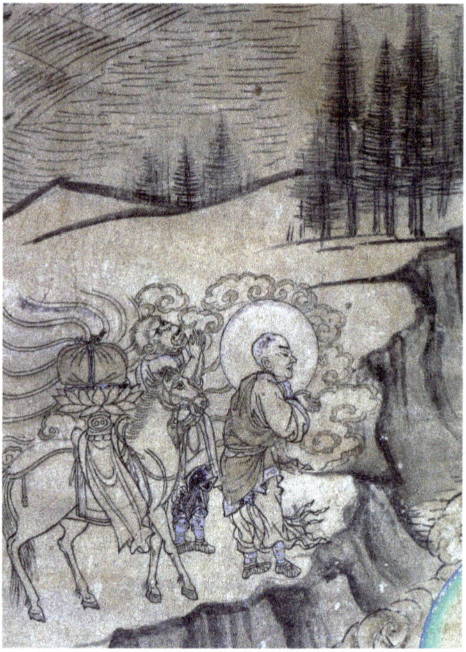

166. Monk Xuanzang Going on a Pilgrimage for Buddhist Scriptures

Yuan

Unearthed from eastern wall of the 3rd grottoes of Yulin Cave, Anxi, Gansu

Mural painting of grottoes. It depicts a scene people at their wits' end in front of cliffs and deep gullies. It shows Monk Xuanzang praying whole-heartedly for the Bodhisattva to help them get out of their predicament and Sun Wukong's worry and impatience. The master and the apprentice contrast greatly, while the white horse stands quietly and waits. Through it is regarded as a wash painting, the painting is almost made by line drawing in a traditional link and brush style. The painting indicates that the story of Pilgrimage to the West had existed in the Yuan Dynasty.

Calligraphy

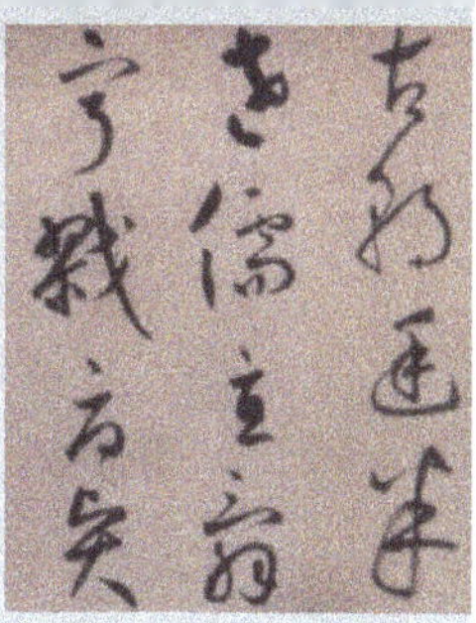

In the early Yuan Dynasty, calligraphy was strongly influenced by the Northern Song Dynasty and the Jin Dynasty. Scholar-bureaucrats mostly imitated Yan Zhenqing or the "Four Great Masters", Su, Huang, Mi, Cai in Northern Song Dynasty. The famous calligraphers in the transitional period from the Song to the Yuan Dynasty were Dai Biaoyuan and Bai Ting, etc. In the year of Dade and Yanyou, Zhao Mengfu, Xianyu Shu and Deng Wenyuan who were known as "Three Great Masters in the early Yuan Dynasty" emerged in succession. They advocated learning from previous times and emulating the styles in the Jin and Tang dynasties which resulted in a Yuan Calligraphy style based on the standardization of ancient traditions and reverting to the declination of calligraphy in Southern Song Dynasty.

Zhao Mengfu accomplished most among many calligraphers in the Yuan Dynasty. His calligraphy, praising highly that of Wang Xizhi and Wang Xianzhi (the "two Wangs"), advocated a return to ancient ways and promoted the formation of a style in the new era considered eminent enough to exert great influence on future generations. Many calligraphers in the Yuan Dynasty imitated Zhao Mengfu, including Yu He, Qian Liangyou, Guo Bi, Zhao Yong and Zhang Yuan, etc., forming the Calligrapher Group of the Zhao School which was rather influential at that time.

Many calligraphers were vocal in wanting to restore ancient ways and objected to Song period advocacy of meaning while neglecting mode and harked back to Jin and Tang traditions; they sought to learn from the ancients at the source. This led to the emergence of a batch of calligraphers good at seal script, clerical script and regular cursive script such as the seal script of Zhou Boqi and Tai Buhua, the seal script and clerical script of Wu Rui as well as the regular cursive script of Deng Wenyuan, etc.

However, there existed many eye-catching calligraphers not following common practice but insisting on their own style, among them being Taoist calligraphers. Their calligraphy emphasized the expression of meaning, did not seek similarity in form, but stressed personality and yearned for the realm of "leisure" to form one of the aesthetic traditions of Chinese calligraphy. Zhang Yu was the representative of this approach. In addition, it seemed that the calligraphy of Yang Weizhen was also out of line. Its structure and pattern lacked elegance, polish and delicacy; the tip of its writing brush was hard and stern, strong and forceful and its pattern was queer and the style distinctive, violating the previous normal calligraphy state and corresponding to the social unrest in the late Yuan Dynasty. Therefore, it was said to possess the "vigor of turbulent days".

The Yuan Dynasty was set up by a minority ethnic group, so the political status of each minority was accordingly elevated greatly. The cultures of all nationalities fused so that a batch of minority calligraphers became noted masters, such as Kang Linao, Tai Buhua and Nai Yan.

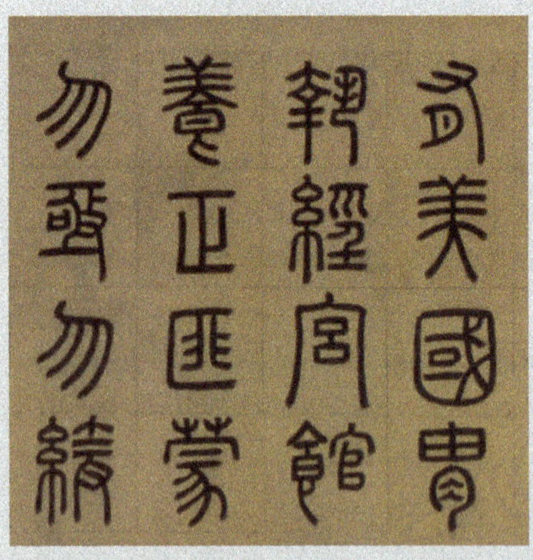

167. Qiu Yuan: Self-written Poem

Yuan

Length: 34.5 cm Width: 455.4 cm

Preserved in the Palace Museum in Beijing

Paper painting, running script. It records 38 separate octaves and is presented to Sheng Yuanren and noted down in the *Notes of Poetry in the Yuan Dynasty* and *Poetry Anthology of the Yuan Dynasty*. The structure is rigorous and mannered, the potential of the characters somewhat queer and harsh, but it is written in a delicate and fine way. Among Qiu Yuan's books that have been preserved, this is the only voluminous masterpiece. It is signed at the end of the volume with "Wulin Qiu Yuan visits again ceremoniously three days before China's Valentine's Day in the years of Wuyin". At the very beginning of the quotation are inscriptions of Wang Hong and Zheng Yongyan and at the end of the volume is a preface and postscript produced by Shi Yan, Hu Yan, Gong Xianglin, and so on, respectively from the Yuan, Ming and Qing dynasties. It is sealed with many connoisseur seals.

Qiu Yuan (1247-?), also known as Renjin and Shancun Min, was born in Qiantang (present-day Hangzhou of Zhejiang). He is famous for his poems as early as during the years of Xian Chun in the Southern Song Dynasty. His calligraphy was influenced by Song Emperor Gaozong and Zhao Mengjian. In his early years, the chirography of his calligraphy was thin and forceful while in later years it became open and clear and liberated.

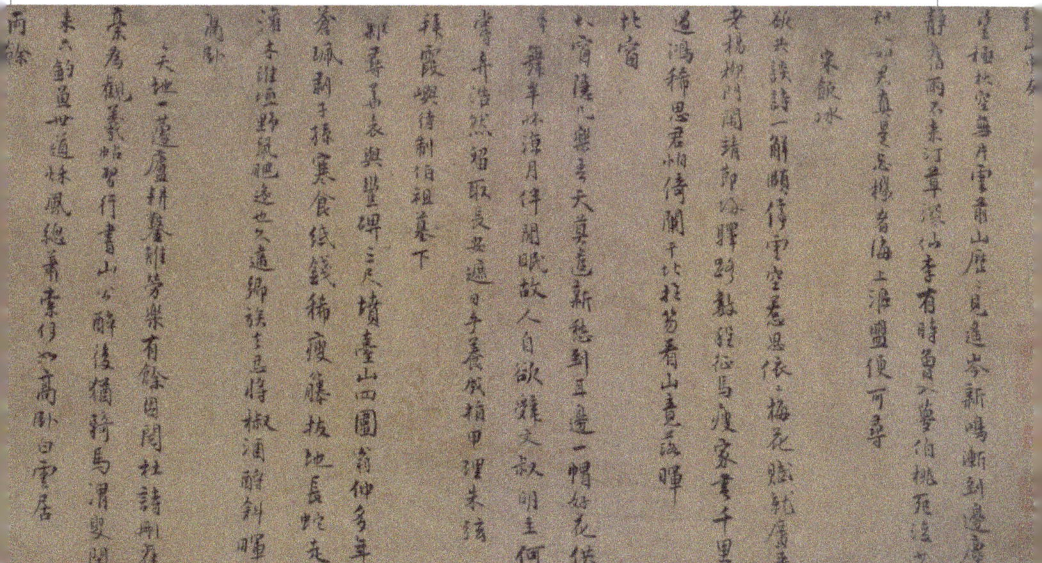

168. Yang Huan: Wuyi Part

Yuan
Length: 27.2 cm Width: 64.5 cm
Preserved in the Palace Museum in Beijing
Paper painting, seal script. It records the full text of the Shangshu: Wuyi Part. Being the only preserved voluminous seal script, its character font is slender, the stroke is smooth and the tip of the writing brush is strong and forceful. It is signed "Written by Donglu Yang Huan in the Dade Jihai Year (1299) " and sealed by "Wuzi Yang Huan". This calligraphy model is mounted together with Xiao S3's clerical script and Zhao Mengfu's *Wuyi Part* in lower case in the same scroll, and later poems of Jie Xisi and Geng Yao Ba (Ba is a postscript) in the Qing Dynasty are included. The overall volume is sealed with 58 squares and half a seal is one square. *Spectacular Life, List of Grand View, Record of Jiangcun Xiaoxia*, and *Precious Collection of the Stone Moat Sequel: Third Edition* and *Catalogue of Lost Paintings and Calligraphy in the Palace Museum in Beijing* record it.
Yang Huan (1234-1299), also known as Wuzi and Xinquan, was born in Yunzhou (present-day Shandong). He used to be Jiaoshu Minister of Court Historian Institution, investigating censor and vice-curator of the imperial library mending the Dayitong Zhi in advance. He was good at calligraphy, especially Zhuanzhou.

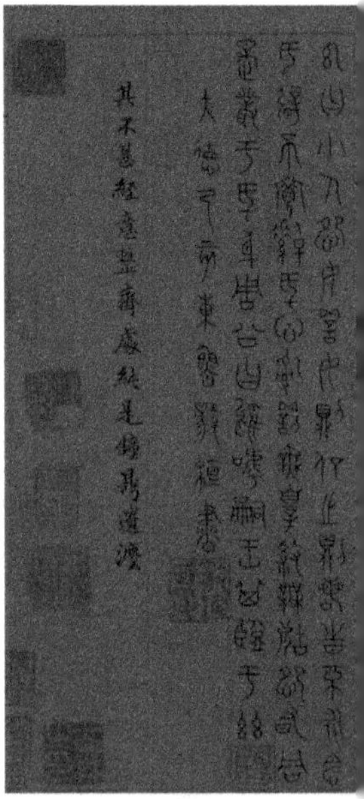

169. Xiao Shi Dou: Wuyi Part

Yuan
Length: 27.4 cm Width: 60.3 cm
Preserved in the Palace Museum in Beijing
Paper painting, clerical script. It collects the full text of the Shangshu: Wuyi Part. The structure is steady and solid and he wrote in a delicate and fine way. This is his only work preserved. It is signed with "Han clerical script written by Xiao Shi Dou in Guanzhong District during the second period of hot season in the Dade Xinchou Year (1301) attached to The Ancient Books of Yang Wuzi and is also sealed with "Father of Xiaoshi Weidou". This panel is equipped with seals of Yuan and Ming people as well as the Imperial Household Department of the Qing Dynasty.
Xiao Shi Dou (1241-1318), also known as Weidou and Qinzhai, was born in Jingzhao (present-day Xi'an of Shaanxi). He used to be the Right Lunde of the Prince. Although his name is not recorded in history books, the Huanyu Fangbei Record contains several book steles written by him.

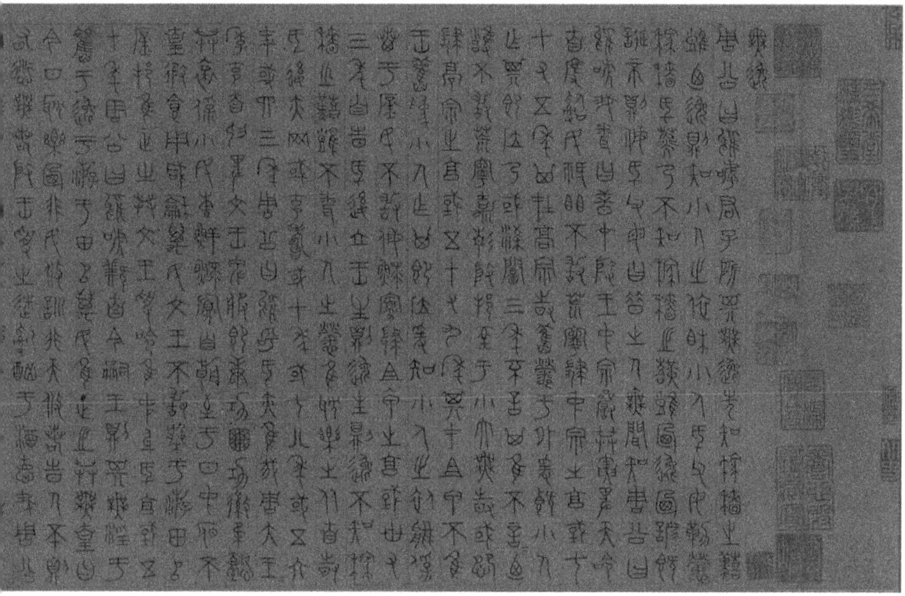

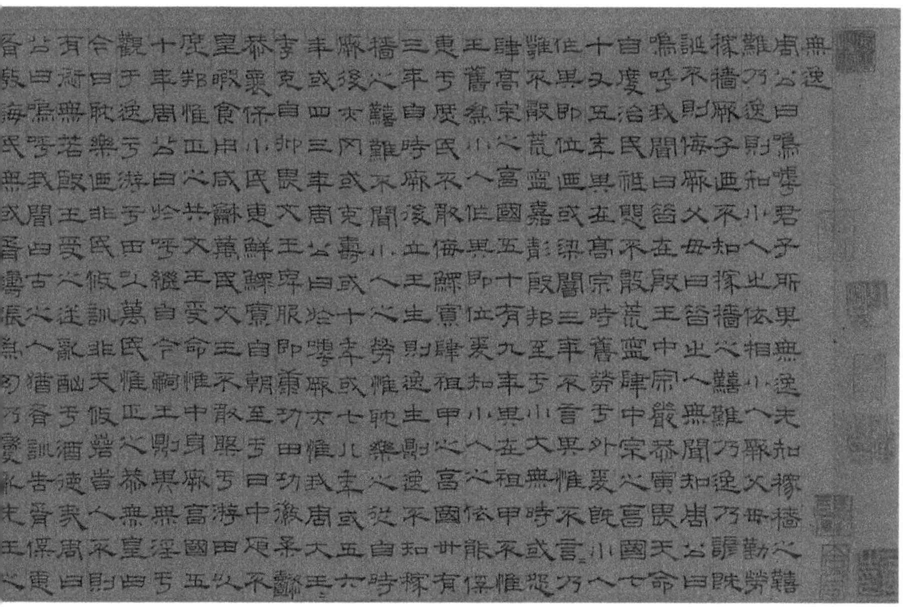

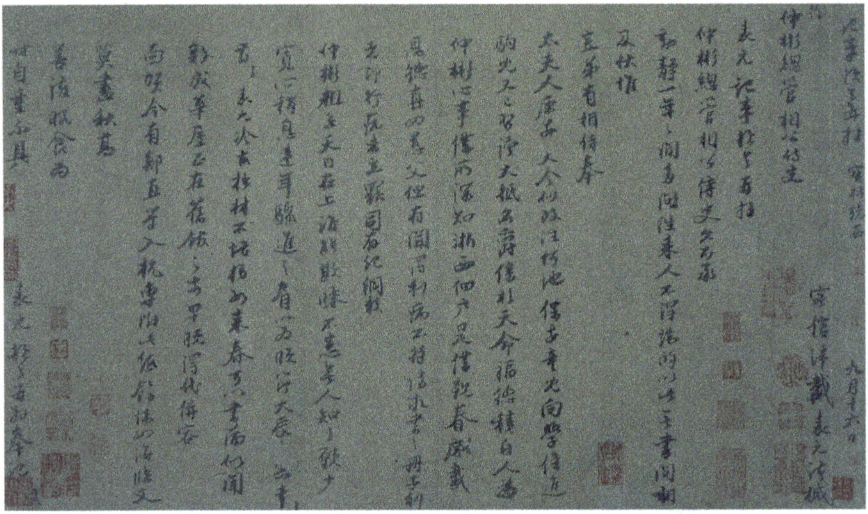

170. Dai Biaoyuan: Calligraphy Model of Movement and Silence
Yuan
Length: 30.2 cm Width: 52.4 cm
Preserved in the Palace Museum in Beijing
Paper painting, running script. They are the letters written to "Zhongbin Supervisor". The calligraphy is smooth and easy, deep and elegant. It is signed with "record of a second visit of Biaoyuan who makes a ceremonious nod". It used to be collected by Xiang Yuanbian, An Qi and Zhang Daqian, etc.
Dai Biaoyuan (1244-1310), also known as Shuaichu and Cengbo as well as Mr. Shanyuan in his later years, was born in Fenghua Shanyuan Yulin of Qingyuan County (present-day Zhejiang). He is famous for his poems.

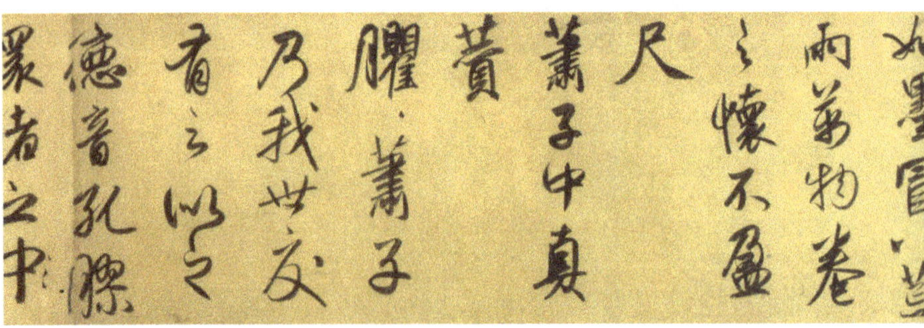

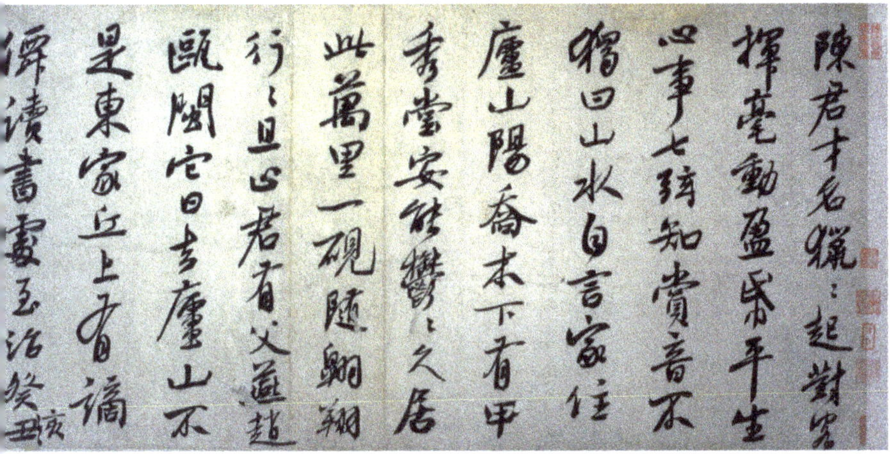

171. Bai Ting: Album of Calligraphy Model of Chen Jun's Poems

Yuan

Length: 31.2 cm Width: 68.2 cm

Preserved in the Palace Museum in Beijing

Paper painting, running script. He wrote one classical seven-character poem. Its structure is rounded, its brushwork powerful, its gesture liberated and its stroke written at will with the messages passed down from Mi Fu. It is signed with "written on the dawn of August in Autumn in the year of Zhikuihai (1323)" and is also sealed with "Zhanyuanzi Bai Ting" and "Qixia Shanren". *Moyuan Huiguan* and *Catalogue of Paintings and Calligraphy in Sanyutang Studio* mention it.

Bai Ting (1248-1328), also known as Tingyu and Zhanyuan, was born in Qiantang (present-day Hangzhou). He lived by the West Lake and then moved to Qixia, becoming known as Qixia Shanren. He was good at writing poems and enjoyed equal popularity with Qiu Yuan. As far as calligraphy is concerned, he imitated Mi Fu.

172. Zhao Mengfu: Two Odes and Two Poems

Yuan

Length: 27 cm Width: 456.3 cm

Preserved in the Palace Museum in Beijing

Paper painting, running script. He wrote in high spirits upon meeting with good friends. His calligraphy style mostly possesses the intended conception in Yan Zhenqing's and Mi Fu's works and this volume is representative of running script in big characters. It is signed with "Meng Fu". There is a preface and postscript of Dong Qichang and Yong Xing, etc. in the Ming and Qing dynasties. It is sealed with connoisseur seals of Wang Shizhen and Ying He, etc. The *Recording in Passing the Xinchou Summer, Catalogue of Paintings and Calligraphy in Sanyutang Studio, Coral Net*, and *The Sequel to Paintings and Calligraphy of Guoyun Building* mention it.

Zhao Mengfu is the most famous Great Master of Painting and Calligraphy and in the history of calligraphy ranks as the first of the "Three Great Masters in the early Yuan Dynasty". He acquired the strong points of the forefathers and has a style of his own by achieving mastery through a comprehensive study of them, which is called the "Zhao School".

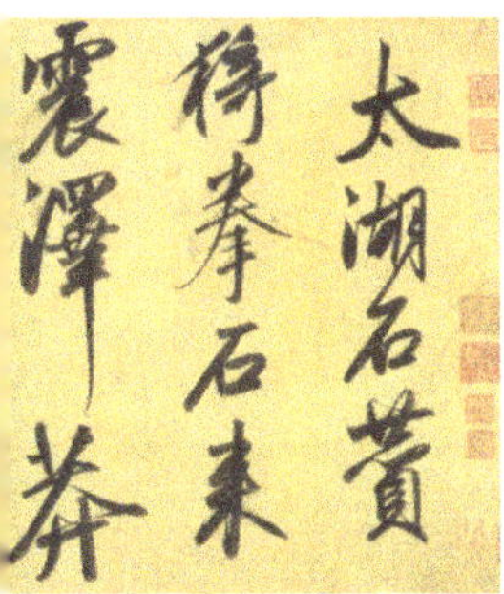

173. Zhao Mengfu: Thousand Character Classic in Two Scripts

Yuan
25-and-a half-open
Length: 24.7 cm Width: 25 cm
Preserved in the Palace Museum in Beijing

Paper painting, regular and cursive scripts. The Thousand Character Classic is recorded in regular and cursive scripts. The brushwork is smooth and strong and the structure is square and long with a little looseness; but it is still possessed with the strength of character of being smooth and beautiful and energetic, which are the features of Zhao Shu. It is signed with "by Zhao Mengfu of Wuxing " and is also sealed with "Zhaoshi Zi'ang" and "Songxue Zhai". Shixue Jushi signed "Thousand Character Classic in true cursive script of the style of Zhao School by Min'gong" on the cover. It is sealed with many connoisseur seals.

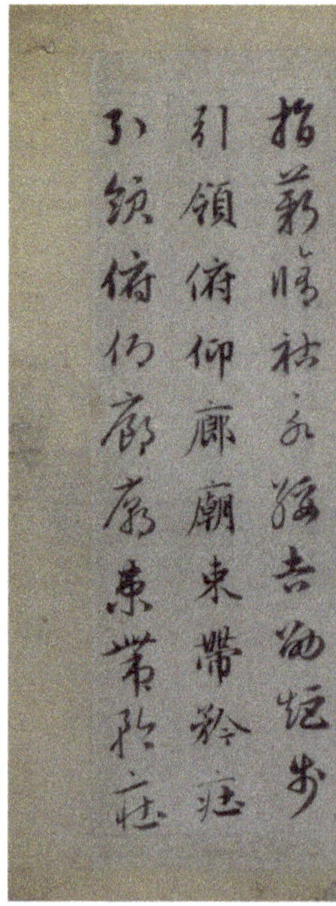

174. Zhao Mengfu: Dishi Danba Stele (Dishi: teacher of the Emperor)

Yuan
Length: 33.6 cm Width: 166 cm
Preserved in the Palace Museum in Beijing

Paper painting, regular scripts. This was written by Zhao Mengfu to give an account of the life stories of Dan Ba, who wasimperial tutor under Emperor Renzong of Yuan Dynasty. The calligraphy is elegant, long and straight. We can see the vividness from being regular and grace from being rigorous. And it is the most famous representative work of regular script. This volume was written in the third year of Yanyou (1316). Yang Xian, Pan Zuyin and other people wrote preface and postscript and *Nanyang Model Calligraphy Chart, Dongtu Xuanlan, Collective Study on Shigutang Studio Calligraphy and Paintings, Records of Renyan Xiaoxia* as well as *Catalogue of Paintings and Calligraphy of Sanyu Hall* mention it.

Dan Ba (1230-1303), also named Jiage Lasi, was born in Tugansidanma of the Tibetan Empire (present-day Shiqu of Sichuan). He was granted the name of Dishi in the seventh year of Zhiyuan of Kublai Khan (1270). Later in the first year of Huangqing, he was named "Dajue Puci Guangzhao Wushang Dishi Danba".

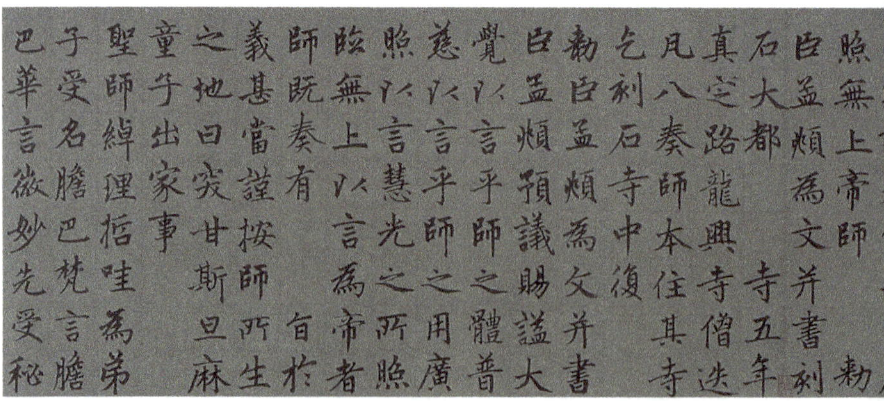

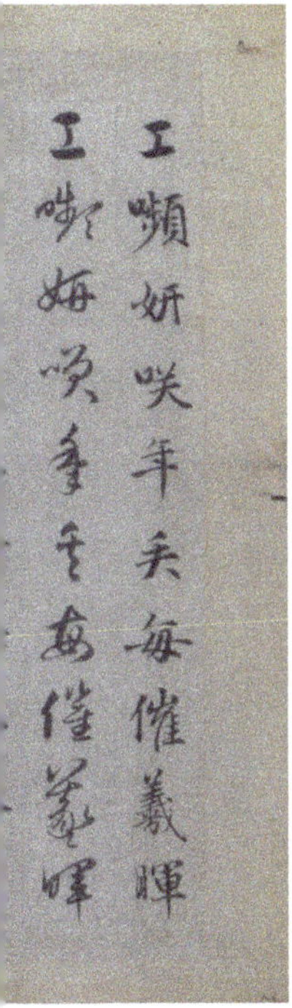
工顰妍笑年矢每催羲暉

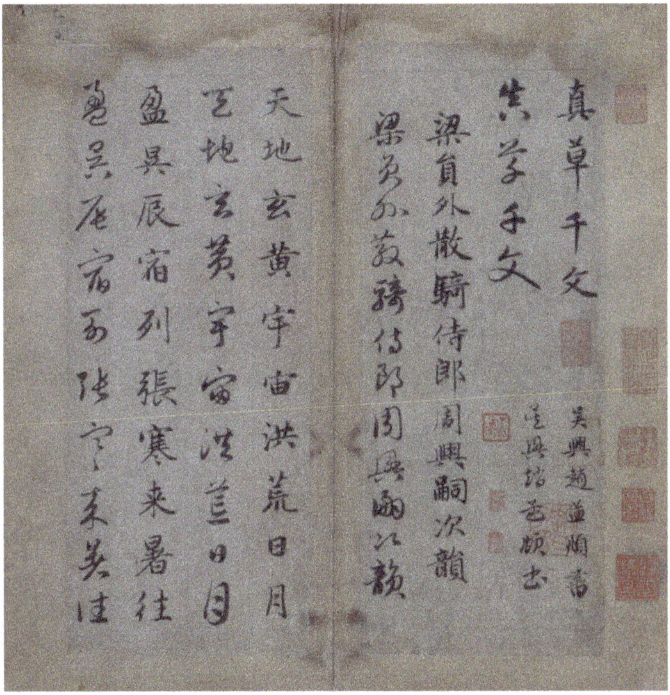
真草千文
梁員外散騎侍郎周興嗣次韻
天地玄黃宇宙洪荒日月
盈昃辰宿列張寒來暑往

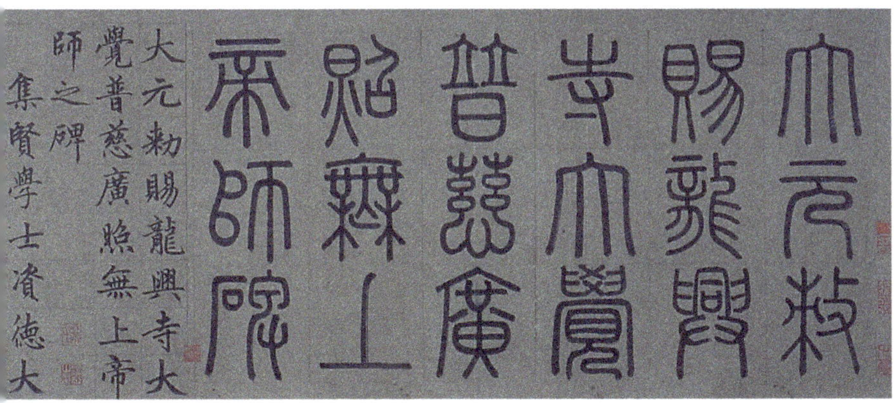
大元勅賜龍興寺大覺普慈廣照無上帝師之碑
大元勅賜龍興寺大覺普慈廣照無上帝師之碑
集賢學士資德大

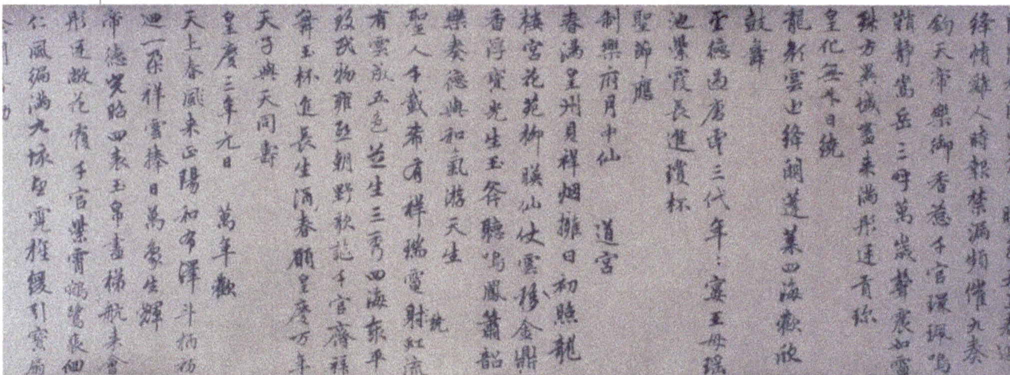

175. Zhao Mengfu: Wanshou Song

Yuan

Length: 27.5 cm Width: 144 cm

Preserved in the Palace Museum in Beijing

Paper painting, running and regular script. It is a Yuefu hymn with four chapters produced by him when the Jixian Shidu Scholar during the years of Huangqing. Its brushwork is exquisite and the style is natural and elegant and forceful; therefore, it is an elaborative work made by Zhao Mengfu in his mature period. This volume is written in the third year of Huangqing (1314). It is signed with "subject Mengfu" and is also sealed with "subject Mengfu" by white square seal. This is his only work signed with the character of "subject". At the end, a preface and postscript from Ke Jiusi of Yuan Dynasty is attached. It used to be preserved by the Inside House of Qing Dynasty. *Spectacular Life and Precious Collection of the Stone Moat Sequel: First Edition* record it.

In his later years, Zhao Mengfu mainly took office in the Jixian Academy and Hanlin Academy and this was written when he was in office.

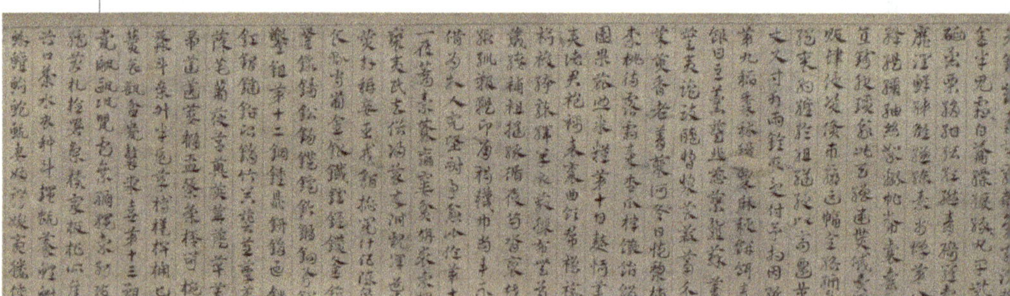

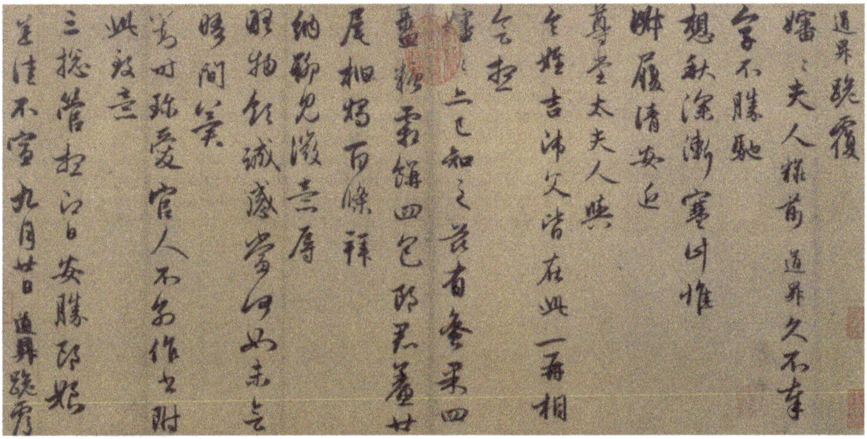

176. Guan Daosheng: Shenqiu Calligraphy Model

Yuan

Length: 26.9 cm Width: 53.3 cm

Preserved in the Palace Museum in Beijing

Paper painting, running script. These are the greeting letters written by Zhao Menfu on behalf of his wife. The strokes are sturdy and the body potential is long, elegant and graceful, fluent and vigorous. It is signed with "Daosheng kneels for Aunt Fu" at the preface and with "Daosheng kneels for Fu" in the end; as the characters under "Daosheng" have traces of being altered, we can assume that Zhao signs his own name and later changes it. It is also sealed with the connoisseur seals of the Inside House and Li Zhaoheng and others during the years of Xuantong in the Qing Dynasty. Guan Daosheng was good at painting and his books are mentioned in the history of calligraphy, but his works preserved were mostly written by Zhao Mengfu on his behalf.

177. Deng Wenyuan: Jijiu Part

Yuan

Length: 23.3 cm Width: 368.7 cm

Preserved in the Palace Museum in Beijing

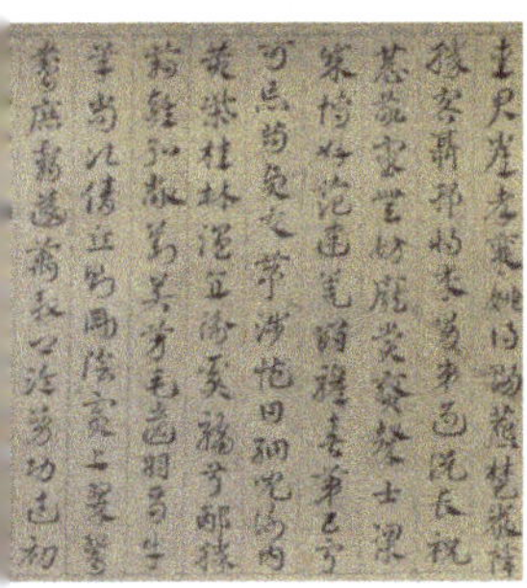

Paper painting, cursive clerical script. This is Wu Huangxiang's full text of Jijiu Chapter in clerical script copied by Deng Wenyuan for Li Zhongyong (named Xi and born in Yutian) at the monk's dormitory of Qingshou Temple in Dadu (present-day Beijing) when he was selected as Juren in Hanlin Academy through the imperial examination. As a representative work of Deng Wenyuan in his early period, its brushwork is refined and stern, expressive and vivid. It was written in the third year of Dade (1299). Seven Masters of Yuan and Ming dynasties such as Yang Weizhen wrote prefaces and postscripts, and this volume is sealed with Xiang Yuanbian and others of Ming Dynasty. *Preface to Shan Hu Wang* etc. is recorded here.

Deng Wenyuan (1258-1328), also known as Shanzhi and Feishi, was born in Mianzhou (present-day Mianyang of Sichuan). He was good at regular script, running script and cursive script writing, especially cursive clerical script. He enjoys equal fame with Zhao Mengfu and Xian Yushu together being called the "Three Great Masters in the Early Yuan Dynasty".

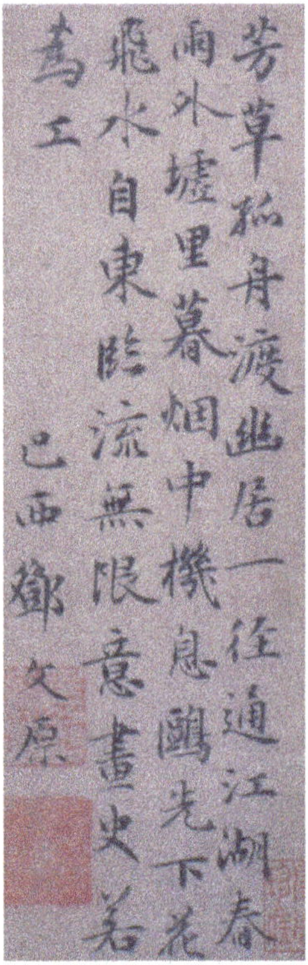

178. Deng Wenyuan: Calligraphy Model of Fangcao

Yuan

Length: 20.8 cm Width: 7.1 cm

Preserved in the Palace Museum in Beijing

Paper painting, regular script. It includes one five-character octave. This calligraphy inherits the tradition of being strict passed down from the Jin and Tang dynasties, and is characterized by extensive structure, balanced ink use, neat blank, high and steep and handsome character pattern, and vigorous and smooth brushwork. And it is the preserved representative work of his regular script in small characters. It is signed with "Deng Wenyuan of Baxi" and is sealed with "Dengshi Shanzhi of Baxi". It used to be preserved by An Qi of the Qing Dynasty.

179. Deng Wenyuan: Calligraphy Model of Five-character Octave

Yuan

Length: 32.7 cm Width: 40.9 cm

Preserved in the Palace Museum in Beijing

Paper painting, running script. Originally, it was the preface and postscript written in the end of Ode to BoYi by Fan Zhongyan of Song Dynasty written in the fourth year of Dade (1300). The calligraphy is vigorous and expansive, natural and unrestrainedly self-congratulatory, mindful and well-ordered. It is signed with "Baxi Deng Wenyuan of Shu" and is sealed with "Deng Wenyuan Seal" and "Dengshi Shanzhi of Baxi". In addition, it is sealed with many connoisseur seals. *Fencing Coral* and *List of Grand View* mention it.

Ode to BoYi was produced by Han Yu of Tang Dynasty to sing highly of BoYi and was written down by Fan Zhongyan of the Song Dynasty; however, it was not kept until the present time.

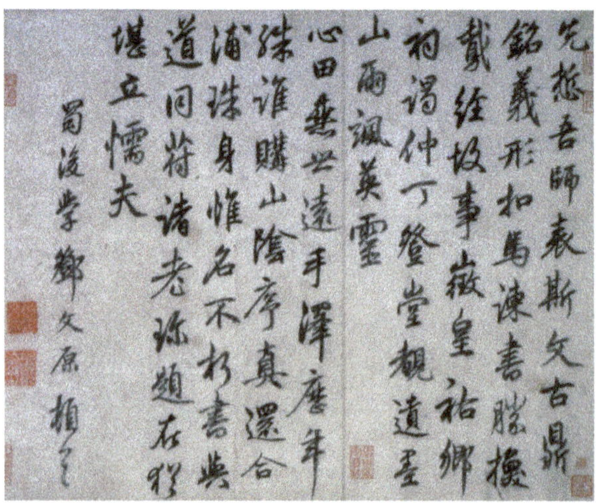

180. Chen Yizeng: Preface of Jingchun Hall Poem

Yuan

Length: 31.2 cm Width: 49.5 cm

Preserved in the Palace Museum in Beijing

Paper painting, regular script in small character. It is a preface of *Poetry Anthology of Jingchun Hall* produced by Chen Yizeng for Yuan Yi. Being the representative work of Chen Yi, the brushwork is delicate and fine, forceful and neat, elegant and graceful. It is signed with "until 16 of March in the 1st year of Zhizhi (1321), a preface by Chen Yizeng from Wuxing ".

Chen Yizeng, also known as Bofu, was born in Huzhou (present-day belongs to Zhejiang). He wrote Wen Shuo, Wen Quan,Tips on the Hanlin Academy. The history books mention he was good at calligraphy, but his work is rarely found.

Yuan Yi(1262-1306), also known as Tongfu, was born in Changzhou of Pingjiang (present-day Suzhou of Jiangsu). He was a writer. After he passed away, his second son named Yuan Zhongchang compiled his posthumous manuscript into Poetry Anthology of Jingchun Hall.

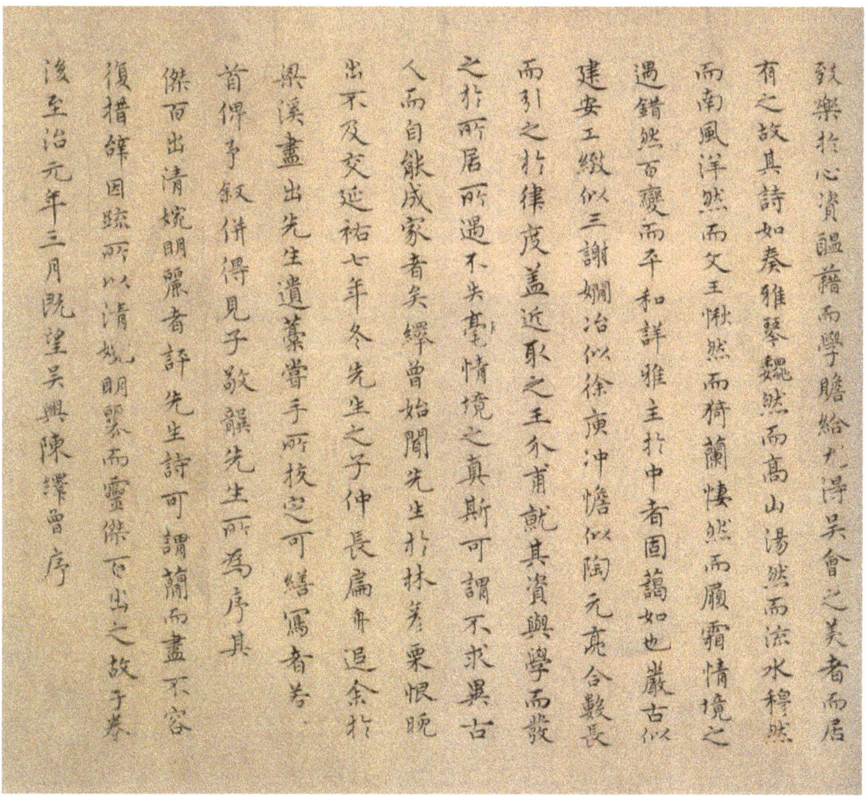

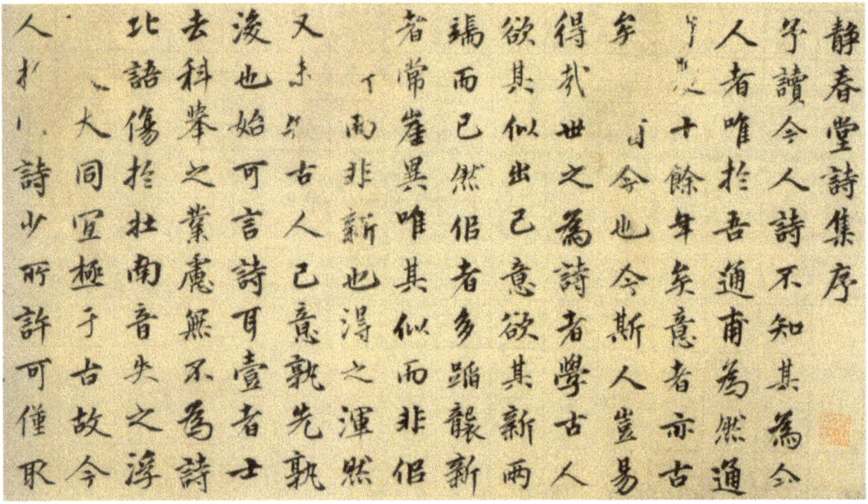

181. Gong Su: Preface of Jingchun Hall Poem

Yuan

Length: 31.2 cm Width: 151 cm

Preserved in the Palace Museum in Beijing

Paper painting, running and regular script. It is a preface of *Poetry Anthology of Jingchun Hall* produced by Gong Su for Yuan Yi. The calligraphy is dignified, the character style neat and square, with a painted boundary lattice. The volume is signed with "the year of Yanyou Gengshen (1320)" and is sealed with "Guyang Study" and "Gongshi Zijing".

Yuan Yi (1262-1306) also named Tongfu, was a native of Changzhou (today's Suzhou of Jiangsu).The Yuan literary writer left behind many works compiled by his second son Yuan Zhongchang into *Poetry Anthology of Jingchun Hall.*

Gong Su (1266-1331), also known as Zijing and Guyang Sheng, was born in Gaoyou of Jiangsu. He produced poetic prose work and was good at calligraphy retaining the ancient style.

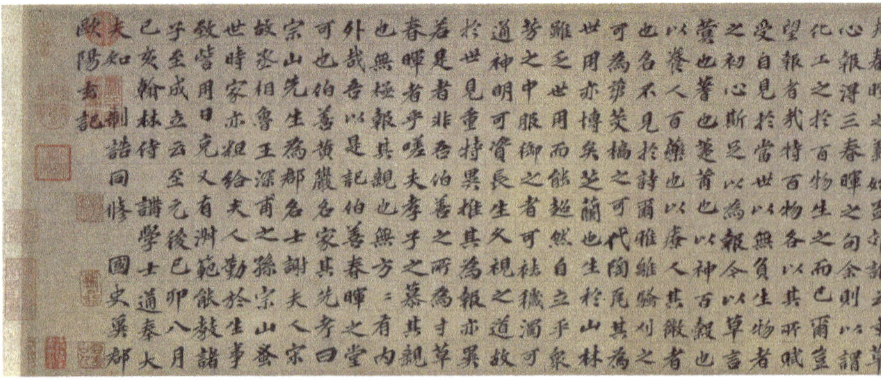

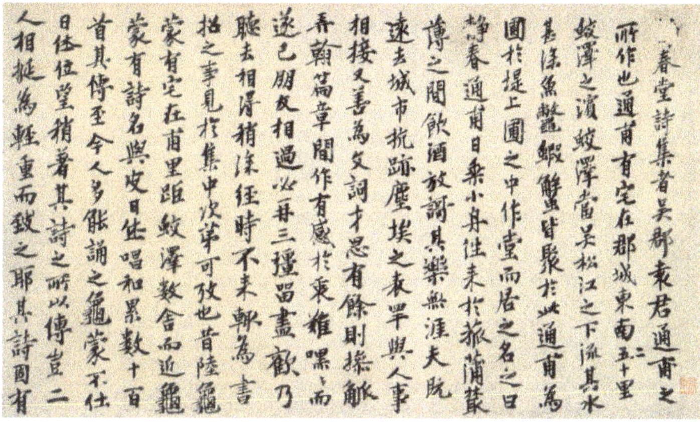

182. Yang Zai: Preface of Jingchun Hall Poem

Yuan

Length: 31 cm Width: 99.6 cm

Preserved in the Palace Museum in Beijing

Paper painting, running script. It is a preface of the *Poetry Anthology of Jingchun Hall* produced by Yang Zai for Yuan Yi. Being the only long calligraphy work of Yang Zai, the character style is rich, the handwriting is ancient and light in color, structure thick and clumsy. However, the brushwork is loose, and the way he uses brush is gloomy. It is signed with "the 2nd year of Zhizhi of Yuan Dynasty (1322)" and is sealed with "Zai", "seal of father of Zhonghong" and "Yangshi of Pucheng".

Yang Zai (1271-1323), also known as Zhonghong, was born in Pucheng (present-day belongs to Fujian) and moved to Hangzhou later. He was erudite and used to be the editing officer in the National History Courtyard of Hanlin Academy as a result of a Vivlian Summon; later he won the title of Jinshi granted with the official title of Chengwu Lang and subsequently was promoted to be TuiGuan of the Explorer House on Ningguo Road.

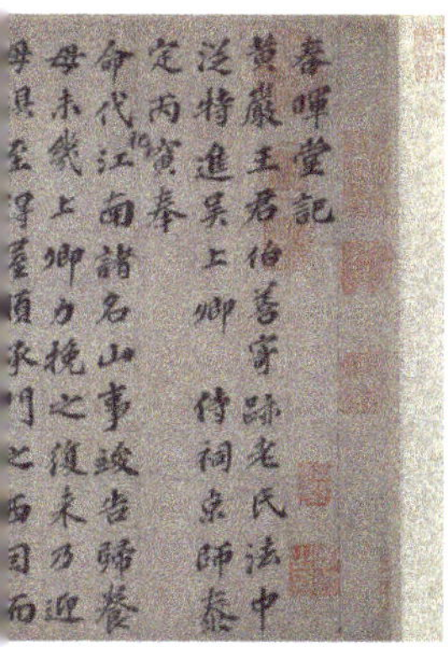

183. Oyang Xuan: Record of Chunhui Hall

Yuan

Length: 29 cm Width: 102.9 cm

Preserved in the Palace Museum in Beijing

Paper painting, regular script. The record is composed and written by Oyang Xuan for Fengqinzhi Hall of Wang Boshan. Its brushwork is sincere and steady, the character potential is square and flat, which is the calligraphy style of Su Shi. This is Oyang Xuan's representative work with the beauties of both composition and calligraphy. It is signed with "Jimao Year after the year of Zhiyuan (1339)" and is sealed with "seal of Oyang Xuan from Ji County". There is a preface and postscript written by Zhang Zhu and others of the Yuan Dynasty at the end of the volume, which used to be collected by An Qi of the Qing Dynasty and the Inside House of Emperor Qianlong. *Precious Collection of the Stone Moat*, *Moyuan Huiguan* and others record it.

The ancestral home of Oyang Xuan (1274-1358), also known as Yuangong and Guizhai, was Luling (present-day Ji'an of Jiangxi), but he later moved to Liuyang (present-day belongs to Hunan). Being good at calligraphy, he composed poetry and learned from Su Shi.

184. Xianyu Shu: Poem on the Place of Zhaoling Mausoleum

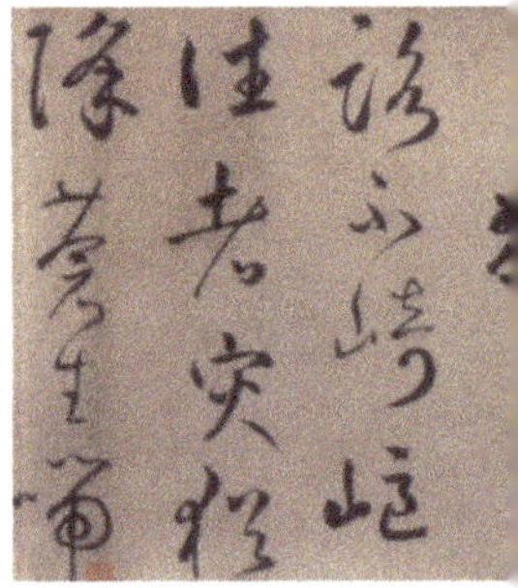

Yuan

Length: 32 cm Width: 342 cm

Preserved in the Palace Museum in Beijing

Paper painting, running script. It presents the *Poem on the Place of Zhaoling Mausoleum* produced by Du Fu of the Tang Dynasty. Being Xianyu Shu's representative work of running script, the calligraphy is queer and vigorous, structure smooth and clear, and the brushwork is forceful, natural and smooth. It is signed with "written by Kunxuemin" and is sealed with five seals. At the end of the volume is the preface and postscript written by Wang Yi and Song Lian of the Ming Dynasty. It used to be collected and preserved in the Inside House in the early Ming Dynasty, Liang Qingbiao and the Inside House of the Qing Dynasty. *Spectacular Life, Precious Collection of the Stone Moat Sequel: First Edition* and *Catalogue of Lost Paintings and Calligraphy in the Palace Museum in Beijing* mention it.

Xian Yushu (1265-1301), also known as Boji and Kunxuemin, etc., was born in Yuyang of Hebei (present-day belongs to Jixian County of Tianjin). He was good at poetry, familiar with rhythm and an outstanding connoisseur. He shares equal fame with Zhao Mengfu regarding calligraphy and followed the trend of restoring the ancient imitating the Tang style and did well in running cursive script in big characters.

185. Xian Yushu: Tao Te Ching of Lao Tze

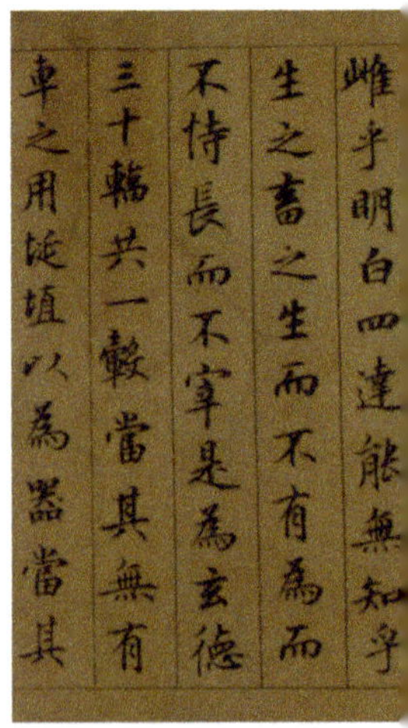

Yuan

Length: 26.7 cm Width: 642.5 cm

Preserved in the Palace Museum in Beijing

Paper painting, regular script. It presents the Tao Te Ching, although lacking the beginning and end. The character style is elegant and upright. The stroke is delicate and fine, but the brushwork is obviously forceful. At the end of the volume is written "1st Volume of Tao Te Ching". There is no signature. This is his only long masterpiece in regular script that has been preserved. There are five paragraphs of preface and postscripts written by Weng Fanggang and Wu Rongguang, etc. And it is sealed with many connoisseur seals. *Collection of Privately Preserved Paintings* mention it.

186. Qian Liangyou: Antiphony Poem of Wu Zhong

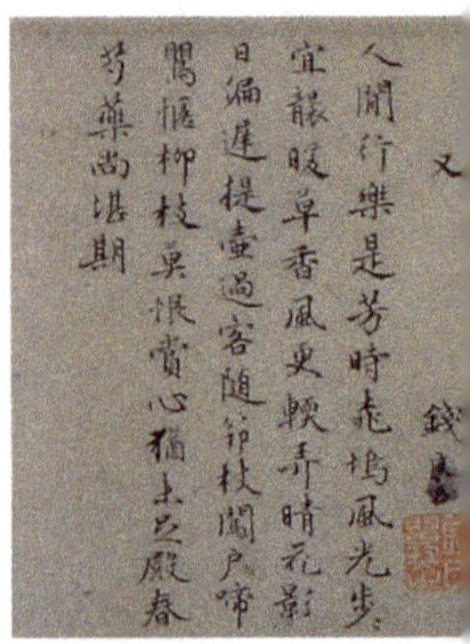

Yuan

Length: 17.5 cm Width: 519.8 cm

Preserved in the Suzhou Museum

Paper painting, running script. Its contents are antiphony poems produced by Wu Zhongren and his companions when they went on a springtime excursion during the Southern Song Dynasty. The stroke is delicate and exquisite, the frame has symmetry from both of which his calligraphy skills can be seen. At the blank of this mounting volume, there exists "Essence of Wuxing" in clerical script by Weng Fanggang. At the end, Du Mu, Du Qi and Wen Zhengming of Ming Dynasty and Weng Fanggang of Qing Dynasty wrote preface and postscript on it.

Qian Liangyou (1278-1344), also known as Yizhi and people called him Mr. Jiangcun because he named himself Jiangcunmin, was born in Pingjiang (present-day Hunan). He was good at painting and excelled in seal script, clerical script and running script. As his running script is clear and loud, outstanding and brilliant, his style is not inferior to Xian Yushu.

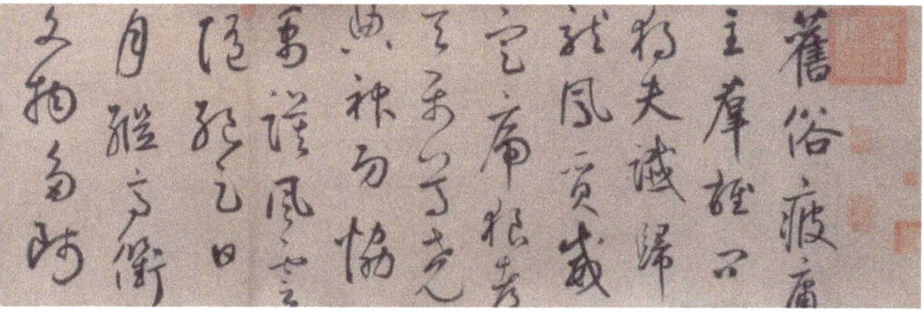

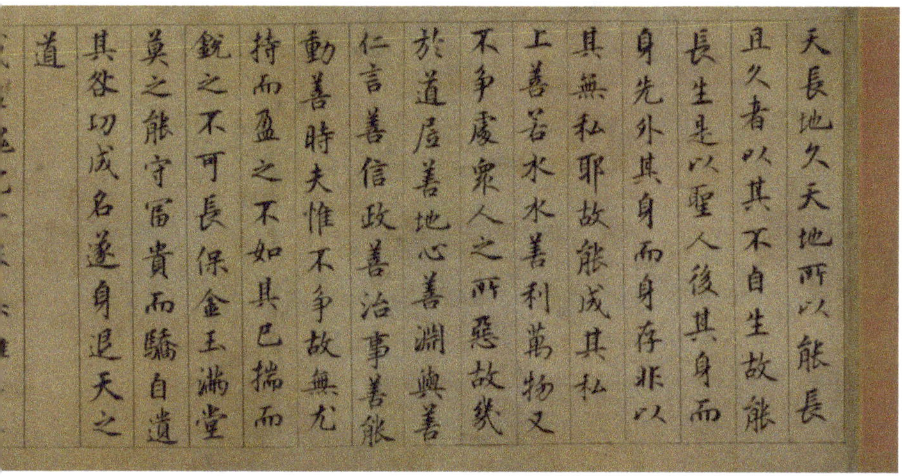
天長地久天地所以能長
且久者以其不自生故能
長生是以聖人後其身而
身先外其身而身存非以
其無私耶故能成其私
上善若水水善利萬物又
不爭處衆人之所惡故幾
於道居善地心善淵與善
仁言善信政善治事善能
動善時夫惟不爭故無尤
持而盈之不如其已揣而
銳之不可長保金玉滿堂
莫之能守富貴而驕自遺
其咎功成名遂身退天之
道

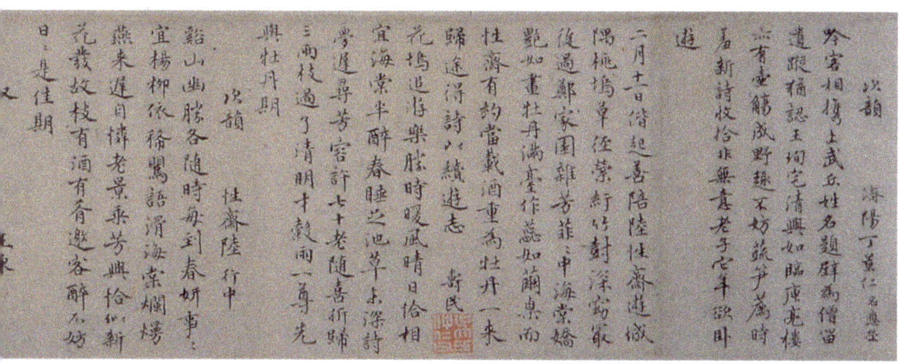

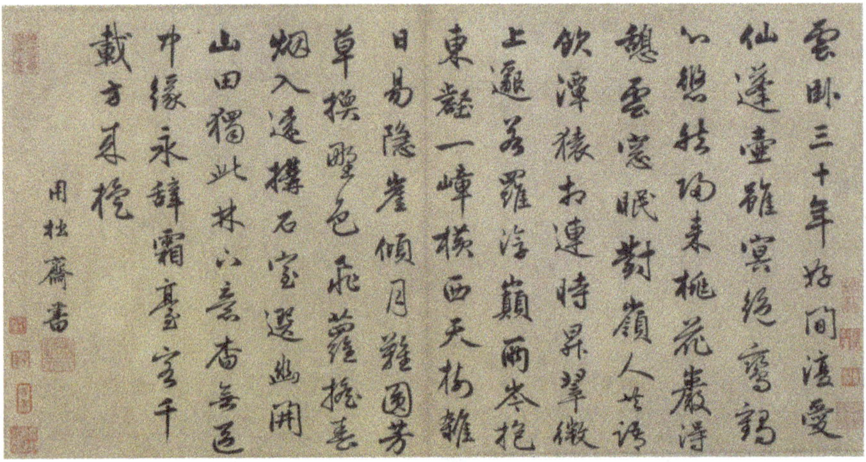

187. Zhang Yuan: Calligraphy Model of Ancient Five-character Poem

Yuan

Length: 27.4 cm Width: 52.7 cm

Preserved in the Palace Museum in Beijing

Paper painting, running script. He wrote down one piece of an ancient five-character poem. The stroke is clear, smooth and forceful, the structure square and expansive, and stipplings are delicate and beautiful, neat and graceful. He imitated the calligraphy style of Zhao Mengfu. This is his only work handed down. It is signed with "written in Yongzhuo Zhai" and is sealed with "Zhangshi Qingfu". This volume is sealed with many connoisseur seals.

Zhang Yuan (1264-?), also known as Qingfu and Yongzhuo Daoren, was born in Wujiang of Jiangsu. Famous for his poetry, he also practiced calligraphy. In his early years, he was a student of Zhao Mengfu to learn calligraphy.

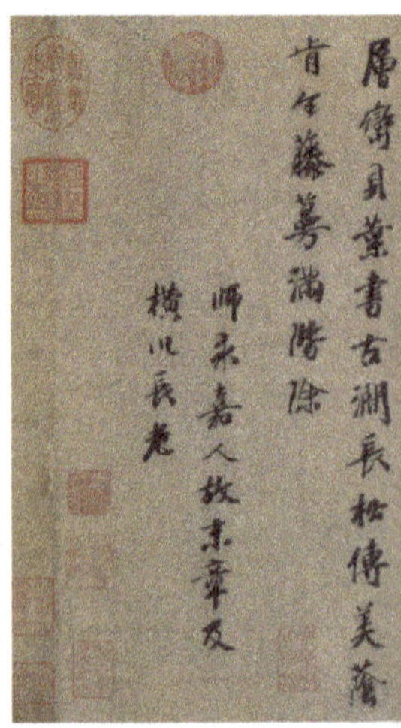

188. Yuan Jue: Calligraphy Model of Poems Produced by Chief Monk Yi'an

Yuan

Length: 31.5 cm Width: 89.7 cm

Preserved in the Palace Museum in Beijing

Paper painting, running script. This volume is about four poems produced by master Yi'an whose name was Bai Shouning, also known as Wuwei and Yi'an, born in Yongjia and later the abbot of Jiang'an Temple in Shanghai. Being the representative of Yuan Jue's running script preserved, the layout of this calligraphy is neat and liberated, the style is soft and smooth and the entire chapter seems to be simple and elegant. At the end of this volume, it is sealed with "Yuan Bochang" and "Qingrong Zhai". It was authenticated and collected by Li Zhaoheng, Bian Yongyu, An Qi and other people.

Yuanxian Jue (1266-1327), also known as Bochang and Qingrong Jushi, was born in Yinxian County of Qingyuan (present-day Ningbo of Zhejiang). His way of writing is graceful, elegant and simple. His calligraphy follows Jin and Tang dynasties in style and draws on the calligraphy of Mi Fu.

189. Jie Xisi: Copy Lin Zhiyong's Thousand Character Classic in Regular Cursive Script

Yuan

Length: 28 cm Width: 342.5 cm

Preserved in the Shanghai Museum

Paper painting, regular and cursive scripts. It is the *Thousand Character* Classic produced by Lin Zhiyong in regular and cursive scripts. The brushwork is ease, refined and elegant, antique and forceful, showing all the attainments of Yuan calligraphy. It is signed with "imitation in September of theJiaxu Year, that is the 2nd year (1334) of Yuantong when I directly learned from Jie Xisi in Hanlin Academy". It used to be collected by Zhou Lianggong and Yan Shiqing of the Qing Dynasty and Ye Gongchao in contemporary times.

Jie Xisi (1274-1344), also known as Manshuo, was born in Fuzhou of Longxing (present-day Fengcheng of Jiangxi). He was good at regular script and running script, and especially cursive script and imitated the calligraphy of the Jin Dynasty.

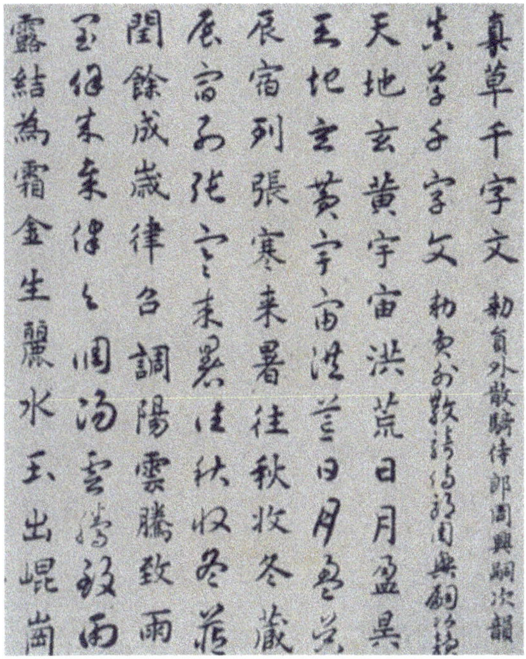

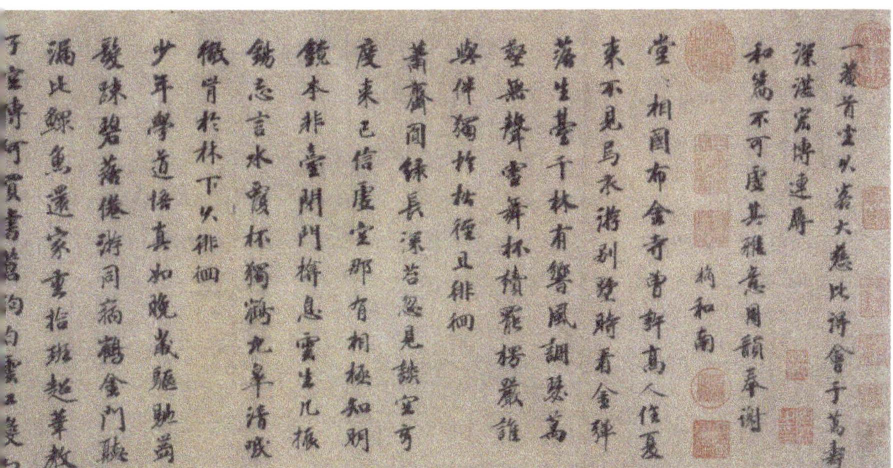

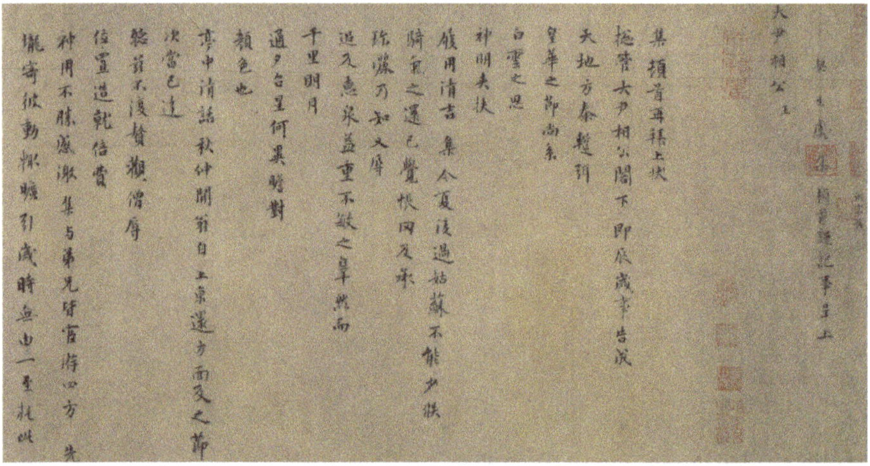

190. Yu Ji: Calligraphy Model of Jichen

Yuan

Length: 32.3 cm   Width: 93.2 cm

Preserved in the Palace Museum in Beijing

Paper painting, regular script. This is letter. The writing is concise, clumsy and simple with exuberant ancient meaning. Although it is regular script, it possesses the calligraphy style of running script and the stippling is charming. This leaf is sealed with "Yuji". It is sealed with many connoisseur seals of Xiang Yuanbian and there is a Collection Number on it. *Fencing Coral and Spectacular Life* record it.

The ancestral home of Yu Ji (1272-1348), also known as Bosheng and Shao'an, was Renshou (present-day belongs to Sichuan), but he lived in Chongren (present-day belongs to Jiangxi). Both his poetry and calligraphy have high attainments and he wrote down many of the nobilities' epigraphs.

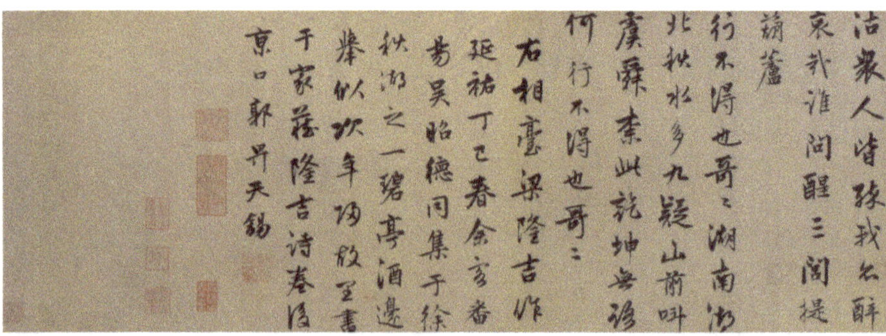

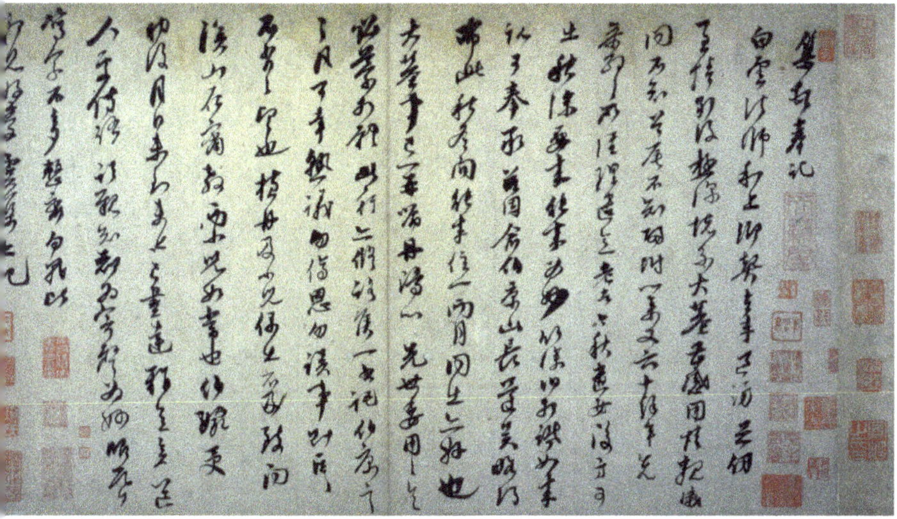

191. Yu Ji: Calligraphy Model of Master Baiyun
Yuan
Length: 30.7 cm Width: 51.8 cm
Preserved in the Palace Museum in Beijing
Paper painting, running and cursive scripts. This is the letter written by Yu Ji to Master Baiyun. Running script alternates with cursive script, and this approach appears to be natural and in accordance with the rules, forceful, antique and elegant. As there is a sentence that "the characters are not so neat because of faint eyes", we can assume that this was the work he produced in his later years. The leaf is sealed with many connoisseur seals of Xiang Yuanbian in the Ming Dynasty, An Qi, He Zizhang and Zhao Shuyan in the Qing Dynasty, etc. *Sanxitang Copybook* and *Moyuan Huiguan*, etc. record it.

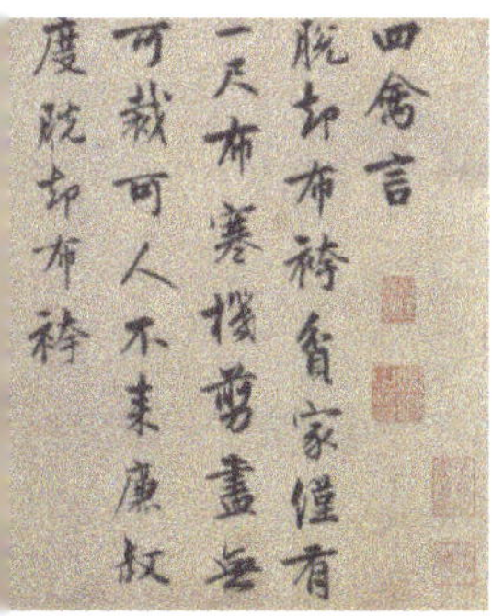

192. Guo Bi: Four Birds Speech Poem by Liang Dong
Yuan
Length: 30.5 cm Width: 112.4 cm
Preserved in the Palace Museum in Beijing
Paper painting, running script. The *Four Birds Speech* was produced by poet Liang Jilong of the Southern Song Dynasty. The calligraphy is gentle and even, smooth and graceful, and the brushwork is adept; the structural alignment, pauses and transitions and the stippling of writing imitate Zhao Mengfu. It is signed "Tianxi, Guo Bi of Jingkou" and is sealed with "Tianxi, Guo Bi". It is sealed with many connoisseur seals of An Qi and the Inside House of Qing Dynasty, etc.
Guo Bi(1280-1335), also known as Tianxi and Yunshan, Jingxingzi, was born in Dantu (present-day Zhenjiang of Jiangsu). He was an official in the Yuan Dynasty and was good at painting and calligraphy imitating Zhao Mengfu.

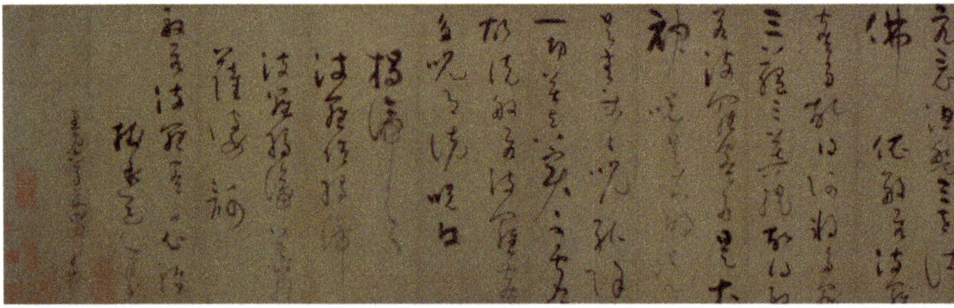

193. Wu Zhen: Heart Sutra

Yuan

Length: 29.3 cm Width: 203 cm

Preserved in the Palace Museum in Beijing

Paper painting on Buddhist sutra cursive script. The structure of the calligraphy imitates Huai Su and gains its attainments. As the representative of Wu Zhen's cursive script, the writing style is grand and magnificent, dull alternating with embellishment, smooth and fresh, and the handwriting is graceful and real. It is noted that this volume was written late in the sixth year of Zhiyuan (1340). It is signed with "written by Meihua Daoren respectfully" and is sealed with "record of painting and calligraphy of Zhongkui, Wuzhen of Jiaxing". Liu Yong, Yongxing and Yang Shoujing provide a preface and postscript at the end of the volume and it is sealed by 18 connoisseur seals. *Records of Haogutang Calligraphy and Paintings* record it.

Although famous for his painting, Wu Zhen was also good at cursive script and mostly inscribed the paintings with cursive script. His brushwork slightly resembles Huai Su but still has a unique style.

194. Zhang Yu: Calligraphy Model of Song Gan Poem

Yuan

Length: 26.5 cm Width: 29.4 cm

Preserved in the Palace Museum in Beijing

Paper painting, running script. This is a seven-character poem. The writing is bold and forceful, high and steep, possessing the tough style of Li Yong; however, it still shows the style of Zhao calligraphy, which is fresh and cute, graceful and elegant. It is signed with "Tianyu" and is sealed with "Juqu Waishi". And this volume is sealed with four connoisseur seals.

Zhang Yu (1283-1350), also known as Tianyu, Boyu and Juqu Waishi, was born in Qiantang (present-day Hangzhou). At young age he left home and became a Taoist. His poetry and painting is fresh, smooth and beautiful with the styles of the Jin and Tang dynasties. As for his calligraphy, he imitated Zhao Mengfu at the very beginning when Zhao advised him to learn from that in the Tang Dynasty.

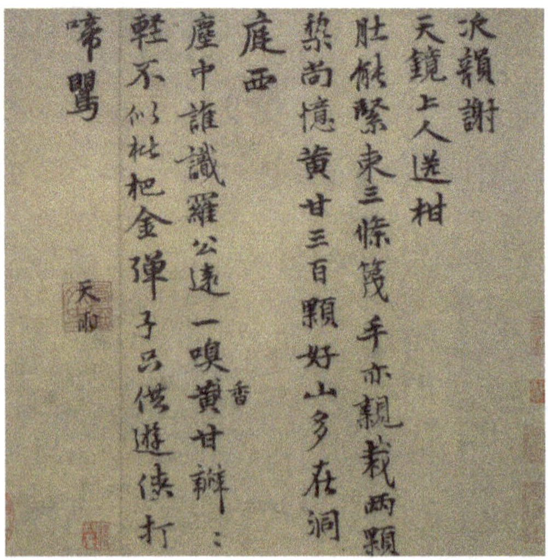

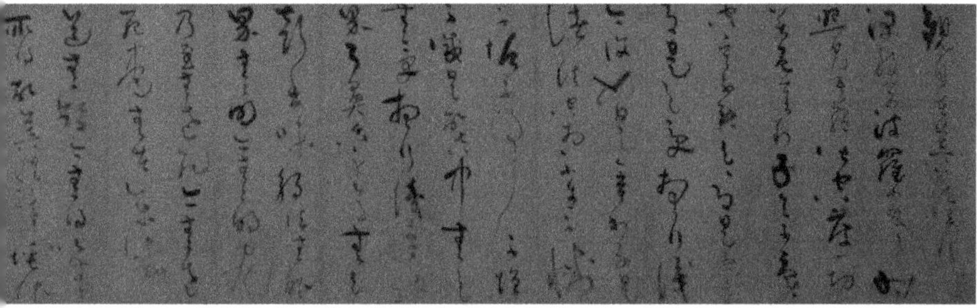

195. Zhang Yu: Calligraphy Model of Poems of Inscriptions on Painting

Yuan

Length: 29.3 cm Width: 148.5 cm

Preserved in the Palace Museum in Beijing

Paper painting, running script. It records two poetic inscriptions on the painting of Zhang Yanfu. Being representative of Zhang's long running script, the calligraphy is clear, forceful and liberated; the brushwork varies with miraculous and novel artistic conception and already possesses some differences comparing with Zhao School Calligraphy. At the end of this volume, he wrote an inscription , "on the right are the inscriptions on Xueshan Louguan and Yunlin Yinju, two paintings of Zhang Yanfu, by Yu" and it is sealed with "Zhang Yusi Seal" and "Juqu Waishi Zhang Tian Yu Seal". At the front blank of this volume is clerical script by Shen Zengzhi saying "the poem keeps the meaning of the painting". There is a poetic inscription written by Zheng Yuanyou and entitled by Luo Tianchi at the end.

Zhang Yanfu, a Taoist in the Yuan Dynasty, also known as Liuyi, lived in Yanjing (present-day Beijing). He was good at landscape painting and also painted bamboos, stones and hidden birds, etc.

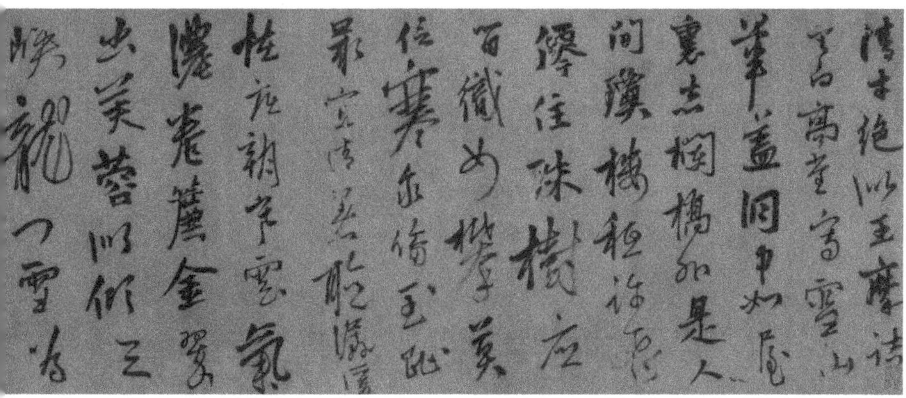

196. Wei Ze: Universalism Preached in Huiqing Temple

Yuan

81 Pages Length of Each Page: 27.3 cm Width of Each Page: 17.4 cm

Preserved in the Nanjing Museum

Paper painting, running and regular scripts. It is the lecture notes narrating Buddhist doctrine. The calligraphy is steady and forceful, the space between characters is scattered and spacious in the style handed down from Zhao Calligraphy. It is signed, "written by Wei Ze of Luling living in Huanzhu nunnery on the 3rd month of this year" and produced in the Zhenyuan Year (1341) of Yuanzhi. Wang Zhideng and others wrote a preface and postscript at the end of the leaf.

Wei Ze (1286-1354), whose real surname is Tan, a monk in Huiqing Temple, was born in Yongxin of Ji'an, Jiangxi. After 20, he entered Tianmu Mountain in Jiangxi and became a student of Chan Master Zhongfeng until he was a very inspiring teacher. Famous temples on famous mountains in regions of Jiangsu and Zhejiangs invited him to be the chief monk time and again. In his later years, he disappeared into Wu Men to cultivate himself according to the religious doctrine and thus rarely connected again with the outside world.

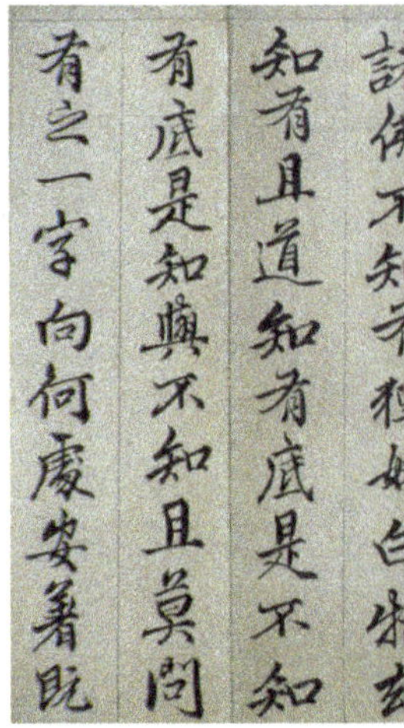

197. Zhao Yong: Eight Odes to Zhangnan

Yuan

Length: 30.8 cm Width: 227.9 cm

Preserved in the Palace Museum in Beijing

Paper painting, running script. It records "Eight Odes to Zhangnan" by Ling Mengfu of Yuan Dynasty at the very beginning of the volume. The structure of this calligraphy is steady and the character is graceful, smooth and elegant from which we can see his skill, and the stippling and structure still possesses the style of Zhao Calligraphy. And this is the representative of his running script. It is signed, "poem of Ling Mengfu and written by Zhao Zhongmu" and is sealed with "Zhongmu". At the front is "Eight Odes to Zhangnan" in seal character by Zhirou Daoren and at the back is the poetic inscription composed by Liu Lin and Gu Yingxiang. It is sealed with many connoisseur seals.

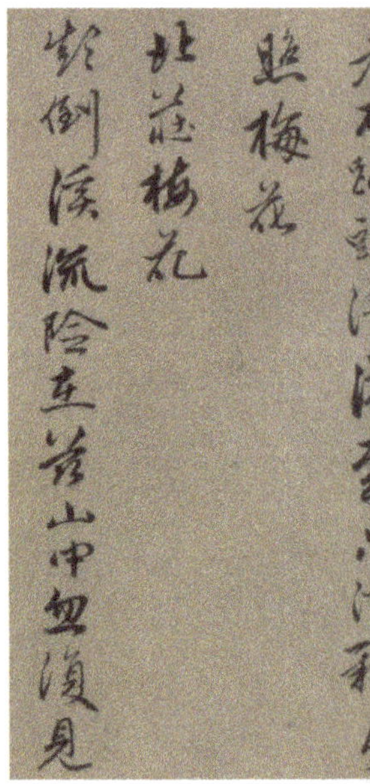

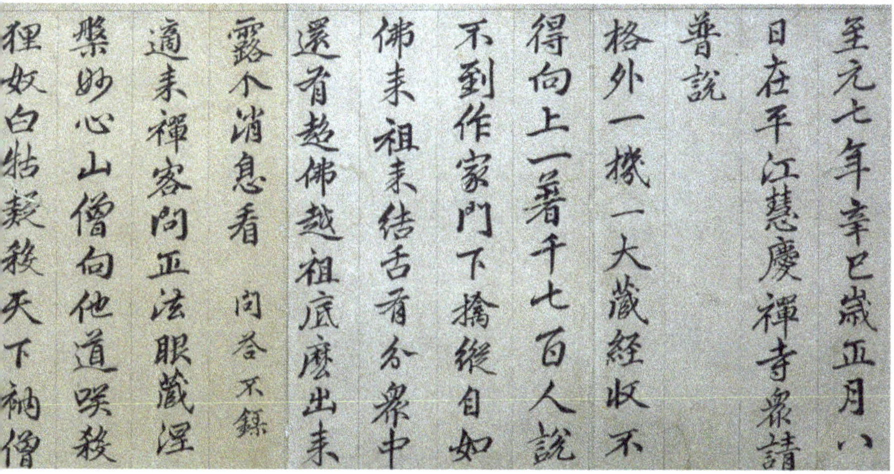
至元七年辛巳歲五月八
日在平江慧慶禪寺衆請
普說
格外一撥一大藏經收不
得向上一着千七百人說
不到作家門下擒縱自如
佛來祖來結舌看分衆中
還有超佛越祖底麼出來
露个消息看 問答不錄
適來禪客問正法眼藏涅
槃妙心山僧向他道咲殺
狸奴白牯鬆殺天下衲僧

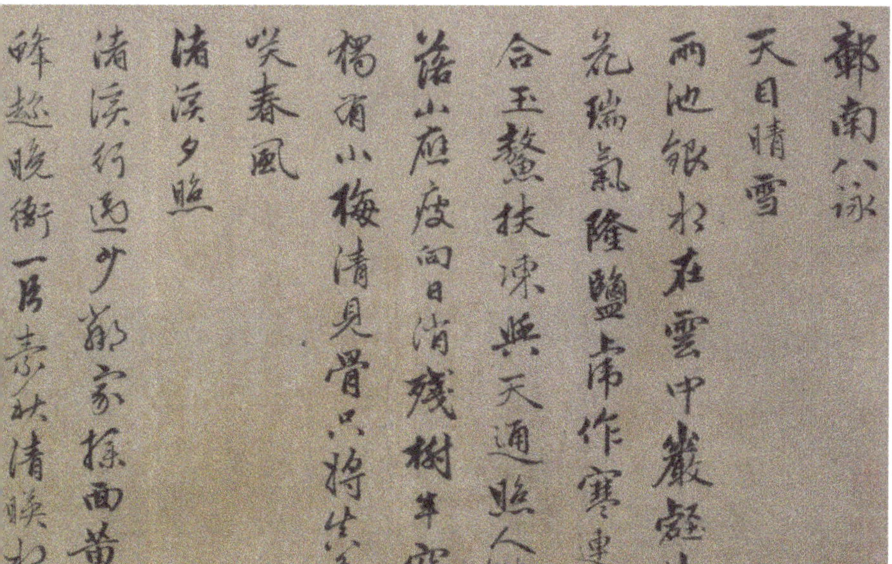

198. Li Xiaoguang: Calligraphy Model of Letter Sent to Jianye

Yuan

Length: 31.2 cm Width: 38 cm

Preserved in the Palace Museum in Beijing

Paper painting, running script. Letters written for Monk Daxin (Monk Xiaoyin). The calligraphy imitates that of Su Shi. The handwriting is bold, the structure square and flat and lateral sharpness appears from time to time, while the stippling, turn and the connection between lines and characters are delicate and neat. According to what is noted down in the leaf, this letter may have been written in the Zhengyuan Year of Zhiyuan (1341). It is sealed with two connoisseur seals.

The secular surname of Daxin was Chen. He was born in Nanchang, and was the chief monk of Jiqing Temple in Longxiang of Jiankang (present-day Nanjing) when he named himself Xiaoyin Jushi. He wrote poetry and used to be one friend of Zhao Mengfu, Gao Kegong, Yu Ji and Ke Jiusi, etc.

Li Xiaoguang (1297-1348), also known as Jihe, was born in Yueqing (present-day Wenzhou of Zhejiang) and used to live in Yandang Mountain in seclusion. He was famous for his poems. In the 7th year of Zhizheng, he was recalled to the capital and later became an official entitled Wenlin Lang and Mishu Jiancheng. He was good at calligraphy imitating Su Shi.

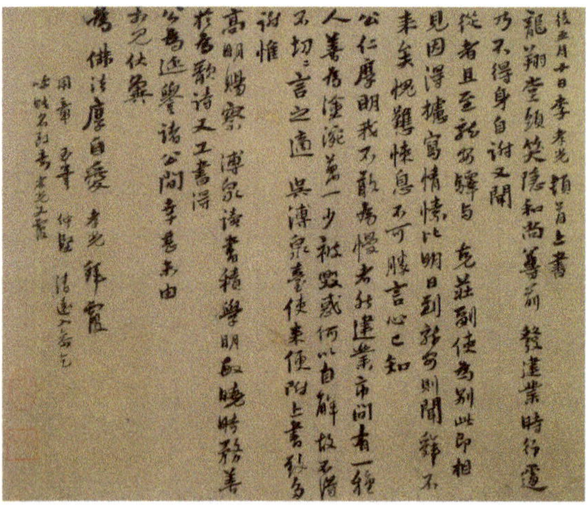

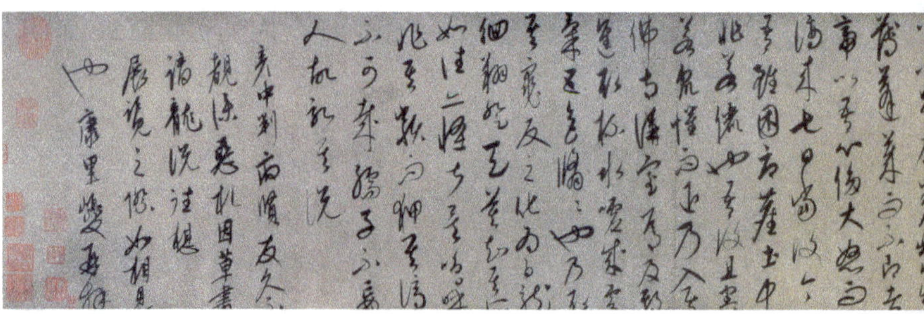

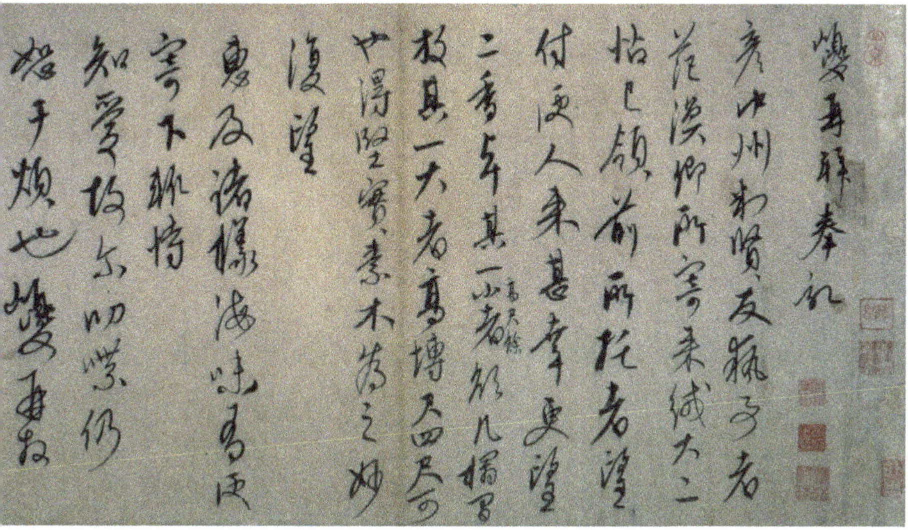

199. Kangli Nao: Calligraphy Model of Fengji

Yuan

Length: 29.8 cm   Width: 55.7 cm

Preserved in the Palace Museum in Beijing

Paper painting, running and cursive scripts. Letters discussing the articles sent. The way he wrote is rapid and vivid with much sharp handwriting. He imitated the style of the Jin and Tang dynasties and his works reflect the concept of being forceful and charming. It is signed with "a second visit by Nao". It is sealed with many connoisseur seals.

Kangli Nao (1290-1345), also known as Zishan, Zhengzhai and Shusou, etc., was born in the tribe of Kangli (Turks Tribe, nomads from the region around the Ural River). He was good at running and cursive scripts and he wrote with the wrist raised. He wrote rapidly and the ink is glorious and shining under the influence of the calligraphy style of Zhao Mengfu, although also forming his own unique style.

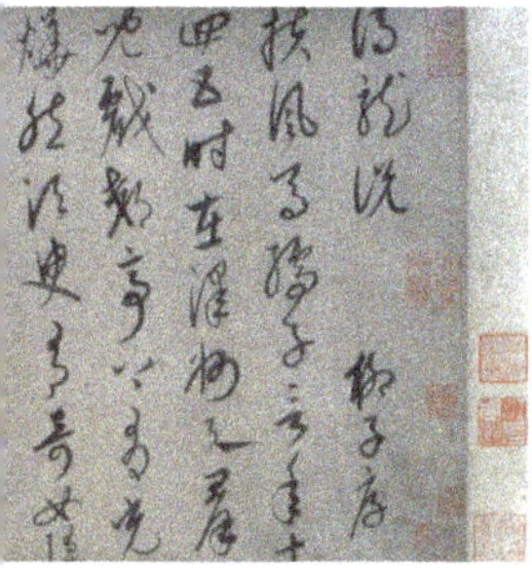

200. Kangli Nao: Zhelong Saying

Yuan

Length: 28.8 cm   Width: 137.9 cm

Preserved in the Palace Museum in Beijing

Paper painting, cursive script. It records Zhelong Saying by Liu Zongyuan of the Tang Dynasty. The handwriting is brisk and neat and its turns are smooth and natural. Not only is neatness and steadiness retained in the process of rapid writing, but also the stippling and structure is in accordance with the rules. This is the representative of his cursive script. It is sealed with "Kangli Zishan" and in the blank sealed with "Songfeng Hall". There is one preface and postscript written by Qu Zhi of Yuan Dynasty and an inscription written by Yongxing of Qing Dynasty at the front as well as the preface and postscript written by Zhou Boqi and others of Yuan Dynasty at the end. *Spectacular Life, List of Grand view* and *Precious Collection of the Stone Moat* mention it.

201. Yang Weizhen: Preface for Yueh-Fu Produced by Student Shen

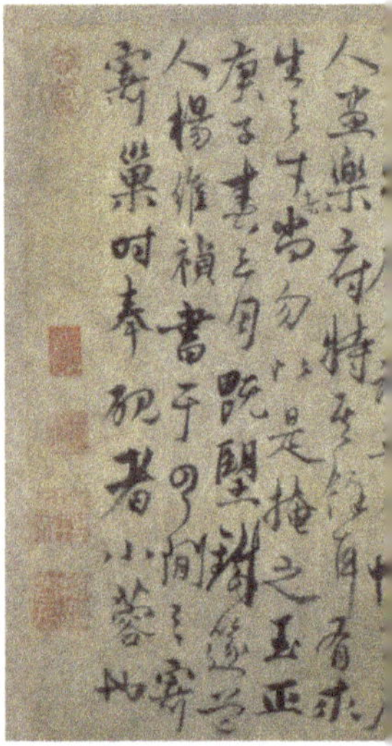

Yuan

Length: 28.3 cm Width: 76.8 cm

Preserved in the Palace Museum in Beijing

Paper painting, running script. It is the preface written by Yang Weizhen for Yueh-Fu Collections produced by Sen Guorui. The stippling of this calligraphy is forceful and steady with variable changes, thick ink alternating with light ink and the style is robust. It is written "on Zheng Gengzi of the year of Yuanzhi (1360)" and is sealed with "Yang Weizhen from Kuaiji Seal" and "Yangshi Lianfu of Kuaiji", etc. Record of Renyin Xiaoxia mentions it.

Yang Weizhen (1290-1370), also known as Lianfu, Tieya and Tiedi Daoren, etc., was born in Shanyin (present-day Shaoxing of Zhejiang). An erudite person, he developed a poetry style of being miraculous and queer, which is called "Tieya Style". He was good at calligraphy with the style being strong and forceful; thus he formed his own style, amid the tide in the Yuan Dynasty towards restoring ancient ways, showing a sense of being out of line.

202. Yang Weizhen: Antiphony Poem in Chengnan

Yuan

Length: 31.6 cm Width: 216.6 cm

Preserved in the Palace Museum in Beijing

Paper painting, cursive script. He wrote down 20 antiphonal poems of Chengnan produced by Zhang Shi (Nan Xuan) of the Southern Song Dynasty. Being the representative of his cursive scripts, the calligraphy structure is miraculous and steep, the handwriting is extensive and liberated, the brushwork antique, clumsy and steep, and the style fresh and forceful. It is signed "the old man Dongwei, Yang Zhenjin wrote on a second visit in December of the year of Zheng Renyin (1362)", and at the end it is marked with "proud evaluation by Zhen" and sealed with "Yang Weizhen of Kuaiji seal". Sun Chengze and others wrote a preface and postscript at the back. *Fencing Coral, Record of Gegzi Xiaoxia* and *Precious Collection of the Stone Moat Sequel: Third Edition* record it.

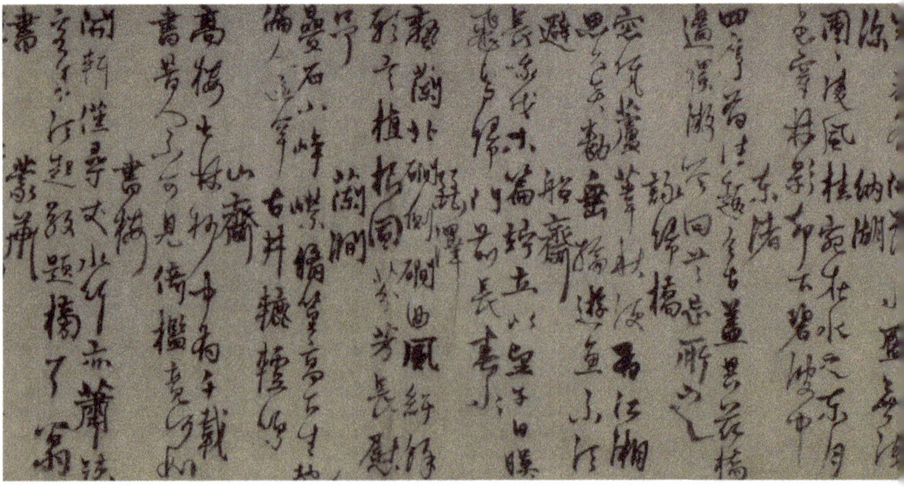

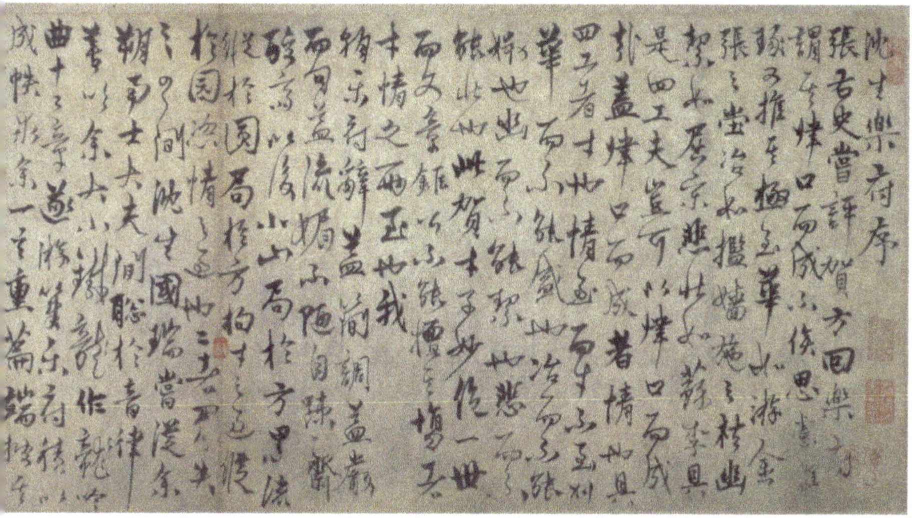

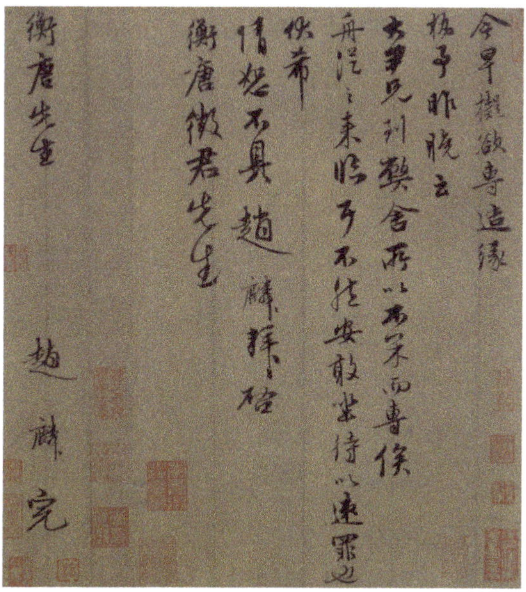

203. Zhao Lin: Calligraphy Model of Hengtang

Yuan

Length: 28.2 cm Width: 25.2 cm

Preserved in the Palace Museum in Beijing

Paper painting, running script. Letters. The calligraphy is vivid, fresh and graceful, bright, clear and unconventional. However, in structural planning and stippling, they are largely inferior to his father and grandfather. It is sealed with many connoisseur seals.

Zhao Lin (time of birth and death unknown), also known as Yanzheng, was the second son of Zhao Yong and the grandson of Zhao Mengfu. While good at painting figures and horses, he also wrote calligraphy. He was able to hand down their household's domestic discipline.

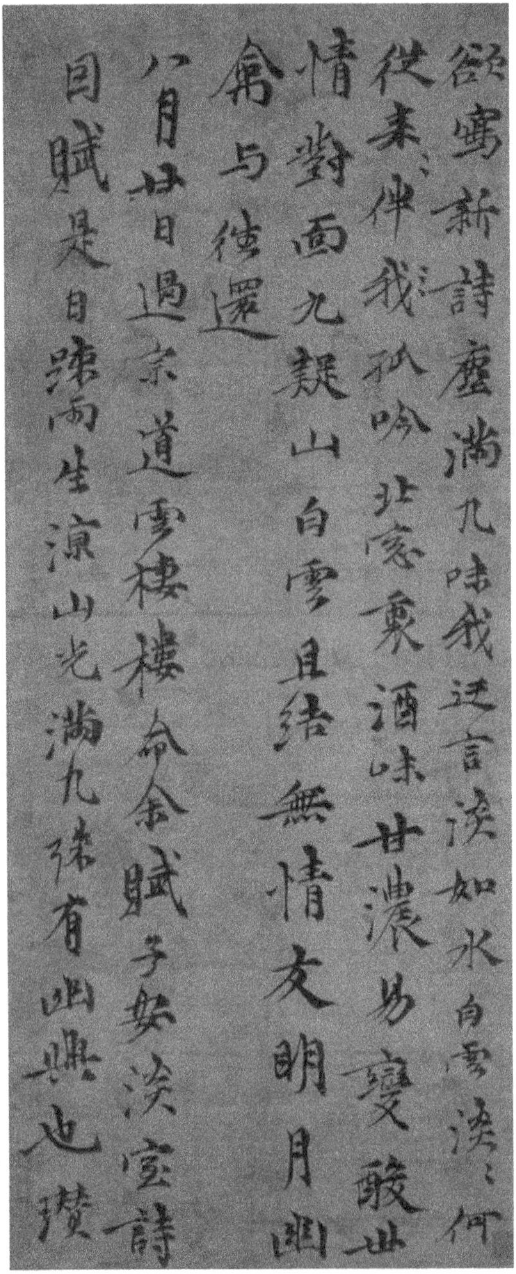

204. Ni Zan: Danshi Poem

Yuan

Length: 64 cm Width: 27 cm

Preserved in the Palace Museum in Beijing

Paper painting, running and regular scripts. It is one piece of seven-character octave produced by Ni Zan for "Zi'An". The calligraphy takes the potential of clerical script; the stippling is rigorous, the structure even and straight and neat and steady, the font size is well distributed and the art of composition is arranged in an orderly way. This is the only example preserved of his running and regular scripts. It is sealed with the connoisseur seal of Dai Zhi.

Ni Zan was famous for his painting and self-appraised his calligraphy as "being liberated and cursive, not pursuant of any form similarity" and the style of "complication implied in simpleness", which exerted a great influence on later ages.

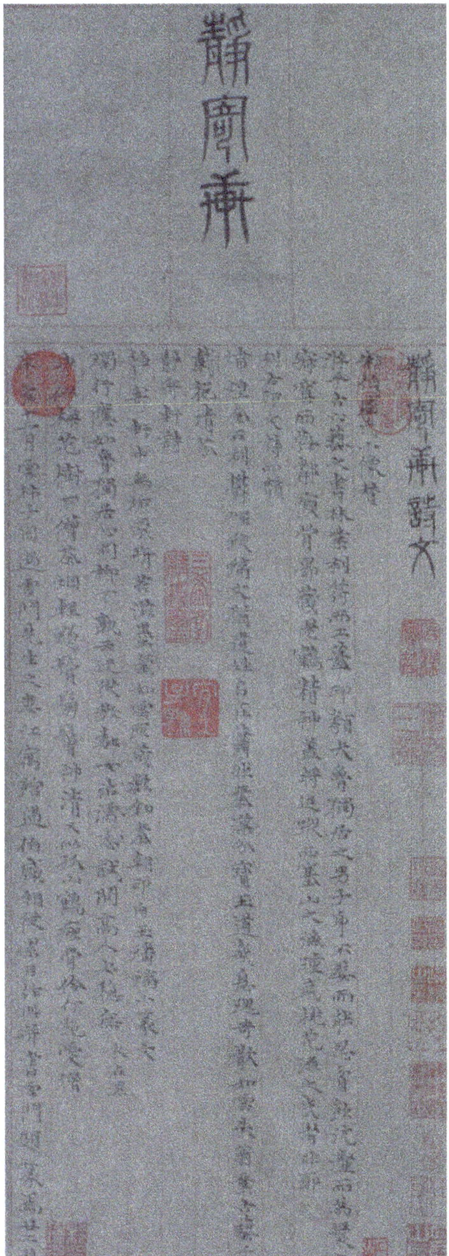

205. Ni Zan: Poems of Jingji Pavilion

Yuan

Length: 62.9 cm Width: 23.2 cm

Preserved in the Palace Museum in Beijing

Paper painting, regular script. Its contents include Ode to statuette of Zhu Bosheng, Poem of Carved Ancient Seals and Poem of Jingji Pavilion. The way he wrote is sincere and elegant, vivid and graceful and the script tends towards cross-potential. It possesses the calligraphic style of clerical script - antique and light, easy and elegant. The top of the leaf is Zhang Shen's seal script. Yang Shoujing of the Qing Dynasty wrote a preface and postscript. It is sealed with the connoisseur seals of the Inside House of Qing Dynasty, etc. *Collective Study on Shigutang Calligraphy and Paintings* and *Calligraphy and Painting Records of Luyun Building* mention it.

The real name of Zhu Bosheng was Gui, who was born in Suzhou and learnt seal script from Wu Rui and liked engraving seals. "Jingji Pavilion" is the name of his pavilion.

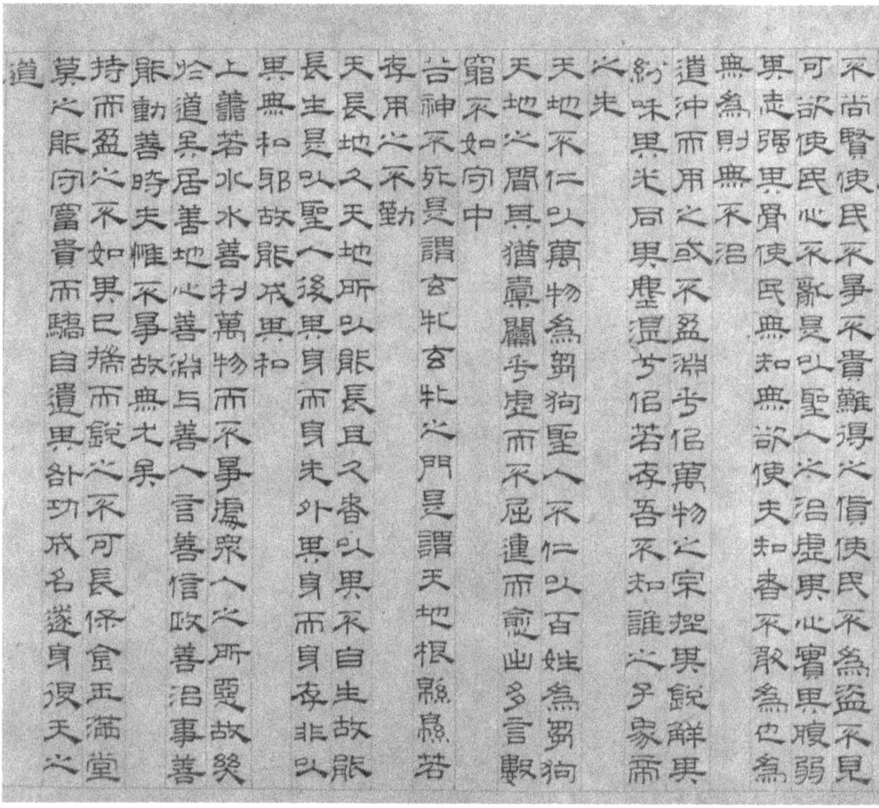
不尚賢使民不爭不貴難得之貨使民不為盜不見
可欲使民心不亂是以聖人之治虛其心實其腹弱
其志強其骨使民無知無欲使夫知者不敢為也為
無為則無不治
道沖而用之或不盈淵兮似萬物之宗挫其銳解其
紛和其光同其塵湛兮似若存吾不知誰之子象帝
之先
天地不仁以萬物為芻狗聖人不仁以百姓為芻狗
天地之間其猶橐籥乎虛而不屈動而愈出多言數
窮不如守中
谷神不死是謂玄牝玄牝之門是謂天地根綿綿若
存用之不勤
天長地久天地所以能長且久者以其不自生故能
長生是以聖人後其身而身先外其身而身存非以
其無私邪故能成其私
上善若水水善利萬物而不爭處衆人之所惡故幾
於道居善地心善淵與善人言善信政善治事善
能動善時夫唯不爭故無尤矣
持而盈之不如其已揣而銳之不可長保金玉滿堂
莫之能守富貴而驕自遺其咎功成名遂身退天之
道

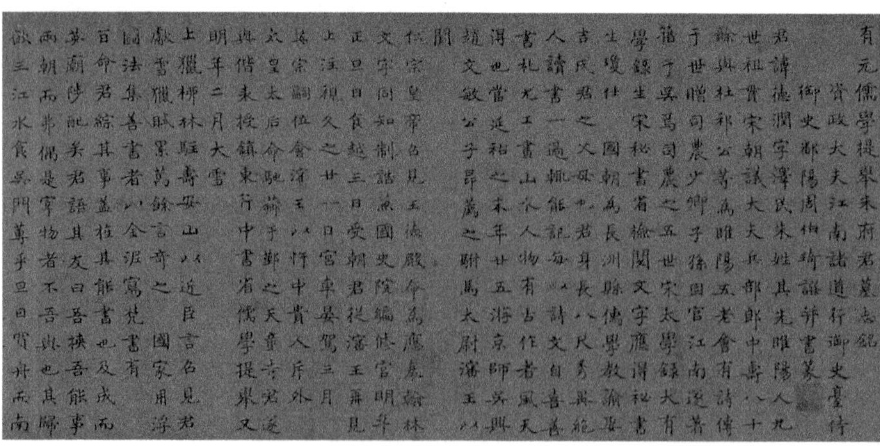

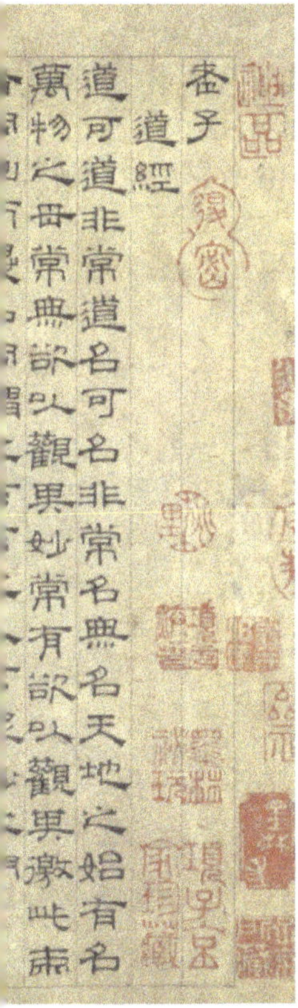

206. Wu Rui: Tao Te Ching of Lao Tze

Yuan

Length: 24.8 cm Width: 400.7 cm

Preserved in the Palace Museum in Beijing

Paper painting, clerical script. It records the full text of *Tao Te Ching*. The brushwork shows dominant square stippling, but the round and the square alternate; the structure is neat and uniform. Throughout the text, he wrote in a steady, neat, delicate and refined way. This is the representative work of Wu Rui's clerical script. It is signed, "the third year of Yuantong (1335)" and is sealed with "the private seal of Wu Rui". At the front of the leaf is fake line-drawing *Picture of Lecturing by Lao Tze of Sheng Mao*, and the paper in the rear carries an inscription by Hu Zi'ang of the Ming Dynasty. It is sealed with many connoisseur seals of Xiang Yuanbian, etc.

The ancestral home of Wu Rui (1298-1355), also known as Mengsi and Xuetao Sanren, Qingyun Sheng and Suyang Chushi, was Puyang (present-day belongs to He'nan), but he lived in Hangzhou, although in his later years he moved to live in Kunshan of Jiangsu as a retiree. He was a student of Wu Qiuyan and was a civlian all his life. He was good at calligraphy, especially seal and clerical scripts.

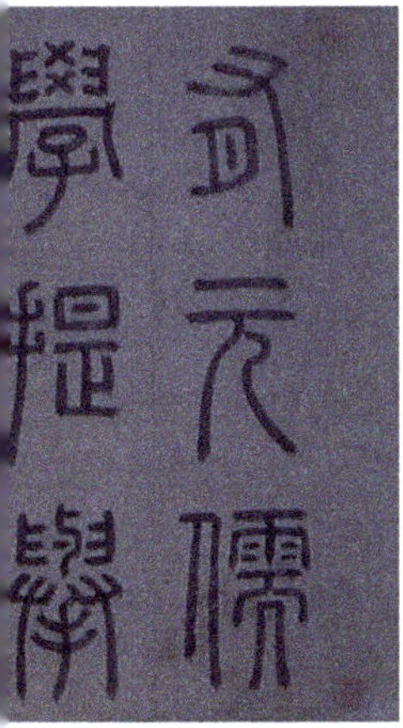

207. Zhou Boqi: the Epigraph of Zhu Derun

Yuan

Length: 34.9 cm Width: 270.8 cm

Preserved in the Palace Museum in Beijing

Paper painting, regular script. This is the epigraph written and produced by Zhou Boqi for Zhu Derun, a painter of the Yuan Dynasty. It is written in both seal script, used at the top, and regular script, used in the body; in addition, the former is neat and steady and the latter displays square characters; the style is profound and elegant. This is the representative calligraphy of Zhou Boqi. It is signed, "seal script written and composed by Zhou Boqi of Poyang" and is sealed with "Zhou Boqi, the Taishishi", "Zhuxia Shi", "home in Poyang of Marquis founding the empire" and "Hanlin of three generations", etc.

Zhou Boqi (1298-1369), naming himself Yuxuepo Zhenyi and Jianbai Jushi and also known as Bowen, was born in Raozhou (present-day Poyang of Jiangxi). He used to hold the official title of Daizhao of Hanlin and Zhi Xueshi, plenipotentiary of checking the incorruptive government in the regions on the east of Jiangxi and the west of Zhejiang, Zizheng Dafu and Left Prime Minister of Jiangsu and Zhengjiang. Famous for being good at seal script, clerical script, regular script and cursive script, he was erudite and wrote articles and calligraphy.

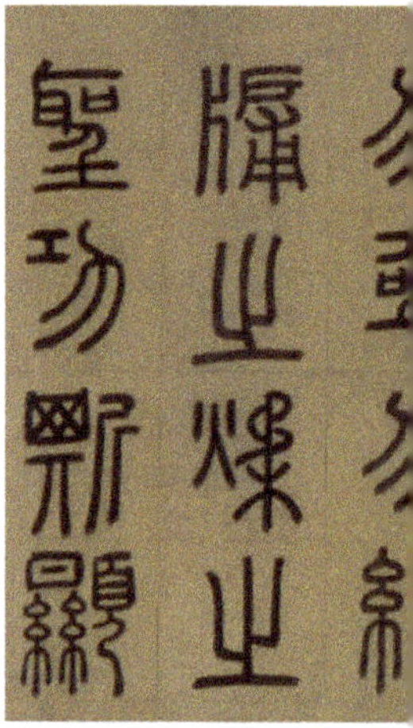

208. Zhou Boqi: Two Pieces of Gong Xue National History
Yuan
Length: 26 cm Width: 284.5 cm
Preserved in the Palace Museum in Beijing
Paper painting, seal script. It was written in Zhengyuan year of Yuanzhi (1341). The calligraphy is square and steady with little conception of clerical script; regarding its structure and brushwork, it leans towards the approach of "stone drum inscription". This is the masterpiece of Zhou Boqi's seal script. It is signed, "narrated and written by Zhou Boqi from Poyang" and is sealed with "Zhiyong Zhai", "Zhoushi Bowen" and "Yuxuepo Zhenyi". Later, Zhang Yu of Yuan Dynasty wrote a preface and postscript on it.

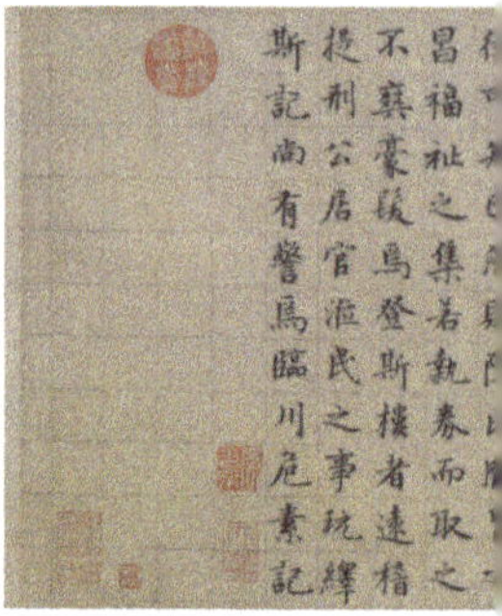

209. Wei Su: Record of Fangcun Building
Yuan
Length: 23.4 cm Width: 102 cm
Preserved in the Palace Museum in Beijing
Paper painting, regular script in small character. It is mounted together with calligraphies of Zhao Mengfu and Yang Weizhen in one volume. The calligraphy is neat and uniform, smooth and graceful, natural and fluent, elegant and easy; the structure is clear and pretty with a style similar to that of Yu Shinan. It is Wei Su's representative calligraphy preserved. It is signed, "recorded by Wei Su of Linchun", and is sealed with "Wei Su" and "Tai Pu". It is also sealed with the connoisseur seals of the Inside House of the Qing Dynasty, etc.
Wei Su (1303-1372), also known as Taipu and Yunlin, was born in Jinxi (present-day belongs to Jiangxi). He restored the history books of the Song, Liao and Jin dynasties, composed Er Ya and restored the History of Yuan Dynasty together with Song Lian. He was good at calligraphy and used to be a student of Kangli Nao. Although composing regular, running and cursive scripts, his strength was regular script.

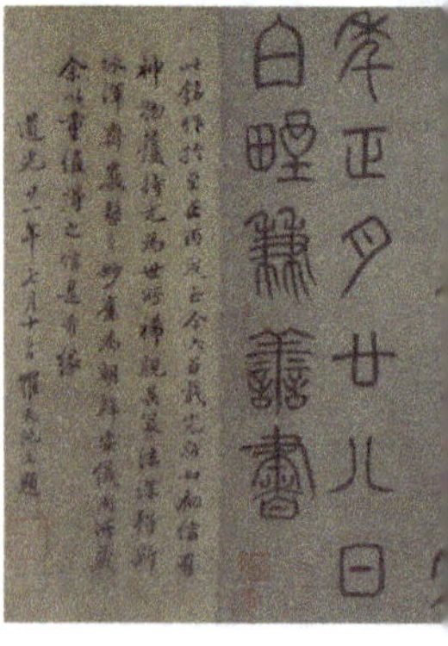

210. Tai Buhua: On My Modest Room
Yuan
Length: 36.9 cm Width: 113.6 cm
Preserved in the Palace Museum in Beijing
Paper painting, seal script. He wrote down the full text of On My Modest Room by Liu Yuxi. The structure is clear and neat and the handwriting is beautiful and forceful; the end of each stroke is mostly sharp and this is called "suspension needle" brushwork. It is the representative seal script work of Tai Buhua. It is signed, "written by Baiye, Jianshan on the 28th day of the first month in the 6th year (1346) of Zhizheng". There is inscription and collection seals of Luo Tianchi and others in the Qing Dynasty.
Tai Buhua (1304-1352), also known as Jianshan and Baiye, was originally named as Da Puhua until Emperor Wen Zong granted him the new name. He was a Mongolian and lived in Taizhou (present-day Linhai , Zhejiang). He was good at seal, clerical and regular scripts.

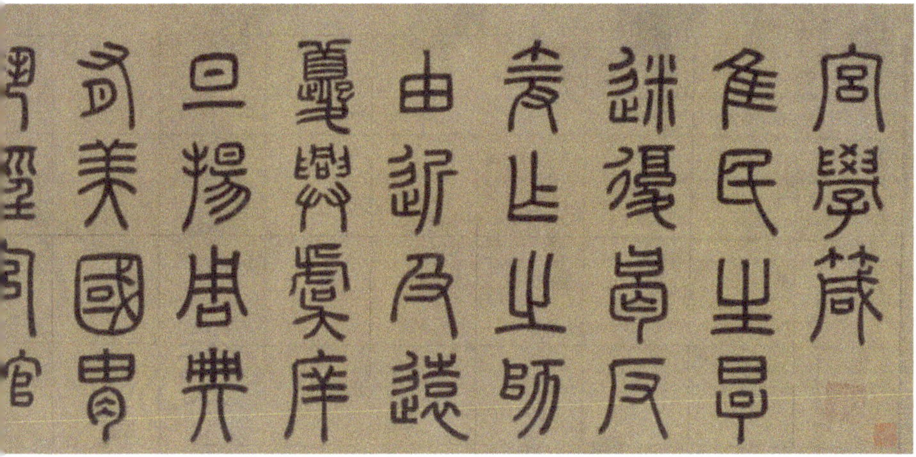

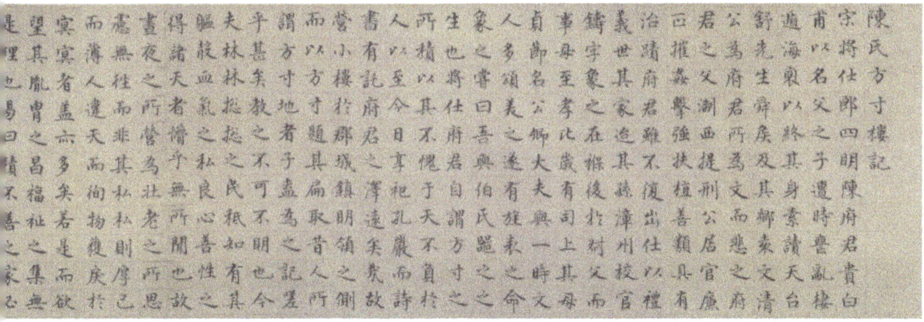

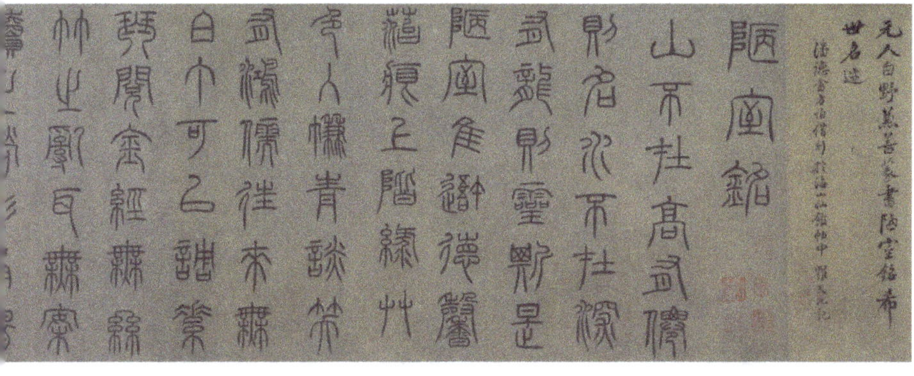

211. Yu He: Orchid Pavilion Series by Lin Dingwu

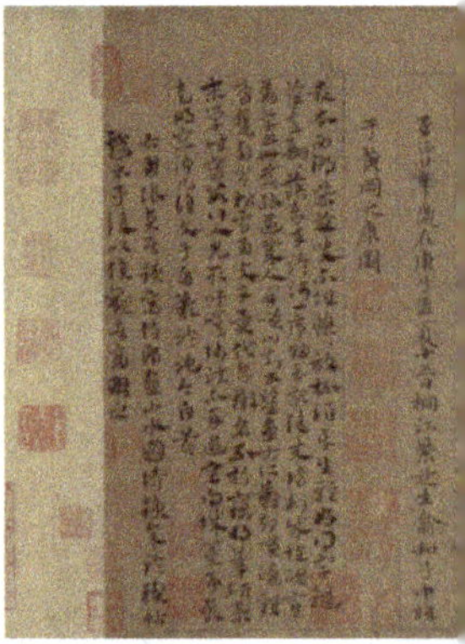

Yuan
Length: 26.7 cm   Width: 83.7 cm
Preserved in the Palace Museum in Beijing

Paper painting, running script. It is the calligraphy model of Lin Dingwu's Orchid Pavillion Series and was written in the 20th year (1360) of Zhizheng. At the end of this model, two poems in regular and cursive script in small characters are written. The calligraphy is forceful and charming, fresh and graceful, displaying the concepts handed down from Wang Calligraphy. However, the style is much more like Zhao Mengfu's. Chen Jiru and others wrote preface and postscript.

The Dingwu version of *Orchid Pavillion Series* was a transcription engraved in the Song Dynasty by Oyang Xun. As it is discovered in Dingwu (present-day Zhending, Hebei), it is called in such a way. The original engraving has been long lost, and only the rubbing is handed down and preserved.

Yu He (1307-1382), also known as Zizhong and Zizhi, was born in Tongjiang (present-day Tonglu of Zhejiang) and later moved to Qiantang (Hangzhou). He liked composing poems and using a writing brush. In his early years, he saw the way Zhao Mengfu wrote and, as a result, his running and cursive scripts were pretty much like that of Zhao Mengfu. His regular script displays the Jin style.

212. Wang Meng: Calligraphy Model of Aihou

Yuan
Length: 33.3 cm   Width: 58.7 cm
Preserved in the Palace Museum in Beijing

Paper painting, running script. This is a letter written by Wang Meng to Zhang Jing to recommend Lin Zishan (nephew of Zhao Yong and grandson of Zhao Mengfu). The structure is elegant and graceful; he started to write in a forceful and steady way with strict rule implied in straightness. The font structure and the stippling and turning imitate Zhao Mengfu. It is sealed with connoisseur seals of "highly valued appreciation of Yeyuan" and "Shishou Hall".

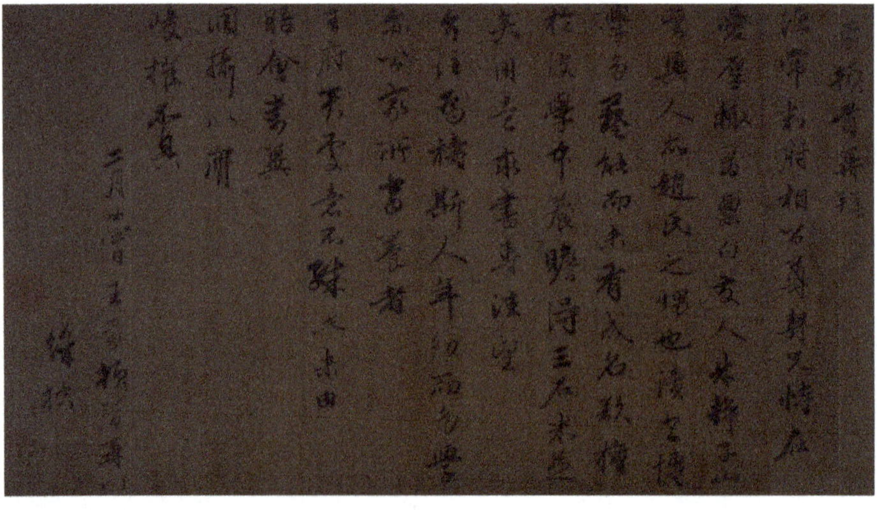

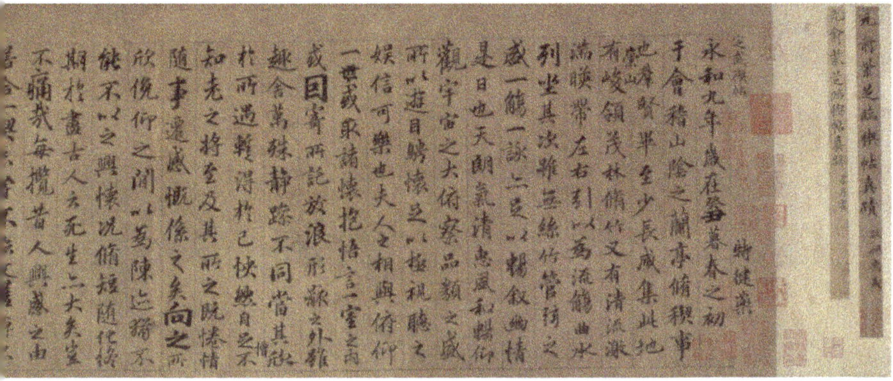

213. Nai Xian: Ancient Poem Calligraphy Model of Ode to Nancheng
Yuan
Length: 23.5 cm   Width: 156.6 cm
Preserved in the Palace Museum in Beijing
Paper painting, running and regular scripts. It recorded 16 pieces of five-character poems produced when he traveled through Nancheng with his friends. The strokes are forceful and the space between characters is broad and clear. And under the influence of Zhao Mengfu and Ni Zan, etc., ease and liberation is implied in neatness and uniformity. This volume was written in the 11th year (1351) of Zhizheng. It is sealed with connoisseur seals of the Inside House of the Qing Dynasty, etc. *Precious Collection of the Stone Moat* and *Sanxitang Copybook* mention it.
Nai Xian (1309-1364), also named Naxin and Nayan and known as Yizhi, was a member of the Karluks Tribe and his alias was Heshuo Waishi. He lived in Jinshan (to the west of Altai Mountain) and later moved to the hinterland, calling himself "native of Nanyang." He was known for his poems.

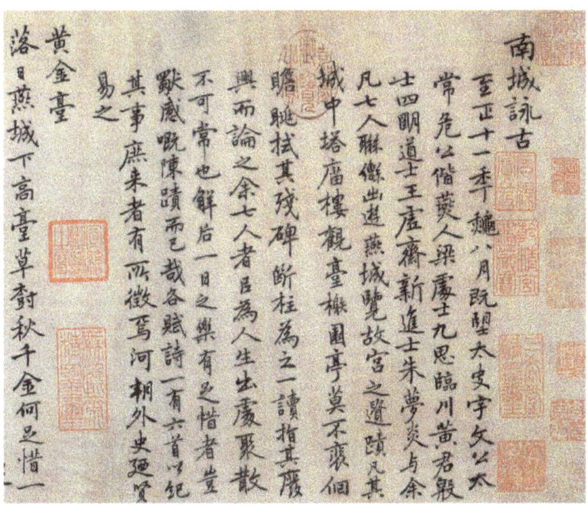

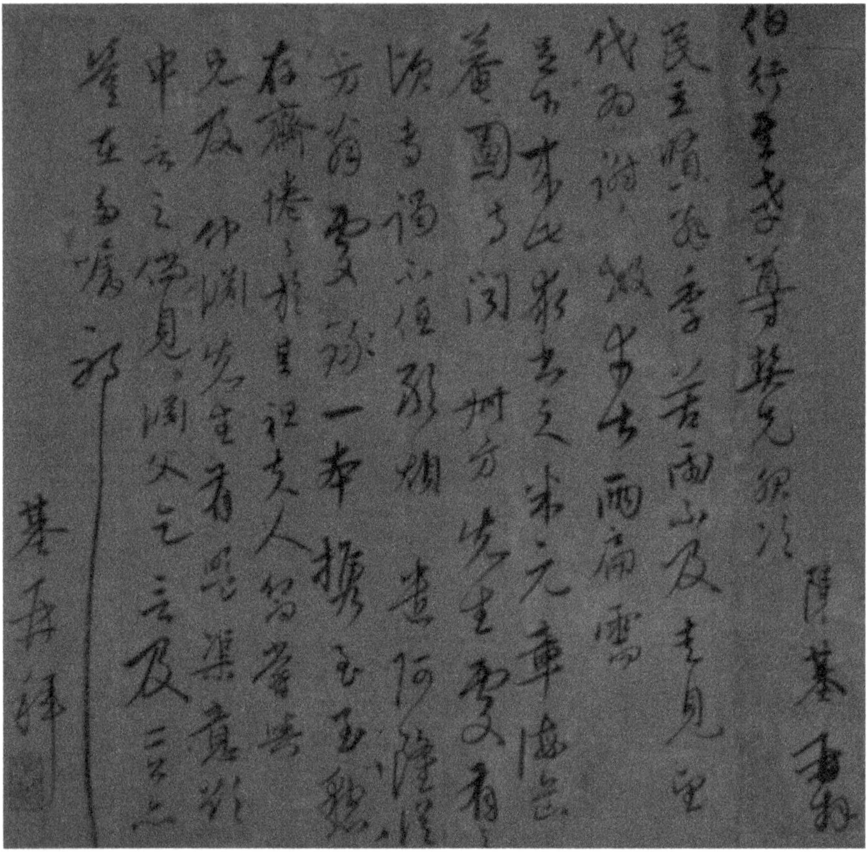

214. Chen Ji: Calligraphy Model of Kuyu

Yuan

Length: 23.9 cm Width: 29.6 cm

Preserved in the Palace Museum in Beijing

Paper painting, running script. This is a letter written to Qian Boxing narrating the whereabouts of Shen You, Boxing, Yu Zhai, Ren Qing, Shu Fang and others. The calligraphy is easy and free. The last stroke of the character ye (simple Chinese:耶) exhibits a kind of heroic spirit directly. Persons and events, etc. mentioned in the letter are of historical value as well. It used to be collected by the Inside House of the Qing Dynasty and was engraved into *Sanxitang Copybook*.

Chen Ji (1314-1370), also known as Jingchu, was born in Linhai (Taizhou of Zhejiang). He used to be the student of Huang Jin, a famous scholar. He could compose articles and was good at writing calligraphy influenced by Li Yong. He was good at seal script.

215. Ma Zhi: Calligraphy Model of Shu'nian

Yuan
Length: 28.5 cm Width: 46.2 cm
Preserved in the Palace Museum in Beijing
Paper painting, running script. It includes letters for consolation of nostalgia and two pieces of five-character octave. The calligraphy is antique and light and elegant with the concept of regular cursive script. This is his representative preserved work. It is signed "Zhi".
Ma Zhi (dates of birth and death unknown), also known as Xiaochang, was born in Yixing (present-day Jiangsu). At the end of the Yuan Dynasty, he lived in Xijian in seclusion together with Zhou Di to escape social upheaval. In the early years of Hongwu of the Ming Dynasty, he became an official. He was good at regular and running scripts.

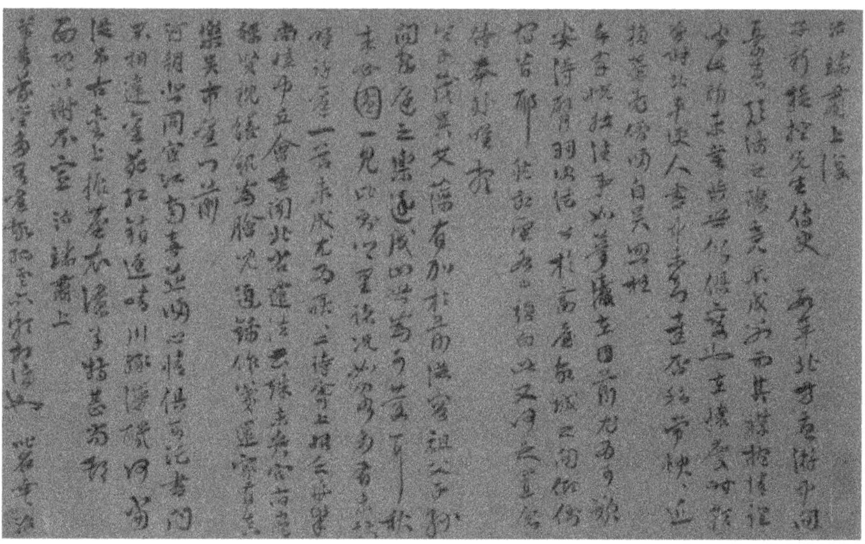

216. Lu Guang: Calligraphy Model of Shijian

Yuan

Length: 29.7 cm Width: 32.4 cm

Preserved in the Palace Museum in Beijing

Paper painting, regular script. These are two poems written to Yu Kan, a bibliophile and poet. The calligraphy style is thin and hard, fresh and vigorous, natural and light and is enriched in romantic charm reflecting the Jin style. It is sealed with the connoisseur seals of Xiang Yuanbian and An Qi, etc. *Moyuan Huiguan* and *Category of Paintings of Sanyutang Studio* record it.

Lu Guang (time of birth and death unknown), also known as Jihong and Tianyou Sheng, was born in Wu (present-day Suzhou). He was good at landscape paintings and imitated Huang Gongwang and Wang Meng. He could compose poetry and also wrote regular script in small characters.

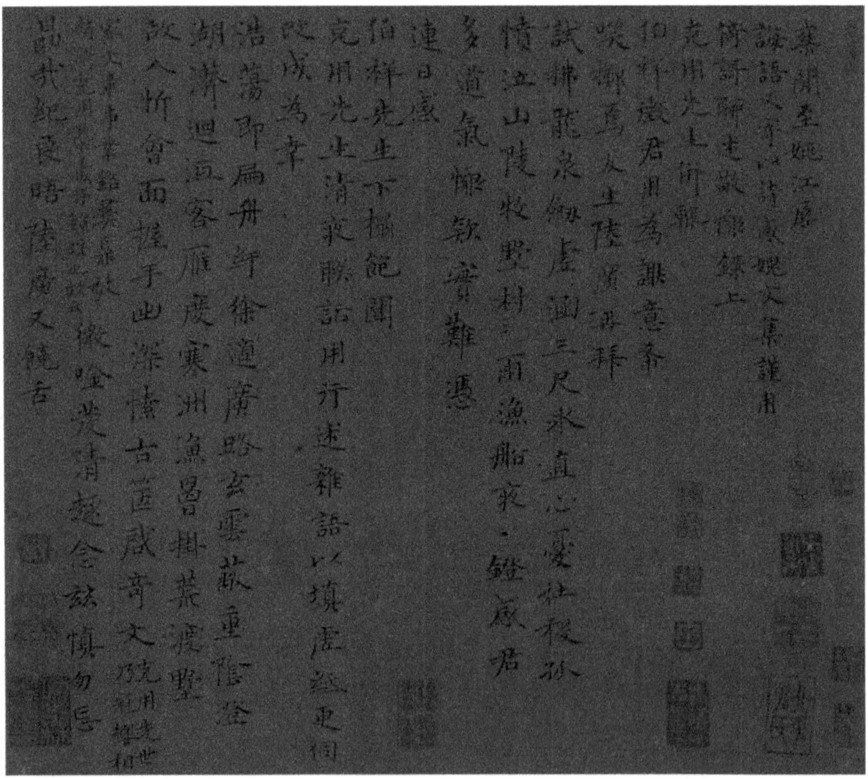

217. Shen You: Calligraphy Model of a Miscellaneous Poem of Drunkenness

Yuan

Length: 27 cm Width: 40.5 cm

Preserved in the Palace Museum in Beijing

Paper painting, regular script. This is a personal letter written to Chen Zhi, the poet and painter-calligrapher. The calligraphy potential is upright and expansive, each stroke is fitting and the whole text is naturally coordinated reflecting the charm of the Jin and Tang dynasties. It is sealed with connoisseur seals of Xiang Yuanbian and An Qi, etc. *Fencing Coral, Collective Study on Shigutang Calligraphy and Paintings, Spectacular Life, Moyuan Huiguan* and *Category of Paintings of Sanyutang Studio* all mention it.

Shen You (time of birth and death unkown), also known as Zhongshuo and Yuzhai, was born in Wu (Suzhou). He was good at composing poetry and imitated the style of Oyang Xun. His running cursive regular script in small characters is famous for being delicate, charming and antique.

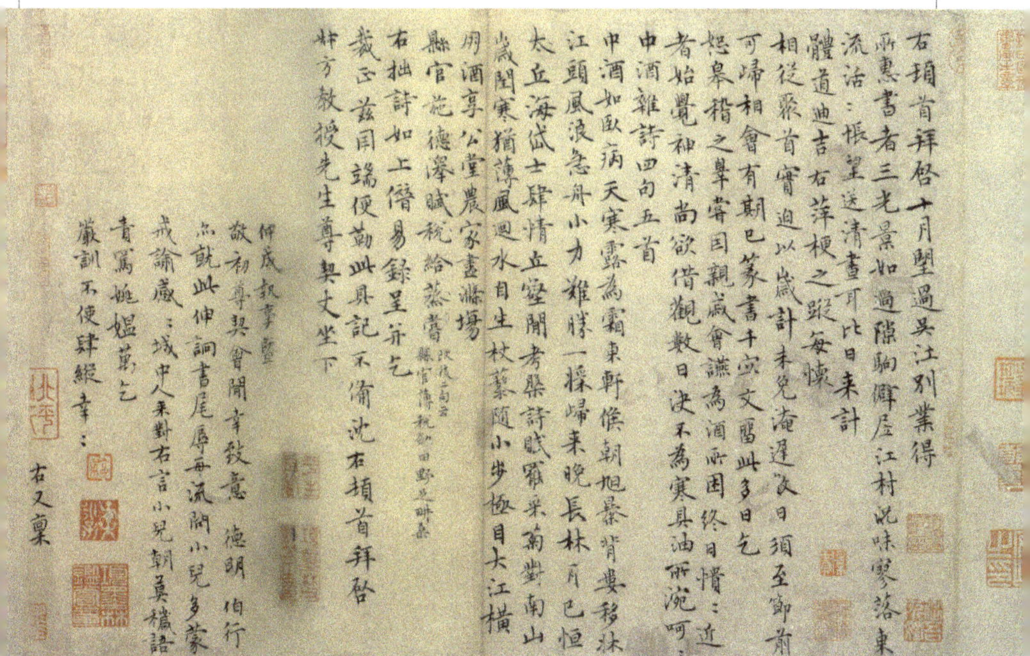

218. Lu Juren : Poem on the Water of Shao

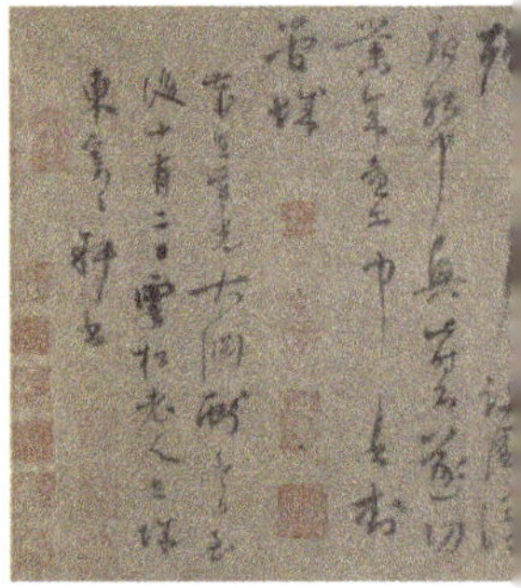

Yuan
Length: 28.2 cm Width: 130.7 cm
Preserved in the Palace Museum in Beijing

Paper painting, cursive script. It records a seven-character poem to highly praise Lu Wenjuan, a brush worker, saying the brush he made is superior and endurable and creative. The calligraphy is easy and graceful reflecting concepts handed down from the Tang Dynasty. It was written on the date of XinHai of the 4th year of Hongwu of the Ming Dynasty (1371) and was signed, "written by the old man named Yunsong in Jiji Pavilion on the east of the city" and was also sealed with "Zhaizhi" and "Lushi Juren", etc. The latter is Zhang Shu's poem in regular script of Yuan Dynasty, which is his famous work handed down. In addition, there is a preface and postscript written by Chen Pu and others of the Yuan Dynasty. It used to be collected by Xiang Yuanbian, Bian Yongyu, An Qi and the Inside House of the Qing Dynasty. *Moyuan Huiguan* mentions it.

Lu Juren (time of birth and death unknown), also known as Zhaizhi, Chaosong Weng, Songyun Yehe and Maohu Jushi, was born in Huating (present-day Sungkiang of Shanghai). His poetry complements the works of Yang Weizhen and Qian Weishan. After their deaths, the three were buried on the eastern foothills of Qianshan, the place becoming known as "Tomb of Three Superior Scholars".

219. Rao Jie: Calligraphy Model of Lanteen

Yuan
Length: 21.7 cm Width: 21.9 cm
Preserved in the Palace Museum in Beijing

Paper painting, running script. This is a letter written by Rao Jie to the painter Chen Ruyan. At the beginning of the work is in regular script, before changing to running script followed by cursive script. He starts to write in a forceful, steady and vigorous way; the structure is elegant and unconventional. It is the classic among the letters of Rao Jie. *Precious Collection of the Stone Moat Sequel: First Edition* mentions it.

Roa Jie (time of birth and death unknown), also known as Jiezhi and named as Woodman in Huagai Shan and Drunken Old Man by himself, was born in Linchuan (present-day Jiangxi). At the end of the Yuan Dynasty, he was promoted to be Xianqian of the western region of Zhejiang from the Hanlin Academy based on the order of the Emperor and later again was promoted as Canzheng of thes south of Huai River. When Zhang Shicheng entered Wu as its head official, he asked Rao Jie to remain in his original position. When the region of Wu perished, he was captured and sent to Jinling to be killed.

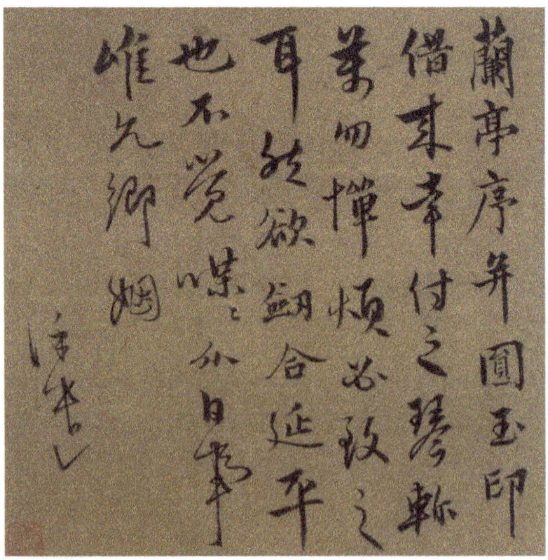

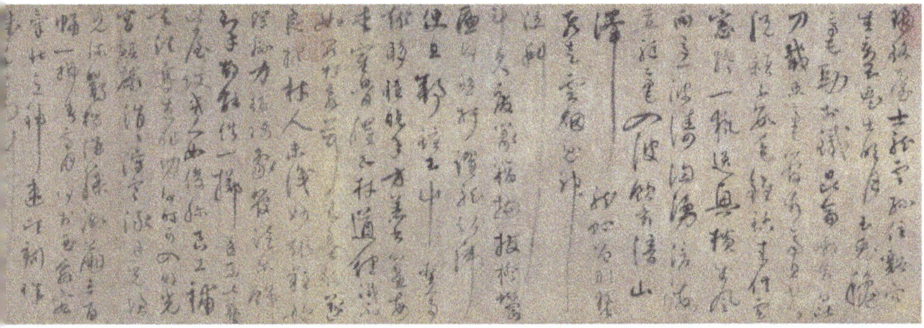

220. Wang Lizhong: Calligraphy Model of Ci Poetry of Warrior Lanling

Yuan

Length: 27.2 cm   Width: 43.4 cm

Preserved in the Palace Museum in Beijing

Paper painting, running script. This is a Ci poetry named Warrior Lanling written by Wang Lizhong to Shao Hengzhen as a present. The character imitates the style of Mi Pei, which is inclined and risky accompanied with a gentle and plain pattern. This is a rare preserved work of Wang Lizhong. It is signed, "the year of Zhizheng which is the change of the designation of an imperial reign (1341)" and is also sealed with the ink seals of "Wangshi Lizhong" and "Yanqiang". It used to be collected by An Qi and Heng Yong, etc. *Moyuan Huiguan* and *Records of Renyan Xiaoxia* record it.

Wang Lizhong (time of birth and death unknown), also known as Yanqiang and Zhongzhai, was born in Suining (present-day Sichuan). In the 17th year (1357) of Zhizheng of Yuan Dynasty. He used to be the ZhouPan of Wuxi and the Prefect of Songjiang at the end of the Yuan Dynasty. In the Ming Dynasty, he retired to a quiet life. He was an able painter.

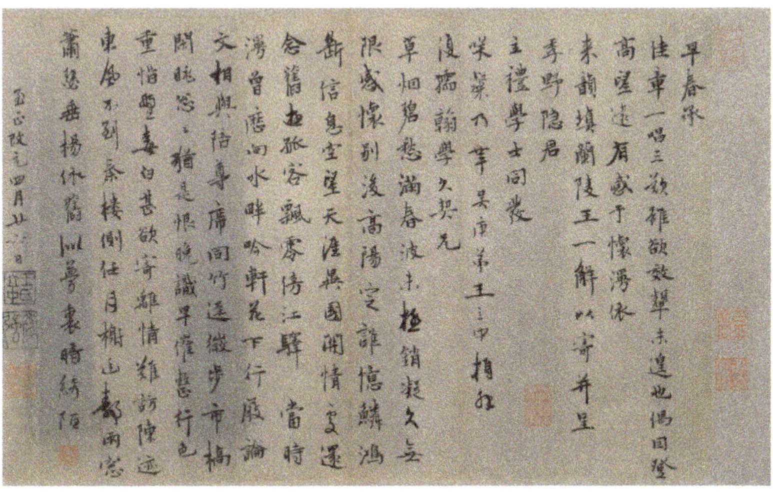

221. Yu Kan: Calligraphy Model of Qiyue

Yuan

Length: 22.6 cm Width: 34.1 cm

Preserved in the Palace Museum in Beijing

Paper painting, running and cursive scripts. Letters. The calligraphy imitates that of Wang Xizhi and the way he uses the brush and the structure reflect the Jin Dynasty calligraphy style as well as showing the influence of Zhao Mengfu. Its style is vigorous and steady and its conception is elegant and graceful. It used to be collected by Xiang Yuanbian. *Precious Collection of the Stone Moat Sequel: First Edition* records it.

Yu Kan (time of birth and death unknown), also known as Keyong and Shengbo, was born in Changzhou (present-day Suzhou of Jiangsu). He was the grandson VIII of Yu Yunwen who was a prime minister during the Song Dynasty. He liked poetry and could paint and was a great bibliophile. At the end of Yuan Dynasty, he lived in seclusion. During the years of Hongwu of the Ming Dynasty, he was a teacher in an education institution founded by the government in Yunnan.

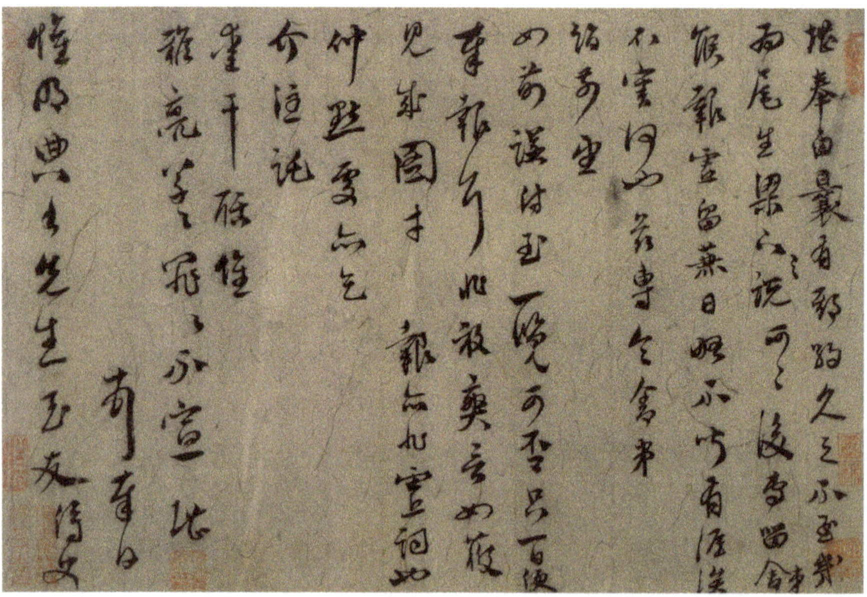

Handicrafts

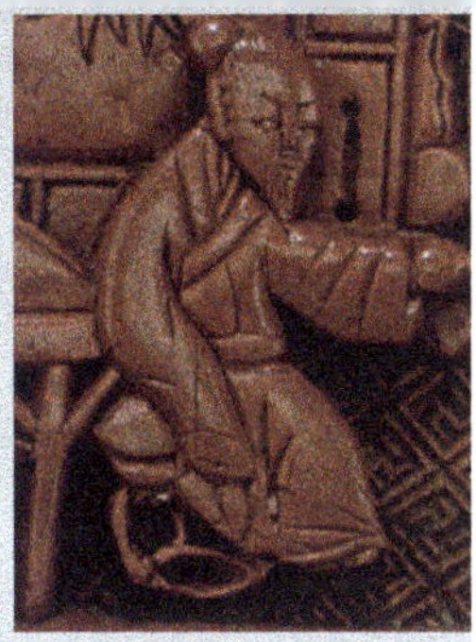

Pottery for daily use in the Yuan Dynasty declined, being replaced by porcelain. Meanwhile pottery figurine for burial objects also decreased in favor of paper-made burial objects. Most excavated pottery figurines inherited features of the Tang and Song dynasties and were largely horse and man pottery figures.

Lacquer style in the Yuan Dynasty was similar to that of the Song, mostly daily use wares. Edged and petal-shape were two dominant features of Yuan lacquer. Lacquering workmanship had developed to a mature stage with superior handicrafts, in particular gold-inlaid, engraved and other lacquer ware carving techniques. Although the lacquering workmanship appeared quite late, it had developed a high degree of excellence and many famous artists appeared. Yuan Dynasty representative artists with top workmanship included Zhang Cheng, Yang Mao and Zhang Minde.

Gold and silver output in the Yuan Dynasty increased, as rulers spent money like water. Indeed, usage of gold and silver ware could be called “extravagant”. Compared with Song Dynasty, types kept increasing, especially the gold and silver ware found in southern China were all fine pieces. Decoration followed the style of Song, being authentic, pure and simple. Most were simply structured and only a few were partly decorated. Mythology, legend and historical stories were decorative themes. A pool of gold and silver ware masters emerged, like Zhu Bishan.

Metal enamel handcraft having been introduced to China combined with local handcrafts and became art-ware for the imperial family. Cloisonné of the Yuan Dynasty was quite simple, mainly palace decoration, like bottles, stoves and jars or appliances for daily use. But no matter the ware model, filigree skill, various glazes or color expression, all reached a superior level.

Gold-wefted brocade developed to an unprecedented level during the Yuan Dynasty. Satins also began to mature, not only increasing the type of silk fabric, but also the techniques for colorful satins. K'o-ssu and embroidery inherited the tradition of the Song Dynasty and kept developing. K'o-ssu took painting as the foundation and added many works based on the figure of Buddha and offering birthday congratulations. Folk embroidery demonstrated great vitality and lively paintings and embroidery of Buddha figures also prevailed at that time.

Chops in the Yuan Dynasty were carved with Phags-pa Mongolian script. Most chops at that time were engraved with Mongolian and Han characters, Mongolian character chops for military officers and Chinese character chops or Mongol character combined with Chinese character chops for civilian officials appeared. Most military officers were Mongolian and while civil officials were both Han and Mongolian. Private chops in the Yuan Dynasty were also engraved with Mongol and Han characters. Ethnic Han men of letters still kept using Han character chops engraved with Zhu style (characters carved in relief). In the unrest of the Late Yuan Dynasty, rulers of the rebellious military force issued chops largely were similar with the Jiu Die seal character of the Song Dynasty.

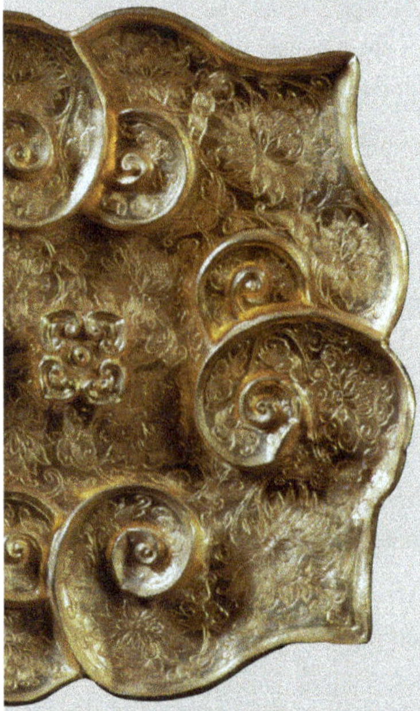

222. Painted Terracotta Rider

Yuan
Height: 38.5 cm
Collected in Qinshui, Shanxi in 1964
Preserved in the Shanxi Museum

Burial object. It wears a bamboo hat with nice looking and solemn facial expression, wearing having round-neck over-knee clothes, long thigh boot and waist-belt, with the belt head drooping on the right side. The saddled horse, with hair shaved and tail tied, stands on a rectangular pedestal looking down. The hands of the rider hold the halter. It is painted with red, white, black, etc.

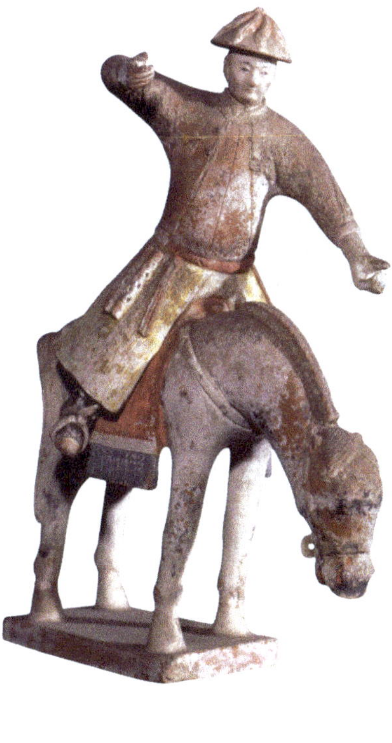

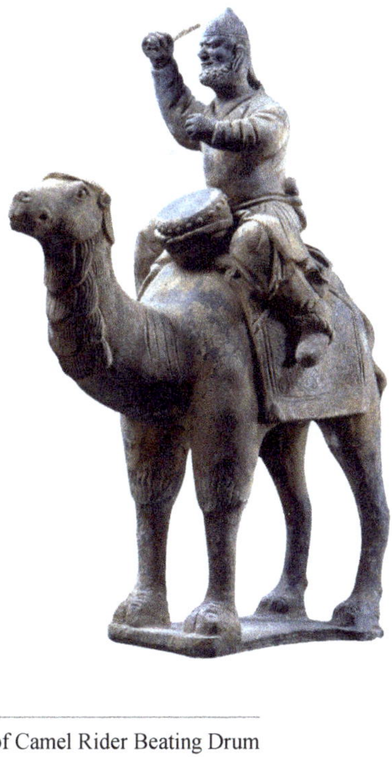

223. Gray Clay Pottery of Camel Rider Beating Drum

Yuan
Height: 42 cm   Length: 35 cm
Unearthed from Hes Tomb in Huxian, Shanxi in 1978
Preserved in the Huxian Bureau of Cultural Relics

Burial Object. It is gray clay pottery. The camel raises its head and stares frontwards with a Tartar rider on its back who is wearing a sharp-topped hat, round-collar short shirt, long trousers and felt boots. With a drum tied to the waist, the rider raises his right hand and holds the drumstick in his hand in a posture of beating the drum.

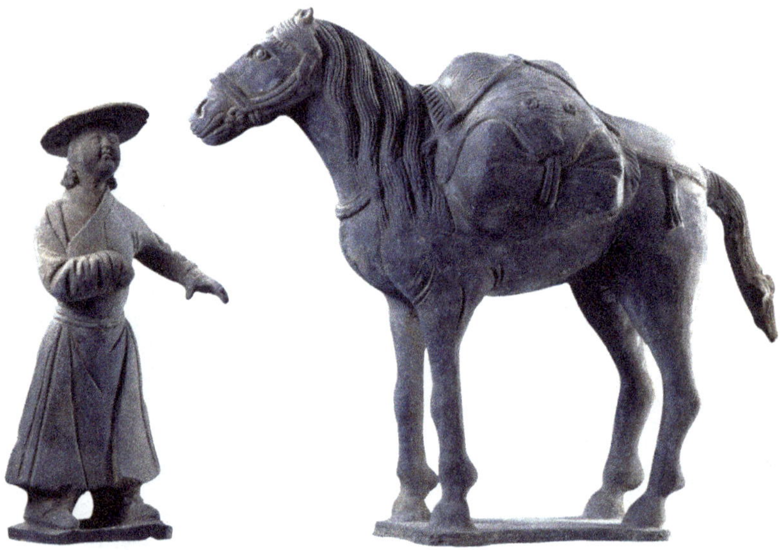

224. Gray Clay Pottery of Horse and a Warrior Leading a Horse
Yuan
Height of figure: 28 cm Height of horse: 34 cm Length: 41 cm
Unearthed from Hes Tomb in Huxian, Shanxi in 1978
Preserved in the Huxian Bureau of Cultural Relics
Burial Object. The horse and the warrior stand on a rectangular pedestal. The warrior wears a wide-brimmed sunbonnet with a round face, eyes looking upwards and hair being combed into two braids. It wears a long robe, waist belt and felt boots with the left hand reaching out and the right hand in front of the chest, as if pulling the reins. The horse is tall with large hooves and eyes staring to the front, hair and tail scattered. Luggage is tied on its back.

225. Carved Red Lacquer Ware of Box Painted with Picking Chrysanthemums in Dongli

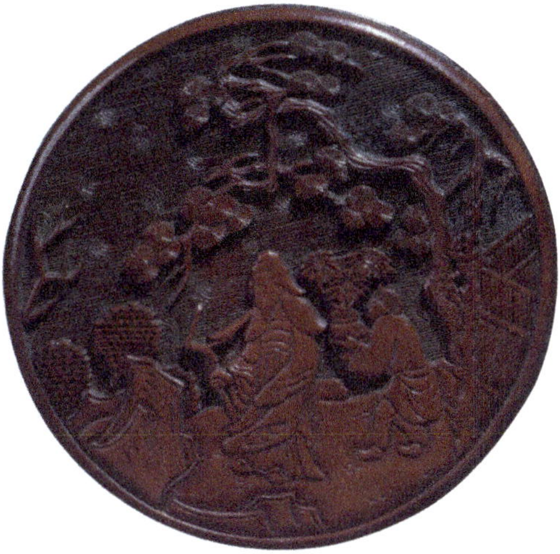

Yuan
Height: 3.9 cm Diameter: 12 cm
Unearthed from Rens Tomb in Qingpu, Shanghai in 1953
Preserved in the Shanghai Museum
Cellar ware. Round wooded body painted red like a date with hard and thick paint. The substrate layer has a cloud design; the box surface is engraved with an old man accompanied by a boy picking chrysanthemums in the shade of a pine tree in Dongli, which presents a picture of an idyllic life. The periphery of the box cover and box bottom is decorated with fret.

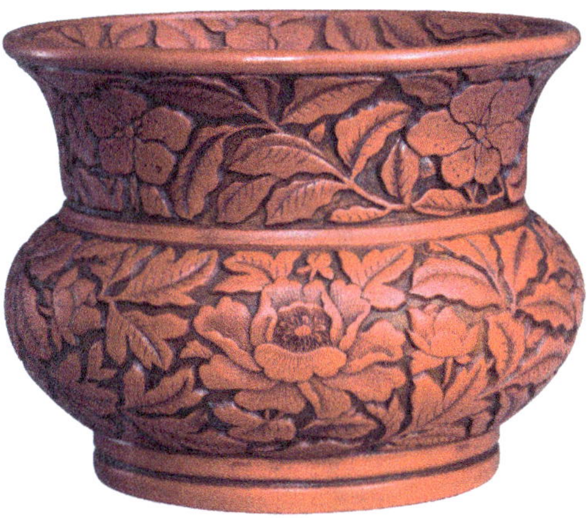

226. Yang Mao Carved Red Lacquer Ware of Flower Statue

Yuan
Height: 9.4 cm
Mouth Diameter: 12.8 cm
Bottom Diameter: 8.8 cm
Preserved in the Palace Museum in Beijing
Vessel. It is a wooden-body vessel with open mouth, short neck, big belly and ring footring feet. The mouth interior and exterior wall are coated with red paint on a yellow base about 70 times, being carved with twigs and flowers. The inner wall and the outer bottom are painted with light-fading paint. The left of the bottom has an inscription in regular script, "Made by Yang Mao" made by a needle.

Yang Mao came from Yanghui, Xitang County, Jiaxing City, Zhengjiang, was well known for his carved red lacquer ware and was good at gold and silver-inlaying skills. Only three of his works are preserved in China.

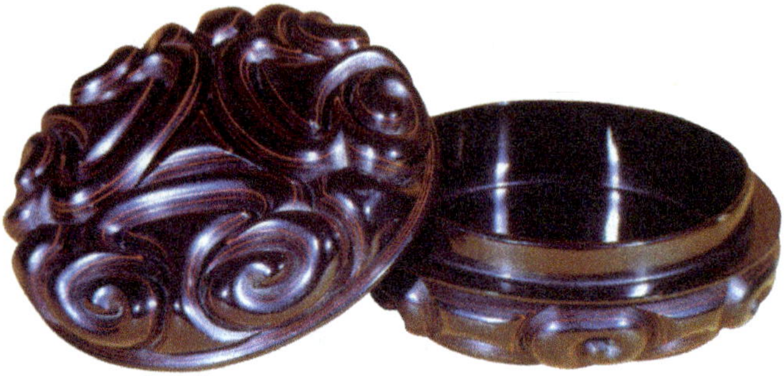

227. Zhang Cheng Carved Marbled Lacquer Ware of Cloud Pattern Box

Yuan

Height: 6.5 cm Mouth Diameter: 14.5 cm

Preserved in the Anhui Museum

Cellar ware. It has a round wooden-body box locked by buckles on the cover and body. The box cover and bottom are painted with black and carved with three patterns of clouds, and three red paint patterns on the middle. The bottom of the box is purple black. Close to the bottom is written "Made by Zhang Cheng" using a needle.

Zheng Cheng, from Yanghui, Xitang County, Jiaxing City, Zhejiang, was a lacquer ware carving master enjoying the same fame as Yang Mao.

228. Zhang Cheng Carved Red Lacquer Ware of Plate with Gardenia Pattern

Yuan

Height: 2.6 cm

Mouth Diameter: 16.5 cm

Bottom Diameter: 12.3 cm

Preserved in the Palace Museum in Beijing

Cellar ware. This is a round wooden-body plate. Painted red for almost a hundred times on a yellow layer and engraved with gardenia pattern, it has a blossom gardenia carved in the middle with four flowers in bud surrounded by leaves. The wall is carved with a vanilla pattern. The bottom is painted black and is inscribed in regular script "Made by Zhang Cheng" by a needle.

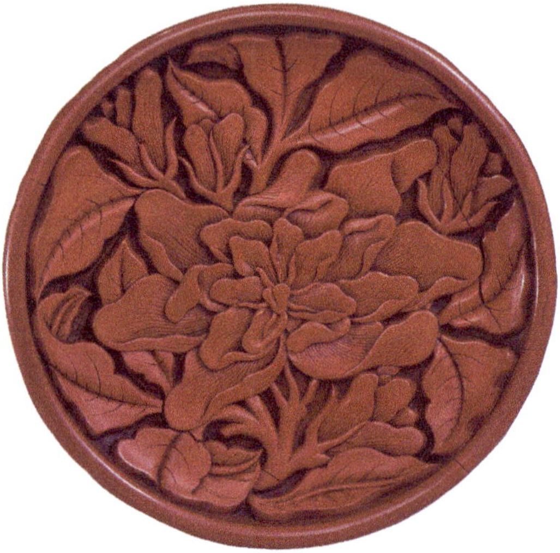

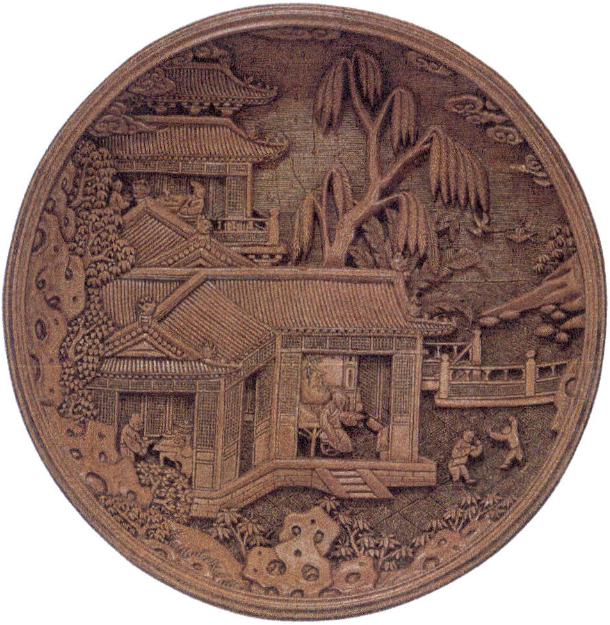

229. Carved Red Lacquer Ware of Plate Painted with Figures from the Red Mansion

Yuan
Height: 3.2 cm
Mouth Diameter: 17.6 cm
Preserved in the Palace Museum in Beijing
Vessel. This round metal-body vessel has round ring feet. The plate rim is decorated with a raised bowstring pattern. A pavilion and courtyard is painted in the platen with weeping willows and verdant Chinese banana trees. A child plays in the courtyard, while an old man reaches out his hand to restrain it as a woman turns round to watch. The external wall is decorated with a grass pattern and the bottom is painted black with a line of regular script "Made in the Period of Emperor Xuande" carved by a knife with gold inlay.

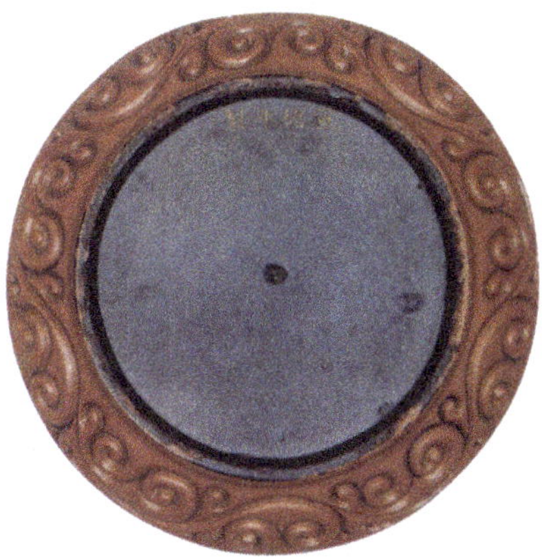

230. Black Lacquer Ware Inlaid with Mother-of-pearl of Boat-shaped Basin Painted with Flowers and Birds

Height: 7.8 cm Length: 38.5 cm
Width: 21.7 cm

Preserved in the Palace Museum in Beijing

Vessel. It is an oval rubber-body vessel with a flat bottom. The basin is divided into two parts by a partition, just like a boat. It is painted black and inlaid with mother of pearl. Just two mother-of-pearl inlaid lacquer wares from the Yuan Dynasty are preserved in the good condition in China, both in the Palace Museum in Beijing, representing superior and mature workmanship.

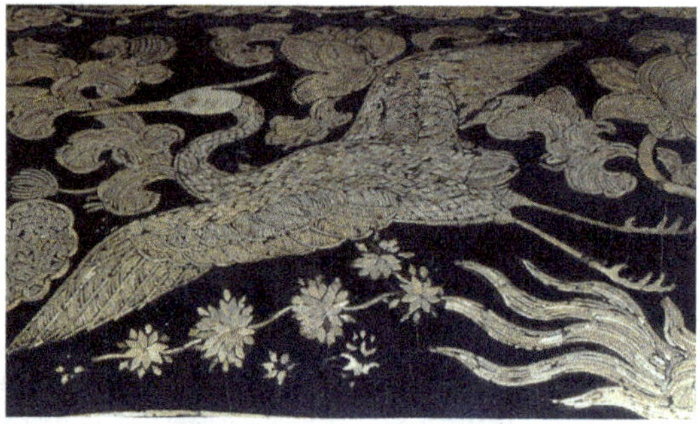

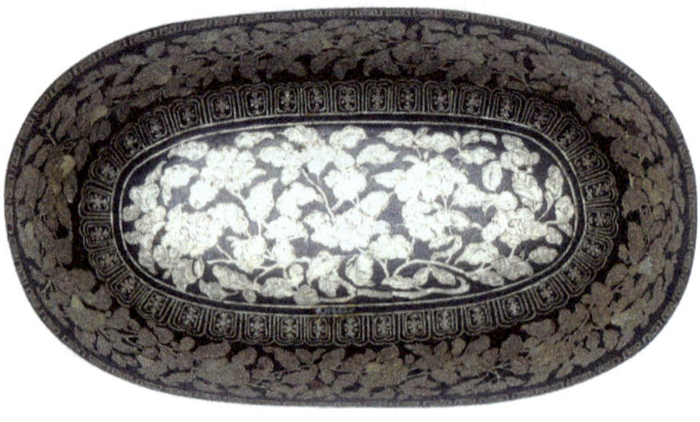

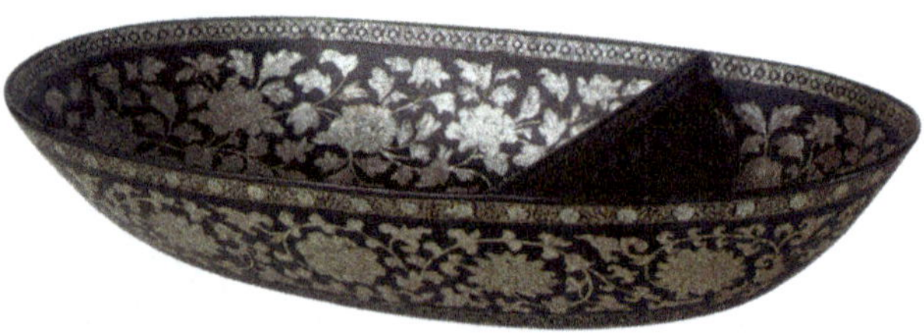

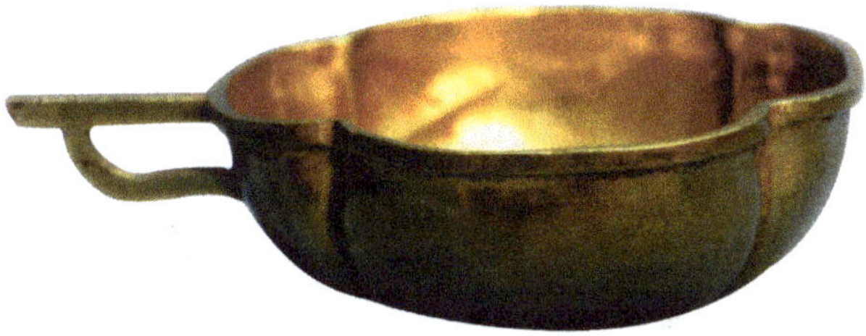

231. Zhang Zhongying Gold Cup

Yuan

Height: 2.5 cm Mouth Diameter: 7.5 cm Foot Diameter: 4.9 cm Weight: 80.5 grams

Unearthed from cellar of the Confucian Temple foundations in Hefei city, Anhui in 1955

Preserved in the Anhui Museum

Vessel. With a contracted mouth, it is shaped like a pumpkin with open mouth and flat bottom. The edge of the cup center is intaglio with regular script stating "Made by Zhang Zhongying". Many gold and silver wares in this cellar were so ascribed, indicating Zhang was a famous gold and silver engraver at that time.

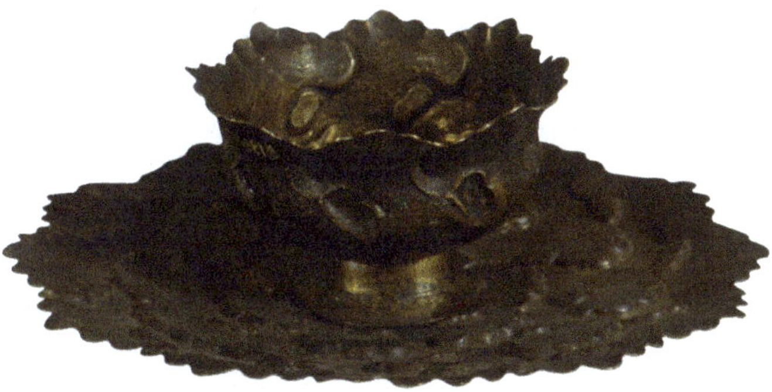

232. Gilt Three Petal-shaped Silver Cup

Yuan

Total Height: 5.8 cm

Cup Height: 5.5 cm Mouth Diameter: 8.8 cm

Bas Height: 1.5 cm Diameter: 18 cm

Unearthed from Qianyu Tomb in the southern suburbs of Wixi City, Jiangsu in 1960

Preserved in the Wuxi Museum

Vessel. The cup and the base body are shaped like a flower by beating silver slices. With an open mouth and flower shape, it has high ring feet. The tray is shallow with layered petals. Those on the cup and the tray are intaglio with twig patterns. The surface is painted with gold.

233. Zhu Bishan Silver Raft Cup

Yuan

Height: 18 cm Weight: 616 grams

Preserved in the Palace Museum in Beijing

Wine vessel. The raft cup is like some old branches intertwined. An old, long bearded man sits on the raft cup, wearing a long robe and smiling as he reads a book. Poems are carved at the bottom of the front face and the middle part of the raft. At the end of the raft, lines of "Zhu Bishan from Weitang crated in Changchun Hall in Dongwu in 1345" and stamp of "Hua Yu" are engraved. The vessel was welded after casting, and then carved into shape combined with carvings and poems.

Zhu Bishan, also known as Hua Yu, from Wutang, Jiaxing, was a famous silver craftsman well known for his unique raft cup skill.

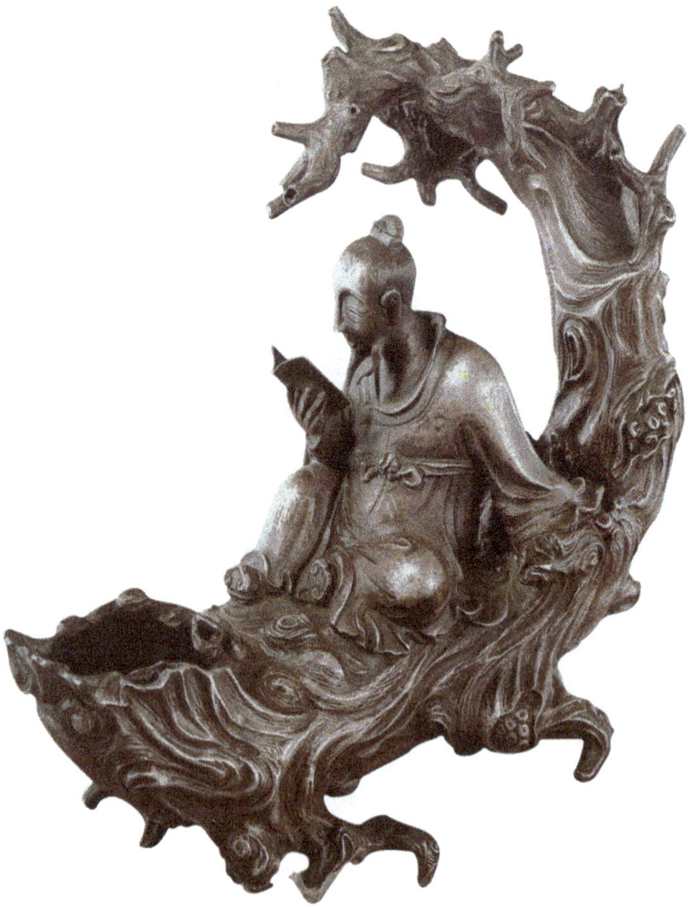

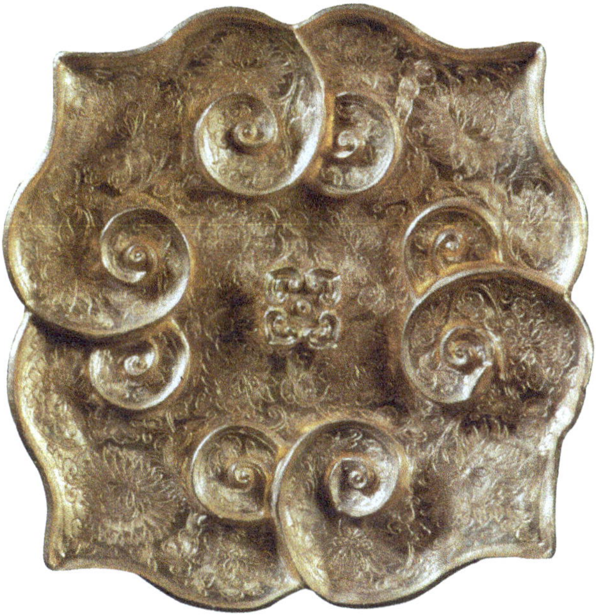

234. Golden Ruyi Plate Painted with Cloud Pattern
Yuan
Height: 1.3 cm Length: 16 cm Width: 16 cm Weight: 236.44 Grams
Unearthed from Lushimeng Tomb in Wuxian, Jiangsu in 1959
Preserved in the Nanjing Museum

Vessel. It was made by hammering and carving. It looks like four lucky clouds overlapping, the center of the cloud head forming the plate center, which is decorated by a flower of four petals. Twigs and flowers intertwine in the center of the plate. "Made by Wen Xuan" is carved at the center of the plate bottom. Many other unearthed gold and silver vessels of different styles are also carved with the same line, suggesting Wen Xuan was a famous gold and silver craftsman.

235. Gilt Anthocephalus Silver Box

Yuan

Height: 8.9 cm Bottom Diameter: 17.5 cm Weight: 236.44 grams

Unearthed from Lushimeng Tomb in Wuxian, Jiangsu in 1959

Preserved in the Nanjing Museum

Vessel. This is an eight-diamond-shaped, straight opening and straight belly box with flat bottom. The external wall is engraved and gilded with more than 20 flowers, like peony, narcissus, peach and lotus. The basin center of the box is engraved with a round phoenix and "Made by Wen Xuan" is engraved on the bottom of the box.

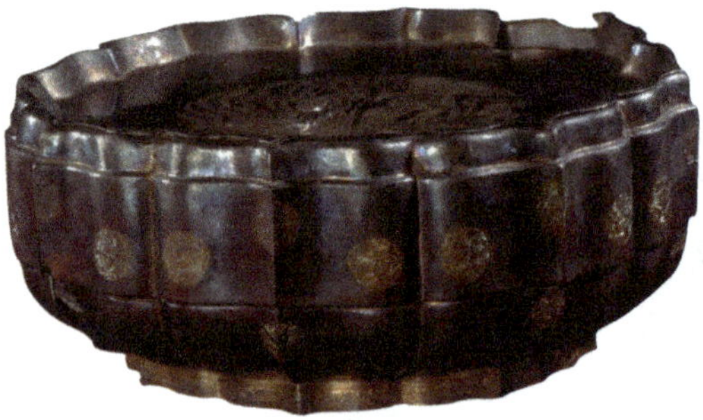

236. Anthocephalus Silver Jewellery Box

Yuan

Height: 24.3 cm

Mouth Diameter: 16 cm

Unearthed from Zhang Shicheng's Parents Tomb in Suzhou, Jiangsu in 1964

Preserved in the Suzhou Museum

Article for combing and make-up. It is shaped like a six-petal begonia with three layers, locked by buckles. The cover and the bottom tray are painted with peony; the box is carved with seven sets of gilt anthocephalus. The brim of the tray is painted with creeping weed. The box is divided into three layers, all for storing combing and make-up articles. Except for the welded bottom of the three layers, other parts were beaten into shape with silver chips.

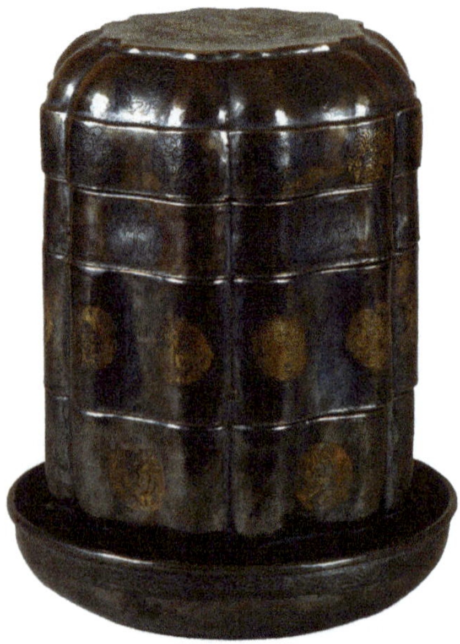

237. Mirror Frame of Jade Rabbit with Lucid Ganoderma Pattern

Yuan

Height: 32.8 cm Width: 17.8 cm

Unearthed from Zhang Shicheng's Parents Tomb in Suzhou, Jiangsu in 1964

Preserved in the Suzhou Museum

Article for combing and make-up. It consists of three frames with a lucky symbol at each head of the beam. The main frame is rectangular with fully arranged hollowed-out decorations in the upper part, flying dragon pattern in the middle, hollowed-out peony on the two sides, hollowed-out two phoenixes playing around the peony and diamond-shaped Ruyi at the four corners. The sub-frame is square connected by a rotatable rivet. The horizontal bar under the two frames connects a plate painted with sparrows flying around flowers, which is also rotatable. Another frame is rectangular with a plate painted with moon, hade rabbit, lucid ganoderma and lucky grass; it is the place for mirror to put onset.

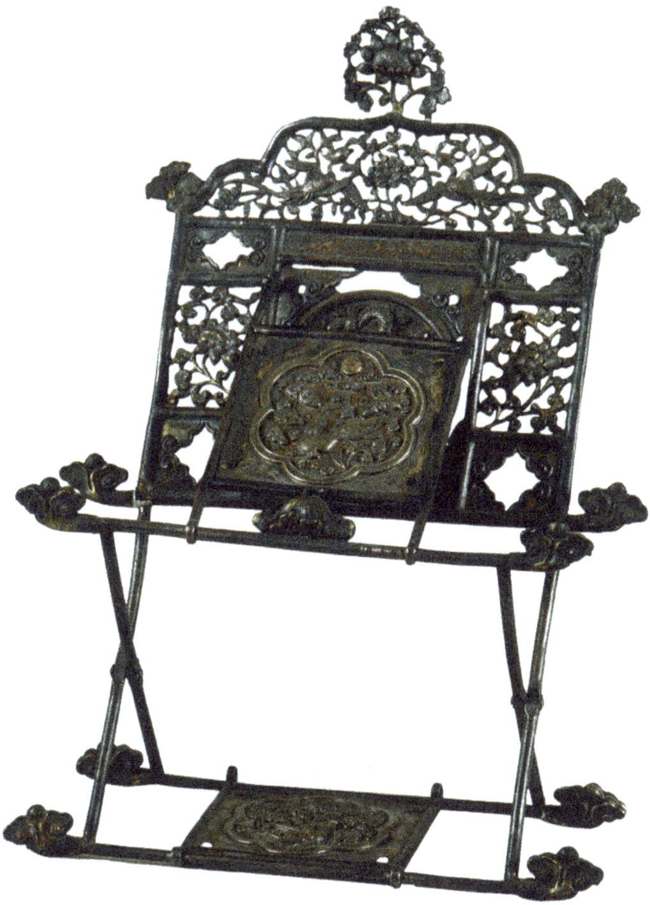

238. Gold Sachet Painted with Frolic Mandarin Duck

Yuan
Length: 7.5 cm Width: 5.1 cm Weight: 21.98g
Unearthed from Lushimeng Tomb in Wuxian, Jiangsu in 1959
Preserved in the Nanjing Museum
Accessory. It is a heart-shaped sachet beaten by two gold leaves. The belly bulges with spice in it. Flowers are carved in the hollowed-out leaves with three sets of lucky symbols on the upper part and bottom, "He He" picture on the upper, mandarin duck on the middle and lotus at the bottom, which are connected by lotus branches, meaning "heart to heart mandarin duck". With a little hole on the upper end, it could be tied on the waist with a strand.

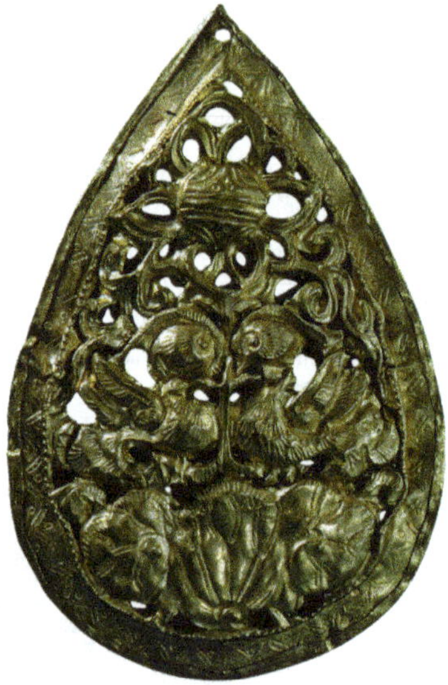

239. Gold Belt with Tapir Pattern

Yuan
Length: 8 cm Width: 5.5 cm Weight: 84.3k
Unearthed from Qianyu Tomb in southern suburbs of Wixi City, Jiangsu in 1960
Preserved in the Wuxi Museum
Accessory. It looks like a Chinese flowering crabapple in the ends, hollowed-out in the middle and rectangular in the right side. An animal symbol is carved in the face with a strong body, straight ears, short feet and sharp paw, and short tail, like a tapir. The back is carved with six sets of flower patterns, lines of "100% gold, made by Chen PuJ4". Tapir means exorcising evil spirits.

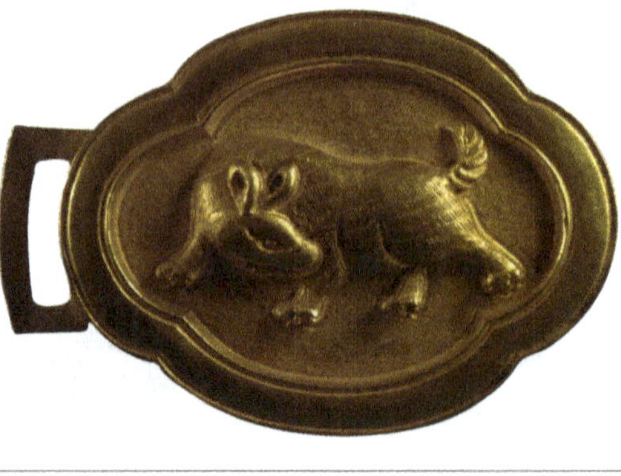

240. Cloisonn Three-ring Jar

Yuan

Height: 70.6 cm Mouth Diameter: 36 cm Foot Diameter: 23.1 cm

Preserved in the Palace Museum in Beijing

Decoration. It was originally a jar and then used as a decoration. The neck and the gold three-animal bottom was added later. Two sides of the jar neck are decorated with two gilded animal ears, and the shoulder of the jar is decorated with three animal heads holding a ring in their mouth. Taking blue as the basic color, the jar is adorned with cloud patterns on the mouth and the shoulder, grape pattern and banana leaf pattern on the neck and feet and lotus pattern on the belly. Lines of regular script "Made in the Year of Jingtai in Ming Dynasty" is carved on the bottom.

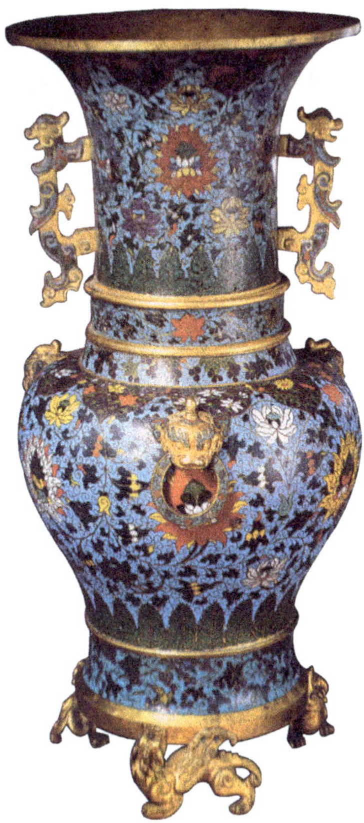

241. Cloisonne Elephant Ear Furnace with Pattern of Lotus Intertwined with Creeping Seed

Yuan

Height: 13.9 cm Mouth Diameter: 16 cm Bottom Diameter: 13.5 cm

Preserved in the Palace Museum in Beijing

Decoration but changed into vessel later. It is a copper gilded elephant head and ears furnace carving with flowers. It looks dignified and graceful. The mouth is made from copper coated with gold, all kinds of chrysanthemums painted on a light blue enamel glaze below the mouth. The furnace takes dark blue enamel glaze as the foundation painted with six red, yellow and white lotuses on the body and lotus-petal-shaped pattern around the belly of the furnace.

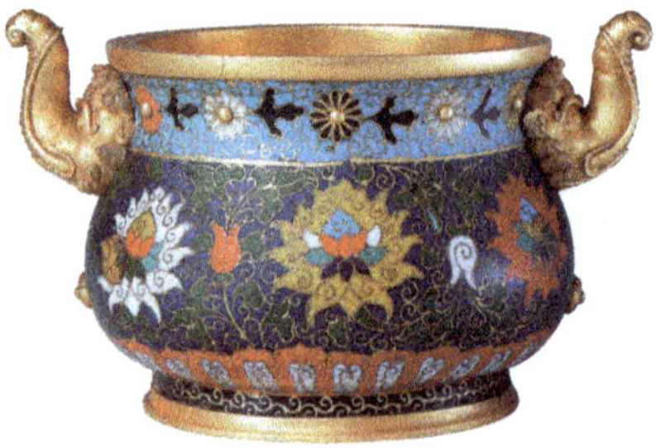

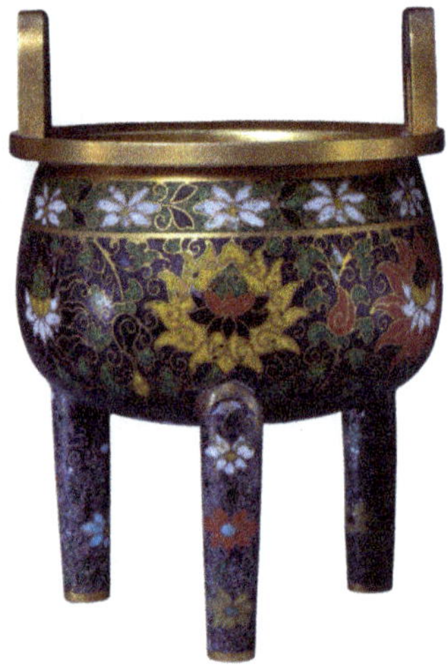

242. Cloisonne Three-legged Furnace with Pattern of Lotus Intertwined with Creeping Seed

Yuan

Height: 20.5 cm Mouth Diameter: 15.3 cm Bottom Diameter: 12.8 cm

Preserved in the Palace Museum in Beijing

Decoration, later changed into a vessel. The three legs and other wares were matched later. It imitates an ancient cooking vessel with two straight ears and three legs. The furnace inner's wall, mouth and the two ears are gilt with gold. With grass green glaze as the foundation, the furnace mouth is decorated coated with white flowers paintings. The belly of the furnace takes sapphire blue as the foundation and is decorated with six red, white, yellow and purple flowers. The three legs and furnace bottom are painted with flowers intertwined with twigs.

243. Cloisonn Bottle of Grass Pattern

Yuan

Height: 23.5 cm Mouth Diameter: 7.5 cm Bottom Diameter: 9 cm

Preserved in the Palace Museum in Beijing

Decoration, later changed into a vessel. It has an open mouth, straight neck and flat footring feet. The neck and the belly consist of different articles of different periods, in which the belly is of the Yuan Dynasty. The neck has gold strings and two gilt dragons twisted on the shoulder; the bottle uses sky blue as the foundation. The neck is painted with chrysanthemum and plum blossom. With twine lotus pattern on the belly, banana tree leaf painted under the belly, the copper bottle bottom is intaglio with gold and carved with "十" symbols.

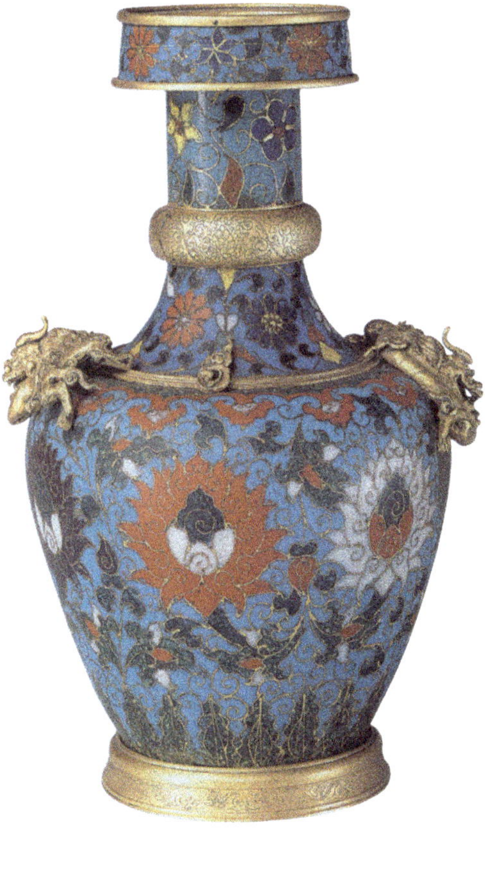

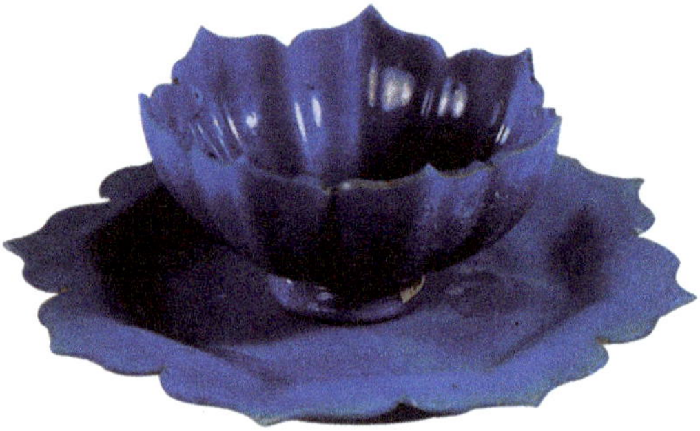

244. Glass Cup Pained with Lotus

Yuan
Cup Height: 4.8 cm
Mouth Diameter: 8.6 cm
Support Diameter: 1 cm
Mouth Diameter: 12.5 cm
Unearthed from Yuanwang Shixians Tomb in Zhangxian, Gansu in 1959
Preserved in the Gansu Museum
Wine Vessel. It is blue, translucent with a lot of bubbles in it. The mouth and the belly like seven lotus petals with fake ring footring feet and little concaved bottom. The support is also blue that lighter than the cup and filled with bubbles. Flat brimmed, it is shaped with eight lotus petals, and the belly rises slightly.

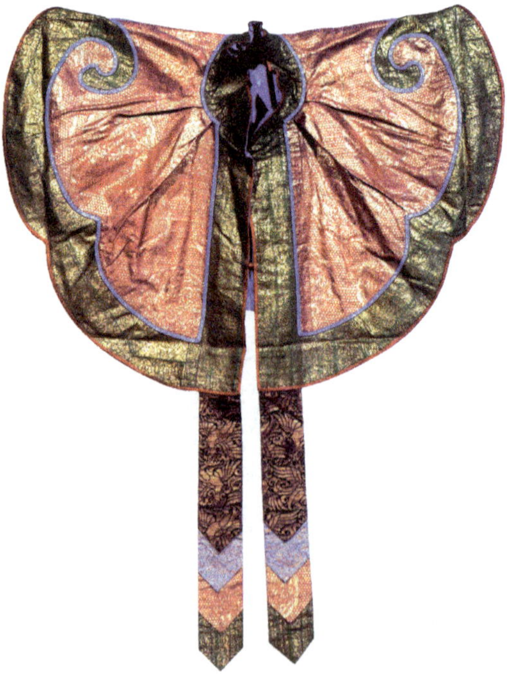

245. Nasich Cape of Buddha with Tortoise, Dragon and Phoenix Patterns

Yuan
Length: 43 cm Width: 70 cm
Preserved in the Palace Museum in Beijing
This butterfly type cape has a high collar with two green silk braids. One loops ties in the front with the red one on the right and round coral button in the left. It is made from Nasich interwoven by warp lines, including ground warp, and weft lines, including twill. The dragon and the phoenix pattern are interwoven by warp lines and ground warp.
"Nasich" is Farsi that means gold brocade interwoven by gold lines or round gold lines.

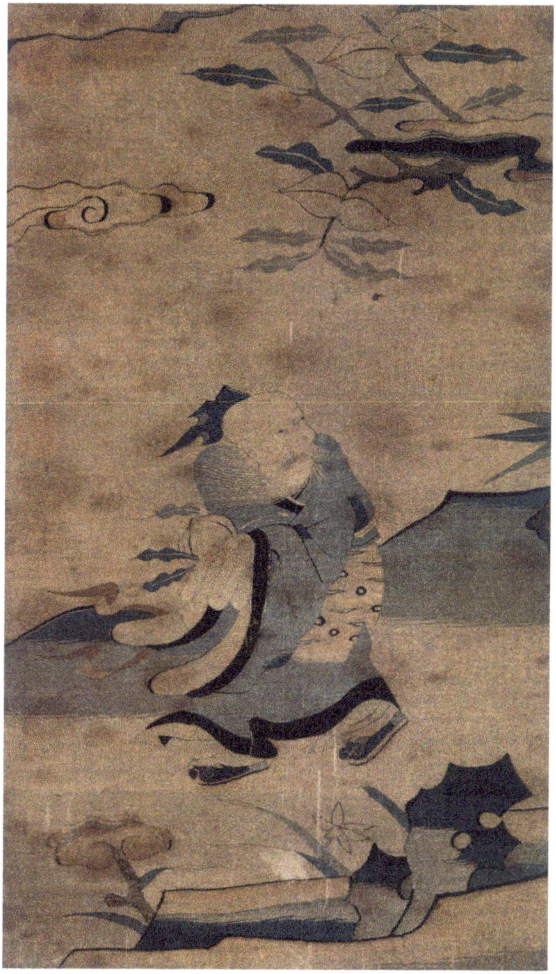

246. Kesi Dongfang Shuo Stealing the Peach

Yuan

Length: 58.5 cm   Width: 33.5 cm

Preserved in the Palace Museum in Beijing

Silk fabric. It weaves the view of Dong Fangsuo looking back with his grey beard flying around his head after stealing the peach of immortality and beginning to run away. With several kinds of kesi-weaving methods, it is woven on a plain kesi fabric. Structure weaving is employed to weave the picture and the long-and-short qiang is used to fill in the color at the brink of one grain or where two colors cross. The agalmatolite is woven and colored in dark blue, blue and light blue to show its three-dimensional effect. It is unique to weave with two threads joining into one string.

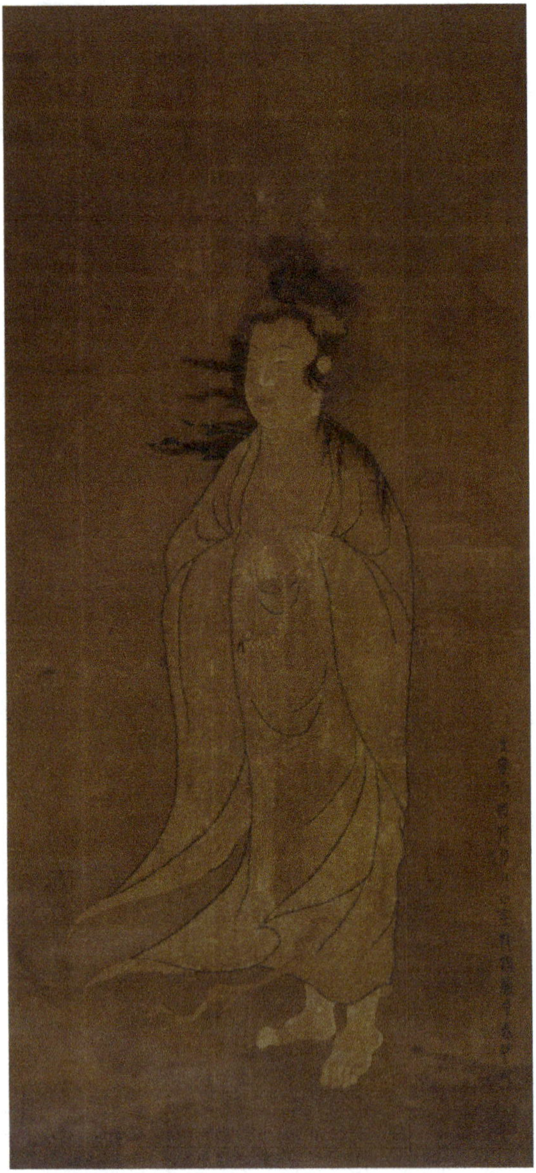

247. Zhao Guanzhong Embroidery of Guanyin

Yuan

Length: 104.9 cm Width: 49.8 cm

A treasure of ancient times in Nanjing Museum

Preserved in the Nanjing Museum

Embroidery. It is woven on the deep beige damask silk with rolling stitch and long-and-short stitch. A barefoot Guanyin carries a set of beads in her hand. Her hair is woven by silk. The upper part of the body is plump, the face rectangle with a wide jaw; her waist is strong and her feet large in the male style. It bears the note in Zhuan Calligraphy: "Woven by Zhao Guanzhong of Wuxing City in the year of 1309".

Zhao Guanzhong, wife of the renowned painter Zhao Mengfu in the Yuan Dynasty, excelled at painting, calligraphy and embroidery.

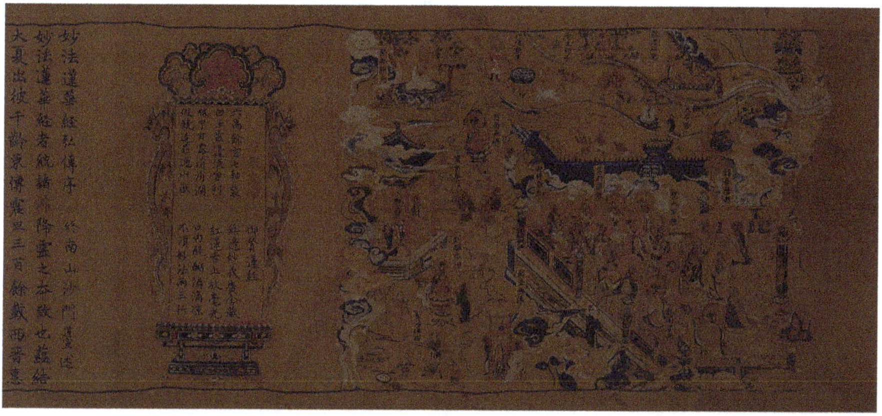

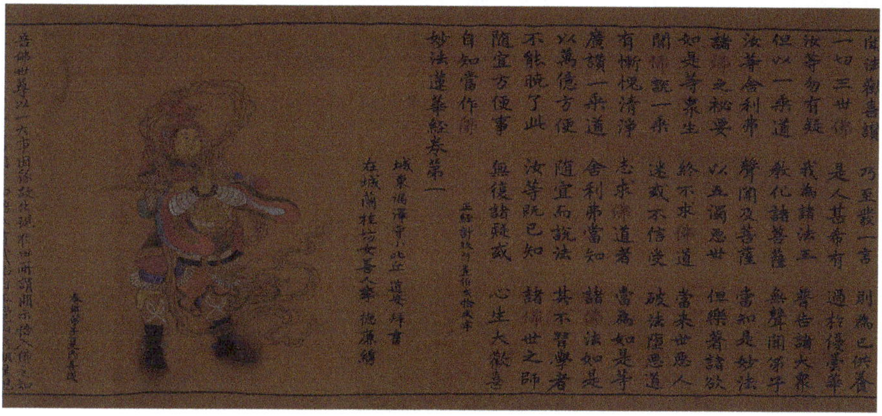

248. Li Delian Embroidery of Saddharma Puṇḍarīka Sūtra

Yuan

Length: 44.1 cm Width: 1953.3 cm

Preserved in the Shanghai Museum

Embroidery. It is woven on light green damask. At front of the scroll, there are some figures of Buddha and an arched bridge woven in colored threads with a seven-character poem "Ode to Saddharma Puarīka Sūtra". Before the sutra, the first half of the poem is woven and behind the preface the second half of the poem is woven. After the sutra, characters are woven as follows "it is woven by Li Delian who is good at embroidery". The Buddha Wei Tuo is woven by colored threads with his left side writing some characters in ink "a follower of Buddhism Xia Shancheng". At present, only the first roll of the sutra is kept, with the last six lost. There are 9,122 characters in the first roll written in regular script and are woven in dark blue threads.

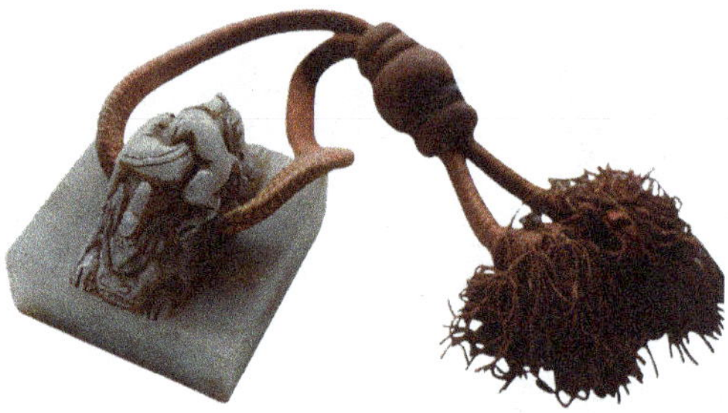

249. Jade Seal of Ba Basi to Revive the Buddhism

Yuan

Height: 8 cm Side Length: 9.5 cm

Preserved in the Administrative Committee of Archaeology of the Tibet Autonomous Region

Royal seal. The shape is square with two dragon-style buttons of red tassels. It is carved in Zhuan Calligraphy "Pagba, the royal preceptor in the Yuan Dynasty, leads the monks to revive Buddhism" in four lines. The royal preceptor is the title for the monk of highest level.

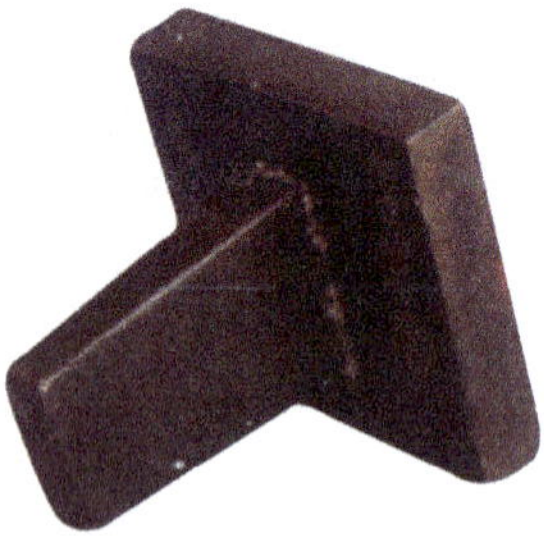

250. Copper Seal of a Marshal by Military Ministry

Yuan

Height: 8.8 cm Side Length: 8.4 cm

Excavated from the Yanzi River in Jinzai County in Anhui in 1975

Preserved in the Historical Relic Administration in Jinzai County

Royal seal. The shape is square with the rectangle button. It is curved with the Zhuan Calligraphy "Seal of Marshal by Military Ministry" in two lines and the right of the back is curved "Seal of Marshal by Military Ministry" , the left "Made by the Ministry of Rites", "in August of the year 1358". The side is carved "the forty-sixth" and the upper carved in regular script. It was an official seal for the leaders of peasant uprisings.

CPSIA information can be obtained
at www.ICGtesting.com
Printed in the USA
FSHW022103290320
68606FS

9 781925 371505